Being a Man

'This important book, both fascinating and instructive, seems to be the first of its kind in probing masculinity and masculinities in a wide range of societies of the ancient world that lay outside the orbit of Greco-Roman culture'.
David J.A. Clines, *Professor of Biblical Studies, University of Sheffield, UK*

Being a Man is a formative work which reveals the myriad and complex negotiations for constructions of masculine identities in the greater ancient Near East and beyond. Through a juxtaposition of studies into Neo-Assyrian artistic representations and omens, biblical hymns and narrative, Hittite, Akkadian, and Indian epic, as well as detailed linguistic studies on gender and sex in the Sumerian and Hebrew languages, the book challenges traditional understandings and assumed homogeneity for what it meant "to be a man" in antiquity. *Being a Man* is an indispensable resource for students of the ancient Near East, and a fascinating study for anyone with an interest in gender and sexuality throughout history.

Ilona Zsolnay (University of Pennsylvania, Lecturer and Consulting Scholar) is an Assyriologist who specializes in ancient Near Eastern religion(s) and gender theory (Ph.D. Brandeis University). She is the author of several articles which investigate the intersection between deities, clergy, and the body politic. Zsolnay is also the Ancient Near East area editor of the *Oxford Encyclopaedia of Bible and Gender* (ed. Julia O'Brien, 2014).

Studies in the History of the Ancient Near East
Series editor: Greg Fisher, Carleton University, Canada

Advisory Board of Associate Editors

Studies in the History of the Ancient Near East provides a global forum for works addressing the history and culture of the Ancient Near East, spanning a broad period from the foundation of civilisation in the region until the end of the Abbasid period. The series includes research monographs, edited works, collections developed from conferences and workshops, and volumes suitable for the university classroom.

Forthcoming:

Reconstructing Israelite and Judean Religions
Alice Mandell and Jeremy Smoak

A Story of YHWH
Shawn Flynn

Comparative Urbanism in the Greco-Roman and Early Islamic Near East
Walter Ward

The Reign of Nebuchadnezzar I in History and Historical Memory
John Nielsen

On the Edge of Empires
Rocco Palermo

Being a Man

Negotiating ancient constructs of masculinity

Edited by Ilona Zsolnay

Routledge
Taylor & Francis Group
LONDON AND NEW YORK

First published 2017
by Routledge
2 Park Square, Milton Park, Abingdon, Oxon OX14 4RN

and by Routledge
711 Third Avenue, New York, NY 10017

Routledge is an imprint of the Taylor & Francis Group, an informa business

British Library Cataloguing-in-Publication Data
A catalogue record for this book is available from the British Library

Library of Congress Cataloging-in-Publication Data
Names: Zsolnay, Ilona, editor.
Title: Being a man : negotiating ancient constructs of masculinity / edited by Ilona Zsolnay.
Description: Abingdon, Oxon ; New York, NY : Routledge, 2016. | Series: Studies in the history of the Ancient Near East
Identifiers: LCCN 2015042639 | ISBN 9781138189362 (hardback : alk. paper) | ISBN 9781315641614 (ebook)
Subjects: LCSH: Masculinity—Middle East—History—To 1500. | Men—Middle East—History—To 1500. | Men—Middle East—Identity. | Men in literature. | Men in art. | Middle East—Civilization—To 622. | Middle East—History—To 622.
Classification: LCC HQ1090.7.M628 B45 2016 | DDC 305.310956/09—dc23
LC record available at http://lccn.loc.gov/2015042639

ISBN: 978-1-138-18936-2 (hbk)
ISBN: 978-1-315-64161-4 (ebk)

Typeset in Sabon
by Apex CoVantage, LLC

Contents

Preface

An anthology such as this one does not happen overnight. Its germination began as the conference *Mapping Ancient Near Eastern Masculinities*, March 24–27, 2011, at the Penn Museum, which I arranged with generous funding from the Mellon Cultural Diversity Fund, The Center for Ancient Studies, and various departments within the University of Pennsylvania and the Penn Museum. The aim of this conference was to provide a venue for scholars to investigate representations of masculinity and their importance in defining various roles within the cultures of the ancient world. Presenters were invited to examine such representations within their areas of specialization using the methodologies developed by gender studies departments. The participants in this workshop were: Julia Assante (Münster), Mary R. Bachvarova (Willamette University), Marc Brettler (Duke University), Simon Brodbeck(Cardiff University), J. S. Cooper (Johns Hopkins University), Ann K. Guinan (University of Pennsylvania), Stephen W. Holloway (James Madison University), Hilary Lipka (University of New Mexico), Martti Nissinen (University of Helsinki), Ann Macy Roth (New York University), and Joan Westenholz. At its conclusion, all took part in a round-table discussion in order to ascertain how best to move forward and incorporate our conclusions into more general studies.

It is my great pleasure, now, to present the culmination of this work. Several of the investigations presented here appear in their more or less original oral forms; however, others have been considerably reworked as their authors continued to tease out their core theses. As there was much provocative discussion after each presentation and lively, yet productive, interaction among the participants during the various more informal gatherings, it is hoped that the volume sparks the same level of dynamic debate and further scholarship. I would like to conclude this preface by offering my gratitude to all who have participated in this endeavor with me. It has truly been both a pleasure and an honor to work with each of these authors who were, at times, pulled out of their comfort zones yet each responded with enthusiasm and, at times, great fortitude.

Ilona Zsolnay (Philadelphia, 2015)

Contributors

Julia Assante is an art historian who received her Ph.D. from Columbia University. She has written on eroticism, sexuality, and magic in the ancient Near East. A number of her scholarly works are targeted at the widespread distortions in scholarship that impose over-sexualized interpretations (e.g., prostitution) on women in Mesopotamian images and texts. She is the author of "From Whores to Hierodules: The Historiographic Invention of Mesopotamian Female Sex Professionals" in *Ancient Art and Its Historiography*. Ed. A. A. Donahue et al. (Cambridge University, 2003), "The Erotic Reliefs of Ancient Mesopotamia" in *Sex and Gender in the Ancient Near East* (Neo-Assyrian Text Corpus Project, 2002) and "Undressing the Nude: Problems in Analyzing Nudity in Ancient Art, with an Old Babylonian Case Study" in *Images of Gender: Contributions to the Hermeneutics of Reading Ancient Art*. Ed. S. Schroer (Freibourg University, 2006).

Mary R. Bachvarova has been committed to investigations of Indo-European textual transmission since her graduate work at the University of Chicago. She is the author of numerous articles devoted to Hittite, Hurro-Hittite, and Greek literature and the interplays and borrowings which occur between them. She is currently preparing *From Hittite to Homer: The Anatolian Background of Greek Epic* (Cambridge University Press).

Marc Brettler is a Biblicist and the author of multiple books devoted to reading, teaching, and understanding the Hebrew Bible in its original historical and linguistic context. He is recently the winner of the Gold Medal in Independent Publisher Book Award, religion category, for participation in *The Three Testaments* and has received the National Jewish Book Award, scholarship category, for *The Jewish Study Bible* (2014). Brettler is currently completing *Book of Four Psalms Commentary* for the Jewish Publication Society.

Simon Brodbeck is Reader in Religious Studies at Cardiff University, Wales. He is co-editor of *Gender and Narrative in the Mahābhārata* (Routledge, 2007) and the Equinox journal *Religions of South Asia*, and author of *The Mahābhārata Patriline: Gender, Culture, and the Royal*

Hereditary (Ashgate, 2009) and some two dozen articles on aspects of the *Mahābhārata* and *Rāmāyaṇa*.

J. S. Cooper's main research interests are Sumerian literature, Mesopotamian history, gender and sexuality in the ancient world, and the early history of writing systems. He has published and lectured extensively in each of these areas. Cooper's articles include: "Genre, Gender and the Sumerian Lamentation" (*Journal of Cuneiform Studies*, 2006), "Buddies in Babylonia. Gilgamesh, Enkidu and Mesopotamian Homosexuality" in *Riches Hidden in Secret Places: Ancient Near Eastern Studies in Memory of Thorkild Jacobsen*. Ed. T. Abusch (Eisenbrauns, 2002), and "Gendered Sexuality in Sumerian Love Poetry" in *Sumerian Gods and Their Representations*. Ed. I. Finkel et al. (Styx, 1997).

Joan Goodnick Westenholz received her Ph.D. in Near Eastern Languages and Civilization from University of Chicago and is a former chief curator of the Bible Lands Museum Jerusalem. She has published extensively on Babylonian religion and literature as well as numerous articles concentrating on issues of gender, women, and goddesses. Her most recent book, written together with Near Eastern Art Historian Julia Asher-Greve, *Goddesses in Context: On Divine Powers, Roles, Relationships and Gender in Mesopotamian Textual and Visual Sources* (Vandenhoeck & Ruprecht, 2013), is a work of profound importance for understanding the development of Mesopotamian religion.

Ann K. Guinan is a specialist in Mesopotamian omen research and an editor of the series *Magic and Divination in the Ancient World* (Brill Academic Press). Guinan is interested in comparative and theoretical approaches to divination. Her research deals with the human behavioral omens of *šumma alu*. She is preparing a text edition of the third and final section of the omen compendium.

Steven W. Holloway is a graduate of the Divinity School of the University of Chicago. His research interests cover the nexus between Assyriology and biblical studies (*Aššur is King! Aššur is King!* Brill, 2002) and the long-standing fascination with and bias against the East that we call Orientalism (*Orientalism, Assyriology and the Bible* (ed.) [Sheffield Phoenix Press, 2006]). He is also a co-editor of *In the Wake of Frymer-Kensky* (Gorgias Press, 2009), an anthology devoted to Tikva Frymer-Kensky's *In the Wake of the Goddesses: Women, Culture, and the Biblical Transformation of Pagan Myth* (Ballantine Books, 1993). Frymer-Kensky was one of the first academics to apply gender theory to the ancient Near East.

Hilary Lipka is a Biblicist who studies the intersection of sexuality, gender, and religious transgression. In addition to presenting several papers devoted to the nature of purity and defilement, she is the author of *Sexual Transgression in the Hebrew Bible* (Sheffield Phoenix Press, 2006) in which she addresses the sex laws of the Hebrew Bible.

Peter Morris is a critic and dramatist. His work has appeared in The Paris Review, the Guardian, and the Independent. His essay "Harold Bloom, Parody, and the Other Tradition" is included in *The Salt Companion to Harold Bloom*. His plays include *The Age of Consent, Guardians, and Gaudeamus*. He also writes for Golden Globe-winning television comedy *Mozart in the Jungle*.

Martti Nissinen's scholarly work focuses on biblical and ancient Near Eastern texts – "biblical" referring to the Jewish and Christian Bible and the "ancient Near East" referring to the Eastern Mediterranean cultures in a broad sense. His main research interests have concentrated on prophecy and gender and their interpretation in the Bible and in the ancient Near East. His study of prophecy is motivated by the opportunity to make scholars aware of "new" sources, such as the Neo-Assyrian prophecies, contributing to a new understanding of prophecy as a common phenomenon in the ancient Near East. The gender perspective also enables an important contribution of biblical scholarship to modern society: the encounter between historical study and modern concerns.

Ilona Zsolnay is an Assyriologist who specializes in ancient Near Eastern religion(s) and gender theory (Ph.D. Brandeis University). She is the author of several articles which investigate the intersection between deities, clergy, and the body politic. Zsolnay is also the Ancient Near East area editor of the *Oxford Encyclopedia of Bible and Gender* (ed. Julia O'Brien, 2014).

Introduction[1]

Ilona Zsolnay

The importance of masculinity to the ancient world is patent. As is apparent in the texts and visual representations which have come down to us, a preoccupation with masculinity permeated multiple aspects of ancient societies. From Hittite and Sumerian texts, we learn of symbols without whose reception masculinity could not be properly conferred (Hoffner 1966; Asher-Greve 2002), while in the Akkadian ša.zi.ga texts, we read of ordinary men who feared a loss of potency if their masculinity was not constructed in a certain way (Biggs 1967). That this was a very real hazard is revealed by Assyrian royal inscriptions, treaties, and soldiers' oaths, in which men are threatened with the removal of their masculinity if they do not comply with certain conditions.

At its heart this volume is dedicated to identity, specifically to a man's identity (it is a volume titled *Being a Man*, after all). Like modern men, yesterday's men struggled with the somewhat existential question "What does it mean to be a man?" ("What does society believe the ideal construct of masculinity to be?") and the more practical "How do I demonstrate my masculinity, my 'manliness'?" ("How do I negotiate my performance of it?"). Factors such as class, ethnicity, and environment will inform culturally desired constructs of masculinity. As an identity, a *performance*, masculinity is therefore a project, one which is under constant surveillance. Frankly stated by sociologist Michael Kimmel, "We [men] are under constant and careful scrutiny of other men. Other men watch us, rank us, grant our acceptance into the realm of manhood. Manhood is demonstrated for other men's approval" (Kimmel 1994: 214). Strictly speaking, to enact a version of masculinity considered less than a societal ideal cannot only be undesirable, but humiliating.

Using the theory of multiple masculinities first purposed by R. W. Connell and later refined by Connell and James W. Messerschmidt as a guide, in this volume scholars of the greater ancient Near Eastern realm revisit works from Mesopotamia, Israel, Anatolia, and India in order to ascertain and illuminate what the application of this seemingly modern concept might expose with regards to ancient societal constructs of masculinity. The results of this project are both fascinating and somewhat unexpected. They reveal not only that the concept of "doing gender" was already well understood in the ancient world, but that the performance of multiple masculinities was both acknowledged and considered in text, art, and (written) oral tales. It quickly becomes evident that no construct (ideal or "alternative") or system was identical in all cultures. The chapters of this volume expose a panoply of methods employed to consider, legitimate, police, negotiate, refine, and amend differing qualities for ideal performances of masculinity and an equally disparate set of structures for addressing "alternative" constructs.

Patriarchal societal systems, such as today's persistent Western model and yesterday's ancient Near Eastern model, answer the question "What does it mean to be a man?" by informing their participants that they are members of a social hierarchy. As a group, men are at the top of this hierarchy; however, certain men, such as the patriarch, can receive "highest billing." At this point, the vast majority of men reading this, fathers in particular, will shake their heads and declare that they by no means feel that they have been awarded this entitled position. They will decry that most of the time, they feel power*less*. Their wives, bosses (male and female), friends (male and female), and children rarely, if ever, defer to them. They will state that they are in a constant struggle to get even a modicum of respect, let alone this Atlantean control or authority, in their lives. And herein lies the rub: in the patriarchal system, analogous to the monarchical one (to which the system gives rise), masculinities are constantly in a state of flux, negotiation, and outright war. A patriarch, as any ruler, can only maintain his authority if he has convinced his family as well as his society that he is worthy/able to embody, maintain, and sustain that power. Because men must constantly legitimate themselves within this system, they must be forever vigilant that they are practising/demonstrating their performance of a dominant and/or hegemonic masculinity.

This does not, however, mean that this construct must be positive, negative, violent, or abusive (although it certainly can be). Nor does it mean that all men performing (attempting) a hegemonic construct are in positions of power. As Connell and Messerschmidt emphasize, it is the *relational* quality of hegemony which is key. The Gramscian understanding of hegemony, upon which the theory of masculinities is based (but not cemented), is conceptualized as that construct which both seizes and is allotted the "power" position in a hierarchy. According to the theory of Marxist thinker Antonio Gramsci, hegemony, from the Greek ἡγεμών, "leader or guide," is a process by which not only the controlling class or state asserts and justifies its right to dominate (have hegemony), but through which subordinated subjects are complicit in their own domination by that controlling class or state. When applied to gender relations, hegemony can occur at several levels: local (face-to-face, family, communities); regional (society wide/nation); and, global (transnational, global politics) (Messerschmidt 2010: 41).

By default, not every male can perform a hegemonic masculinity. Alternative masculinities are then referred to as dominant, subordinate, or marginal, sometimes even oppositional (Charlebois 2011: 33). These latter are the masculinities performed by the majority of men and they are the constructs which validate the hegemonic. Easily miscomprehended as hegemonic, dominant constructs of masculinity are in practice "the most powerful or the most widespread types in the sense of being the most celebrated, common, or current forms of masculinity in a particular setting" (Messerschmidt 2010: 38). These are non-hegemonic constructs which embody the ideal, yet do not overtly oppress (e.g., the star athlete who expresses tolerance toward homosexuality or does not deride women). Subordinate and marginalized masculinities are those constructs which are stigmatized. A man attempting to perform a hegemonic construct must, by necessity, group other men and all women into the category of "other," frequently referring to those characteristics which differ or conflict with that construct as being feminine. While it may or may not be true that the stigmatized men are performing constructs of masculinity which incorporate characteristics generally deemed feminine by their society(ies), as biological males, they are performing masculine constructs. Yet, it is the fear elicited from the very suggestion that they are *less* masculine, *less* powerful, which aids in legitimating the claim that the hegemonic performance is the true and *natural* construct. To be hegemonic is to distance oneself from other constructs and continually (re)affirm that they are inferior while at the same time asserting that your construct is superior. Hegemonic is defined oppositionally, by that which it is not: marginalized and/or subordinated (Hirose and Pih 2010: 191).

Masculinities are ever-changing cultural projects that fluctuate in response to variables. These constructions may be influenced by class distinctions, sexual orientations, religious precepts, racial views, and/or economics. We may see this variation illustrated most concretely in our modern society and the way it is grappling with definitions of masculinity. Previously, two assumed aspects of an ideal masculinity were to be both breadwinner and protector of the family. As women have entered the paid workforce over the years, and now receive salaries which may exceed those of their male partners, the definition of this construct has begun to be redefined. Further, with the rise of the "metrosexual" and "hipster" man, the man not defined by his rough exterior and actions, the role of man as natural protector has also been thrown into question. In Western societies, the coarse masculinity of the laborer is conceptualized far differently from the genteel masculinity of the affluent tenured professor. In blockbuster American cinema, it is the fighter who is lauded as being the most "manly," because he performs the desired construct (Hirose and Pih 2010: 194–195), while in China the genteel construct (*wen*) is given priority, as a laborer's or soldier's masculinity (*wu*) is derided as non-contemplative and reactive.

Multiple (and shifting) constructions of masculinity are also evident in works throughout the ancient arena. Even a cursory reading of the Sumerian wisdom text *The Instructions of Šuruppak* presents a construction of masculinity which differs significantly from those presented in the Old Babylonian legend The Epic of Gilgameš. Although each could be argued to be an advisory text (i.e., wisdom), the main character of the Epic, Gilgameš, performs magnificent physical feats of valor for which he is rewarded, while Ziudsura, the recipient of the directives listed in *Instructions*, is advised to be a prudent and disciplined gentleman. This difference is also present in artistic renderings. The depiction of the Sargonic king Narām-Sîn's lithe male body is in radical opposition to that of the severe and impenetrable body of the Neo-Assyrian king Aššurnaṣirpal II (Winter 1996: 15). This dichotomy of presentation is also apparent in Egyptian royal depictions. The languid body of Akhenaten is startling when compared to the austere postures which earlier pharaohs take. Egyptian artisans were therefore instructed not to depict Akhenaten as other pharaohs, including Ḥatshepsut, the female pharaoh. An example of a discordant alignment of modern gender constructions with ancient ones is found in Greco-Roman society. While in many modern societies, it is considered a masculine role to be promiscuous (i.e., "boys will be boys"), in Roman society, the promiscuous man was considered to be performing an inferior construct of masculinity because promiscuity was deemed a feminine characteristic (Williams 1999: 3). A high sex drive, heroism, and a strong musculature were therefore not steadfast traits of an ideal or normative construct of masculinity.

The lack of recognition of these evolving paradigms of ideal masculinity has led to a broad application of the nineteenth-century Western construction of normative masculinity onto ancient societies. This, in turn, has led scholars to propose, at times, creative solutions and to commit rather gross scholarly gaffes. Perhaps one of the most fascinating examples of erudite inventiveness is in the case of Akhenaten. Depicted with a supple physique, Akhenaten was, and still may be, labeled "effeminate." So confusing has his appearance been to scholars that he has been argued to have been a homosexual – even though he is frequently portrayed with his beautiful wife Nefertiti and their children (Montserrat 2003: 168). So sinuous are his features that he has been thought to have had myotonic dystrophy, a muscle-wasting illness which would bring about soft (i.e., feminine) features (Cattaino and Vicario 1999: 60). An even more significant example of this phenomenon occurred over one hundred years ago, yet is still accepted today. Perpetuated by nineteenth-century Scottish folklorists (e.g., James Frazer), the notion of a vast ancient fertility cult presided over by women and whose head was a great mother-goddess has recently been largely debunked. Since fertility has been assumed to be a feminine trait, it has been understood to be the domain and concern of women and female deities. As demonstrated by Jo Ann Hackett, it is, in fact, male gods (generally weather deities) who regularly preside over fertility, for they were deemed in charge of the life-giving rains (Hackett 1989: 74). These rains were in turn analogized to semen, a uniquely male product.

Although a topic embraced by Classicists (Laqueur 1990; Osborne, 1997; Williams 1999; Foxhall 2000) and recently addressed by New Testament scholars (Moore and Anderson 2003) and Biblicists (Creangă 2010, 2014), a more systematic review of constructions of masculinity has only sporadically entered into the conversations of scholars whose focus is on these even more remote cultures (Clines 1995; Nissinen 1998; Asher-Greve 2001, 2008; Montserrat 2003; Parkinson 2008). Gender in general and masculinities specifically as topics of analysis have been much-needed and-omitted additions to the scholarly discourse, for, as the articles collected together in this volume demonstrate, the negotiation and maintenance of certain constructions of masculinities, as they are today, form a, if not *the*, keystone of societal organization.

The volume

In order to ground or root this volume dedicated to unraveling various ancient attitudes toward, and guidelines for, being a man, it seems apropos that it should begin at the beginning; thus, the study which launches the collection addresses the very concept of societal gender/biological sex in the earliest written language: Sumerian. A language which to this day has no known cognates, Sumerian was first inscribed on cuneiform tablets over five thousand years ago. In "Categorizing Men and Masculinity in Sumer," Joan Goodnick Westenholz and Ilona Zsolnay survey and contextualize specific lexemes for male mortals in administrative, lexical, and literary texts. They determine that, broadly speaking, men were categorized by age and that each age had a corresponding construct (e.g., the ĝuruš "able-bodied youth" performed namĝuruš "youthful masculinity"). Men were also divided by societal position such as dependent or independent. While the finer distinctions between these divisions continue to be debated by modern scholars, that a general term "masculinity (namnita)" is not attested is striking as is the lack of a generic term, devoid of *any* societal classification.

A very different phenomenon is evident in the contributions of Julia Assante, Mary R. Bachvarova, and J. S. Cooper. Examining the negotiation of hierarchical masculinities in Mesopotamian relief, in "Men Looking at Men," Assante demonstrates that in the homosocial environment of a military culture the renegotiation of a man's status was through territorial conquest and its equation with sexual dominance. Because she focuses on Middle Assyrian and Neo-Assyrian works, her conclusions suggest a radical new formation of an ideal construct of masculinity and Assyrian relations with "outer" lands. Gone is the Old Assyrian patriarch who, in order to trade goods, negotiated his way through the hinterlands with savvy and payment. Instead, Assante's investigation reveals an elaborate and brutally depicted method for defining the hegemonic construct of masculinity vis-à-vis forced subordinate and marginalized performances.

Domination of land is also paramount in the Hittite text known as the Kumarbi Cycle. In "Wisdom of Former Days: The Manly Hittite King and Foolish Kumarbi, Father of the Gods," Bachvarova investigates the manner by which the authority of the *paterfamilias* (be he the storm god, king, or father), was repeatedly justified, legitimated, and policed in Hittite proverb, narrative, and art. Without his dominion, the fields would not be fertile and chaos would reign. The maintenance of the normativity of this construct of masculinity informed every level of society, for the life of each person dwelling in Hittite territory was at risk if the king's hegemony was not properly enacted and supported. Bachvarova unfolds a morality tale which portrays with apocalyptic imagery the horrors which occur when a ruler does not perform this "correct" dominating construct. Dissimilar from the Assyrian precedence of force over others, as is shown by Bachvarova, a key component of the Hittite construct of normative masculinity was the conflicting belief that to be masculine was to be both wild and irrational *and* to have the innate potential for rational thought with the ability to dominate this wild irrationality. If the hegemonic male cannot dominate himself, how then can he dominate and so save and protect the weaker world?

A re-envisioning of hegemonic masculinity and the legitimation of new characteristics is at the heart of the Akkadian epic The Enūma Eliš in Cooper's "Female Trouble and Troubled Males." Reading like a modern libretto for assuring generals before an attack, in the Enūma Eliš, the young male warrior god Marduk, facing the female chaos monster Tiāmat, tells his concerned progenitors that "a woman's force may be very great, but it cannot match a man's." Marduk uses hewn weapons, not merely the spells employed by previous (male) warriors (and Tiāmat). He fights with what are specifically deemed masculine implements, armaments wielded by neither women nor, apparently, unsuccessful men. Moving away from the Epic, to augment his reading, Cooper then utilizes the letters of the very real Šamšī-Adad, in which the Amorite king derides his son for not participating in such brutal and bodily forms of combat and lifestyle.

Ancient texts and visual works not only normalize and legitimate hegemonic constructs, they also reveal an awareness of the conflicting characteristics which lead to an unsustainability of certain hegemonic and dominant performances. Complex negotiations and contemplations are illuminated by Simon Brodbeck and Ann Guinan. In "Mapping Masculinities in the Sanskrit *Mahābhārata* and *Rāmāyaṇa*," Brodbeck explores the interactions of the varied and richly portrayed male characters in the two great Indian works. By focusing on the relational aspects of the *kṣatriya*, a class of rulers and warriors, and the brahmin, an elite social class which includes a yogic renouncer, Brodbeck is able not only to lay bare the multiple and differing constructs of masculinity evident in the texts, but also, reveal their intricate interactions. Brodbeck demonstrates that the texts themselves are very much aware of the "problem of masculinity" through their consideration, debate, and concern for which construct is supreme, for, as the texts divulge, each performance has a fatal flaw.

In "Mesopotamia before and after Sodom," Ann Guinan, with Peter Morris, interrogates the inescapable subconscious of Mesopotamian men. Using two Middle Assyrian Laws, an omen from the first-millennium compendium of terrestrial omens *šumma ālu*, and the erotically charged language that is used to portray the relationship between Gilgameš and Enkidu in the Epic of Gilgameš, Guinan contends that there was a certain acceptance and incorporation of marginalized and stigmatized masculinities. According to the strict hierarchical ordering of society presented in the laws codes, and which must always be maintained, it was essential to condemn publically homosexual acts. While this same hierarchical ordering is present in the terrestrial omens, because omens address and deal frankly with subconscious thought and private action, they reveal a recognition of societally taboo urges. In the omens, these natural *accepted* inclinations are then rationalized into the hierarchical system.

It is the chapters of Hilary Lipka, Marc Brettler, Martti Nissinen, and Steven Holloway which shed a more direct light on our own Western heritage. Using primarily historical texts, in "Shaved Beards and Bared Buttocks: Shame and the Undermining of Masculine Performance in Biblical Texts," Lipka teases out the characteristics of a dominant masculinity which is repeatedly endorsed. Broadly, she determines that its primary markers are both physical: an unblemished strong capable body with great stamina made complete by an intact penis and luxuriant beard, and psychological: a rational and skilled mind and a demeanor which is above all confident, able to navigate aggression and violence with great self-control. Arguably the most unforeseen marker of this construct is that a key aspect of this unblemished male body is fertility. The man performing this ideal construct must maintain sexual vigor and production, for, as Lipka establishes, not to perform this characteristic is an open invitation to a challenge of one's masculinity and therefore one's hierarchical positioning in society. Even more damaging is that a performance of a lesser construct of masculinity is depicted as an affront and abomination to the god of Israel; thus, its characteristics are divinely sanctioned and so naturalized.

In "Happy is the Man who Fills his Quiver with Them," Brettler opens his analysis with a systematic philological scrutiny of the biblical text in order to determine whether the language distinguishes gender from sex, and whether the authors conceptualized gender as that which can be and is performed. Not only does he conclude that yes, the text demonstrates that there are different terms for the conceptually distinct categories of sex and gender, but he also notes that the man performing the hegemonic construct, referred to as a *geber* and detailed by Lipka, is disproportionately present in the book of Psalms. That psalms are celebratory in nature and may be sung by either individuals or communities makes them an ideal channel through which values may be conveyed and internalized. Thus, the latter portion of this chapter is devoted to a contemplation of how, why, and for whom these songs were created.

The strict monitoring of an ideal masculinity is not present in all biblical books. As Nissinen's study of alternative masculinities demonstrates, the strict seemingly blanket proscriptions found in Leviticus are not consistently adhered to or policed throughout the Bible. Through an interrogation of the narrative texts, in "Relative Masculinities in the Hebrew Bible/Old Testament," Nissinen reveals that certain biblical characters perform actions that are not sanctioned. The unmarried prophet Jeremiah, young princes who seem to engage in homosexual relations, and non-procreating eunuchs all find accepted stations in Israelite society. Jeremiah, who is so elevated that he speaks for his god, is hailed as a knower of truths; David, the prince who so often seems to perform seemingly scandalous activities, comes to be the paragon of monarchy; and, eunuchs, who so ordinarily are assumed to be lesser by modern scholars, have pride of place next to the king himself.

The final chapter of this anthology takes us (almost) full circle to the volume's point of departure. The Victorian gender system still resonating today was informed by biblical texts as much as the texts were synthetically utilized to confirm it. In "The Masculinity of Male Angels on the Make," Holloway investigates pre-Victorian Romantic interpretations of the biblical tale of divine-mortal coupling. He demonstrates that by using Genesis 6:1–4 as a foil, these artists could express, consider, and judge the paradox inherent in the assumed normative construct of masculinity: to be a mortal male is to perform a masculinity whose key characteristic is an *uncontrollable* lust for women. Because a second component of this ideal was thought to be *control* over one's emotions and the management of power, to perform both aspects simultaneously is untenable and ultimately leads to banishment and/or unsanctioned violence. Masculinity, in these depictions, is a fragile construct which can be torn down by the mere presence of a woman. It is also revealed that a key characteristic of femininity is the innate power to impede and indeed destroy proper masculine performance.

Together then these investigations establish that the ancients were very much aware of gender as a social construct separate from biological sex, that the performance of masculinities, particularly desired constructs of masculinity, required constant monitoring and enforcement by affirming the ideal and deriding vying constructs. However, several of the discussions presented here also reveal an awareness, tolerance, and indeed celebration of what seem normally to have been considered subordinated and marginal constructs. To learn that during the Middle Assyrian period even the thought of homosexuality between men could be tolerated defies conventional beliefs. That eunuchs find societal niches in both Assyria and India, in some cases even being elevated, enlightens. Indeed, it is the collective aspect of this volume that exposes and corrects the traditional assumption – an assumption so elegantly revealed by the inclusion of an exposition into Romantic art – that one construct of masculinity should be assumed to be common to all cultures.

Several of the investigations confirm that the maintenance of patriarchal power was very much a preoccupation of the societies of Mesopotamia, Israel, Anatolia, and Persia. Its legitimation and normalization justified the masculine authority of gods, kings, and fathers. Yet, as this power was rooted in the proper performance of culturally defined and mutable hegemonic masculinities, it was tenuous. These studies demonstrate that the threats to their performance were great and varied depending on the culture, medium, and characteristics which were thought to define them. Contrary to modern expectations, it is only the artistic interpretations of the Romantics which suggest that it can be the mere presence of a woman which is a crucial factor in the impairment of an ideal masculine performance. Also divergent is that fertility was primarily a feminine characteristic, for a formidable obstruction to the enactment of the biblical hegemonic construct was infertility. Not emphasizing fertility in their reliefs, the Middle and Neo-Assyrian kings instead accentuated *forced* domination over others as a prime characteristic of hegemonic masculinity. While in the Hittite Kumarbi cycle, internal discipline takes precedence over external submission; a lack of restraint is deemed a personal flaw, suggesting that a male, mortal or god, possessing it is unable to elevate himself by enacting a man's masculinity instead of a boy's.

The juxtaposition of investigations into Neo-Assyrian artistic representations and omens, biblical hymns and narrative, Hittite, Akkadian, and Persian epic, as well as detailed linguistic studies on gender and sex in the Sumerian and Hebrew languages, exposes and substantiates that no set of characteristics was either fundamental to any one construct of masculinity, hegemonic or otherwise, or consistently conceived of as normative throughout a period, region, or literary genre. As no complete set of markers was common to any culture, in order to better understand a society's evolutions (e.g., from an Old Assyrian trader economy to the rape and pillage approach of certain later Assyrian rulers), it is remiss of us as scholars if we do not begin to recognize and unravel these deeper, more intricate, and ever fluctuating factors. To do so can only strengthen our understanding of the seemingly minute internal forces which are foundational to intricate social systems and feed great transformations.

Note

1 Although this introduction briefly addresses gender theory (that gender is a social construct while sex is biological), it does not delve further into the vast corpus of scholarship dedicated to gender studies. "Doing Gender," first coined by Candace West and Don H. Zimmerman, is the theory that gender is a production, "a routine, methodological, and reoccurring achievement" (West and Zimmerman 1987: 126). As an achievement, gender is something which needs to be performed and produced daily and so becomes foundational to one's identity. Furthermore, because gender is defined by the society in which one is living, it is culturally guided, influenced, and made mandatory.

Bibliography

Asher-Greve, Julia. "The Essential Body: Mesopotamian Conceptions of the Gendered Body." *Gender & History* 9 (1997): 432–461.

———. "Decisive Sex, Essential Gender." In *Sex and Gender in the Ancient near East: Proceedings of the 47th Rencontre Assyriologique Internationale*, Helsinki, July 2–6, 2001. Eds. Simo Parpola and R. M. Whiting. Helsinki: Neo-Assyrian Text Corpus Project, 2002, pp. 11–26.

———. "Images of Men, Gender Regimes, and Social Stratification in the Late Uruk Period." In *Gender Through Time in the Ancient Near East*. Ed. Diane Bolger. Lanham: Alta Mira Press, 2008, pp. 119–171.

Berger, Maurice, Brian Wallis, and Simon Watson, eds. *Constructing Masculinity*. New York and London: Routledge, 1995.

Biggs, Robert D. *ša.zi.ga: Ancient Mesopotamian Potency Incantations*. Locust Valley, NY: J.J. Augustin, 1967.

Cattaino, G. and L. Vicario. "Myotonic Dystrophy in Ancient Egypt." *European Neurology* 41 (1999): 59–63.

Charlebois, Justin. *Construction of Hegemonic and Oppositional Femininities*. Lanham: Lexington Books, 2011.

Clines, David J. A. *Interested Parties: The Ideology of Writers and Readers of the Hebrew Bible*. Sheffield: Sheffield Academic Press, 1995.

Connell, R. W. *Masculinities*. Los Angeles: University of California Press, 1995.

Connell, R. W. and James W. Messerschmidt. "Hegemonic Masculinity: Rethinking the Concept." *Gender & Society* 19 (2005): 829–859.

Creangă, Ovidiu, ed. *Men and Masculinity in the Hebrew Bible and Beyond*. Sheffield: Phoenix Press, 2010.

Creangă, Ovidiu, and Peter-Ben Smit, eds. *Biblical Masculinities Foregrounded*. Hebrew Bible Monographs 62. Sheffield: Sheffield Phoenix Press, 2014.

Foxhall, Lin and John Salmon. *When Men Were Men: Masculinity, Power and Identity in Classical Antiquity*. London: Routledge, 2000.

Glover, David and Cora Kaplan. *Genders*. London: Routledge, 2000.

Graves-Brown, Carolyn, ed. *Sex and Gender in Ancient Egypt*. Llandysul: The Classical Press of Wales, 2008.

Hackett, Jo Ann. "Can a Sexist Model Liberate Us? Ancient Near Eastern 'Fertility' Goddesses." *Journal of Feminist Studies in Religion* 5 (1989): 65–76.

Haddad, Tony, ed. *Men and Masculinities: A Critical Anthology*. Toronto: Canadian Scholars' Press, 1993.

Hirose, Akihiko and Kay Kei-ho Pih. "Men Who Strike and Men Who Submit: Hegemonic and Marginalized Masculinities in Mixed Martial Arts." *Men and Masculinities* 2 (2010): 190–209.

Hoffner, Harry A. "Symbols for Masculinity and Femininity: Their Use in Ancient. Near Eastern Sympathetic Magic Rituals." *Journal of Biblical Literature* 85 (1966): 326–334.

Hörschelmann, Kathrin and Bettina van Hoven, eds. *Spaces of Masculinities*. London: Routledge, 2004.

Keuls, Eva C. *The Reign of the Phallus: Sexual Politics in Ancient Athens*. New York: Harper & Row, 1985.

Kimmel, Michael. "Masculinity as Homophobia: Fear, Shame and Silence in the Construction of Gender Identity." In *Theorizing Masculinities*. Eds. Harry Brod and Michael Kaufman. London: Sage Publications, 1994, pp. 119–141.

Laqueur, Thomas. *Making Sex, Body and Gender from the Greeks to Freud*. Cambridge: Harvard University Press, 1990.

Lorber, J. and S. A. Farrell, eds. *The Social Construction of Gender*. Newbury Park: Sage, 1991.

Mac an Ghaill, Mairtin, ed. *Understanding Masculinities: Social Relations and Cultural Arenas*. Buckingham & Philadelphia: Open University Press, 1996.

Messerschmidt, James. *Hegemonic Masculinities and Camouflaged Politics: Unmasking the Bush Dynasty and Its War Against Iraq*. London: Paradigm Publishers, 2010.

Montserrat, Dominic, ed. *Changing Bodies, Changing Meanings: Studies on the Human Body in Antiquity*. London: Routledge, 1998.

———. *Akhenaten: History, Fantasy and Ancient Egypt*. London: Routledge, 2003.

Moore, Stephen and Janice Capel Anderson, eds. *New Testament Masculinities*. Atlanta: Society of Biblical Literature, 2003.

Nissinen, Martti. *Homoeroticism in the Biblical World: A Historical Perspective*. Minneapolis: Fortress Press, 1998.

Osborne, Robin. "Men without Clothes: Heroic Nakedness and Greek Art." *Gender and History* 9 (1997): 504–528.

Parkinson, R. B. "'Boasting about Hardness': Constructions of Middle Kingdom Masculinity." In *Sex and Gender in Ancient Egypt: "Don Your Wig for a Joyful Hour."* Ed. C. Graves-Brown. Swansea: Classical Press of Wales, 2008, pp. 115–142.

Penner, Todd and Caroline Vander Stichele, eds. *Mapping Gender in Ancient Religious Discourses*. Brill: Leiden, 2006.

Spencer-Wood, Suzanne M. "Gendering Power." In *Manifesting Power: Gender and the Interpretation of Power in Archaeology*. Ed. Tracy Sweely. London: Routledge, 1999, pp. 175–183.

Synnott, Anthony. *Re-Thinking Men: Heroes Villains and Victims*. London: Ashgate, 2009.

Whitehead, Stephen M. *Men and Masculinities: Key Themes and New Directions*. Cambridge: Polity Press, 2002.

Whitehead, Stephen M. and Frank J. Barrett, eds. *The Masculinities Reader*. Cambridge: Polity Press, 2001.

Williams, Craig A. *Roman Homosexuality: Ideologies of Masculinity in Classical Antiquity*. Oxford: Oxford University Press, 1999.

Winkler, J. J. *The Constraints of Desire: The Anthropology of Sex and Gender in Ancient Greece*. London: Routledge, 1989.

Winter, Irene. "Sex, Rhetoric and the Public Monument: The Alluring Body of the Male Ruler in Mesopotamia." In *Sexuality in Ancient Art*. Ed. N. B. Kampen. New York: Cambridge University Press, 1996, pp. 11–26.

Wylie, Alison. "Gender Theory and the Archaeological Record: Why Is There No Archaeology of Gender?" In *Engendering Archaeology*. Eds. J. M. Gero and M. W. Conkey. Cambridge: Cambridge University Press, 1991, pp. 31–54.

1 Categorizing men and masculinity in Sumer[1]

Joan Goodnick Westenholz and Ilona Zsolnay

Biological sex and social gender are categories that we, in Western culture, assign to human beings. Traditionally, Male mortals perform masculine activities, modes of dress, behaviors, while female mortals perform feminine activities, modes of dress, behaviors, et cetera. These performances allocated to, adopted by, or, in some cases, forced upon, individuals can be identical (e.g., family driver) or different (e.g., men tend not to wear dresses). Western culture also expects certain activities, modes of dress, behaviors, and the like to be performed during certain stages in a man's or woman's life. Both sexes are thought to pass through culturally defined chronological stages: infancy, childhood, adolescence, "prime of life," middle age, and old age. The chronological parameters of these stages have changed through the decades, centuries, indeed, even, millennia. When once there was no childhood, in the United States, it has become common for adult "children" to remain dependent upon their parents well into their twenties and even thirties. Middle age, stereotypically defined as the time when one settles down into a chosen life, may occur in one's early thirties or late fifties. Conversely, a person may pass through this stage chronologically, but never actually *perform* it.

Today, men are categorized by age, racial and ethnic background, class, or financial status. In this chapter, we investigate if, how, and when men were designated by sex and/or gender in Sumerian administrative, lexical, and "literary" texts. We begin by identifying, defining, and contextualizing those pictographs (logograms) which signified categories of men in texts which date to the Archaic period (c. 3350–3000 BCE). We then review the later attestations of the Sumerian terms these logograms came to represent. Less an analysis of social characteristics, here we survey the most basic categories to which a man could be assigned (not choose to enter). Many of the classifications discussed are familiar to the Sumerologist: dependent, independent, worker, and upper class "person." What is exposed by this survey is that there seems to have been no true generic category "male human," that is, one devoid of social status with an accompanying generic construct of masculinity. From the Archaic period onward, the southern Mesopotamian writing system demonstrates a complex system for designating men that is dependent upon social class, age, text type (e.g., lexical versus ration list), and period in which it was written.[2]

Categorizing by sex and gender

In the Archaic sign repertoire, mammals are first divided according to their more general categories, for example, ovicapridae, bovidae, cervidae, suidae, felidae, and hominidae.[3] In order to indicate a more specific class, the sign that indicated the general category was either modified or supplemented. For example, the generic sign for goat is a simple cross (MAŠ) and the generic sign for sheep is an encircled cross (UDU).[4] In order to specify a fat-tailed sheep, a "fat" tail was amended to the UDU sign. In order to mark the sex of either a sheep or a goat, the sign HI (ŠIR$^{?}$), which represented a testicular sac, was added to the more general pictograph (e.g., MAŠ or UDU) to indicate a male, while teats (no independent sign) were added to indicate a female.[5] The sex of nonovicaprids is otherwise indicated. Cows and bulls were each designated by slightly modified versions of a triangle (i.e., cows were depicted with floppy ears [AB$_2$] and bulls with upright horns [GU$_4$]).[6] For young animals of all types (including calves, kids, and lambs), and adult cervidae, suidae, and felidae, an additional pictograph was inscribed next to the generic-family sign to designate sex. If the animal was female, the additional pictograph is the image of a pubic triangle (SAL); if the animal was male, the pictograph was either the image of an ejaculating erect penis (UŠ) or a set of mountains (KUR$_a$):[7]

SAL		female; woman[8]
UŠ		male; independent man[9]
KUR$_a$		male/subjugated; subjugated man; mountains[10]

Hominidae – that is, humans – could also be designated as either UŠ, KUR$_a$, or SAL. When substantivized, UŠ and SAL referred to seemingly nondescript people, for example, ATU5 W7024 lists a man (UŠ) and woman (SAL) together; ATU5 W7227,a lists 11 men (UŠ) and six subordinate$^{?}$ men (UŠ RU); and ATU5 W9311,q lists an old man (UŠ GI$_4$).[11] Substantivized KUR$_a$ was used to refer specifically to a subjugated man. Because KUR could also be used adjectivally with an ever morphing signification, it will be dealt with extensively in the following discussion.

The independent, dependent, and subjugated

The pictograph for "person/individual" was SAG, an unmarked hairless head: .[12] As a generic sign, SAG could be modified in a numerous of ways. It could be marked to indicate various facial features (e.g., teeth, mouth, or nose) or accompanied by additional signs to indicate actions (e.g., drinking or eating) or certain objects (e.g., rations). In much later Ur III (c. 2112–2004 BCE) sale documents, SAG refers to a particular social class and is qualified by sex. The terms SAG UŠ "individual man" and SAG

SAL "individual woman" refer to people who had not yet been sold or were in the process of being purchased.[13] In his study of the Ur III corpus, Piotr Steinkeller refers to these individuals as independent (versus the dependent $arad_2$ and $geme_2$, discussed below), persons designated by the SAG sign were independent in so far as they were in a transitional state. The SAG individual would become dependent once purchased. In these administrative texts, unmodified/unqualified SAG is employed when people were treated as countable entities or objects, just as we would speak of a head count and not of a person count, as pointed out by Gertrud Farber.[14] Eventually, SAG came to reference people in both the subjugated and quasi-independent working classes (e.g., farmer and baker), when saĝ-hi-a "assorted head(s)" became the collective term that includes men, women, and children.[15]

The generic and unisex nature of SAG is emphasized in the Archaic corpus.[16] One does not find lists that include or total a number of male and/or female SAG, and it is difficult to assesses its full range of meaning and function during the Uruk period.[17] In Archaic texts, a single SAG, or several, are mentioned alongside animals (e.g., ATU7 W19948,37 and ATU5 W7227,d) or in a group listed with various officials, perhaps receiving rations (e.g., MSVO 3,68).[18] That SAG needed to be qualified when indicating subjugated people is indicated by a very specific set of tablets from the Archaic corpus (MSVO 1,212–14), discovered in the administrative building in the northern city Jemdet Naṣr. MSVO 1,213 contains a listing of people, many of whom are individually labeled SAGxMA "noosed SAG."[19] MSVO 1,214 seems to be an additional set of persons not individually labeled SAGxMA, but connected to the group present on MSVO 1,213. MSVO 1,212 contains a summary of those persons listed on MSVO 1,213 and 214 (minus two women). MSVO 1,212 also contains a subtotal and a total. What is of particular note is the difference in the manner of recording. In addition to some people being labeled SAGxMA, on MSVO 1,213, every person is designated as either KUR_a, SAL KUR_a, or TUR ("young").[20] MSVO 1,212, recording the same people, does not designate anyone as SAGxMA and, although each is qualified by sex and age, the terms used are KUR_a, SAL, and TUR (i.e., SAL not SAL KUR_a). The totals for these persons are given on the reverse of the tablet.

Reading backwards, MSVO 1,212 col. 3 gives a total of 27 SAL and KUR_a. In col. 2, 17 of these persons are identified as SAGxMA "noosed" and ten are defined as ERIN, which may mean "yoked":[21]

col. 2	1. $1(N_{14})$ $7(N_1)$ SAL KUR_a SAGxMA
	2. $1(N_{14})$ SAL KUR_a $ERIM_a$ X [. . .]
col. 3	1. [$2(N_{14})$] $7(N_1)$# SAL# KUR_a# UB PA_a#? SAGxMA# $SANGA_a$# X EN_a# $1(N_4)$

The conclusion then is first that SAGxMA is a unisex signifier, which could be sexed if the conditions warranted. Additionally, when the situation regarded a group class, it was unnecessary to qualify individually each person as belonging that class. The overarching category is only noted in the total, or subtotal; thus, in MSVO 1,212, KUR_a SAL "men and women" is the generic class, while the subtotals, categorized as SAGxMA and ERIM, reflect more specific classes. In this instance, the categories denoting the sex of the individuals, KUR_a *and* SAL/SAL KUR_a, are less important as a means by which to classify the groups. They are of the same value. That KUR_a *and* SAL, not SAG, is the collective term is also attested in the Archaic tablets from Uruk; for example, ATU5 W9827 has a grand total of 211 "KUR_a *and* SAL."[22] Since neither MSVO 1,213 nor 214 gives a total, the SAGxMA status of those individuals who were "noosed" (whether KUR_a or SAL KUR_a) must be designated separately. This indicates that those persons labeled KUR_a or SAL KUR_a were not automatically considered to be in the category unqualified SAG.

Of further note is the seeming difference between the two terms unqualified SAL and SAL qualified by KUR_a. KUR_a, when functioning adjectivally, described a noun as "male," and, when substantivized, signified a "subjugated man"; however, as this registry indicates, KUR_a could also be used to describe a woman. In these instances, she is not a male woman, she is a subjugated woman. To be KUR_a was not to simply be male, but to be of the chattel class.[23] That the SAL KUR_a on MSVO 1,213 are referred to simply as SAL on MSVO 1,212 is a shorthand permissible by context.[24]

Following the Archaic period, the KUR, SAL, SAL KUR system is standardized[25]. KUR is no longer attested as a sex designation for any animal (or human), only as a status indicator. At this time, the designations became consistently UŠ KUR ($arad_2$), "male slave or servant," and SAL KUR ($geme_2$), "female slave or servant." The earliest clear attestation for $arad_2$ and $geme_2$ is UET 2, 259, which lists 23 masculine personal names followed by 12 feminine names. These are then totaled 23 $arad_2$ and 12 $geme_2$.[26] There is no greater unisex or generic category (e.g., SAG). In sale documents from the Ur III period, $arad_2$ and $geme_2$ are used to reference owned people. As SAG UŠ and SAG SAL are the categories which designate people *before* they are owned, $arad_2$ and $geme_2$ are those that designate them *once* they are purchased. They have become dependent.

In addition to the states of chattel servitude intrinsic to the labels $arad_2$ and $geme_2$, southern Mesopotamia also had a state-organized system of labor in which able-bodied male workers were characterized by the lexeme ĝuruš.[27] In the Archaic sign repertoire, the pictograph GURUŠ is an abstract image of a sledge with a litter on top. From its representation on seals it has been determined that this sledge was pulled by a bovine of some sort and was used for ceremonial, in addition to agricultural, purposes. In ceremonies, the notable figure (male or female) would sit in the litter while a driver would stand before it, still on the sledge, and goad the animal. When used as a threshing implement, the sledge's bottom would have been covered in sharp flints and an animal of some sort would drag it repeatedly over grain while a person would serve as a guide. From ĝuruš "sledge" developed the meaning "field-hand," which eventually came to mean able-bodied workers of all sorts, including those in military units;[28] thus, at this point, ĝuruš signified not simply a type of worker, but a man in his physical prime.

That these persons were not wholly independent and had an overseer even during the earliest periods is indicated on Archaic inscription ATU7 W19851,b + W19948,28, which lists an official referred to as the GAL GURUŠ "overseer of the ĝuruš."[29] That GURUŠ fell into the category SAG is apparent on an Archaic tablet from Kiš, MSVO 4,74 (see Figure 1.1).

On MSVO 4,74, the grand total of persons is defined as three SAG GURUŠ. The subtotals inform that one is a DA and two are DU. One of these DU is

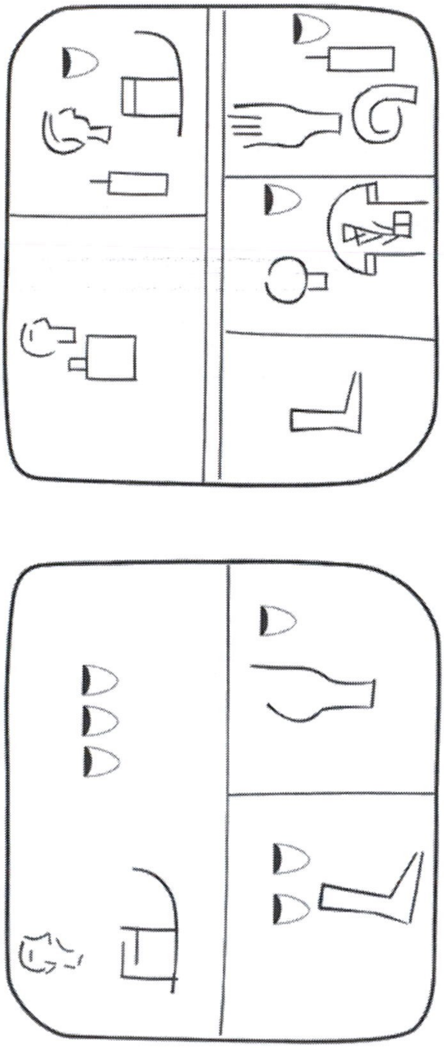

O0101 1(N1) SAĜ UŠ ĜURUŠ
O0102 SAĜ URUDU

O0201 1(N1) DA UŠ ZATU697?
O0202 1(N1) EZENb
ZATU651+ENa
O0203 DU

R0101 1(N1) DA
R0102 2(N1) DU

R0201 3(N1) SAĜ ĜURUŠ

Figure 1.1 MSVO 4, 74 (Ashm, 1926, 56). Archaic Uruk III, Kiš. National Museum of Iraq, Baghdad, Iraq.

Image in public domain. http://cdli.ucla.edu/P005476 (accessed 2 Dec 2015).

qualified by UŠ, whereas the one DA is designated as SAG UŠ GURUŠ. It is impossible in either instance to confirm if the UŠ is a sex marker; however, because SAG GURUŠ (the collective designation for all three people), does not contain a sex marker, one might conclude that one of the individuals listed as DU was female. This would indicate that GURUŠ, in this case, was not a sexed category; however, this is unlikely as when totaled the bi-sex collective is GURUŠ SAL, as on MSVO 1,1, a tablet that records a number of men and women working in the fields of higher officials; thus, SAL, not SAL GURUŠ, is the female counterpart to GURUŠ. Most likely, UŠ, in the examples on MSVO 4,74, signifies location.[30]

By the Early Dynastic period (c. 2900–2350 BCE), SAL is no longer the counterpart to GURUŠ. Instead, as "man in the prime of his life," becomes the more general meaning of ĝuruš, $geme_2$ replaces SAL as its female equivalent. In ration lists, ĝuruš and $geme_2$ represent "adult male worker" and "adult female worker," respectively. In these lists, if the worker is young, they are designated as dumu "child"; however, if they are "old," yet still working, the terms ĝuruš and $geme_2$ are qualified by the unisex adjective $šu\text{-}gi_4$.[31] In these texts, groups of ĝuruš and $geme_2$ are categorized simply as SAG or lu_2 didli-me "assorted people."[32]

Professional classes

It is unclear if the Sumerian term for an independent unsexed person paid wages for their work, ḫuĝ(a), "hireling," appears in the Archaic corpus; however, lexemes for specific professions are attested. In Sumerian, the terms for members of professional classes are usually singular and devoid of categorization by sex or gender. The profession of scribe, official, farmer, and others is each separately labeled (e.g., dubsar "scribe/tablet writer"). There are sporadic instances in which these professional classes are sexed and, in ration lists, persons classified as "X professional" can be totaled by sex. Examples of the latter are attested in the earliest writings. Archaic ATU5 W9579,ci lists one KAB UŠ "male shepherd," and W9579,o records the presence of a SAL SANGA KISAL "female a kisal-bookeeper."[33] Perhaps unexpectedly, VAT 09091, which is dated to the ED IIIa period, records two ENGAR SAL "female farmers." In ED administrative lists from Girsu, totals of professionals are regularly divided by male and female; for example, a series of persons can be listed as unsexed "X professional." This list is then subtotaled with the phrase nita(UŠ) me, "these are the men," or by munus(SAL), me "these are the women."[34] The entire group of professionals can then be totaled as lu_2, just as in the case of the ĝuruš and $geme_2$.

The elite

In texts, members of the elite, and ruling families of Sumerian cities, referred to themselves and others of equal rank as lu_2, at least as early as the ED period. For example, E-anatum, king of Lagaš, describes himself as lu$_2$-inim-si-sa$_2$-kam, "the lu$_2$ of correct laws."[35] While Uru-ka-gina refers to himself as the lu$_2$ e$_2$-ninnu du$_3$-a, "the lu$_2$ who built the E-ninnu."[36] Of his enemy the lu$_2$ of Umma, Uru-ka-gina says:

> lu$_2$ ^{giš}#KUŠU$_2$#.KI#-ke$_4$# eger#-lagaš# ŠIR.BUR# [LA].KI ba-hul-a-ta nam-dag ^{d}nin-ĝir$_2$-su-da e-da-ak-ka-am$_6$
>
> The lu$_2$ of Ĝiša (Umma) having sacked Lagaš, has committed a sin against the god Ninĝirsu.[37]

The high standing of a lu$_2$ may be seen in the reform texts of Uru-ka-gina, who speaks of the abuses performed by this class of person: e$_2$ lu$_2$ gu-la-ke$_4$ e$_2$ RU-lugal-ka ab-us$_2$-sa, "(When) the house of an important lu$_2$ adjoins the house of a subordinate."[38] Additionally, this king promises that the prerogatives of the powerful will be curtailed: nu-siki nu-ma-nu-kuš$_2$ lu$_2$ a$_2$-tuku nu-na-ga$_2$-ga$_2$-a, "that he would never subjugate the orphan (or) the widow to the powerful lu$_2$."[39]

The pictograph that signifies the lexeme lu$_2$ is the abstract image of an anthropomorphic being .[40] Because its form may well be yet another modification of SAG, "head," the hatched "body" could have indicated a type of garment (elite?) or other social-class marker.[41] In the Archaic materials, there are fewer than ten attestations for the pictograph LU$_2$.[42] The sign is attested in combination with KU$_6$, "fish," in Archaic Fish (ATU3 W22101,9b and W17902,d). In these instances LU$_2$ is simply one of many types of fish. LU$_2$ is also attested in Archaic Plants (W20266,20), where it seems to be a type of location that would contain a SUKKAL, "secretary."[43] In ED Plants, the same entry adds a lil$_2$, "fool"; thus, the entry is traditionally read e$_2$ lu$_2$ lil$_2$ sukkal, "secretary of the house of fools."[44] In four additional attestations, LU$_2$ is modified by either MUD or MUD$_3$.[45] It is unclear how this should be understood. The pictograph for MUD$_3$ is a modified DUG, "jar," and the sign is attested in several exemplars of Archaic Vessels and Archaic Metals. As later lexical lists equate MUD$_3$ with Akkadian *hubur*, "beer jar," the LU$_2$ MUD$_3$ may have been involved in the beer industry.[46] Bolstering this conclusion is MSVO 3,42, which lists LU$_2$ MUD$_3$ in connection with large quantities of barley, a key ingredient in the making of beer and, notably, a plant.

In the ED administrative documents, persons designated as lu$_2$ who receive rations may be totaled under the generic classification nita me, "these being the men." Similar to SAG, that lu$_2$ itself does not mean "man" or "male" is indicated by the need to state that these person are designated in the total as nita, "men," not simply lu$_2$. That lu$_2$ could refer to ĝuruš is evidenced in texts from Fara in which series of ĝuruš are totaled as lu$_2$ dab$_5$, "conscripted lu$_2$," rather than *saĝ dab$_5$, "conscripted heads." (This once again throws confusion on the exact status of the ĝuruš.) In Thorkild Jacobsen's discussion of *The Marriage of Martu*, he proposes that lu$_2$ denotes a person having economic responsibility for, and charge of, others; he also considers this the basic meaning of the lexeme. This would certainly accord well with modern understandings of those professions that are designated as gal, "chief."[47]

Referring to the literary composition *The Marriage of Martu*, Jacobsen highlights the culturally assumed differences between ĝuruš and lu$_2$ and contends that ĝuruš must always refer to a subordinate man. A description of the distribution of food rations at the end of the working day reads:

> ud ne ud ten-na um#-[ma-te]-a#-ra ki niĝ$_2$-ba-ka um-ma#-[te]-a-ra igi ^{d}EŠ$_2$.LIL.DU niĝ$_2$-ba na#-ni#-ĝa$_2$#-ĝa$_2$ niĝ$_2$-ba lu$_2$ dam tuku 2-am$_3$ i$_3$-ĝa$_2$-ĝa$_2$ niĝ$_2$-ba lu$_2$ dumu tuku 3-am$_3$ i$_3$-ĝa$_2$-ĝa$_2$ niĝ$_2$-<ba> ĝuruš saĝ-dili 1-am$_3$ i$_3$-ĝa$_2$-ĝa$_2$
>
> One day, as the evening came, and they had reached the place of rations, they established the rations before the god EŠ$_2$.LIL.DU. The ration of a [lu$_2$ with a spouse] was established as double, the ration of a [lu$_2$ with a child] was established as triple; the ration of a ĝuruš was established as single.[48]

Although in certain administrative documents, ĝuruš (and geme$_2$) are totaled as lu$_2$, in this text, a decided status difference is indicated: those assumed to have, and not have, dependents.

While it may seem that lu$_2$ would designate a high-born male, as will be demonstrated by the following investigation into the categories present in early lexical lists, lu$_2$ probably refers to a freeborn person in general, as has been suggested by Raymond Westbrook and others, while, outside of the lexical tradition, the more general lexeme nita was used of independent males more broadly.[49]

Lu$_2$ nita, ĝuruš, and saĝ in early lexical lists

Lexical texts are a characteristic feature of Mesopotamian culture from the earliest period. In them is represented a (somewhat) systematic picture of their world, as they enumerate and classify everything animal, vegetable, and mineral as well as man-made objects, societal structures, and spiritual entities.[50] The list commonly referred to as Lu$_2$ A exists in two recensions: Archaic Lu$_2$ A, which dates to the end of the fourth millennium, and ED Lu$_2$ A, which was compiled during the third. Despite its name, Archaic Lu$_2$ A does not provide any evidence of the lexeme lu$_2$. This list, also referred to as the Standard Professions List, seems to be mostly concerned with the managerial classes, as many of the titles begin with gal "overseer."[51] Furthermore, none of the professions listed are sex-classified, e.g., accompanied by nita. The enlarged ED recension of Lu_2 A also contains no evidence of lu_2, nor does it sex-classify any of the occupations listed. It does, however, list two professions that demonstrate a differentiation of the masculine classes that may be based on either age class or social status: nita and ĝuruš:

110	gal nita	"nita overseer"
111	gal ĝuruš	"ĝuruš overseer"

As has been mentioned above, the GAL GURUŠ is attested in the Archaic corpus.[52] The gal nita is unique to this lexical text. It is also of note that the GAL SAL does not occur in these lists as it is present in the Archaic materials. Lu_2 A has been analyzed as having a hierarchical arrangement.[53] If the listing of gal nita before gal ĝuruš indicates a higher status, the nita might be considered a higher-class male; thus, the nita may be an independent man performing some form of servile or general labor just as the ĝuruš is a dependent single man performing a similar service. It is also of note that, unlike, say, in the case of the gal $kiri_6$, "overseer of the garden/ers," there is no obvious or specific workload associated with either ĝuruš or nita. As discussed above, a ĝuruš may have performed field labor, but he could also have been conscripted into other forms of service.

Unlike Lu_2 A, which is attested in the Archaic corpus, Lu_2 B, C, D, and E were likely composed during the ED period. B and D are singular and differing manuscripts from Fara, while C occurs in both a Fara and an Ur III manuscript.[54] The latest of this group of "professions" lexical texts, ED Lu_2 E, was more popular from the ED IIIb through Old Akkadian (c. 2300–2150 BCE) periods.[55] The earliest attestations of lu_2 in these lexical texts occurs simply as a semantic classifier or relative pronoun lacking any sex or class distinction. It appears with occupations that may well have been performed by either a man or a woman (e.g., lu_2 nar "singer"). As with Lu_2 A, Lu_2 B, C, and D, ED Lu_2 E contains no professions that are sex-classified; however, it can be observed that Lu_2 B lists a lu_2 ĝuruš:

r ii 1	lu_2 ninda-kum_4	"person who makes (particular ingredient in) beer"
r ii 2	lu_2 ĝešpu_2	"person who wrestles"
r ii 3	lu_2 ĝuruš[56]	"person who is able bodied"
r ii 4	lu_2 GIŠ:KID	"person who weaves mats?"[57]

Since the lu_2 ĝuruš is listed alongside workers who perform specific tasks, it may well be that ĝuruš was a profession of sorts (e.g., "the one who is a field-hand"). That the lu_2 ĝuruš entry is grouped with a series of individuals needing strength to perform their jobs reinforces the meaning "able bodied."

Although not referred to as a Lu-list, there are several entries listing ĝuruš in the ED version of the rarely attested Officials list that may shed some light:

89	ĝuruš	"ĝuruš"
90	1(AŠ) ĝuruš	"1 unit ĝuruš"
91	niĝin ĝuruš	"total ĝuruš"

This series is followed by:

93	saĝ	"saĝ"
94	2(AŠ) saĝ	"2 unit saĝ"
95	niĝin saĝ	"total saĝ"[58]

As these lines bear a great resemblance to the manner by which units of ĝuruš are listed in the administrative tablets discussed above, the scribe is likely writing down the proper method for entering data. That the series is followed by a parallel sequence of saĝ indicates a differentiation between ĝuruš and saĝ. That an unqualified lu_2 or a gal lu_2, "overseer of the lu_2," does not appear in these lists suggests that lu_2 is not a class of worker and certainly not one that would have an overseer (gal).[59]

Not strictly hierarchical,[60] Lu_2 E also may have been composed during the ED period, perhaps in Kish, as proposed by Biggs.[61] In Lu_2 E, there are two juxtaposed categories: one unmarked category and one marked, the marker being munus "female":

49	Ø agrig	"steward"
50	^{munus}agrig	"female steward"[62]

Here we know that munus is likely acting as a determinative or signifier simply because, if it were acting as an adjective, we would expect it to come after the noun agrig "steward." It may also be noted that, in so far as the profession steward is concerned, there arose a need to delineate the social gender category: feminine. As agrig is a proper rather than descriptive noun, there may have been no need for either a determinative or relative pronoun, thus the term need not have been marked with lu_2; however, it would seem that there must have been a reason to specify that there were two different types of steward. Perhaps, in the culture in which the list was created, it was socially obvious which jobs were performed by men and which by women (e.g., $šag_4$-zu, "midwife," or lukur, a type of priestess). If agrig was one of the few jobs with an originally unsexed title, it is also possible that the distinction was made because the feminine form of the job differed in some way from the masculine. It may be also have been related to the differentiation in the Semitic languages, which do have grammatical gender ("the so-called Kish area").[63]

In the first half of the second millennium, new word lists were composed that became the staple of the education system. Two thematic catalogues of humans were produced by the pedagogues: (1) OB (Old Babylonian) Proto-Lu$_2$ (the forerunner of the canonical Lu$_2$ = *šá*),[64] which exists as a very long monolingual Sumerian vocabulary of offices, titles, professions, and kinship terms and in shorter bilingual editions; and (2) a bilingual thematic word list "with a wider anthropological outlook, that includes terms for psychological qualities, bodily characteristics, morbid states, and general human activities."[65] This word list was published as OB Lu$_2$ and is now referred to by its incipit as Lu$_2$-azlag$_2$ = *ašlāku* "fuller." Although Archaic/ED Lu$_2$ and OB Proto-Lu$_2$ are mostly, if not entirely, nouns and nouns phrases, Lu$_2$-azlag$_2$ = *ašlāku* has verbal phrases. Many entries don't have titles per se; they are listed as "the one who does/holds the. . . ."[66]

In OB Proto-Lu$_2$, the first line contains the entry lu$_2$ which must be regarded as a title of the composition meaning "[list] of persons"; the actual list begins with the entry lugal, "king."[67] Here again are categories of persons; however, there are also sets: unmarked category followed by category marked with the unspoken classifier "female":

ø : munus

317	kisal luḫ	"courtyard sweeper"
318	^{munus}kisal luḫ	"female courtyard sweeper"
499	ensi	"dream interpreter"
500	^{munus}ensi	"female dream interpreter"

These pairs also occur in which lu$_2$ appears as a relative pronoun in each case:

ø lu$_2$: munus lu$_2$

102	lu$_2$ ^{kaš}kurun$_2$-na	"one who is a brewer/innkeeper"
103	^{munus}lu$_2$ ^{kaš}kurun$_2$-na	"female one who is a brewer/innkeeper"

Finally, since OB Proto-Lu$_2$ is not merely a list of professions, it adds a section devoted to family relations. Here we find the pairs:

371	nita	"independent male"
372	munus	"independent female"
373	arad$_2$	"dependent male"
374	geme$_2$	"dependent female"

It is of note that there is no set lu$_2$/munus, instead we find the sets nita/munus and arad$_2$ /geme$_2$. It is likely that here we have the difference again between the broad categories of dependent and independent listed hierarchically.

Unlike OB Proto-Lu$_2$, bilingual Lu$_2$-azlag$_2$ = *ašlāku* truly confirms the unsexed nature of lu$_2$ for throughout the catalogue lu$_2$ is used as either a relative pronoun or as a determinative. Again, several of the entries also include categories *additionally* marked by the classifier munus:

21	lu$_2$-^{kaš}kurun$_2$-na	= *sà-bu-ú*	"brewer/innkeeper"
22	^{munus}lu$_2$-^{kaš}kurun$_2$-na	= *sà-bi-i-tum*	"female brewer/innkeeper"
23	lu$_2$ gub-ba	= *mu-úh-hu-um*	"one who is frenetic"
24	^{munus}lu$_2$ gub-ba	= *mu-hu-tum#*	"female one who is frenetic"

Or entirely lacking munus:

61	[lu$_2$ dinĝir tuku]	= *ša i-lam i-šu-ú*	"one who has a protective god"
62	[lu$_2$ dinĝir tuku nu]- tuku#	= *ša i-lam la i-šu-ú*	"one who does not have a protective god"
63	[lu$_2$ ^{d}šedu tuku]	= *ša še-e-dam i-šu-ú*	"one who has a *šedu* spirit"
64	[lu$_2$ ^{d}lamma tuku]	= *ša i-lam i-šu-ú*	"one who does not have a *lamma* spirit"

Finally, just before the final entries, a series of people who died horribly, is listed:

492	lu$_2$	*a-wi-lum*	"man"
493	lu$_2$	*ša-a*	"one who . . . "
494	lu$_2$	*a-wi-il-tum*	"woman"

The Akkadian lexicographers who had to provide translations of the Sumerian terms were struggling with the translation of the Sumerian lexeme lu$_2$ in these lines. They put forward three different translations into Akkadian: *awīlum* "man," *ša* "who," and *awīltum* "woman."

Lu$_2$, nita, ĝuruš, and saĝ in "literary" texts

In the Sumerian judicial system, the emphasis was on the actions of the individual person (lu$_2$), regardless of gender, age, or sex. In her discussion of the terminology of the legal texts, Martha Roth puts emphasis on the subject of the laws, the lu$_2$ as "person" rather than "man."[68] The Sumerian Law Collection of Ur-Namma contains a set of laws that employ the three terms lu$_2$, ĝuruš, and nita, and provide clarification for the use of these lexemes.[69]

¶6 tukum-bi dam ĝuruš-a a nu-gi$_4$-a[70] nig$_2$-a$_2$-gar-še$_3$ lu$_2$ in-ak-ma a bi$_2$-in-gi$_4$ nita-bi i$_3$-gaz-e

¶7 tukum-bi dam ĝuruš-a ni$_2$-te-a-ni-ta lu$_2$ ba-an-us$_2$-ma ur$_2$-ra-ne$_2$ ba-an-na$_2$ munus-bi i$_2$-gaz-e nita-bi ama-ar-gi$_4$-ni i$_2$-ĝa$_2$-ĝa$_2$

If a lu$_2$ violates the rights of another and deflowers the virgin wife of a ĝuruš, they shall kill that nita.[71]

If the wife of a ĝuruš of her own initiative, approaches a lu$_2$ and initiates sexual relations with him, they shall kill that munus; that nita shall be released.[72]

According to Jacobsen, in these laws, lu$_2$ ceases to be seen as a responsible person for the lu$_2$ becomes a mere sex specimen, a male (nita).[73] Although it well may be true that the lu$_2$ is reduced to this "sex specimen," it is more likely that the lexeme nita is employed for clarification. It is the nita male, not the ĝuruš male, or the dam ĝuruš (spouse of the ĝuruš), who is to be killed. The juridical situation described in these two legal paragraphs depends on the clear understanding of dam ĝuruš. A ĝuruš is not a married man but has only contracted an inchoate marriage. The wife-to-be is living in her father's house and susceptible to sexual advances. Roth notes that this change clearly identifies the outsider male who violates the husband-to-be's rights. Because of the different statuses of a nita and a ĝuruš, lu$_2$ needed to be clarified.[74]

The Nippur Homicide Trial, a text that dates to the beginning of the second millennium, deals with the case of three men who conspired to murder a priest; after committing the murder they informed his wife, who then kept silent about the crime.[75] The verdict was:

lu$_2$-lu$_2$-u$_3$ in-gaz-eš-am$_3$ lu$_2$-ti-la nu-me-eš nita# 3-a-bi u$_3$ munus-bi . . . i$_3$-gaz-de$_3$-eš

As lu$_2$ who have killed lu$_2$, they should not be allowed to live (lit. they should not be living beings [lu$_2$]). Those three nita and that munus . . . shall be killed.[76]

Again, there is a change from lu$_2$, general, in the first sentence, to nita and munus, specific, in the second. If, instead of specifying three nita and one munus, the verdict had merely referred to all as lu$_2$, it would have lacked clarity; it was necessary to specify that the woman, who had merely been told of the murder, was also being assessed as a lu$_2$ who "had killed lu$_2$" and "should not be allowed to live."

The lexeme lu$_2$-ulu$_3$, "civilized person," and its abstract namlu-ulu$_3$, "civilized life," are employed as more encompassing terms to express "civilized human, humanity" as in:

nam-lu$_2$-ulu$_3$ munus nita zi-gal$_2$ mu-tuku-bi[77]

(he crushed with weapons) its civilized life, women and men, those possessing life (and) having a name . . .

In this line, the Ur III king Šu-Sîn is referring to the people of Šimaški, his enemies, and describing his wiping out of all *civilized* life. The term lu$_2$-ulu$_3$ is formed using the logogram for person and city:

LU$_2$ + ULU$_3$ (URU × MIN)[78]  human body + urbanization[79]

LU_2 + ULU_3 is a concatenation of two nouns. In this compound, the lu_2, rather than a marker of semantic category, forms part of the word. On the basis of the meaning of these two nouns, one might hazard a suggestion that the compound refers to civilized human beings (human beings living in cities). This term would have its antonym in the usage of KUR, mountaineer (non-city-dwellers), for the socioeconomic lowest classes.

A Sumerian proverb presents a parallelism between the two lexemes lu_2 and lu_2-ulu_3: $šag_4$-$ĝa_2$ lu_2-ulu_3-me-en igi-$ĝa_2$ lu_2 nu-me-en, "in my heart you are a lu_2-ulu_3, but in my eyes you are not lu_2."[80] In his commentary, Bendt Alster reads that "this apparently refers to a discrepancy between a man's outer appearance and his inner qualities. In the speaker's opinion, the man about whom this is said is considered suitable for the designation 'man,' although his outer appearance does not qualify him as such."[81] Perhaps, this enigmatic proverb can be nuanced that the coarse outer appearance of this person does not even qualify him as lu_2: "in my heart you are a civilized person (lu_2-ulu_3), but in my eyes you are not *even* a human being (lu_2)."

In his quest for the Cedar Forest, Gilgameš declares to Enkidu:

> en-na lu_2-bi lu_2-u_{18}-lu $ḫe_2$-a im-ma-zu-a-a-aš diĝir $ḫe_2$-a im-ma-zu-a-aš $ĝiri_3$ kur-$še_3$ gub-ba-$ĝu_{10}$ iri^{ki}-$še_3$ ba-ra-gub-be_2-en
>
> Until I discover whether that lu_2 (i.e., Huwawa) is a lu_2-ulu_3 or a god, I shall not direct back to the city my steps which I have directed to the mountains.[82]

Note that the title of this literary work, which modern scholars designate as *Gilgameš and Huwawa*, was identified by the ancients by its incipit, that is, the first line of the composition: en-e-kur-lu_2-ti-la-$še_3$, "The-Lord-towards-the-Mountain-where-the-lu_2-lives."[83]

Among the examples of saĝ, used in the general sense of individual that were collected by Farber, is one minimal pair with lu_2.[84] The example comprises two lines from an ED royal inscription of Lugalzagesi of Uruk in which lu_2 and saĝ appear in synonymous parallel lines:

> lu_2 $^{d}PISAN_2$.SAG.UNU^{ki}-ga
> saĝ a_2-e_3-a ^{d}Nin-$girim_3$ nin Unu^{ki}-ga-ka
> the lu_2 of (the god) Mes-saĝ-Unuga
> the saĝ raised by Ningirima, the nin of Uruk.[85]

Two divergent published translations of these lines are: " 'servant' of the god Mes-saĝ-Unug, who was brought up by the goddess Ningirim, the mistress of Uruk"[86] and "dem Mann Messanga-Unuga(s), dem von Ningirim, der Herrin Uruks großgezogenen Diener."[87] Whereas in the former Douglas Frayne treats the two lexemes differently, Claus Wilcke considers them as a synonymous pair. Another example, which Farber cites, indicates a further use in the literary language of the replacement of lu_2 by saĝ in the Uruk

Lament: saĝ lul-la saĝ zid-da šu bal mi-ni-ib-ak-a-a-aš, "how honest saĝ are transformed into traitors."[88] Not only do these two passages suggest a fluidity of the term typically used to represent different classes of human in administrative documents, their parallelism also reflects their inherent unsexed natures.

Masculinity and the life cycle

The physical unit that is the human body was studied by ancient Mesopotamian scholars and lexicographers. The results of their research are found in an anatomical vocabulary titled Ugu-mu, "my cranium."[89] Usually translated "my head," this list contains a compendium enumerating all known parts of the human anatomy as well as terms related to the essential elements of human nature. This latter section of this vocabulary includes five abstract age classes or states:

nam-lu$_2$-tur-ĝu$_{10}$	my status as young lu$_2$
nam-ĝuruš-(tur)-ĝu$_{10}$	my status as able-bodied (young) male
nam-kalag-ga-ĝu$_{10}$	my status as strong
nam-ur-saĝ-ĝu$_{10}$	my status as hero
nam-ab-ba-ĝu$_{10}$	my status as male elder

Each of these Sumerian words is composed of the abstract derivational prefix nam + the lexeme for a category of human, male, or characteristic. As a noun, nam is commonly translated as "fate," though its actual meaning is probably closer to something like "status or state";[90] thus, here, it would seem that five states are presented. It should be noted that a beginning student's exemplar of this list concludes with the Akkadian abstract term *awīlūtum* "personhood" or, perhaps better for this discussion, "life cycle."[91] Using this passage as a guide, we may surmise that these are the perceived states through which a male mortal passes as he ages. It should also be noted that general terms for person saĝ and lu$_2$, or the broad category for male/man, nita, are not present in the list.

The first age-class compound, nam-lu$_2$-tur, is composed of the abstract derivational prefix nam + the lexeme for "person," lu$_2$, + the adjective for "little/young," tur; thus, the age class could be termed "childhood."[92] As to the age range, this is perhaps weaned toddler, as indicated by the Sumerian proverb lu$_2$-tur ga nu-un-da#-gu$_7$-a, "O little child, who is no longer nursed with milk,"[93] as well as the simile šeg$_5$-šeg$_5^{\text{mušen}}$-e lu$_2$-tur er$_2$ pad$_3$#-[da-gin$_7$] sig$_7$ na-ĝa$_2$-ĝa$_2$, "The *šegšeg* bird sheds tears like a crying baby."[94] The term may also be applied to slightly older children of either sex and even adolescents that are pubescent or possibly even postpuberty, but sexually inexperienced: both female Inana and male Šukaletuda are referred to affectionately as lu$_2$-tur. Furthermore, in the Sumerian tale *Enki and Ninhursaĝa*, the god Enki looks at his young daughters one after the other and remarks "Is this nice lu$_2$-tur not to be kissed? Is this nice Ninnisig not to be kissed?"[95] It should also be noted that lu$_2$-tur is unsexed and had no gendered delineation, masculine or feminine.

The second listed age class nam-ĝuruš-(tur) does specify sex and gender.[96] Similar to nam-lu$_2$-tur, nam-ĝuruš-(tur) is composed of the abstract derivational prefix nam + the lexeme for young able-bodied male, ĝuruš, + / – tur, the optional adjective for "little/young," thus, it may be translated "young able-bodied manhood" or "adolescent masculinity." The designation ĝuruš-tur, "adolescent male," is found in various Sumerian literary passages indicating the time before marriage. The most famous instance is the passage in *Enlil and Ninlil*: ^{d}En-lil$_2$ ĝuruš tur-bi na-nam ^{d}Nin-lil$_2$ ki-sikil tur-bi na-nam, "Enlil was one of [Nippur's] adolescent men, and Ninlil was one of [Nippur's] adolescent women."[97] Thus, the difference between lu$_2$-tur, a compound composed of the lexeme for person, lu$_2$, + the adjective for "young/little," and ĝuruš, "able-bodied male," + "young/little" is the difference between lu$_2$ and ĝuruš, the first term lacking any sexual/gender identification and the second incorporating a specific male designation.

The abstract nam-ĝuruš renders also the concept youthful masculinity as opposed to nam-ki-sikil youthful femininity as in Išme-Dagan K:

> ki-sikil-e-ne nam-ĝuruš-e tug$_2$ zid-da mu$_4$-mu$_4$
> ĝuruš-e-ne nam-ki-sikil-e-eš$_2$ tug$_2$ gab$_2$-bu mu$_4$-mu$_4$
> to make young women dress in nam-ĝuruš on their right side,
> to make young men dress in nam-ki-sikil on their left side[98]

Nam-ĝuruš as a term for a youthful masculinity is made explicit in proverbial sayings such as:

> šul diĝir-ĝu$_{10}$ ĝiri$_3$ ^{d}lamma-ĝu$_{10}$
> nam-ĝuruš anše kar-ra#-[gin$_7$] ḫaš$_2$-ĝa$_2$ ba-an-[taka$_4$]
> I was a youth – now my personal god, and access to my protective deity,
> and my nam-ĝuruš have all left my loins, like a run-away donkey.[99]

Characteristics of this construct of masculinity are strength, hard work, and martial activities as in the Song of the Hoe: ^{giš}al u$_3$-šub-ba ^{giš}al saĝ ĝal$_2$-la-am$_3$ ^{giš}al-am$_3$ a$_2$ nam-ĝuruš-a-kam, "The hoe is brick molds, the hoe has made saĝ exist. It is the hoe that is the strength of nam-ĝuruš."[100] And in Lugal-e: ^{giš}tukul sag$_3$-ge ezen nam-ĝuruš-a ešemen ^{d}inana-ke$_4$ a$_2$-zu ba-ra-ni-zig$_3$, "Do not lift your arm to the smiting of weapons, to the festival of nam-ĝuruš, to Inana's dance!"[101]

Nam-ĝuruš is also associated with the lexeme nam-šul. Šul is a poetic synonym meaning male or female at the "prime of life" who can be the possessor of valor and bravery. This is demonstrated by its juxtaposition with nam-ab-ba "elder masculinity," in *An Elegy on the Death of Nawirtum*: dam-zu ḫe$_2$-til$_3$ nam-šul nam-ab$^?$-ba ḫe$_2$-ak-e, "May your [spouse] maintain his health so that he may be able to perform nam-šul and (then) nam-ab-ba."[102] Nam-šul might also be understood to mean "excellence," given its equation with Akkadian *meṭelūtum* in OB Proto-Izi II (Bilingual Version)[103] and in the bilingual Edubba text:[104]

> nam-šul-la-a bí-til nam-a[b-ba sá bí-in-du$_{11}$]
> *[meṭ-lu-ta tag-da-m]ar tak-ta-šad lit-tu-tu*
> "Du hast das nam-šul beendent und das nam-ab-ba erreicht."[105]

The poetic language used in Sumerian literary compositions provides a multiplicity and fluidity of designations. In the following citations, the lexemes šul, saĝ, and ĝuruš are used synonymously. These terms alternate in the naming of the kings Gudea and Šulgi: ĝuruš [X] an-ne$_2$ zu-me, "you are the ĝuruš whom An knows,"[106] šul an-ne$_2$ zu diĝir-re-ne mu-še$_2$ mu#-ri$_2$-in-sa$_4$, "called your name: šul-whom-An-knows(-well)-among-the-gods',"[107] and šul-gi sipa kalam-ma saĝ ^{d}en-lil$_2$-le zu, "Šulgi, the shepherd of the Land, the saĝ whom Enlil knows."[108] They exhibit that one age-class, ĝuruš, can be paralleled by one poetic lexeme, šul, and one generic referent, saĝ. This synonymous parallelism demonstrates the interlocking and overlapping dynamic and fluid gradient of these lexemes. As already established, saĝ could refer to a status of servitude. Consequently, it can be used as an epithet of a king describing his relationship with a deity. Moreover, the dependent able-bodied worker ĝuruš became the sobriquet of the most active age class, the male in his prime, so it was an apt description of a ruler. Šul and nam-šul, as discussed above, seem to be poetic synonyms of ĝuruš and nam-ĝuruš. Ultimately, these three lexemes were listed together as a series of masculine identities listed in the order of their hierarchical ranking attested in the administrative documents as in OB Nippur Lu$_2$:

310 gir$_{15}$
311 šul
312 mes
313 ĝuruš
314 ĝuruš dili
315 ĝuruš AŠ
316 ĝuruš# saĝ# dili
316a saĝ#-nita
316b saĝ-[. . .]
316c saĝ-[. . .]

Yet, although šul and ĝuruš are synonymous categories of "specifically aged" biological males, since saĝ is merely the term for "head/individual" it thus must be further augmented by nita "male" (line 316a) to indicate a masculine identity.

The third listed state in Ugu-mu is tied to the abstract concept of kalag(a), "strength, might, power," nam-kalag(a).[109] As a substantive, kalag(a) means "strong one" or "mighty one." Nam-kalag(a) is a compound composed of the abstract derivational prefix nam + the nominalized adjective kalag(a), "strong," and thus seems to not necessarily signify a male status, only a state of strength. This is similar to the fourth-class, nam-ur-saĝ, which is composed of the abstract derivational prefix nam + the noun ur-saĝ, "warrior," or "hero." The two lexemes are commonly found in parallelism in royal descriptions and literary texts:

> nam-ur-saĝ ba-<e-de$_6$>
> nam-kalag-ga ba-<e-de$_6$>
> You have brought with you nam-ur-saĝ,
> You have brought with you nam-kalag(a)[110]

As a term used to classify human categories, nam-kalag(a) is attested once in OB Nippur-Izi, another lexical text that proceeds from the status of powerless to the status of powerful:

214	nam-lu$_2$ u$_2$-tur
215	nam-ibila
216	nam-a$_2$-e$_3$
217	nam-LA$_2$
218	nam-maḫ
219	nam-gal
220	nam-kalag-ga

Nita-kalag(a), "mighty male," also occurs as a royal title. For example, Enanatum I of the state of Lagaš declares that the deity Ninĝirsu spoke of him as: Enanatum, nita-kala-ga-ĝu$_{10}$, "my nita-kala-ga," and a priest dedicated a mace head to Ur-gigira of Uruk "for the life of Ur-gigira, nita-kala-ga, king of Uruk."[111] It is difficult to determine whether a specific age is connected to either state of being, nita-kala-ga or nam-ur-saĝ; however, it can be established that men performing these constructs are theoretically older than children/adolescents, yet younger than elders. Using the list found in Proto-Izi as a guide, the statuses may be less physical and more class or psychological; it would be the time of independence, rather than dependence. It would be the time during which a man could affect his world. Certainly, a more in-depth investigation into these terms is warranted, particularly since both the goddess Inana and the goddess Bau can be referred to as šul and Inana is considered an ur-saĝ.[112]

The last listed age class is nam-ab-ba, "male elderhood."[113] The components of this compound are again the abstract derivational prefix nam + the lexeme ab-ba, "father," or "male elder." The class nam-ab-ba can be found in list of me (abstract principles that govern society), as attested in

Inana and Enki: nam-ab-ba ba-<e-de$_6$>, "You have brought with you male elderhood."[114] Sometimes "elderhood" involves a definite chronological milestone that must be surpassed, while at other times the required age is simply relative to the ages of all of the other members of the group in question. The elders held a position of respect in Mesopotamian society, as the father instructs his son in the *Instructions of Šuruppak*: "the instruction of an old man is something precious, pay attention to it."[115] PSD A/II 131 §8 lists documentary and legal references to the male elder in general and the city-elder in particular.

The pairing of nam-šul and nam-ab-ba in *An Elegy on the Death of Nawirtum* highlights the last age class. The social structure of ancient Sumer inculcates respect for the elderly and in *The Curse of Agade* goddess Inana endowed the old women with the gift of giving counsel/advice (ad-gi$_4$-gi$_4$) and the old men with the gift of counsel/eloquence (ka-inim-ma).[116] The binary pair ĝuruš and ab-ba is a leitmotif in the composition *Gilgameš and Agga*:

> ^{d}Gilgameš$_2$ igi ab-ba iri^{ki}-na-še$_3$ inim ba-an-ĝar . . .
> 2-kam-ma-še$_3$ ^{d}Gilgameš$_2$ igi ĝuruš iri^{ki}-na-še$_3$ inim ba-an-ĝar
> Gilgameš presented the issue before the ab-ba of his city, ...
> Gilgameš presented the issue again, this time before the ĝuruš of his city.[117]

This literary juxtaposition between a council of elders and a council of juniors serves as the framework for the events of the plot. That certain differing constructs of masculinity are associated with the two separate age classes/statuses can been seen in the playful quote: ab-ba nam-ĝuruš-na ba-an-ku$_4$ "the ab-ba (geezer) will (re-)enter (the state of) nam-ĝuruš (youthful masculinity)."[118]

Conclusions

From this brief survey, it has been shown that Sumerian constructions of masculinity are rooted in class distinctions and societally understood age parameters. There would seem to have been little practical use for the construction "man = male mortal." In administrative registers, groupings of men are subsumed under the various social and age classes according to which they are ranked and/or are conceived to pass through during their lifetimes. Since the Archaic period, differentiation between males is more dependent on categories indicative of existing societal construction: superior versus subordinate and independent versus dependent. Even lexicographic evidence suggests linguistic differentiation and interest in only age/sex/economic/legal class/status.

While the lexeme nita could be used adjectivally (male) or as a substantive (generic man), attestations of the latter are rare and meant more for clarification, thus continuing to serve a more adjectival function. Furthermore, when employed, nita refers not to a man generally, but rather to an independent man specifically, again confirming a status orientation. Unisex lu_2 is the most common sobriquet used of any human being, male or female, even more so than unisex saĝ. Similarly, although sexual dualism is encoded in the Sumerian cultural system, this investigation has produced three concrete terms for masculinity whose constructions are based on age: nam-ĝuruš-tur, "adolescent masculinity," nam-ĝuruš, "youthful masculinity," and nam-ab-ba, "elder masculinity."[119] Very young males, that is, children, do not have a specific masculine gender construct. In fact, the generic nam-nita, "masculinity," is attested in only five pieces of Sumerian literature. Four occur with mortals and in the phrase ki-nam-nita-ka, "place of masculinity," i.e., place where masculinity is performed: the battlefield. For example, the Sumerian version of *Gilgameš, Enkidu and the Netherworld*, contains the line:

> ki-nam-nita-a-ke_4 me_3-a nu-un-šub kur-re im-ma-an-dab_5
> He did not fall in battle at the place of nam-nita, the Netherworld seized him![120]

The later Akkadian version embedded in the XII tablet of the Standard Babylonian *Epic of Gilgameš* makes explicit the implicit, that the ki-nam-nita-a-ke_4 is *ašar tāḫāz zikarī*, "where men do battle": *ašar tāḫāz zikarī ul imqut erṣetu iṣbassu*, "He did not fall where men do battle, the Netherworld seized him!"[121] And again in OB bilingual text of *Instructions of Šuruppak*:

> ki-nam-nita-ka um-me-te šu nam-gu_4-gu_4-dè
> *a-[šar zi-k]a-ri ina teḫêka la muppišāta*
> When you approach the place of "masculinity," don't conclude a sale![122]

Presumably, the ki-nam-nita-ka was a place where all three constructs of masculinity could be performed. Certainly, one can envision the ĝuruš-tur, the ĝuruš, and the ab-ba, all having (differing) martial roles, all performing differing constructs of masculinity.

It is hoped that this survey has provided a framework into which more specific and detailed investigations can be placed, for as the Akkadian language superseded the Sumerian as a method by which ideas were conveyed, so too did new constructions replace their older versions, while others continued unchanged for millennia.

Notes

1 It was with a heavy heart that I took over this project after the untimely death of Joan Goodnick Westenholz, a great scholar and dear friend. Although we had worked jointly on the paper since its inception, it was truly born from Joan's desire to finally eradicate the ever-persisting translation of Sumerian lu_2 as "man," rather than as the unisex relative pronoun "who," or the nouns "person" or "anthropomorphic being." As these latter understandings of the lexeme

have long been acknowledged by certain scholars (see particularly Gelb, 1982, 86), evidence for the unisex nature of lu_2 will be presented here; however, any arguments concerning its attestations are meant more as a foil. It must also be noted that this chapter does not focus on how women were categorized (e.g., nursing). Reference to female categorization is only given when it can shed light on male categorization. This study also does not consider the more specific worker classification system, worker distribution, or familial lines, or present any investigation into the determinative maker. Finally, both authors wish to thank Aage Westenholz and Philip Jones for reading earlier drafts of this work and providing useful comments, discussion, and suggestions. As always, any error is the responsibility of the authors.

2 Locality is also extremely relevant, but this is beyond the scope of this inquiry.

3 Archaic tablets which date to the Uruk IV (c. 3200 BCE) and Uruk III periods (c. 3100 BCE) provide the earliest information for how the peoples of Mesopotamia categorized their surroundings. This statement must, however, be qualified. Not only are the texts inscribed on these tablets almost entirely administrative, that is, they are not literary and do not attempt to convey spoken syntax, but they also originate exclusively from the southern Mesopotamian city Uruk and from town(s) within the more northerly Kiš region. To make the situation even more suspect, those tablets from Uruk were discovered primarily in secondary contexts (e.g., dumps) while those from the Kiš region may have come from any of three different sites: Jemdet Naṣr, Uquir, or Kiš. (Also, now with the possible addition of Larsa.) For a comprehensive contextualized overview of the Archaic corpus see Bauer, Englund, and Krebernik (1998).

4 A note on transliteration. For those discussions specifically referencing signs attested in the Archaic corpus, the most basic value for the sign is given (e.g., UŠ) and these are presented in capital letters (as is the tradition). Further, although it may be frustrating to some, the terms "sign" and "pictograph" are used somewhat interchangeably. Sumerian words (transliterations) are given in lowercase (nita). In transliterations, the # symbol is used in lieu of half-brackets to notify that the text/sign is broken. Unless otherwise noted, transliterations are presented in their published formats. For Assyriological abbreviations see the Bibliography.

5 The differentiation and relationship between the signs HI(ZATU 254), HI@ *gunû* (ZATU 258) and ŠIR(ZATU 526), is not yet fully understood. See Steinkeller (1995a, 258) for references.

6 This is with the exception of the sign for breed bull, which, like UTUA (breed ram), had an appended HI. There are several studies on animal husbandry and pictographic representation in the Archaic period. See particularly Green (1980).

7 A few scholars contend that KUR_a does not represent a set of mountains, and is instead an abstract rendering of mortal male genitalia (Nissen, Damerow, and Englund, 74). This seems impractical since UŠ already served this purpose. Furthermore, if the intent of the KUR_a pictograph was to depict male genitalia, there would then be no sign that symbolically represented a mountain. Given the region, this seems improbable. More likely is that the individuals designated as KUR_a were simply drawn from prisoners of war taken from the mountain (KUR_a) tribes surrounding Mesopotamia (Gelb, 1982, 81); however, it may also be that this use of the sign KUR_a is one of the earliest examples of homophony and is in fact a homophonic substitute for KUR_2 "to be hostile or strange." This latter solution may also have been a practical one as KUR_2 can also be read PAP, a ubiquitous term that appears in the designations of multiple officials in the Archaic corpus and could be a source for confusion.

8 ZATU 443.

9 ZATU 228/604, following Steinkeller (1995a, 702), who considers UŠ/NITA(ZATU 604) the same sign as $GIŠ_3$(ZATU 228). For the UŠ/NITA representational development into UŠ/NITA and $NITA_2$/$NITA_x$(NITAxKUR) see Gelb (1982, 96, Chart 1). Also, it should be noted that all pictographs date to the Archaic period. These versions of the signs give the clearest visuals (versus the later more abstract versions of the signs).

10 ZATU 304. There are numerous examples for KUR_a and SAL as adjectives (see Green, 6, and Gelb, 1982, 81). That KUR_a stood for male is demonstrated persuasively by two lines of text inscribed on MSVO 4, 8: O0102 $1(N_1)$ UTUA KUR_a GUM and O0303 $1(N_1)$ UD_5 NI SAL. An utua was a breed ram signified by the addition of testicles (HI) to the sign for sheep (UDU). An uzud (UD_5) was a nanny goat whose sign includes teats. In this example, the utua is described as a "crushed(?) KUR_a" as the nanny goat is a "dairy female" (for NI_a as "dairy fat"? see Bauer, Englund, and Krebernik, 1998, 168); thus, KUR_a "male" can be understood to parallel SAL "female," for both KUR_a and SAL would be redundant.

11 For RU "subordinate" see Ukg. 4–5 xi 32–34 and RIME 1.9.9.1 col xi 32–34.

12 ZATU 437.

13 See Steinkeller (1989, 128–133). Examples of listed SAG NITA and SAG SAL also occur in the ED records from Lagaš, for example, Nik 174 r. 3–5 8 SAG NITA 2 SAG SAL ti-u_4-su_3-$še_3$ "8 male SAG and 2 female SAG from Ti'usuše"; however these are somewhat rare.

14 Farber (2005, 109f). One might even go so far as to wonder if perhaps SAG is hairless and lacking any discernible features because, for example, a particular hairstyle or mode of dress could indicate a specific class of person.

15 See Gelb (1973, 76) and Zettler (1992, 163). For an overview on the position of slaves in households, see Culbertson (2011). It should also be noted that Archaic Lu_2 A contains the entry SAG SUG_5 (ED Lu A saĝ DUN_3) "land recorder" followed by the UB SAG (UB perhaps being some sort of official), who is also listed in ATU6 W15692,a3; thus, SAG during the Archaic period may not automatically indicate the lowest status.

16 The broken ATU7 W19416,b perhaps containing an example of SAG SAL.

17 There is also the added encumbrance that the signs SAG and UŠ could represent the concepts of "width" and "length," and, in the case of SAG, "front," "best," and "first."

18 It may be that the inherent worker class status of the SAG is indicated by the sign for GU_7 "ration" (SAG sign + a ration bowl). As noted by Nissen, the plethora of mass-produced Uruk period bowls and cups discovered may well be those signified by the sign (Nissen, Damerow, and Englund, 14). See Gelb (1965), for the inherent chattel status of any person receiving a "ration" versus a "wage" and Englund (2009, 15).

19 And here the sign SAG is depicted with a "noose" around its neck. Discussion of these tablets is in Nissen, Damerow, and Englund, 72–75. It should be noted at the outset that these tablets are not fully understood and that several sections of text are broken. For prisoners of war during the Sargonic (c. 2350–2100) and later periods see Gelb (1973).

20 Those that are not SAGxMA are three that seem to be connected to the EN E_{2a} $ŠU_2$, and those noted as N_2 (meaning unclear) as opposed to N_1 "1 unit."

21 Cf. Damerow and Englund, who suggest that $ERIM_a$ may signify the status "dead" (Nissen, Damerow, and Englund, 74). In their discussion of these texts, Damerow, and Englund read that the individuals noted as N_1 on MSVO 1,213 are the 17 SAGxMA subtotaled in MSVO 1,212. The situation is a bit more complex. The scribe summarizing those listed in MSVO 1,213 neglected to notice that r. col. 1 1.a. is actually two people ($2[N_1]$ SAGxMA SAL KUR_a AL).

Furthermore, three people listed in MSVO 1,213 as N_1 are noted as N_2 (which Damerow, and Englund logically seem to equate with $ERIM_a$) on MSVO 1,212; thus, at some point their status changed so that the two women designated as SAGxMA on MSVO 1,213 are not listed on MSVO 1,212 as either SAGxMA or $ERIM_a$ ($N_2^?$). Finally, the number of people listed as N_2 on MSVO 1,212 is not ten, but nine. Since there are many breaks in the text, it may well be that one of the entries should be corrected to read 2(N_1); however, this would still not align with the listings in MSVO 1,213 and 214.

22 See discussion by Nissen, Damerow, and Englund (1993, 71).

23 E.g., MSVO 1,222 O0101 2(N_1) SAL KUR_a GAL SAL, perhaps to be read "two: [one] servant woman and [one] overseer of women." See also MSVO 1,223 O0101 1(N_1) SAL KUR_a. This tablet is quite fragmentary. (Cf. ATU5 W07024 R0301 2(N_1) SAL UŠ.)

24 Of course it could also simply be the difference between a pedantic thorough scribe and a more efficient/less careful recorder, as there would seem to be several discrepancies between the lists.

25 In tablets dated to the ED period, a subjugated person is no longer signified by SAGxMA, but by lu_2 dab_5 "one who is seized" (see Nissen, Damerow, and Englund, 77–88, for a discussion of these particular tablets). Like SAG, this designation is also used as a collective, e.g., the ĝuruš counted on VAT 12736 and VAT 12454 are listed as ĝuruš and labelled according to the city from whence they came, but totally as lu_2 dab_5. During the Sargonic period (c. 2350–2200 BCE) captives may be referred to as lu_2 kar_2 (Gelb, 1973, 80).

26 See also the contemporaneous OIP 104, no. 7 obv. i 1. For the development of the sign combinations and formations in third-millennium texts, the best chart is that prepared by Gelb (1982). The clear break of the latter sign form from the highly standardized use of its individual components to represent female and male slaves, respectively, in the preceding Uruk phases, may be due to an indication of the disruption in the writing system of cuneiform brought on by the break between Uruk III/Jemdet Naṣr and ED I (Englund, 2009, 6 and n. 13). That this paired formulation becomes standardized in the writing system and in the lexical system can be seen in OB Proto-lu_2 373–374.

27 Gelb distinguishes ĝuruš "serf" (1965). For ĝuruš, "able-bodied men capable of doing a full day's work," see Foster (2010) (Sargonic period). For further terms see Steinkeller (1987). Cf. Wilcke (1985, 216).

28 ZATU 247. For the designation of the sign as a depiction of sledge, see Steinkeller (1990, 22). For the ancestor of GURUŠ probably being ZATU 281 (KAL acc to ZATU), see Steinkeller (1995a, 702). See further, Englund (2009, 8f., n. 19). Cf. Civil (2007, 28, no. 172), who suggests a possible derivation from a compound ĝir-uš.

29 See also Jacobsen (1993).

30 See also ATU5 W9579,ac in which GURUŠ are listed separate from SAL: O0101 1(N_1) SAL O0102 3(N_1) GURUŠ; O0201 SUKKAL UŠ# UNUG KUR_a MAGUR. Cf. ATU5 W9311,a. That GURUŠ seems to modify ewe (U8) in a list of sheep (W9579,du) is somewhat unexpected.

31 Gelb (1965, 238).

32 See particularly the enormous list in *ASJ* 20, 106 6.

33 For kisal "bookkeeper" see Bauer, Englund, and Krebernik (1998, 197, n. 450). In the Archaic corpus there are several officials seemingly designated as female, e.g., EN SAL. According to Damerow and Englund (1993, 55) this particular combination should be read "city ruler's wife." Perhaps in conflict with this understanding is the broken ATU5 W2352 O0201 EN:UŠ X [].

34 This is not the only group classification. Subtotals of various kinds of workers (e.g., muhalidim me, "these are the bakers"), temple affiliates, and so forth can

also be subtotaled. On a side note, there is no evidence in these lists for any third or fourth gender/sex category. The gala (Akk. *kalû*), frequently debated to be third-gender individuals, are listed as nita (e.g., CT 50, 036).

35 Ean 1 x 12–13 and RIME 1.9.3.1: col. x 13.
36 Ukg. 10, 4: 8–9 and RIME 1.9.9.6: col. iv 8–9.
37 Ukg. 16.1.1 and RIME 1.9.9.5: col. i 1–5 & col vii 10–col viii 3.
38 Ukg. 4–5 xi 32–34 and RIME 1.9.9.1 col xi 32–34.
39 Ukg. 4–5 xii 23–25 and RIME 1.9.9.1 col xii 23–25.
40 ZATU 332. Piotr Michalowski (2004), contends that early texts indicate that lu_2 may have been pronounced as /nu/, as evidenced by such syllabic spellings as nu-gal for lugal "king."
41 This is, however, complete conjecture.
42 Although CDLI hazards that W1872,2 should be dated to the Uruk IV period, the sign in question and the tablet itself are in such poor condition it is impossible to confirm this.
43 ATU3 W20266,20 O0207 $1(N_1)$ SUKKAL E_{2a} LU_2#.
44 This reading would seem to be contrary to ATU3 W20511,1 O0103 $1(N_{14})$ DI HI E_{2a} LU_2 TUN_{3a} NUN_a. Unless noted, for all lexical lists see DCCLT: http://oracc.museum.upenn.edu/dcclt/
45 CUSAS 1,083, MSVO 3,42, ATU7 W19851,b+W19948,28, and W20493,6+32. Cf. MSVO 1,80 and particularly its attestation in MSVO 4,67, a list of female beer workers. The appearance of the sign in the fragmentary ATU5 W1872,2 and ATU6 W17586 allows for no context.
46 This would also then suggest another homophonic substitution in the instances using MUD.
47 Although the juxtaposition of the signs GAL LU_2, which in later Sumerian (lugal) and Akkadian (*šarrum*) is confirmed to signify "king," is attested on several Archaic tablets (Cf. ATU7 W20274,21; W20274,26; and, W20274,34), the designation lu_2 of a city has been confirmed only in texts which date to the ED IIIa period.
48 ETCSL 1.7.1: 19–24.
49 Westbrook (2003a: 333, 2003b: 197).
50 The most recent and comprehensive treatment of lexical lists is Veldhuis (2014). See also Civil (1969) and Michalowski (2003).
51 On use of the sign GAL in this text, see Wilcke (2005, 444).
52 See W6966,b, which may list multiple GURUŠ as differentiated from UŠ.
53 Cavigneaux (1980–83, 613), and Wilcke (2005).
54 Cavigneaux (1980–83, 614), and Taylor (2003).
55 Abu Salabikh, Ebla, Gašur, and Kiš, see Buccellati (2003).
56 The lu_2 ĝuruš also appears in administrative texts, for example, OSP 2, 176 1 and UTI 6, 3524 2.
57 SF 070.
58 MEE 3, 50 + o iv 9–15.
59 This would seem to only emphasize that the role of lugal "king" is simply to be the overseer of *all* people.
60 Cavigneaux (1980–83, 614) suggests that the order reflects a Tempelwirtschaft (the temple economy) and references in Buccellati (2003).
61 1981, 132.
62 ED Lu_2 E also contains multiple "professions" qualified as lu_2, the pair $arad_2$ and $geme_2$, and an entry simply as ĝuruš (in an unhelpful context).
63 For references to adoption of Semitic terminology in the south, see Steinkeller (1993, 121) and Civil (2007, 11).
64 See Cavigneaux (1980–83), §18.2, and Gesche (2000, 124–125).
65 Civil (2010, 163). For a detailed discussion of this text, see Böck (1999).

66 See Civil (1969).

67 Although the text is attested in copies from Nuzi, Ugarit, and Hattuša, the best preserved and most extensive comes from Nippur and lists high professions, categories for social relations (e.g., mother, brother), and agricultural occupations. It also contains multiple insertions, many of which are not anthropomorphic. These insertions, such as lists of farm implements, may have been added due to thematic or graphic (similar/same sign) attraction. The insertions are lacking in later exemplars of the composition.

68 1997, 8.

69 For the most recent edition of this law collection, see Civil (2011). For a discussion of the usage of these three lexemes in the text, see Roth (1995, 17).

70 In place of the interpretation of the phrase a-gi$_4$ as "to have sexual relations," Civil reads a as *e$_2$ (see comments, Civil, 2011, 255f.) "to incorporate the daughter-in-law into household = to marry." Thus, he translates these two laws as: "If a man seduces with guile a betrothed [inchoately married] woman not yet married (lit. not included (yet) in a household) and takes her into (his) household, this man will be killed. If a betrothed girl, on her own initiative, pursues a man (and) sleeps with him, (if) he (the prospective husband) kills the woman, he will be set free." Cf. Claus Wilcke (2002, 313): "Wenn jemand der jungfräulichen Ehefrau eines Mannes Gewalt antut und sie defloriert, wird dieser Mann getötet. Wenn die Ehefrau eines Mannes freiwillig einem Manne folgt und er in ihrem Schoße liegt, diese Frau wird getötet werden. / diese Frau wird der Mann tötet. Für diesen Mann wird seine Freiheit festgesetzt."

71 Cf. OB Lu$_2$-azlag$_2$ B-C Seg.2, 95 [lu$_2$ dam] ĝuruš na$_2$# *ša aš-ša-at a-wi-li#* "one who sleeps with the spouse of a man."

72 Translation Roth (1995, 17).

73 1993, 76.

74 1998, 176 n. 9

75 Most recently Westbrook (2010)

76 Jacobsen (1970, 198, 30–35).

77 RIME 3/2: 1.4.3 v 32–34. Translation ours. For this meaning, see Sjöberg (1973, 125, note to line 70).

78 ZATU 229 s.v. GIŠGAL; ePSD reads this logogram as ĝišgal "station, attendant."

79 The reading of this compound sign is given in ePSD s.v. lulu "man, humanity." For a reading lullu$_x$, see Marchesi (2001, 673). An etymology < lu$_2$-lu$_2$ "men" is given by Steinkeller (1995b: 67, n. 67). For OB phonetic Sumerian lu$_2$-ulu$_3$ and standard Sumerian lu$_2$-u$_{18}$-lu and lu$_2$-ulu$_3$ in different versions of same incantation, see Geller (1989, 195, l. 9); note the Akkadian translation of this word is not preserved.

80 SP 1.95. Alster (1997, 22).

81 351.

82 ETCSL 1.8.1.5: A 94–95. The translation given by Marchesi (2001, 673 n. 1) is: "Until I know whether that being (i.e., Huwawa) is a man or a god, I will not turn to the city my mountain-turned foot." Unfortunately, the Oxford Electronic Text Corpus of Sumerian Literature (ETCSL) consistently translates "man" for "person," which makes poor sense in the context: en-e kur lu$_2$ til$_3$-la-še$_3$ ĝeštug$_2$-ga-ni na-an-gub, "Now the lord once decided to set off for the mountain where the man lives; Lord Gilgameš decided to set off for the mountain where the man lives (1)."

83 Cited in OB catalogue from Nibru, at Philadelphia, ETCSL 0.2.01, line 10; OB catalogue in the Louvre, 0.2.02, line 10; OB catalogue from Urim (U1), ETCSL 0.2.03, line 14; and, OB catalogue from Urim (U2), ETCSL 0.2.04: 9.

84 2005, 111f.

85 RIME 1.14.20.1: 30–33.

86 RIME 1.14.20.1
87 Wilcke (1990, 460f.).
88 ETCSL 2.2.5 Segment E line 31.
89 For an introduction to Ugu-mu, see Sigrist and Westenholz (2008).
90 Tanos (2007); Jagersma (2010, 118).
91 YRL SC 1826-Bx2–7.
92 CBS 6484 ii"1"(?), YRL SC 1826-Bx2–7 o. r. 1, Cotsen 40739 vii 16. For lexical references outside of Ugu-mu cf. nam-lu$_2$-tur Proto-Izi 234 (MSL 13 47), Proto-Izi II (Bilingual: *mi-iṣ-ḫi-ru-*[*tum*]) B ii" 13 (MSL 13 59).
93 Alster (1997), SP 4.14. and ETCSL 6.1.04: 19.
94 *Nanše and the Birds*, ETCSL 4.14.3 C 16 see Veldhuis (2004, 121).
95 ETCSL 1.1.1: 91 and *passim*.
96 CBS 6484 ii″ 2″ (?), YRL SC 1826-Bx2–7 o. /r. 2 nam-ĝuruš-mu and Cotsen 40739 vii 17 nam-ĝuruš-tur-mu. Cf. Lu Excerpt II 31 ĝuruš tur = *batūlu* "adolescent male" (MSL XII 105).
97 ETCSL 1.2.1: 10–11.
98 ETCSL 2.5.4.11: 22–23.
99 Alster (1997, 238): Proverb 17 Sec. B 3 and Alster (2005, 386 line 20). Also the bilingual nam-ĝuruš-mu anše kar-ra-bi(sic!) ḫaš$_2$-mu ba-e-DAB$_5$: *eṭ-le*(?)-*tum*(?)-*ma* x# x# *ki-ma* ANŠE *mu-nàr-bi ḫal-li# iz-ba-am* "my nam-ĝuruš passed from my loins like a runaway donkey" (Alster, 2007, 105 no. 7 and duplicates).
100 ETCSL 5.5.4: 96–97.
101 ETCSL 1.6.2: 136–7.
102 ETCSL 5.5.3: 59.
103 UET 7 78 ii' 9.
104 See Wilcke (1985, 217) and Sjöberg (1975, 140f.) 4 "Examenstext A (earliest exemplar 1st millennium)": u$_4$-tur-ra-(a)-zu-ta nam-šul-la-(a)-zu-(-[šè]) é-dub-ba-a ì-ti-le-en : *ul-tu* (*u$_4$-um* / *iš-tu u$_4$-mu*) *ṣe-ḫe-ri-ka a-di meṭ-lu-t*[*i-ka*] *ina bīt tup-pi áš-bat* "Seit den Tagen, als du klein warst, bis in dein nam-šul hast du im Edubbâ gelebt."
105 Sjöberg (1975, 144: 33).
106 Gudea, Cyl. B xxiv 5 and ETCSL 2.1.7: 1351.
107 Šulgi P Sect. b 38–39, Klein (1981, 26), cf. ETCSL 2.4.2.16 Segment C line 39. ETCSL adds: "(valiant) one." See also Šulgi F 169–170, Klein (1981, 26) and notes ^{d}Nin-hur-saĝ-ĝa$_2$-ke$_4$(!) šul-gi u [1(?)-x] *šul an-*ne$_2$(!) zu mu-še$_3$ mu-sa$_4$, "Ninhursag gave me as (my) name: Šulgi-the-. . .- šul-Whom-An(-Personally) Knows."
108 Šulgi G, line 42, ETCSL 2.4.2.07.
109 CBS 6484 ii" 3" (nam-kalag$^?$-x?[-mu], cf. DCCLT OB Nippur Ugumu 283" nam-ur-saĝ$^?$#-[ŋu$_{10}$] "my heroism"), YRL SC 1826-Bx2–7 o. r. 3 (nam-kalag-ga-mu), Cotsen 40739 vii 18 (nam-kal-la-mu). The variant nam-kal-la-mu "preciousness" or "valuable-ness" is senseless in this context. For further lexical references, see Izi text cited below.
110 *Inana and Enki* II v 53–54, ETCSL 1.3.1 Section I, lines 53–54. Cf. Segment D 2–3: nam-ur-saĝ nam-kalag-ga nam-niĝ$_2$-erim$_2$ nam-niĝ$_2$-si#-[sa$_2$ iri laḫ$_5$ i-si-iš ĝa$_2$-ĝa$_2$ šag$_4$ ḫul$_2$-la] kug ^{d}inana-ke$_4$ šu ba-<ti>, "Holy Inana received nam-ur-saĝ, nam-kalag-ga, wickedness, righteousness, the plundering of cities, making lamentations, rejoicing."
111 RIME 1.9.4.2 x 4 and RIME 2.13.2.2001.
112 It should be noted that we know of no instance when a mortal woman is titled in these ways.
113 Attestations: CBS 6484 ii" 4" (nam-ab-ba[-mu]), Cotsen 40739 vii 19 (nam-a-ab-ba-mu). The latter spelling is probably a mistake on the part of the scribe.

For further lexical references, cf. nam-ab-ba Proto-Izi 253 (MSL 13 48) [before sukkal and judge, probably 'elder']. However, note the equation šu-gi = *šību* in the lexical series of ages in Lu Excerpt II 45ff. (MSL XII 105). Further, see PSD A/2 129ff ab-ba; see also CAD *šibutu* (lex ref to Group Voc. A in CT 51 168 iv 50). For another interpretation of the term nam-ab-ba as "(Kult)Ältester," see Krispijn (1990, 2).

114 *Inana and Enki* II v 52, ETCSL 1.3.1 Section I, lines 52. Cf. Segment F line 33: [niĝin$_3$-ĝar] kug# X AN nu-gig an-na ĝiš-gu$_3$-di nam-nar nam-ab-ba me-a "Where are the holy *niĝin-ĝar* shrine, . . . , the mistress of heaven, loud musical instruments, the art of song, venerable old age?" For their place at the top of the city hierarchy in early periods, see Wilcke (2003, 33) and under the Third Dynasty of Ur, see Sigrist (1992, 366f.).

115 Alster (2005, 58: 13).

116 ETCSL 2.1.5: 29–30.

117 ETCSL 1.8.1.1: 3–4 and 18–19.

118 *Old Man and Young Girl*, Alster (2005, 386: 20).

119 In this connection, it is interesting to note a cross-cultural case in point. Among the Yorùbá of southwestern Nigeria, there was also traditionally no concept of gender classes of masculine and feminine. The primary principle of social organization was seniority, defined by relative age. (Oyěwumi, 1997, 31–79 and 149–156). Yorùbá categories also apply only to adult human beings and not to children.

120 ETCSL 1.8.1.4 228 and 236. Cf. George (2003, 756: 229, 758: 237, 773).

121 George (2003, 730f., XII 62).

122 Alster (2005), 70: 68, and comments, 133.

Bibliography

For the many Assyriological abbreviations consult: http://cdli.ox.ac.uk/wiki/abbreviations_for_assyriology.

Alster, Bendt. *Proverbs of Ancient Sumer: The World's Earliest Proverb Collections.* Bethesda: CDL Press, 1997.

———. *Wisdom Ancient Sumer*. Bethesda: CDL Press, 2005.

———. *Sumerian Proverbs in the Schøyen Collection*. Bethesda: CDL Press, 2007.

Bauer, Josef, Robert K. Englund, and Manfred Krebernik. *Mesopotamien: Späturuk-Zeit und Frühdynastische Zeit*. Göttingen: Vandenhoeck & Ruprecht, 1998.

Biggs, Robert D. "Ebla and Abu Salabikh: The Linguistic and Literary Aspects." In *La Lingua di Ebla. Atti del Convegno Internazionale*. Napoli, Aprile 21–23, 1980, edited by Luigi Cagni, 121–133. Naples: Instituto Universitario Orientale, Seminario di Studi Asiatici, 1981.

Böck, Barbara. "Homo mesopotamicus." In *Munuscula Mesopotamica: Festschrift für Johannes Renger*, edited by E. Cancik-Kirschbaum and T. Richter, 53–68. Münster: Ugarit Verlag, 1999.

Buccellati, Giorgio. "A LU E School Tablet from the Service Quarter of the Royal Palace AP at Urkesh." *JCS* 55 (2003): 45–48.

Cavigneaux, Antoine. "Lexikalische Listen." *RlA* 6 (1980–83): 609–641.

Civil, Miguel. "Old Babylonian Proto-Lu: Types of Sources." In *The Series lu2 = ša and Related Texts*, edited by Miguel Civil and Erica Reiner, 24–73. MSL 12. Rome: Pontificium Inst. Biblicum, 1969.

———. "The Sag-Tablet." In *Materials for the Sumerian Lexicon, Supplementary Series*, vol. 1, edited by M. Civil, O. R. Gurney, and D. A. Kennedy, 1–41. Rome: Pontificium Inst. Biblicum, 1986.

———. "Ancient Mesopotamian Lexicography." In *Civilizations of the Ancient Near East*, edited by Jack Sasson, 2305–2314. New York: Scribners, 1995.

———. "Early Semitic Loanwords in Sumerian." In *Proceedings of the 51st Rencontre Assyriologique Internationale Held at the Oriental Institute of the University of Chicago*, July 18–22, 2005, edited by Robert D. Biggs, Jennie Myers and Martha T. Roth, 11–34. Chicago: The Oriental Institute, 2007.

———. *The Lexical Texts in the Schøyen Collection*. Bethesda: CDL Press, 2010.

———. "The Law Collection of Ur-Namma." In *Cuneiform Royal Inscriptions and Related Texts in the Schøyen Collection*, edited by A. R. George, 221–286. Bethesda: CDL Press, 2011.

Culbertson, Laura. *Slaves and Households in the Near East*. Chicago: The Oriental Institute, 2011.

Englund, Robert K. "Smell of the Cage." *Cuneiform Digital Library Journal* 4 (2009).

Farber, Gertrud. "saĝ as pars pro toto for 'Person' and 'Dead Body." In *"An Experienced Scribe Who Neglects Nothing": Ancient Near Eastern Studies in Honor of Jacob Klein*, edited by Yitschak Sefati, Pinhas Artzi, Chaim Cohen, Barry L. Eichler, and Victor A. Horrowitz, 108–115. Bethesda: CDL Press, 2005.

Foster, Benjamin. "On Personnel in Sargonic Girsu." In *DUB.SAR É.DUB.BA.A: Studies Presented in Honour of Veysel Donbar*, edited by Sevket Dönmez, 143–151. Istanbul: Ege Publications, 2010.

Gelb, Ignace. "The Ancient Mesopotamian Ration System." *JNES* 24 (1965): 232–243.

———. "Prisoners of War in Early Mesopotamia." *JNES* 32 (1973): 70–98.

———. "Terms for Slaves in Ancient Mesopotamia." In *Societies and Languages of the Ancient Near East: Studies in Honour of I. M. Diakonoff*, edited by M. A. Dandamayev, 81–98. Warminster: Aris and Phillips, 1982.

Geller, Markham. "A New Piece of Witchcraft." In *DUMU-E2-DUB-BA-A, Studies in Honor of Åke W. Sjöberg*, edited by H. Behrens, D. Loding, and M. T. Roth, 193–205. Philadelphia: University Museum, 1989.

George, Andrew. *The Babylonian Gilgamesh Epic: Introduction, Critical Edition, and Cuneiform Texts*. Oxford: Oxford University Press, 2003.

P. D. Gesche, *Schulunterricht in Babylonien im ersten Jahrtausend v. Chr.* [1] Ugarit-Verlag, 2001.

Green, Margaret W. "Animal Husbandry at Uruk in the Archaic Period." *JNES* 39 (1980): 1–35.

Jacobsen, Thorkild. *Toward the Image of Tammuz and Other Essays Mesopotamian History and Culture*. Cambridge: Harvard, 1970.

———. "Notes on the Word lú." In *kinattūtu ša dārâti: Raphael Kutscher Memorial Volume*, edited by A. F. Rainey, 69–79. Tel Aviv: Institute of Archaeology of Tel Aviv University, 1993.

Jagersma, A. H. *A Descriptive Grammar of Sumerian* (Doctoral dissertation, Faculty of the Humanities, Leiden University, 2010).

Klein, Jacob. *Three Sulgi Hymns: Sumerian Royal Hymns Glorifying King Sulgi of Ur*. Bar-Ilan: Bar-Ilan University Press, 1981.

Krispijn, Th J. H. "Beitrage zur altorienalischen Musikforschung 1." *Akkadica* 70 (1990): 1–27.

Michalowski, Piotr. "An Early Dynastic Tablet of ED Lu A from Tell Brak (Nagar)." *Cuneiform Digital Library Journal* 3 (2003).

———. "Sumerian." In *The Cambridge Encyclopedia of the World's Ancient Languages*, edited by Roger D. Woodard, 19–59. Cambridge: Cambridge University Press, 2004.

Marchesi, Gianni, "í-a lùllumx ù-luh-ha sù-sù: on the incipit of the Sumerian Poem Gilgameˇs and Huwawa." In S. Graziani, *Studi sul Vicino Oriente antico dedicati alla memoria di Luigi Cagni* 61 (2001): 673.

Nissen, Hans J., Peter Damerow, and Robert K. Englund. *Archaic Bookkeeping: Writing and Techniques of Economic Administration in the Ancient Near East*. Chicago: University of Chicago Press, 1993.

Oyēwumi, Oyèrókẹ. *The Invention of Women: Making African Sense of Western Gender Discourses*. Minnesota: University of Minnesota Press, 1997.

Roth, Martha. *Law Collections from Mesopotamia and Asia Minor*. Atlanta: Society of Biblical Literature, 1995.

———. "Gender and Law: A Case Study from Ancient Mesopotamia." In *Gender and Law in the Hebrew Bible and the Ancient Near East*, edited by Victor H. Matthews, Bernard M. Levinson, Tikva Frymer-Kensky, 173–184. Sheffield: Sheffield Press, 1998.

Sigrist, Marcel. *Drehem*. Bethesda: CDL Press, 1992.

Sjöberg, Åke W. "Nungal in the Ekur." *Archiv für Orientforschung* 24 (1973): 19–46.

———. "Der Examenstext A." *ZA* 64 (1975): 137–177.

Steinkeller, Piotr. *The Foresters of Umma: Towards a Definition of Ur III labor*. New Haven: American Oriental Society, 1987.

———. *Sale Documents of die Ur III-Period*. Stuttgart: Franz Steiner Verlag, 1989.

———. "Threshing Implements in Ancient Mesopotamia, Cuneiform Sources." *Iraq* 52 (1990): 19–24.

———. "Early Political Development in Mesopotamia and the Origins of the Sargonic Empire." In *Akkad, the First World Empire: Structure, Ideology, Traditions, Sargon*, edited by Mario Liverani, 107–112. Padua: sargon srl, 1993.

———. "Review of ZATU." *BiOr* 52 (1995a): 690–714.

———. "Sheep and Goat Terminology in the Ur III Sources from Drehem." *Bulletin on Sumerian Agriculture* 8 (1995b): 49–70.

Tanos, Bálint. "The Polysemy and Productivity of the Formative Element nam in Old Babylonian Literary Sumerian." In *Analysing Literary Sumerian: Corpus-Based Approaches*, edited by Graham Cunningham and Jarle Ebeling, 250–272. London: Equinox, 2007.

Taylor, J. J. "Collations to ED Lu C and D." *Cuneiform Digital Library Bulletin* 3 (2003).

Veldhuis, Niek. *History of the Cuneiform Lexical Tradition*. Münster: Ugarit Verlag, 2014.

Westbrook, Raymond. "A Sumerian Freedman." In *Literatur, Politik und Recht in Mesopotamien: Festschrift für Claus Wilcke Herausgegeben*, edited by W. Sallaberger, K. Volk, and A. Zgoll, 333–339. Wiesbaden: Harrassowitz Verlag, 2003a.

———. "Neo-Sumerian Period (Ur III)." In *A History of Ancient Near Eastern Law*, edited by R. Westbrook, 183–226. Leiden: Brill, 2003b.

———. "A New Look at the Nippur Homicide Trial." In *A Woman of Valor: Jerusalem Ancient Near Eastern Studies in Honor of Joan Goodnick Westenholz*, edited by Wayne Horowitz, Uri Gabbay, and Filip Vukosavovic, 195–200. Madrid: Consejo Superior de Investigaciones Científicas, 2010.

Westenholz, J. Goodnick and Marcel Sigrist. "The Measure of Man: The Lexical Series Ugu-mu." In *Proceedings of the 51st Rencontre Assyriologique Internationale Held at the Oriental Institute of the University of Chicago*, July 18–22, 2005, edited by Robert D. Biggs, Jennie Myers and Martha T. Roth, 221–232. Chicago: The Oriental Institute, 2008.

Wilcke, Claus. "Familiengründung im alten Babylonien." In *Geschlechtsreife und Legitimation zur Zeugung*, edited by E. W. Müller, 215–219. Munich: Karl Alber Freiburg, 1985.

———. "Orthographie, Grammatik und literarische Form: Beobachtungen zu der Vaseninschrift Lugalzaggesis (SAKI 152–156)." In *Lingering over Words: Studies in Ancient Near Eastern Literature in Honor of William L. Moran*, edited by William L. Moran, Tzvi Abusch, and John Huehnergard, 488–498. Atlanta: Scholars Press, 1990.

———. "Der Kodex Urnamma (CU): Versuch einer Rekonstruktion." In *Riches Hidden in Secret Places: Ancient Near Eastern Studies in Memory of Thorkild Jacobsen*, edited by Tzvi Abusch, 291–333. Winona Lake: Eisenbrauns, 2002.

———. *Early Ancient Near Eastern Law: A History of Its Beginnings: The Early Dynastic and Sargonic Periods*. Winona Lake: Eisenbrauns, 2003.

———. "ED Lú A und die Sprache(n) der archaischen Texte." In *Ethnicity in Ancient Mesopotamia: Proceedings of the 48th Rencontre Assyriologique Internationale*, Leiden, July 1–4, 2002, edited by W. H. Van Soldt, 430–445. Leiden: Nederlands Instituut voor Het Nabije Oosten, 2005.

Zettler, Richard L. *The Ur III Temple of Inanna at Nippur the Operation and Organization of Urban Religious Institutions in Mesopotamia in the Late Third Millennium B.C.* Berlin: Dietrich Reimer Verlag, 1992.

2 Men looking at men

The homoerotics of power in the state arts of Assyria

Julia Assante

The royal art of Assyria is about the world of men and made for male viewers.[1] From the socles of Tukulti-Ninurta I (1243–1207) to the great palace reliefs of Assurbanipal (668–627), men looked at pictures of men. Powerful kings, bare-chested warriors, chubby eunuchs and a whole panoply of foreign men, from subjugated royals to anonymous soldiers and captives, thickly populated the steles, orthostats, doors and obelisks of Assyria. How did state art construct the masculinities it portrayed? And what performative effect did they have on the subject formation of male viewers? How did the array of hierarchies from the idea of supreme masculine to the least masculine, all progressively codified in state art, propel state ideology? Or, were the emerging codifications the outward expressions of an irresistible social drive that necessitated the invention of Assyria's ideology in the first place?

As Assyria grew in military might during the Middle Assyrian period, and as more and more disparate peoples were brought into the Assyrian fold, previous class systems were no longer workable. New social orders were called for, particularly to accommodate the rise of a new and problematic class, the military, in the Neo-Assyrian period. Huge communities of deportees of all social stations, growing internationalism in general and the new military class swelled the Assyrian male population and subverted the primacy of the earlier patriarchy whose dominant force was the *awīlu*, the pure Assyrian male citizen class, as well as the older class stratification based on land ownership.[2] In short, the professional standing army of the Neo-Assyrian period, in which Assyrians and non-Assyrians of any class could advance,[3] undermined the earlier *awīlu*-centric social structure that used social status, ethnicity, hereditary economics and gender to uphold itself in the Middle Assyrian period, at least as it was voiced by its members, the lawmakers and writers of royal annals. The new social order was powerfully homosocial and hierarchical, as befits a military state. More than ever before, it was organized around notions of phallic aggression.

What was unprecedented was the strong insertion of another form of masculinity – eunuchism, which seemed to have arisen as a complement to the military class. Eunuchism appeared at first tentatively on the battlefield, in palaces and in the administration during the time of territorial expansion of the Middle Assyrian period, but burgeoned into a vibrant class of its own, the *šūt rešūtti*, by the Neo-Assyrian period. It was then that eunuchs became especially prominent features of state art. Eunuchism was a needed injection of a new, man-made (by the knife!) masculine gender into a homosocial system that had been flagging since the "dark ages" between Assur-bel-kala (1074–1057) and Adad-Nirari II (911–891). It resuscitated the primacy of ideal manliness, once only attributable to the elite *awīlu*, but now to many, reshaped and sharpened distinctions of manhood, and reset the social boundaries for high-ranking men along gender lines. In order to speak across a shifting, heterogeneous and illiterate society, the new social order employed boldly enunciated imagery that carried strong eroticized components. With the introduction of eunuchs into royal compositions, a greater range of masculinities came into play, which was used to compositionally orchestrate broader, clearer, yet more nuanced messages.

The constellation of represented masculinities visibly altered with the reign of Assurnasirpal II (883–859), when a discernible set of visual codes evolved. Calculated to manipulate the sexual identity of individual male viewers, these codes therefore controlled the parameters of visual pleasure. They also incited homosexual desire and directed it toward state-approved aims. Between the time of Tukulti-Ninurta I and the White Obelisk (date uncertain), on the one hand, and Assurnasirpal II, on the other, new mortal masculinities, namely eunuchs, appeared on palace walls, while other types either disappeared (e.g., the kneeling Assyrian king), or were recast (e.g., bearded royal attendants). Each modification to the portrayal of one masculinity necessarily redefined all others, putting them further up or down the ladder of male gender hierarchy. It was not until the more complex reliefs of Assurbanipal when these fixed rules of representation lost some of their standardization. Exploring the shifts in the image-making of men during this period, including the reconfigurations of group scenes, can tell us much about the ideology of male sexualities in Assyria.

Although the subject of men in the scholarship of ancient Mesopotamia has been nearly equivalent to the study of history until recently, little critical attention has been paid to *differences* among masculinities. Especially lacking is theorizing of eunuchism and what it might have signified in Mesopotamian antiquity, despite progress made in identifying eunuchs in the visual and textual records.[4] Fortunately, as this present volume demonstrates, there is a growing body of sensitive work in our field that understands masculinity as a social construction. Megan Cifarelli's laudable analysis of Assyrian alterity, the "otherness"-making, of non-Assyrians in Neo-Assyrian state art (1995, 1998) is particularly provocative for the present discussion.

Images of men from no matter what period of Mesopotamia, even prehistory, consistently share one rule of difference: there are men who dominate and men who submit. An age-old trope in the arts of the elite and one that best describes this asymmetry is, of course, the victor and the defeated or "fallen enemy." The body iconography for each is set in clear opposition. Typically, the former towers over the latter, who lies helpless at his feet, literally fallen, and frequently under a horse (see, for example, Figure 2.10) or chariot. The victor stands upright, usually either smiting the enemy, pointing a weapon at the enemy or simply holding his weapons as emblems of his unquestionable might. By contrast, the defeated is portrayed stripped of his weapons and often his clothing. Cifarelli divides men into two groups: erect men (i.e. Assyrians) and non-erect men (i.e. non-Assyrians). In art, the non-erect take many forms, from milder versions, such as the "crouching tributary," to men in full-scale prostration, which seems to have been a formal gesture of submission made to the Assyrian king (Cifarelli 1998: 218). Tracing such postural and gestural codes in art and texts, she brings to light the social contexts in which they might have been understood by their contemporary audiences. Whereas erect posture would be read as conveying order, dignity and, above all, military discipline, stooped or groveling postures would be seen as subhuman. Portrayals of passivity and cowardice are time after time attached to non-Assyrians (never, of course, to Assyrians), along with other markers of low status, namely nudity, mutilation and physical bondage with yokes, ropes and so forth, which visually equate foreigners with punished criminals and animals.

Body carriage carries easily identifiable notations of male sexuality. Posture, for instance, measures a man's *baštu*, his life force or potency,[5] so that the erect-standing Assyrian soldier, so clearly demonstrated in Figure 2.1, becomes the whole that stands for the part – the erect and ready penis – the phallic potency of the Assyrian army. This is hardly a modern hypothesis. Akkadian sources frequently conflate the male body and the penis. In both, straightness, tension and even length or height are admirable characteristics. The erect penis is, in turn, likened to effective weapons.[6] And few weapons are portrayed as more effective than the Assyrian soldier himself. When

Figure 2.1 City Assault, Tiglath-Pileser III (744–727).
The British Museum, London.

looking at state art, contemporary viewers could not fail to read erectness as real manliness, constructed as inherently belligerent and "naturally" superior over other men. Conversely, non-erectness marks the less manly, constructed as deserving to be conquered by the truly manly.

Overt feminization of "the enemy" occurs from the Middle Assyrian period on in texts that employ gender dualisms in military contexts. Tukulti-Ninurta I's royal inscriptions call on Ishtar to change the enemy from a man to a woman and to cause the enemy's manhood to dwindle away.[7] In Neo-Assyrian curses, especially for soldiers, the warrior is turned into his opposite, the lowly *ḫarimtu*, a female with no standing whatsoever in the patriarchal system, and, consequently, the most sexually vulnerable.[8] In such texts, the enemy-warrior then is physically and socially castrated.

The more Assyria's military power escalated, the more state art became preoccupied with inciting a psychology of difference among men. Because the success of an imperial state relied on the tension of a rigorous hierarchy that maintains a fierce pecking order, obedience within the chain of command and an appetite for conquest, an unambiguous operating recognition of male hierarchy based on ethnicity and gradations of male gender was reiterated relentlessly in art, royal inscriptions, laws and edicts. Conquest obviously belonged to the virile upper end of the hierarchy and was quintessentially Assyrian. Military ideology in images carefully directed desire for conquest away from the Assyrian military body and toward the foreign other, or "right" conquerable body.

To demonstrate, in Figures 2.1 and 2.2 from Tiglath-Pileser III (744–727), the eye first alights on the victor, giving him an immediate, but short-lived,

Figure 2.2 Tiglath-Pileser III and the Defeated Enemy.

The British Museum, London.

primacy. Then compositional techniques quickly channel the eye toward the defeated other, either by placing the other at center or as the terminating point of diagonals that draw the eye toward him, or by making him the object of the action or the gaze of other figures in the scene. Right objects of conquest were also portrayed with objectifying and what were considered feminizing traits, such as nudity and postures signifying helplessness or submission.[9] The Assyrian state seems to have realized that homosexual desire *when sublimated* is an effective way to cultivate the ideal military qualities of loyalty, obedience and a thirst for conquest.

From the point of view of artistry, juxtaposing distinctly articulated masculinities according to degrees of empowered and disempowered, from the king (or sometimes a god) and male members of the royal family down to Assyrian soldiers, eunuchs, enemy soldiers and captives, builds dramatic tension in scenes. The result is more interesting and more powerful pictures. Easily readable and standardized iconography also makes such images less open to misinterpretation. By repetition, coded depictions on obelisks, palace walls, gates and steles schooled audiences to accept definitive, constructed categories of masculinity as natural – if not biological, according to ethnicity – ways of being. Representations also transmitted how these categories were to interact from an Assyrian worldview. In short, for men looking at men they were performative. Inundated as we are today with images, the impact state art made on ancient, usually illiterate viewers, who inhabited a world relatively devoid of representation, can hardly be measured.

Within the hypermasculine milieu of the military and particularly of the battlefield, the sheer physicality, the adoration of men, the harsh observance of male ranking, survival aggression, fear and, finally, the lack of wives and other sexually available women all contrive to foster same-sex desire. The intensity of male bonding must have led to homosexual acts within the Assyrian military and, conversely, to homophobia, which emphatically aims extreme attachments and slavish loyalty at inaccessible icons, such as a general, a king or emperor, a warrior god, a city or nation. In antiquity, the ideal male hero was usually portrayed as possessing military prowess, if not, in the case of Gilgamesh, nearly uncontrollable belligerence, coupled with a strong sexual drive and sexual magnetism, or *kuzbu*, to which either sex was presumably susceptible.[10] In the first-millennium *Gilgamesh Epic* (Gilg. I ii), called the Standard Edition, the poet describes the King of Uruk's unrivaled sexual predatoriness with a martial simile for the royal genitalia: "[Gilgamesh's] weapons are (ever) raised" (l. 54).[11] In an elegant image of the definitive phallic signifier, the poet demonstrates a deep-rooted cultural association between male sexuality and aggression. In this and other texts contemporary to the Neo-Assyrian period, the hero often appears in a discrete homoerotic relationship, highlighted in the story, in which the love of man for another man can surpass the love of a man for a woman. It is specifically said in the Standard Edition that Gilgamesh loved his wild-man companion Enkidu "like a wife."[12] In a much earlier episode of the

Gilgamesh story, however, the love between the king and Enkidu is explicitly sexual. Gilgamesh is described as penetrating Enkidu's "vulva." The later erasure of this homosexual act may indicate a "Don't ask, don't tell" policy in which same-sex activity is assumed but not openly divulged.[13] Witness too the love of Achilles for Patroclos and David for Jonathan (2 Sam 1:26).[14] Within a historical context, Alexander the Great's demonstrations of love for Hephaistion were self-consciously modeled on the Homeric prototype.

Asymmetry between the hero and his beloved are played out personally, socially and narratologically. In all these, the hero has the greater importance (Halperin 1990: 78). The subordinate beloved is also susceptible to physical violation, with fatal results. Differences between the two are drawn in the extreme when the body of the beloved lies limp and passive in inevitable death. The hero's attachment to the lifeless form – disturbingly sensuous images of male vulnerability – becomes obsessive, while lavish mourning exalts and memorializes love between men. Nevertheless, these friendships appropriate heterosexual gender inequalities. David Halperin notes, for instance, that Patroclos performs functions for Achilles that a wife or female dependent normally performs in the Homeric world (1990: 84). And as we have seen, Enkidu, whom Gilgamesh loved like a wife, was a derivative being, made as a complementary companion for the legendary king. Within the high echelons of the power elite of the first millennium to which these characters belong, same-sex bonds take precedence and supplant conjugal and, for that matter, kinship, relationships. Such stories of passionate fidelity undoubtedly influenced male relationships in the palace and especially in military camps. Despite all this and the persistent glorification of men's beauty in these ancient texts, homosexual activity remains an allusion with the one exception just mentioned.

In antiquity, homosexual activity in no way refers to homosexuality as a way of life or as a self-identity as it is today but rather as isolated instances of same-sex interaction. The modern dualism of heterosexual/homosexual came into being at the end of the 19th century. Since the term "homosexual" appeared first, as what Michel Foucault called a new species, it gave rise to the term "heterosexual," which is itself another modern invention.[15] In current usage, the male homosexual most often identifies himself by the biological sex of his lover/s. (So too, for that matter, bisexuals and heterosexuals.) There is no indication from ancient Near Eastern sources that homosexuality was ever a self-identification nor that sexual identity rested on a person's object choice. Although modern scholarship has translated certain terms, usually for male offices of the Inanna/Ishtar cult, as homosexuals, homosexual prostitutes, transvestites and so on, a critical look at these terms shows that such interpretations are seriously in error.[16]

With eunuchs, a feminized male sexual identity was artificially and ineradicably imposed. Yet even here, we cannot speak of a simple dualism of homosexual/heterosexual or even of masculine/effeminate. The eunuch offers instead a considerable array of masculinities, depending on how he was castrated and at what age. The varying sexuality of eunuchs as well as their degree of virility were to a great extent measurable, controllable and predictable. The eunuch was the ultimate designer male. How does the high visibility of eunuchism square with the near silence of textual and visual records on homosexual activity?[17] Are both the result of a deep cultural homophobia? Or did both come about because of a widespread but tacit acceptance of same-sex exploits as common in the course of masculine life?

Two Middle Assyrian laws afford a rare glimpse of how society regarded male sexual interaction. These are the only clauses known from Mesopotamia that regulate homosexual activity, and both refer to sodomy as a chargeable transgression.[18] Although the first, MAL A §19, deals with sexual slander and sodomy is not the actual offense of the clause, the circumstances of the clause tell us that a man who allows himself to be habitually sodomized, literally "fornicated upon," is punishable under the law. What is interesting here is that a man of *awīlu* status, that is, of the adult male citizen class, who allows himself to be frequently sodomized is seen to indulge in unlawful behavior, but *awīlu* sodomizers appear to be penalty free. The next provision, MAL A §20, regards an *awīlu* sodomizer as an offender only if the object of his sodomy is of equal status.[19] If he sexually penetrates another *awīlu*, he is gang-raped and castrated. One can barely imagine how harsh the penalty would have been for a non-*awīlu* man to sodomize an *awīlu*. This violent feminization of the *awīlu* offender clearly casts him forever out of his peer group and asserts a radical gender hierarchy between *awīlu* and criminal. The offender's altered position as the "other," a viable object of male predation, one who can never again penetrate, recovers and exaggerates the lost masculine status of the violated *awīlu*. These clauses offer three different views of same-sex sodomy. If a man is an *awīlu* and frequently wants to be sodomized, that is, if he takes the role of the passive partner, he is a sexual offender. If he is an *awīlu* and sodomizes another *awīlu*, he is a sexual offender, and the humiliation of the sodomized *awīlu* will be harshly redressed under the law. Finally, we learn that sodomizing a man and/or castrating him were legal methods of punishment, presumably enforced by *awīlu*-class men, which physically marked him as a criminal.

Castration was sometimes the penalty for another sexual crime against the *awīlu*, adultery with another *awīlu*'s wife (MAL A §15). Middle Assyrian clauses institutionalize the safeguarding of the *awīlu*'s bodily integrity, which extends to his wife and to a lesser extent his sons and daughters. Violation of his body, from rape, beating, lacerating of the flesh, castration to shaving, not only renders him as less than an *awīlu*, as less than a real man, it may also signify that he has forfeited his legal rights, certainly irreversibly in some cases, among them his right to bodily integrity. An *awīlu* who invites anal invasion willingly abandons his birthright of physical inviolability, and, like an *awīlu* who asserts himself sexually at the expense of another *awīlu*, he subverts the sociosexual values of his class, a crime for which he forfeits his membership. From the sodomy clauses we might infer a certain social milieu in which homosexual acts are overlooked, if not expected, as long as they observe rules about class inequality.

The rules governing the sexual life of an Assyrian *awīlu* appear very similar to those of ancient Greco-Roman adult males of the citizen class.[20] In the world of classical antiquity, the adult male citizen could fornicate with male or female, adult or child, as long as he maintained the masculine stance of the penetrator. As in Mesopotamian law, certain orifices were prohibited: citizen adult males could not penetrate other men of the same sociolegal status nor women married to men of that status. His sexual partners necessarily took the passive-receptive role of the penetrated. Given that these roles were never interchangeable, the sexual protocol of classical Greece and Rome for men of patriarchal status preserved a heterosexual model in same-sex activities, as it did in Assyria, according to the evidence that remains. Sexual identity for a Greek or Roman male citizen and, no doubt, for the *awīlu* as well, did not rest on the biological sex of his partner as it does today but on the phallocentric act of insertion. Yet, sexual identity was also inextricable from sociosexual attitudes that utterly polarized human populations into two opposing groups. Free adult males were the power figures, dominant and active. Not only were they never to be penetrated, they were never to be physically violated in any way. Physical violation, the rubric under which the ancients would have located penetration, reduced the male citizen to the level of the slave, child, woman, criminal or foreigner (Walters 1997), as it seems to have done in Assyrian law. Insertive sex, a "real man's" prerogative indeed, but one to which he was limited, was the very definition of sexual activity, and phallic penetration the only truly performable act.

By contrast, the other group, made up of women, children, foreigners and slaves, that is, everyone who was not an adult male citizen, was characterized as having feminine traits, as submissive and receptive rather than active. As mere recipients of phallic action, those in this group had no sexual autonomy; they did not "do" sex but rather sex was done to them.[21] Just as the sex act in the classical world was not constituted as something that two or more people do together but as something that one person does to another (Dover 1978: 16, 84–106; Foucault 1985: 46–47; Halperin 1990: 29), Akkadian verbs for fornication, copulation and the like are transitive and express a conceptualization of sex in terms of an active male subject who fornicates a passive (accusative) object.[22] Usually in western European languages the expressions for copulation connote mutual action: John makes love with Jane or Jane copulates/fornicates/screws with John. We come closer to the active/passive structure common to the ancient Semitic form when John fucks, screws or mounts Jane, an action that has been understood as exclusively male until very recently. Modern translations from Akkadian into western languages, however, customarily change this original sense into the current modern mutual-action forms.

Whereas the homosexuality of today's western world cuts across class and lends its adherents a kind of instant flash glamour, in antiquity, the very act of one man penetrating another instead instituted social difference. A man who "fornicates" another man is consequentially superior; he who is "fornicated upon" is inferior. The sex between men would not admit relationships based on sameness. Even the disreputable Greek *kinaidos* and Roman *cinaedus*, the *mollis* or "soft" man (what a pun!) who wants to be used as a woman by other men cannot be considered homosexual by today's standards, first, because he seeks "normal" men who would never engage in reciprocal penetration, oral or anal – in fact, the cultural assumption of sexual unsameness was so strong that a *cinaedus* in bed, so to speak, with another *cinaedus* would have been unthinkable (Walters 1997: 58); and, second, because, as in the Middle Assyrian clause cited above, he is no more than an inversion of the values of phallic action attached to high-status manhood for his time (Halperin 1990: 48). Besides imbalances based on legal class (free-born male versus slave, for instance) and ethnicity (e.g., citizen versus foreigner), which operated in Assyria as well as in the classical world, other more complex imbalances are known from Rome and Athens that were weighed out on the scale of age.

To what extent pederasty occurred among the citizen class in the classical world is a topic too vast and complicated to canvas here. A few things can be said, however, namely that males who were too young to assume the legal citizen standing of their fathers were problematic targets of adult male lust. In ancient Rome, penetrating a future *vir* was an offense subject to criminal punishment, so that viable objects of pederastic desire were slaves or ex-slaves, usually of foreign extraction (see Fantham 1991; Richlin 1993). In classical Athens, penetration of the not-fully-fledged male citizen was sidestepped with intercrural (between the thighs) copulation, at least in the ideal (Dover 1978). Needless to say, the penetrator in either case was also citizen class. The sexual ethos of classical Greece arranged elite pederastic relationships into a strictly observed ritual between pursuer and pursued. The older male, an educational mentor of sorts, courted a younger male who was expected to remain demur, like a properly brought-up maiden. If the youth did comply, he did so only for reasons of esteem, gratitude and affection for his suitor, never for reasons of reciprocated desire (see Dover 1978: 52–53; Foucault 1985: 223–225; Halperin 1990: 92). Both cultures concur, however, on the contours of male desirability. A male was sexy only at the age between the onset of puberty and his first beard. The growth of hair then constituted the dividing line between sexual object and sexual subject. In some ancient sources, hair growth on the young male body is sullying and sexually revolting (Halperin 1990: 88). Desirable bodies were not manly bodies.

All the above categories of erotic response – the binaries of superior/inferior, active/passive, dominant/submissive, inviolable/violable and, in particular, penetrator/penetrated – are consistently exploited in Assyrian state art. The other common binary (later discussed) is bearded versus beardless. Despite Assyria's lack of discernible homoerotic imagery in either art or in texts, its official arts stringently observed the psychosexual rules of binary homoerotism known in the ancient world. The images were aimed to hit viewers, quite literally, below the belt. From the Middle Assyrian period through the Neo-Assyrian period such dualisms were usually clothed in ceremonial, ritual, hunt and especially battle scenes – *the* topics of state art. Assyrians are always portrayed as the doers, the dominators, who force submission and frequently death on non-Assyrians and animals, and submission on nature in the form of hewing *lamassu* from rock or cutting through wild terrain. In none of these is a single Assyrian ever portrayed as penetrated. No arrow ever pierces the Assyrian body, no knife, no sword, no lance. No Assyrian nor any of his parts is ever displayed as limp flesh, impaled on a pike or severed. For that matter, in centuries of battle art, no Assyrian lies down. As Figure 2.1 illustrates, he stands "head held high," a Mesopotamian metaphor for pride, shoulders broad, with some penetrating weapon at the ready or already plunged into the adversary's body. In the same scene, we do see an Assyrian bending over, but only to cut off the head of a fallen enemy.

By contrast, portraits of defeat and submission abound for the non-Assyrian enemy, who suffers a vast range of humiliations. Chiefly, he is portrayed as penetrated by an Assyrian weapon. Yet he is also regularly depicted in art and texts as symbolically castrated; innumerable severed heads, arms, hands, eyes, ears, stand metonymically for the physical emasculation of the non-Assyrian.[23] He is also shown paraded nude, or worse, publicly flayed – the ultimate stripping – for the entertainment of Assyrian audiences (Cifarelli 1995: 218). State art captured for Assyrian viewers the enemy's destiny in non-Assyrian regions, where he was set up in public naked and impaled alive, as in Figure 2.1, a terrifying reminder for his people of their utter powerlessness. Image after image of his knife falling from his hands, his arrow going astray, his lance broken, weapons that never will and never could penetrate their mark, capture and showcase his miserable impotence for centuries of Assyrian viewers. By contrast, vignettes in narrative scenes of deportation that involve captive women and sometimes children portray their Assyrian guards as respectful and protective (Reed 2007). Nevertheless, Middle Assyrian private royal pornography, which presents captives in live sex shows, reveals a possible darker side of captivity and the humiliating sexualization of both male and female foreigners in unseemly acts (Assante 2007).

The intransigence of the dominant-submissive/penetrator-penetrated theme, which seems to have driven men's desire in antiquity, speaks volumes about homoerotic anxiety in Assyrian military life. The emphatic turning outward of physical violence onto the bodies of the enemy other attempts to mask the often gruesome reality of Assyrian soldiers. After all, they too fell in the face of maiming, death and the occasional rape. Even more, manliness must also have been at risk within the soldier's own troops, as it was in other armies of the ancient world. In Rome and Greece where texts reveal far more of military life than Assyrian sources do, homoeroticism operates within the military dogma of hypermasculinity differently. Since Rome equated real men with physically inviolability and the soldier was upheld as the very emblem of normative manliness, the fact of his physical vulnerability – in battle as well as within his own legion from beating or rape – presented an ideological conflict. Romans regarded instances of homosexual acts within the ranks as shameful anomalies. The ideal response to sexual advances was forceful resistance, even to death. In one account, Marius, a private soldier, kills an officer who wanted to violate him sexually. Marius's extreme defense was not just condoned, it was publicly lauded (Walters 1997: 40).

Rather than whitewashing the homoerotics of military life, the Greeks exploited it. In the fourth century BCE, for instance, an elite military core of 150 homosexual couples known as the Sacred Band formed in Thebes (see De Voto 1992). Relationships were based on an older *erastes*, a teacher and mentor, and a youth or *eromenos*, and developed during the youth's training. The sexual aspect of the relationship stopped, again, at the appearance of the youth's beard, at which point he was given his armor and sent to war. However, the tension of the psychosexual hierarchical bond continued, spurring the older to impress the younger on the battlefield and the younger to emulate the older. Plato describes the superior fighting force of sexually bonded warriors as the result of a similar ongoing flirtation in the midst of battle.[24] The Theban Sacred Band worked as a shock unit with the express mission to "crush the head of the [enemy] snake."

In later Iraq, under the caliphs, protecting young Mamluk trainees and warriors from the sexual assaults of older military personnel seems to have been a full-time job (Ayalon 1999: 50–51). That job was the responsibility of eunuchs. Eunuchs, who trained Mamluk youths for combat, ran interference between Mamluk youths (never retrieved from Muslim lands) and older Muslim officers, sometimes by offering their own bodies for sex. Eunuchs also saw to it that Mamluks did not engage sexually among themselves. Unlike sources from ancient Rome, Greece and Medieval Iraq, Assyrian visual and textual records do not furnish overt testimony about sexual life and homosexual friction in the military. Nevertheless, Assyria's palace walls, gates and steles communicate a high degree of homoerotic tension. The more it is repressed and sublimated, the greater its force becomes so that sexual aggression turns to violence and dominance to sadism. Assyria's propagandistic art relieves homoerotic tension by picturing release as sadistic acts focused on the foreign enemy. Displacement of desire then instilled in the subject a need for conquest.

The king and the construction of hypermasculinity

State art's primary project was channeling the wrong kind of visual desire away from the king, a project much more important than channeling it away from the Assyrian military. By the wrong kind of visual desire, I mean here a desire to sexually conquer, which I will call here "active desire." As

Commander in Chief, the ruler stood for his army. As King of the Universe, he also stood for the state and what approximates later notions of absolute monarchy. He was the chief signifier for the combined psychosexual, sociopolitical meaning of mighty Assyria. In a certain way, Assyria culminated in the royal body, or perhaps it would be more accurate to say that Assyria itself issued from it. As the king was Assur's earthly representative, he supposedly shared the god's physical likeness and deeply masculine values (see Ornan 2007; Westenholz 2000; Winter 1997). He was also the high priest, the *šangu-elu*. The claim to godlike semblance seems to have begun in Assyria with Assurnasirpal II, the same king who set the canons under discussion. Assyria's myth-making of its own superiority and invincibility necessarily produced king after king as the divinely given template for humanity, the perfection of male virility, the ultimate phallic weapon, around which all else and all others, including female physiques, were derivative.

Within the framework of this brand of homoeroticism, the king is the desirer, never the desired. The dilemma here, which Assyrian art eventually overcame, was that representations of the king thrust him into the role of desirable object and the viewer into the dominant male role, who visually desires and possesses the object in view. The prohibition of this standpoint was so untenable in the domain of Assyrian imperialistic hierarchy that it extended even beyond imagery and into the three-dimensional reality of everyday life. Tellingly, some texts indicate that the king's subjects were even forbidden to gaze on his countenance (Parpola 1980: 172). Objectification of the royal figure in art had to be radically minimized and whatever desire his image provoked properly diverted. Displaced active desire underpinned a powerful, subliminally driven devotion to the king in which a soldier remained inferior and feminized by comparison. Yet the potential for climbing the military ranks and the permission for violent conquest promised the soldier at least a chance at a mimetic royal manliness.

In order to deter men from ogling images of the king, artists developed techniques along two lines: supermasculinizing the royal figure, as mentioned above, and juxtaposing it with forms associated in the ancient mind with feminine characteristics. The latter technique works to deflect active desire away from the royal body. These devices were not fully realized until Assurnasirpal's Northwest palace reliefs. In earlier representation in the written and visual records of Mesopotamia, the king was frequently featured openly as an object of sexual desire. Two obvious examples that come to mind here are found in the court poetry of King Shulgi, where the king's sexual appeal to women is central to his kingship, and in the stele of Naram-Sin (Figure 2.3), in which the ruler's nearly naked body is alluringly displayed.[25] Assyrian kings are, by comparison, de-eroticized. Whether in ceremonial dress as in the socle of Tukulti-Ninurta I (Figure 2.4) or in battle garb, the king is fully, if not elaborately, covered. Gone are the displays of bare-chested warriors, of kings with smooth muscles and slender waists, rounded buttocks and exposed shoulders, or even Hammurabi's silky

Figure 2.3 The Stele of Naram-Sin (2254–2218).

Musée Du Louvre, Paris.

drapery, all of which cause the eye to linger with the wrong kind of fascination.[26] Assyrian kings grow progressively thick set and solid, like impenetrable fortress walls (Figure 2.5). Although they are indeed magnificent spectacles and glorify masculinity, they in no way encourage a visual caress.

Figure 2.4 Socle of Tukulti-Ninurta (1243–1207).
Archaeological Museum, Istanbul.

Body thickness signals viewers that kings are not to be mistaken for youths and therefore, as we have seen, objects vulnerable to sexual assault. Muscle mass conveys instead the mature accretions of power and experience. In an earlier royal representation, Tukulti-Ninurta's sensuous curves, his small, plump buttocks tucked in by fringe, his slender arms, are, in later versions, replaced by a blocky robustness. In the Assurnasirpal stele (Figure 2.5) a fringed apron, worn only by kings, crown princes and a very few officials (Reade 1972: 92), wraps across the bulky royal buttocks, distracting the eye from what it conceals rather than delineating. The forearms bulge, the waist spreads, the neck retreats into massive shoulders, all to convey a portrait of compact potency. Here and elsewhere Assurnasirpal's body is a plethora of busy detail (Figures 2.5 and 2.6) that at once armors the body's vulnerability, scatters the gaze and transfers sensuosity onto flat, neutral, material surfaces. The body is read rather than experienced.

Figure 2.5 Assurnasirpal II (883–859).
The British Museum, London.

The corporal vocabulary of monarchs' positions and sizes also changes over time toward a more explicit enunciation of hypermasculinity. For instance, the earlier Tukulti-Ninurta figure (Figure 2.4) is portrayed in strict

Figure 2.6 Detail of Clothing, Assurnasirpal.

From E. A. Budge. *Assyrian Scuptures in the British Museum* (London 1914), plate 59. In the public domain.

profile, whereas, by the Neo-Assyrian period, the royal body, although more rigid, usually twists to bring both shoulders into view (Figures 2.5 and 2.7). The effect of greater mass and strength, especially in the chest, accentuates ideal masculine traits. In the throne base from Nimrud (Figure 2.7), the foreign ruler and Shalmaneser III appear – for the last time, incidentally – as approximate equals, but because of the twist, the body of the Assyrian king takes up more space. Height in art is obviously another characteristic that

Figure 2.7 Thronebase of Shalmaneser III (858–824).
Iraq National Museum, Baghdad.

communicates a man's position relative to other men. Neo-Assyrian artists frequently conveyed superior height for royal figures through visual devices such as taller headgear. In the White Obelisk (Figure 2.8) such distinctions made in later art between the monarch and his entourage are here absent or poorly drawn, one reason among many to regard this monument as transitional from Middle Assyrian to Neo-Assyrian, although its dating is problematic. The fez-like *polos*, which makes the wearer appear taller, is a case in point. In the obelisk the king and many of his entourage wear the *polos*, although the king's is somewhat distinguished by its inner cone; iconographical differences between ruler and ruled as well as height differences are consequently blunted. By the time of Assurnasirpal II, however, this small intimation of egalitarianism was censored and the king alone wears the *polos*. From then on, it becomes a notable part of the royal insignia and, as such, an object worthy of elaboration. In some scenes, the conical headgear is so high that it pierces the register's frame, as though the king's prominence were so great that it cannot be contained within the bounds of the unreal and the real.

In pre-Neo-Assyrian scenes involving the king and the divine, the king's stature is compromised, whereas by the time of the Northwest palace it is audaciously maintained. The Middle Assyrian plinth (Figure 2.9) depicts Tukulti-Ninurta I as seeming to shrink between two taller supernatural beings, whose frontality and confrontational stares further augment their compositional importance. In the socle of the same king (Figure 2.4), the monarch kneels in obedience to a symbol for the god Nabu. In the *bīt-nat̮hi* scene on the White Obelisk (see Figure 2.8, left side, third register down), the king's diminutive size relative to the divine figure in the scene would most certainly trouble later Neo-Assyrian viewers. Far worse, he appears emasculated and insignificant before a *female* figure and worse still, one who is sitting. As far as I am aware, later public art never again portrays the king before a goddess or standing before any seated figure, divine or

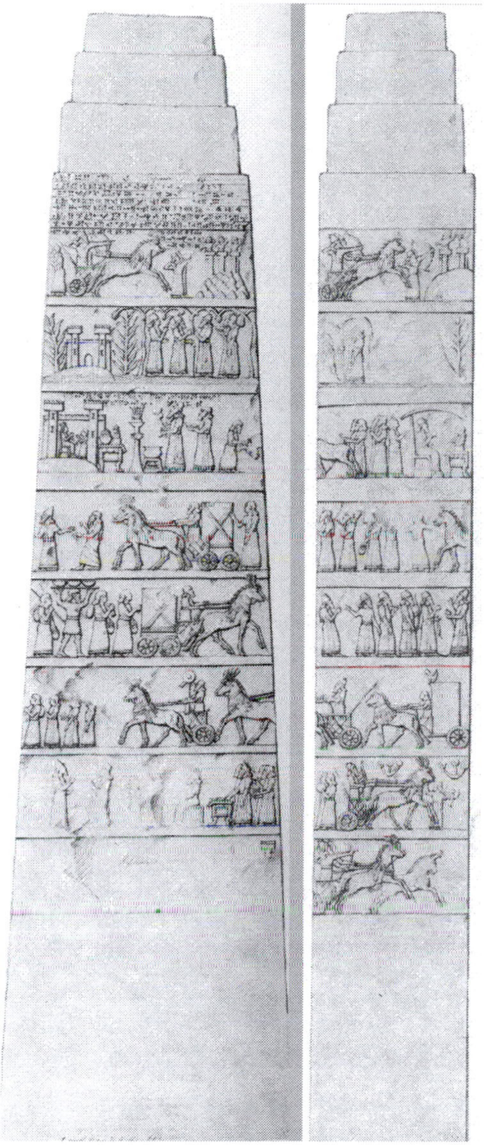

Figure 2.8 The White Obelisk, sides a and b.

Drawn by C. H. Hodder. In Rassam Original Drawings I, 1853.

otherwise. By contrast, Assurnasirpal's sculpture portrays him as equal in size to divine beings. Furthermore, the ruler maintains centrality in such scenes. In other later images, gods are usually compositionally diminutive, reduced to symbols orbiting around the king or miniaturized in cartoon clouds hovering over him (Figure 2.10). The accumulation of such details

Figure 2.9 Plinth of Tukulti-Ninurta I (1240–1207).
Vorderasiatisches Museum, Berlin.

Figure 2.10 Assurnasirpal II (883–859).
The British Museum, London.

form forceful, unconsciously received messages about the Assyrian ruler's standing in both paranormal and normal realms.

Although it remained customary to portray royalty in some gesture of obeisance to deities, the kneeling-king motif of Tukulti-Ninurta's socle (Figure 2.4) was erased in later art; it was no doubt too close to depictions of the defeated other, portrayed so dramatically in Shalmanesser III's Black Obelisk (Figure 2.11). Although Tukulti-Ninurta's manner of kneeling is different from the one in Shalmanesser's obelisk in that he sits on his heels with his upper body erect, it is still capable of blurring lines of distinction. Hierarchical tension is only sustainable when both ends of the spectrum are clearly defined against each other. The later piece does exactly this. In the top two registers sculptors position a tall standing king directly opposite men who kneel in defeat before him. This form of kneeling – head to the ground, buttocks lifted higher than the head – is carefully avoided in the Tukulti-Ninurta socle. There seems to have been two forms of kneeling in Assyria: one partially erect used for worship and the other bending over to signify utter submission.[27] The latter may have been a purely sociopolitical gesture. As female captives are never represented in this degrading position, it implicates submission only among men. Given its use in art, it was the most humiliating posture a man could make, carrying, as it did, unmistakable undertones of sexual capitulation.

Prominently featured at the top of the obelisk, the messages of conquest and homosexual desire set the theme for the entire piece. The bottoms-up posture is one way desire is deflected away from the royal body and aimed at the appropriate conquerable body. The composition itself works toward the same goal. Although the eye is first drawn to the king, the viewer's gaze goes immediately to the groveling figure. The vacuum above the defeated in the obelisk also channels visual attention toward the kneeling figure, while appearing to press him even lower. This placement of the victor and defeated is not dissimilar from Tukulti-Ninurta's pornography featuring foreign captives in which a female, whose vision is restricted, lies naked beneath her standing male partners who do not even deign to look at her. But the viewer does. In such overtly sexual scenes, his dominant eye possesses her body, visually penetrating it like a penis (Assante 2007).

The bow as the phallic signifier

Another signal of the king's hypermasculinity used in state art is his bow. Of all weapons in the arsenals of antiquity the bow and arrow, when employed, graphically imitate the penile passage from a state of highly focused tension to one of release, penetration and, in the social terms of ancient Mesopotamia, conquest. Given the homosocial discourse of the military state, it may come as no surprise then that this weapon was Assyria's chief emblem of mastery over others. It is the bow that the high gods hold in political reliefs (Figure 2.10), as if the bow and the male body were inevitable reflections of a deeply gendered cosmic truth. The celestial archetype finds its most perfect mortal expression in the Assyrian king. It is the bow he carries when

Figure 2.11 Black Obelisk, Shalmaneser III (858–824).
The British Museum, London.

offering trophies from his hunt, despite scenes in which he kills with a lance or dagger. It is again the bow that appears in parallel scenes in which he officially receives submission (Figures 2.2 and 2.11). In the battle scenes of

Assurnasirpal II, Shalmaneser III and Tiglath-Pileser III, (Figure 2.12) when Assyrian monarchs still portrayed themselves as warriors active in the field, the king always appears as an archer, whether in his chariot or on foot (Figure 2.10).[28] The bow, constructed to be shot at someone or something, necessarily describes a penetrator/penetrated relationship between the shooter and the target, the ruler and the ruled, the living and the dead.

When Assurnasirpal draws his bow (Figure 2.10), his stance displays his chest at its greatest breadth and his muscled arms at their maximum tautness, just as the bow is drawn taut and ready; the body and the bow work as one, each an extension of the other, each mirroring the action of the other. In texts of the same king, among a string of self-flattering superlatives about his power and virility, he imagines himself as "the merciless weapon."[29] This visual vocabulary draws power from the root language of the biological phallus and primal drives. In cuneiform texts as in art, the constellation of metaphors for male potency frequently revolves around notions of physical strength, metonymically referred to as the "strong arm" (see Paul 2002: 492; Winter 1989), a first requirement for good archers. The bow in Akkadian curses, incantations and other literature, also directly formed part of this constellation as a particularized simile for the erect penis or for an aggressive male sexuality.[30] It stood in for manhood itself, especially with regard to the sexuality of war. The bow is an added dimension of gender dualisms in military curses of the type mentioned above. In one, for instance, taking away the enemy's bow is enough to turn him into a woman.[31] The enemy-warrior without a bow is then a man without a penis. But a man without a bow/penis is not a eunuch. He is worse. He is a woman. Women as naturally and divinely built to be penetrated, built to be conquered, are so inferior that they fall beneath all other categories known in the militant, homosocial environment of this period, even below the slave and the castrate.

As Cifarelli (1998: 223–224) observes, enemy soldiers making gestures of submission are frequently shown holding their bows in a lowered position with the string on top, a position from which bows cannot be readily used. Or the bows are shown dropped. By contrast, Assyrian archers are depicted holding their bows either at the drawn and ready with an arrow to the string or slung over their shoulders with the string to the back, a position that would allow immediate use. Cifarelli suggests that to Assyrian eyes the consistent image of the non-Assyrian with lowered or dropped bow, featured in nearly every combat scene (e.g., Figure 2.10), signified something specific. In addition to communicating the enemy's lack of discipline, willingness to submit and proximity to death, it also communicated the enemy's lack of virility.

The circumstances in which the bow is presented in Assyrian state art – drawn, carried, dropped and so on – are anything but casual narrative anecdotes; the bow is a symbol that is carefully and deliberately manipulated primarily to alert viewers of differences in masculine genders, although it has political and religious meanings as well. When the king is not holding his bow himself, eunuch attendants carry it for him (e.g., Figures 2.7 and 2.12), as if the bow were a part of the royal body too intimate to be

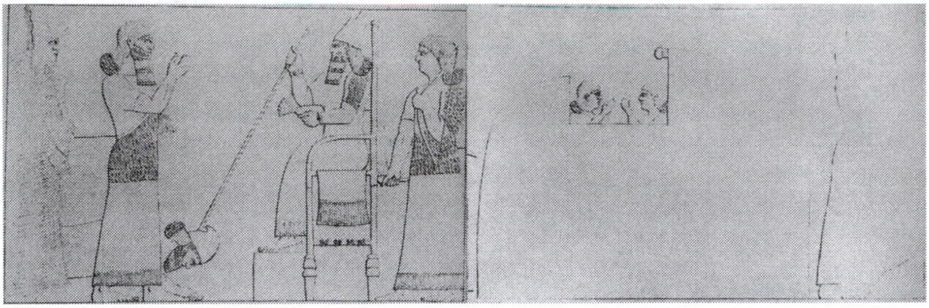

Figure 2.12 Camp Scene of Tiglath-Pileser III (745–727).
The British Museum, London.

touched by so-called real men. The drawn bow also works as a badge for male potency awarded to certain men or classes of men by the king, most obviously the corps of archers in the Assyrian army. Memorializing these awards in art gives even greater prominence to specific groups. All in all, the bow is the symbol of phallic power around which gods, kings and the imperial state are organized.

Eunuchs and the construction of inferior masculinities

The compositional device of placing a king, with all his supermasculinized traits, next to objects with feminine signifiers, such as the enemy ruler in the position of submission, serves several purposes. It arouses homosexual desire by structuring scenes according to homoerotic affinities; it displaces that desire away from the royal body and onto the right or conquerable body; and it heightens homosocial hierarchical tension. All these aims work to reinforce the ideology of imperialism. The numerous hunt and animal offering scenes present the same trope but use maimed or dead animals as the feminized objects in exchange for the enemy.

The true champion of this ideological trope, however, is the beardless, unarmed male who is consistently placed next to the king. His soft face, "unsullied" by hair, and often fleshy body (Figure 2.13) exaggerate the mature, hardened virility of the monarchs he serves. Even a quick glance at the Neo-Assyrian visual corpus gives ample examples of clean-faced men as the king's closest assistants. Although from the roll-out, two-dimensional perspective of reliefs they appear to flank the king in single file,[32] a man participating in the real-life state functions that the artwork depicts would actually see the king surrounded by anxiously attentive beardless males. What messages would a male spectator absorb about masculinities in such instances?

Figure 2.13 Assurnasirpal II (883–859).
The British Museum, London.

Beards and no beards

By the late Neo-Assyrian period, the world of court officials seems to have been conceptualized in two categories: bearded men (*ša zigni*) and eunuchs (*ša rēši*),[33] a divide we have seen earlier that was made in antiquity between active and passive, desirer and desired. Such obvious and opposing signs issuing forth from the face make unavoidable announcements about male gendering. Beards and barefacedness went to the core of a man's identity in Assyria. Shaving, could, for instance, mark a man as a slave. Shaving or cutting off the hair and/or beard also denoted criminal status for men who could not prove sexual slanders of either adultery with the wife of an *awīlu* or of an *awīlu* having passive sex with other men. Were these allegations proved true, the punishment for the offender was often castration. When the slanderer cannot prove these sexual offenses, the punishment is turned back on him in that he suffers a lesser type of emasculation, the loss of his hair. Nevertheless, the penalty shows an inverse association between sexual misconduct, in particular male passive sex, and beardlessness.[34]

Beard styles in art could literally identify a man's ethnicity or social status. Assyrians, of course, generally flaunted longer, fuller beards than their closer-cropped enemies. The royal beard was luxurious and elaborate, sprouting so profusely it nearly envelops the cheeks, and falling to the level of the mid-chest where it is dramatically squared off. The effect is one of generative virility under rigid control. Individual styles of royal beards were crucial. Anyone who studied under Edith Porada, at one time or another, had to count the number of curls in each row and the number of rows of alternating curls and waves in the beard of a given king in order to distinguish which ruler was being represented. In royal imagery beards conveyed power, maturity and that aggressive sexuality that comes with an excess of hair-proliferating testosterone, while fastidious grooming of the beard and the exacting way in which it was curled might have conveyed discipline in addition to identity, high status and luxury. Even if beardless males in reliefs were pubescent boys, as Leo Oppenheim (1973) postulates, a hierarchical dynamic is still at work setting mature and bearded men over youths, the prime targets of pederastic lust. Whether on boy or eunuch (perhaps eunuch slave?), beardlessness exteriorized a gender difference among men that was anchored in biology: on the one hand, a transitory biologic difference, on the other, an artificially imposed but permanent biological difference. The considerable amount of meticulous work in the last decade allows us to assume with a fair degree of certainty, however, that *ša rēši* does indeed mean eunuch and unbearded men on Assyrian reliefs and seals do in fact depict *šūt rēši*. (Watanabe 1999).[35] The device of bearded versus nonbearded impresses on the body the social articulation of opposing sexual categories. Yet what is passed off as difference rooted in biology is just an ideological tool, for it is no more true that all unemasculated Assyrians have the luxurious beards we see in images than that all eunuchs are naturally beardless. In fact, there seem to be instances of Mesopotamian queens portrayed with beards in official art; the beard signified their (male) right to rule, as did the beard of Egypt's Queen Hatshepsut (McCaffrey 2002: 389–391). However, a eunuch who became king (see Watanabe 1999: 320) could not be portrayed bearded or his identity as a eunuch would have been lost. It may be that court eunuchs were forced to appear shaven.

The beardless figure seems to have made his Assyrian art debut in the White Obelisk, (Figure 2.8), although texts document eunuchs in Assyria as early as the reign of Tukulti-Ninurta I.[36] Contrary to later art, the iconography of hierarchically gendered masculinities is unstable in the White Obelisk, once again hinting at the transitional nature of this monument. Bearded attendants and courtiers predominate over unbearded ones, even in domestic scenes (Reade 1975: 145), whereas sculpture of the ninth century onward features beardless men as the king's attendants in domestic scenes. These images are our best source for the roles eunuchs played in Assyria and in particular in the life of the king. In the earlier obelisk, bearded men are also seen performing tasks that are given only to nonbearded men in later state images, such as holding the fly whisk for the king (on side d, not shown) or introducing tributaries to the kings (compare Figure 2.8 side b, fourth register from the bottom, with Figures. 2.2, 2.7 and 2.11).

The eunuch as the king's devoted caretaker

In art from the reign of Assurnasirpal II until the fall of Assyria, unarmed eunuchs appear in abundance, assisting the king. Most of the home-front scenes feature palace activity, such as processions, rituals and hunts. The eunuch's most commonly portrayed tasks – the above-mentioned fly whisking (Figures 2.13 and 2.14), holding sunshades over the king (Figure 2.10) and fans to keep him cool, as well as carrying what seem to be towels for him – describe eunuchs as the primary caretakers of the king's body. They were also used as his personal bodyguards. Nonmilitary eunuchs, then, are in intimate proximity to the king, protecting him from physical dangers and discomforts as well as from the pollutions of everyday life. They also serve him food and drink and carry his state furniture, his animal trophies and, of course, his bow.

There may be more than one reason that safeguarding the royal body – and the intimacy it entailed – evolved as a privilege assigned to pictorially nonvirile males. One might be the growing availability of eunuchs. Another is that some of these ordinary caretaking tasks might have come to be seen as too much like tasks performed by women and therefore too lowly for "real men." The famous garden scene of Assurbanipal and his wife celebrating

Figure 2.14 Camp Scene of Tiglath-Pileser III (745-727 BCE).

Drawn by Austen Henry Layard. From C. J. Gadd, *The Stones of Assyria: The Surviving Remains of Assyrian Sculpture* (London 1936), page 53. In the public domain.

the defeat of the Elamite king, whose head dangles nonchalantly in a nearby tree (Figure 2.14), throws light on the gendering of tasks in the palace. As this is an open-air banquet, there are a number of people working away at the flies. Behind the queen at the left are two women whisking flies away from her head. They are followed by two more women, one who is holding a tray of food, and a eunuch who holds a tray of food and a fly whisk. Behind them are women and eunuch musicians. The king is attended by two men, both waving fly whisks at his head. One is a eunuch and the other is a bearded Elamite. This scene's compositional equation of women with fly whisks on the left to eunuchs and a member of the just-defeated enemies with fly whisks on the right assimilates eunuchs and defeated male ethnicities to women. If J. V. Kinnier Wilson's suggestion that some eunuchs who served at royal banquets be likened to the exceptionally beautiful boy-eunuchs or *ghulams*, who presided at royal banquets of later Islam, deserves merit, and I think it does, the gender equation is all the stronger.[37] Delicate, castrated boy beauties in the service of the king arouses images of extreme helplessness, sexual vulnerability and subjugation in the face of raw masculine power.

In a more general vein, the dyadic relationship of king and eunuch may have been privileged in state art simply because eunuchs were regarded as being incapable of sexual penetration. In the world of the Assyrian military state, the discourse of homoerotic hierarchy could not permit the slightest suggestion of a king in intimate contact with men who also belonged to the active/penetrator upper end of the hierarchy. Any implication that the king indulged in sex with unemasculated attendants in which he conceivably took the receptive role or, more likely, in which he sodomized other virile Assyrians, was scrupulously avoided. From what we know from early Islamic literature, it was acceptable, even expected, that a ruler or any elite man, has sex with his eunuchs (Ayalon 1999: 34). Although we know virtually nothing concrete about the sexual tastes and habits of Assyrian kings, the groups of eunuchs hovering around the king and doting on him in domestic scenes are so evocative of a "harem" of women that male viewers may have inferred a sexual relationship between a monarch and his eunuch attendants. It might be said with some certainty that a king could "take" a eunuch if he wanted to without compromising his reputation for superlative manhood.[38]

From textual rather than visual sources, more structural affinities between eunuchs and women emerge. Eunuchs were known for their loyalty, trustworthiness and devotion to the king (Ayalon 1999; Grayson 1995: 95–96, 1999: 260; Hawkins 2002: 221), in much the same way as wives were expected to be toward their husbands, and, for that matter, slaves toward their masters. Cuneiform records sometimes describe these characteristics directly, as in land grants from Assurbanipal to eunuchs "whose affection to his lord is undivided," or to whom "the palace is his only home," or who "kept watch over my kingship" (Deller 1999: 307). They are clearly reflected in the types of positions eunuchs held, from provincial governors, military commanders and treasurers of the king's tribute (touched on below), to bodyguards for the king, the crown prince and the women of the palace, to name some (Deller 1999; Grayson 1995; Kinnier Wilson 1972). They also served as the king's private secret service (Kinnier Wilson 1972: 47–48). As there are extremely few instances in Assyria of eunuchs marrying and, even more rarely, adopting children, nearly all were without family attachments of their own, leaving their loyalty to the king undivided. Like wives and, again, slaves, eunuchs lacked an independent patrimony and became dependents of the patriarch in whose household they lived. In fact, when cuneiform texts refer to a given eunuch, they do not record the names of his father or grandfather (Grayson 1995: 96). Eunuchs were given new names, such as "god NN, protect the king," which reflects that "safeguarding the king was central to their identities," as Karheinz Deller notes (1999: 306).

The eradication of the eunuch's lineage, his origins, his antecedents as well as his descendants, suggests to me that the king's eunuchs were not Assyrian.[39] Furthermore, given the associations of shaving with state punishment and slavery, of castration with curses, the criminal class and social condemnation, it is not likely that Assyrians turned other Assyrians into eunuchs unless it were to redress a criminal offense. In Achaemenid Iran and Medieval Iraq, the virile masculinity of indigenous males was not to be defaced. Castrated subjects would have disturbed the picture such vigorously male-identified, warrior cultures wished to present of a native, matchless dominance. And quite simply, Assyrians had no need to conscript candidates among their own. Massive deportations, up to 100,000 people at one time, would have supplied a surfeit of foreign boys suitable for castration, as it did for Achaemenid rulers. Some eunuchs may well have come as children from the families of rebellious rulers, in which case sterilization would avert the reemergence of enemy dynasties. Another source for the supply of eunuchs might have been slave traders from outlying countries, as it was in Medieval Iraq (Ayalon 1999). Because castration resulted in a high rate of death, slave eunuchs were extraordinarily expensive;[40] ownership of eunuchs then, as with any luxury item, showcased the wealth of their masters. New identities for castrated boys in general and their Assyrian enculturation would erase lingering sympathies for their homelands or ethnicities. Physical and psychological isolation would intensify dependency on the royal house.

Whether a captive or slave from foreign territories, or a son from an Assyrian family as A. Kirk Grayson suggests (1995: 95), to the masses the eunuch was a display object in public processions and palace ceremonies, a strange and uncommon spectacle, rare because of his peculiar status to king and palace but also because castration frequently resulted in death. He was no doubt accustomed to a good deal of gawking and sexual leers from other men. In art or life, he symbolized the king's power to command devotion so extreme that it required the sacrifice of his rightful social and physical identity as a man. When eunuchs publicly present captive rulers or foreign tributaries to the king, it is a warning to all of the ruler's capacity to utterly crush manhood. The message of domesticated masculinity that eunuchism embodied would have been all the more frightening to captives and tributaries if the eunuch who presented them was himself originally from conquered lands. The eunuch in state art stood as an emblem of the king's hegemonic dominion over men and their sexuality.

As guardians, house stewards and chamberlains of the "inner quarters" (Kinnier Wilson 1972: 46, 83–84), eunuchs also stood for the king's women, his sons and the wealth of their combined possessions. The richer and the more virile the ruler, the greater the number of women and sons in his household, the more tangible wealth owned by each, and the higher number of eunuchs for the care and safekeeping of people and things. The eunuch constituted one side of a triangular relationship, women another and the king the third; relationships between the king and his women and young sons were routed through the eunuch until princes passed the age of sexual ambiguity. The frequency with which a eunuch appears next to the fully grown crown prince in the palace settings of the ninth and eighth centuries (Reade 1972: 95) speaks for an enduring allegiance between the two. It may have been that, as in later Iraqi courts (Ayalon 1999: 39), eunuchs were the primary caretakers and teachers of boys brought up in the royal household, which could include, besides the king's sons and nephews, the sons of military commanders, of rulers from conquered territories and captives. As already mentioned, they served as decoys against rape of high-ranking boys and young Mamluks. Prepubescent boys set aside for castration and young eunuchs must also have been raised in Assyrian palaces in order to develop loyalty to the royal house; learn palace etiquette, which would be important for state functions; and become thoroughly Assyrianized. If later literature is anything to go by, castrated palace youths were regarded as the sexual property of the ruler, available to other men with his permission.

There is surprisingly little direct evidence from Assyrian sources for palace eunuchs preventing uncastrated men from sex with the king's women[41] and, I would argue by extension, children. Oddly enough, there are hints in the records of regulations meant to thwart *eunuchs* from having sex with palace women. Documentation on palace eunuchs comes primarily from the Nimrud Wine Lists and the earlier Middle Assyrian Palace Edicts. Both the Wine Lists and the Edicts divide "eunuchs of the king" into at least two types. In the Edicts they are the "royal eunuchs" and the "court attendants" (MAPD §§8, 9, 20 and 22), a division that seems to correspond to "outer court" and "inner court" eunuchs (Grayson 1995: 94; Kinnier Wilson 1972: 46–48). It would be the eunuchs of the inner quarters we are concerned with at the moment. Although royal eunuchs of the Middle Assyrian Edicts, who appear to have been under direct command of the king, could only enter the inner quarters, where palace women, their daughters and young sons lived, under highly regulated conditions (MAPD §§9 and 20; Roth 1995:

201 and 205–206), there seems to be no prohibition against eunuch court attendants entering those same quarters. However, from two problematic clauses we learn that the genitalia of both types were regularly inspected (MAPD §§8 and 20; Roth 1995: 200–201 and 205–206). If a eunuch was found to be "not *murruru*," a word that literally means "checked" but has been translated as "castrated" in this context, he was to be handed over "to be made into a court attendant *for a second time*" (my emphasis).[42] Modern scholars have understood this to mean he will be handed over for castration, but in view of the enigmatic phrasing, it may signify something more complex. Considering the extraordinarily harsh treatment of palace personnel described in the Edicts, it is not likely that a man who tries to pass himself off as a eunuch but is not in fact a eunuch is simply castrated and sent back to work. Duplicity of this magnitude would have called for severe punishment, if not death. As the Edicts state, it is the officials, including the physician of the "Inner Quarters," instead who pay the penalty (the loss of a foot) for letting such a man enter. The clauses suggest rather that what was inspected was not whether a man was or was not a eunuch but the degree to which he was emasculated. Later literature attests that certain methods of castration, such as crushing the testicles, allowed eunuchs to perform even prolonged penetrating sex (Ayalon 1999: 325) despite their sterility; these so-called partial eunuchs were able to exhaust women and were purported to reach heights of sexual ecstasy never experienced by unemasculated men.[43] Quite obviously, the caliphs of Iraq sought eunuchs for their harems who were castrated too early, that is, before puberty, or too fully to experience lust for women, girls or boys. In the merciless social environment of the Middle Assyrian palace in which the merest unauthorized and unsupervised proximity of a man to a woman warranted death (MAPD §§19: Roth 1995: 204–205), it is not likely that eunuchs whose genitals were still intact enough to sexually penetrate orifices of whatever type would have been admitted into the inner quarters. And it would be those officials, especially the physician, who had the experience to evaluate the degree of a eunuch's impotency. I would suggest then that the phrase "to be made into a (castrated) court attendant for a second time" means that the eunuch is to undergo a second and more extensive mutilation, a process that could well kill him.

Eunuchs in military contexts

There is also a fair amount of textual evidence for military eunuchs. These are not the same as those we see in state art whisking flies away from the royal head. Some military eunuchs could be described as clerks, such as scribes sometimes seen writing on the wax tablets used for writing in Aramaic, and accountants for recording the streams of booty, including animal and human deportees, that flowed into Assur from conquered territories. Eunuchs who present booty, tributaries and prisoners to the king could also be considered part of the clerical military. In a camp scene from one of Assurnasirpal II's campaigns, eunuchs are portrayed in various stages of food preparation. Other military eunuchs performed as the king's private secret service.

Then there were the fighting eunuchs, some of whom rose to great martial and administrative prominence, from provincial governors to military commanders and generals. Fighting eunuchs as lower-level army officers and soldiers are better attested in art, although many images show them waging war in the ankle-length tunics of the court (Reade 1972: 94). Ironically, most military eunuchs seemed to have formed the all-important corps of archers, even depicted in ninth- and eighth-century battle scenes in the full-chested masculine stance of the archer with drawn bow. It is as though the bow and arrow were given in redress for his sacrificed manhood. There is no question that the physically emasculated could be fighters of the greatest aptitude. Not only would the army be a venue for social and political advancement, especially for the proposed non-Assyrian eunuch, it would also be a proving ground for a compensatory manly virility that could rise even to the status of the hypermasculine claimed by the military elite. The eunuch's love of archery, attested throughout the pre-modern Islamic periods, extended beyond the battle arts. At the end of the eighth century in Sargon II's palace at Khorsabad, eunuchs with drawn bows are shown in scenes independent of political or ceremonial content as hunters, a privileged class of masculinity to be sure.

It seems logical that allowing eunuchs in the military, especially as archers, was a way of restoring some measure of male potency. Yet that manliness was not an inherent right but rather fragile, for just as a king could give it, he could take it away. Five years before Sennacherib's reign in 705, a high-ranking officer, who was a eunuch, together with 20 other eunuchs began a conspiracy in the northern land of Urartu. They were arrested and put to death.[44] When Sennacherib came to power he seems to have eliminated the military eunuch. Breaking precedence with Assyrian kings before and after him, his monumental reliefs are singular for their absence of representation of beardless soldiers. He went so far as to eliminate eunuchs from scenes involving hunting, as though to ensure no eunuch had access to weapons. Instead, his assistants are all bearded (Reade 1972: 100–101). I would suggest that evicting eunuchs from the military was the direct outcome of the Urartian conspiracy. Sennacherib's elimination of military eunuchism suggests that the class of eunuchs, the *šūt rešūtti*, had by then formed a power block strong enough to threaten the state. More importantly, it suggests that eunuchs confederated with other eunuchs across political boundaries. If this is so, then we are looking at a sector of society that clearly recognized itself as a disparate third-gender identity.

The warrior eunuch, a phenomenon that continued long after the fall of Assyria in Near Eastern lands, seemed to have been two-sided. Those eunuchs who taught Mamluks the art of warfare and who were themselves renowned military commanders were described as "warlike by day in campaign" but "womanly and docile in bed at night"(Ayalon 1999: 34). Given the eunuch's dualistic attributes of warrior bedmate from Islamic periods, it is left to the imagination what sexual roles eunuchs actually played in Assyrian campaigns. A camp scene from Tiglath-Pileser III, even though it is a daytime scene, tantalizingly suggests that the monarch at least knew and took full advantage of the eunuch's nighttime attributes. The penetration motif here is outrageously evident and takes center stage. Tiglath-Pileser sits before his field tent, elevated on a portable throne. Before him, a man of apparently high rank stands making the formal gestures of homage and submission. The king effortlessly holds a long pike at the top end with one hand. The pike forms a diagonal line between him and the submitted other that quickly directs the viewer's eye away from the royal body. Skewered on the lower end of the pike at the level of the king's feet is the head of the enemy staring at the ground.

So much for the political side of the scene. Behind the eunuch at the right of the panel is the royal tent. Through the opening at the top appear the heads of two eunuchs seemingly in conversation. What are they doing in the king's tent? For that matter, why are they portrayed at all in this scene? Does their presence work as a label for viewers that what they are looking at are indeed the king's living quarters? It would be naïve to assume that such eunuchs merely served as bodyguards or as keepers of the royal toilet. After all, who or what would dare impose on a monarch sexual abstinence at any time, with the possible exception of ritual law? It is far more likely that certain eunuchs on campaigns were the king's transportable bedmates, useful by day in the field and at night in the tent. If we back up and try to look at these panels from the standpoint of a viewer in Tiglath-Pileser's palace, the entire story of hierarchical masculinities is laid out. The left-hand block describes the military significance of penetrator versus penetrated in very bold terms, using nearly all the aforementioned devices that promote the royal body as the primary phallic weapon. The right-hand block sends a more subtle message of the same theme by situating two men who are custom-made for penetration in the king's private quarters. Setting public and private side by side manipulates viewers to yoke the skewered head with sexual castration and conquest. Furthermore, the puzzling hands-up gestures of the tent eunuchs parallel the formal gesture of submission made to the king.

Conclusion

When Assyria's imperial growth caused a breakdown in the old *awīlu*-centric social order, new hierarchies formed and they formed most prominently along gender lines, as they have done in all historical periods of massive social upheaval. The use of the supermasculinized king in a dyadic relationship with the newly injected masculinity of the eunuch, a figure who connoted captivity, foreignness, submission and emasculation, in other words, the ultimate other, set the grammar of active subject and passive object for Assyria's discourse on men. This insertion alone speaks for a high degree of male social confusion and most probably a homophobic fear, for which the eunuch became a convenient target. Nevertheless, the beardless male immortalized in palace reliefs was an icon of a man custom-made for sodomy. For those privileged enough to see these monuments, he was a chilling reminder of the king's power over men, their sexuality and the degree of their manliness. Assyrian narrative images, whether ceremonial or historical, were seen only in the metropolitan centers (Shafer 2007), where threats to the king were most concentrated. Their primary task would probably have been the manipulation of rivals, the ruling and military elite. For these elite spectators, the visual pleasure state art incited would have made them all the more compliant to the imagery's embedded messages. By looking at pictures that glorified the Assyrian male body and degraded the non-Assyrian body, that ranked and gendered masculinities and that aroused and sublimated homosexual desire, all men of whatever rank participated in the maintenance of hierarchical tension and the paradigm of penetrator and penetrated on which the imperial state was built.

Notes

1 This paper was prepared for publication in 2004.

2 Middle Assyrian kings instituted the practice of deporting non-Assyrian populations from outlying territories into the heartland of Assyria, especially into the capital city of Assur. When Assyria's military power resurrected under Assur-dan II, mass deportation was reinstituted and followed on an enormous scale by his successors. By the end of the eighth century, Assyrians represented only a minority of Assyria's population. See Bustany Oded, *Mass Deportations and Deportees in the Neo Assyrian Empire*, Dr Ludwig Reichert, Verlag, Wiesbaden, 1979; and Mayer (1995, 2004).

3 Mayer (1995).

4 i.e. Deller (1999); Grayson (1995); Hawkins (2002); Tadmor (2002); Watanabe (1999)

5 For discussion on *baštu* as it applies to idealized portrayals of kingship, see Winter (1995, 1996).

6 The term used for making the penis "hard" in potency incantations is *tebû*, "to rise up," often written in Sumerian logograms as ZI or ZI.GA. "Erection" itself, *tebûtu*, derives from the same verb. In medical and omen texts the verb has secondary meanings of "to throb" or "pulsate" (Biggs 1967: 9), while the same verb in the stative can mean "standing" or "standing up," applied to the human body in general (*AHw.*:1342a). Also see CAD E:327, *erūtu*, meaning "erect" or literally "tall of back." Besides examples discussed later, a line in a potency incantation makes this clear: "May your penis become long like a club" (Biggs 1967: 32). The notion of hardness is inherent in the simile.

7 TN I A. 0.78.1 vi 2–22, (Grayson 1987: 238). The inscription survives in 18 examples.

8 See the treaty curse of Assur-nirari V (Parpola and Watanabe 1988: 12 v 9–11). Similar curses against soldiers surface in biblical writings, such as Jeremiah 50.35 and Nahum 3.13. See also Assante (1998: 62).

9 See the discussion on female nudity and postures of submission in Assyrian pornography in Assante (2007).

10 Although these qualities belonged to the male province, they were properties of Ishtar, the goddess of war but not necessarily of sex in the Neo-Assyrian period, whose statue led Assyrian armies into battle.

11 *ul īši šāninamma tebû kakkū* [*šu*]

12 As Jerrold Cooper (see Cooper 2002: 80 and especially 1977) notes, in a dream Gilgamesh foresees the coming of Enkidu who appears as an axe. Gilgamesh loves the axe and embraces it like a wife. Whereas *râmu*, to love, is not always meant as sexual love, *ḫabābu*, to embrace, always denotes sexual intercourse when used in connection to human activity. Interestingly, the Old Babylonian version mentions the phrase only once, whereas the Nineveh version repeats it frequently (I, v, 36, 47; I, vi, 4, 14, 19; cf. VIII, ii, 4–6), indicating the growing tendency to sexualize male hierarchical relationships. Tigay (1982: 85) has "[I loved it, and lik]e a wife I caressed it." Different versions of the *Gilgamesh Epic* seem to display both types of homoerotic bonding. In earlier versions, inequality is stressed. Enkidu is Gilgamesh's servant. In first-millennium texts they are nearly equals, the one made for the other, the Eve to Gilgamesh's Adam. Inequalities are still present: Gilgamesh is the king, for instance, and Enkidu is the victim of revenge, and so forth. Such subtle inequalities were not risked in Assyrian art. See also Hammond and Jablow (1987).

13 Personal communication, Andrew George, the leading translator of the Gilgamesh cycle. The reading of the unpublished lines is still disputed.

14 Both the *Iliad* and the Book of Samuel were later, roughly seventh-century BCE remakes of earlier versions. For discussion on biblical homoerotism, see Nissinen (1998) and Ackerman (2005).

15 Foucault (1976: 43 and 105). For discussion of the historical contexts and changing meaning of these terms see Sedgewick (1990: 44–48 and 67–90); Halperin (1990: 15–18 and 155 n.2).

16 These terms are: the sag-ur-sag, the pilipili, the gala singers, the *assinnu*, the kurgarra/*kurgarrû*, the *kulu'u* and to some extent, the *sinnišānu*. For an in-depth discussion on these terms, see Assante (2009).

17 Contra Bottéro and Petschow (1972/1975). An Ur III seal from Mari is the only image from ancient Mesopotamia that could be construed as homosexual (fig. 949, pl. 40 in A. Parrot, *Les Palais. Documents et Monuments.* Mission archéologique de Mari II/3 Paris, 1959). Despite popular scholarly belief, Mesopotamia avoided explicit descriptions and terminology for deviant sexuality, such as homosexuality and prostitution, and it produced very little erotica of any type outside of the Old Babylonian Period. For discussion see Assante (1998, 2000: 289–299, 2003, 2009).

18 MAL A §19: "If a man furtively spreads rumors about his comrade, saying, 'Everybody sodomizes him' (*ittinikkuš* or in *CAD* under *nâku, it-ti-ni-ku-ka*, lit. everybody fornicates him), or in a quarrel in public says to him, 'Everyone sodomizes you,' and further, 'I can prove the charges against you,' but he is unable to prove the charges and does not prove the charges, they shall strike that man 50 blows with rods; he shall perform the king's service for one full month; they shall cut off his hair, moreover, he shall pay 3,600 shekels of lead." Roth (1995: 159).

19 MAL A §20: "If a man sodomizes his comrade and they prove the charges against him and find him guilty, they shall sodomize him and they shall turn him into a eunuch (*ana ša rešen*)." Roth (1995: 160).

20 There is an enormous body of secondary literature on this topic. See especially Cantarella (1992), Dover (1978), Foucault (1976), Golden (1991), Hallett and Skinner (1997), Halperin (1990), Lilja (1983), Richlin (1993), and Williams (1999), among many.

21 This may be why there is no description for a woman loving another woman in ancient Mesopotamia.

22 Nearly all Akkadian verbs designating sexual action take accusative (= direct) objects. See *CAD* L: 55–56 *lamāda*, to know (someone) sexually; N: 197–198 *niāku/nâku*, to (illicitly) fornicate (someone); R: 87–88 *rakābu*, to copulate (someone), to mount; R: 140 *râmu*, to love (someone), to make love ([to] someone) R: 217 *ratāpu*, to sexually approach (someone); but in Ṣ: 69 *ṣalālu*, to sleep with a woman or, literally, in Gilg I iv 18, to sleep on top of a woman, takes a dative (= indirect) object. Verbs such as *reḫû*, to penetrate, to inseminate, *erēbu*, to enter, to penetrate, and *petû*, to open, obviously call for accusative objects.

23 Amputation of hands and arms was more frequent than decapitation, followed by the gouging out of eyes and cutting off of noses and ears. Interestingly, it was in Egypt rather than Mesopotamia where penises were cut off and thrown in piles (see Assante 2010: 6).

24 *The Symposium*, passages 178e-19a, Christopher Gill, tr., London, Penguin Classics, 1999.

25 Irene Winter has written several articles on the royal body. For Naram-Sin see Winter (1996), see also 1989 for Gudea's bare-shouldered statues and the more general discussion of 1995.

26 As in art, the growing tendency to de-eroticize representations of rulers in texts runs parallel with an increasing militancy of hegemonic monarchies, in which dominion is portrayed as absolute and invulnerable. During the Ur III and Isin-Larsa periods, Shulgi and Iddin-Dagan presented themselves in court poetry as hopeful objects of Inanna's lust. The so-called sacred marriage texts factor in a sexual vulnerability into public royal personas, as it is Inanna who tests their desirability and prowess in bed. This type of court literature is no longer attested after the Isin-Larsa period. By the latter half of the Old Babylonian period, an Akkadian hymn modeled on sacred marriage texts and composed for King Amiditana (ca. 1683–1647) presents the relationship between the king and Ishtar as distant and formal rather than sexual. The figure of the eroticized king is expunged. One might attribute its erasure to a changed conception of kingship begun by Hammurabi in which kings no longer claimed divine status and therefore no longer needed carnal union with Inanna/Ishtar to get it. But the erasure seems to be more the result of a growing militancy in which females and the enemy are set in lowly opposition to the idealized truly masculine. Devaluation of the feminine leaves no room for a female king-maker or a goddess who decides whether or not a king is adequate in bed. The passages in the first-millennium *Gilgamesh Epic* that hideously pervert the ancient notion of sacred marriage demonstrate the later male abhorrence of men's sexual vulnerability (Assante 1998: 55–57). Although images of royal sexual prowess are latent in royal inscriptions and palatial art after the Isin-Larsa period, the direct use of an eroticized royal body in state ideologies seems to have ceased.

27 Cifarelli (1998: 223) notes intentional correlations between royal postures assumed during prayer to the gods and those assumed by non-Assyrians in the presence of the king. Both forms of kneeling are still in use for worship today: the upright form of Christianity and the form of head touching the ground, still for men only in Islam. The two forms speak of complicated, subtle differences in the relationships between the Christian and Islamic worshipper and his or her god.

28 According to Julian Reade, later kings from the seventh century on are seen on campaigns but not portrayed as fighting. Reade astutely interprets the change in royal representation as marking the shift from priest-king to imperial despot (1972: 92–93).

29 "At that time my sovereignty, my dominion, (and) my power came forth at the command of the great gods; I am king, I am lord, I am praiseworthy, I am exalted,

I am important, I am magnificent, I am foremost, I am a hero, I am a warrior; I am a lion, I am virile; Assurnasirpal, strong king, king of Assyria, designate of the god Sin, favorite of the god Anu, loved one of the god Adad (who is) almighty among the gods, I, the merciless weapon which lays low lands hostile to him, I, the king, capable in battle, vanquisher of cities and highlands, (i. 35) foremost in battle, king of the four quarters, the one who defeats his enemies, king of the totality of the (four) quarters including all their princes, the king who forces to bow down those insubmissive to him, the one who rules all peoples; these destinies came forth at the command of the great gods and they properly fixed (them) as my destinies." Grayson (1991: 194, A.O.101.1 i 31b–37a).

30 Many incantations combine images of the taut bow with an aggressive sexual potency, for instance, "Wild ass! Wild ass! Wild bull! Wild bull! Who has made you [fall limp] like slack cords?. . ." (Biggs 1967: 19 No. 3:20–21) and "May the [qu]iver not become e[mpt]y! May [my] bow not become [slack]! Let the battle [of] my love-making be waged! Let us lie down by night!" The ritual that accompanies this text includes instructions for making a bow, as do several other potency incantation rituals. One specifies the making of a bow using a mouse tendon for the string and supplying it with an arrow. These magical tools were put at the head of the man and the woman who are lying down in preparation for, one hopes, satisfying sex. See Biggs (1967: 37–38, 2002: 73–74). The bow and arrow also feature in Hittite potency rituals. In one the impotent man is likened to a woman. The sorceress says: "When he comes [fo]rth through the gate, I shall take the mirror (and) distaff away from him. I shall [gi]ve him a bow (and arrows), and while doing so I shall speak as follows: 'See, I have taken womanliness away from you and given you manliness. Cast off the ways of a woman, now (show) the ways of a man!' " Interestingly, a eunuch also participates in the ritual as a foil for the now potent man (*Ancient Near Eastern Texts*, James B. Pritchard, ed., Princeton University Press, 1969 [third edition]: 349).

31 Ishtar is implored to take the bows and arrows away from the enemy and put in their hands instead the mirror and spindle of women, and then dress them like women (*KBo* II 19 I 25–30, quoted in Paul 2002: 493). Similarly, in Hittite oaths, if a soldier breaks his oath, he and his troops will be changed into women and dressed as women. Their bows and arrows will be replaced by the distaff and mirror (*Ancient Near Eastern Texts*, James B. Pritchard, ed., Princeton University Press 1969 [third edition]:354). These texts together with their exact reversals in the potency incantation quoted in the previous note graphically demonstrate the equation between the bow with virile masculinity and penile erectness.

32 The ancient format of the cylinder-seal roll-out, still in use in Assyrian reliefs, was the mode of representation employed in Mesopotamia to officialize imagery. Acanonical, non-roll-out formats, rare as they are, was a visual method of deploying a subversive, anti-official intention. See Assante (2002).

33 See S. Parpola and Kazuko Watanabe (1988: 32, 6. l. 78).

34 The verb for this punishment is *gadāmu*. Another is *gullubu*, meaning to shave all or part of the hair as a punishment or as a slave, as noted in Cifarelli (1998: 227 n. 54).

35 See the review of the scholarship for or against eunuchism in Mesopotamia in Tadmor (2002: 604–607).

36 Deller (1999: 303). Interestingly, overt sexualization of the enemy seems to have begun with Tukulti-Ninurta I, as reflected in his royal inscriptions and his pornographic furniture inlays. Since the first inkling of institutionalized eunuchism also appears during his reign, one wonders if eunuchism was directly connected to sexual objectification of the enemy.

37 Kinnier Wilson (1972: 83). The author quotes an eyewitness account from Minorsky's *Voyages du Chevalier Chardin* V, Paris, 1811: 470.

38 Hawkins relates an instance of a Hittite prince who made a "friend" of a eunuch (2002: 223). Apparently Hittite eunuchs were allowed to form close relationships with men as long as the king approved.
39 For the origins of the institution of eunuchism as possibly non-Assyrian, see Deller (1999: 309–311).
40 The death rate for total castration could be as high as 80 percent until the 19th century CE (Ayalon 1999: 313). The cost of a eunuch was anywhere from four times to twice that of an uncastrated slave; one ruler bought a eunuch in exchange for 50 slaves. A totally castrated male could cost six times more than a partially castrated one (*ibid*: 300).
41 For sexual relations between eunuchs and men of the ruling class in Hittite texts see Hawkins (2002: 224).
42 For *murruru* as meaning "to check," "to check severely," "to check whether a person is castrated" see Grayson (1995: 92) and for earlier bibliography n. 35; also Deller (1999: 305) and Hawkins (2002: 219–220).
43 Although there is no evidence for R. D. Biggs (1969) conjecture that crushing the testicles was the method used to make eunuchs in Assyria (*History of Science* 8, 1969: 100), later scholars have assumed the same, i.e. Grayson (1995: 92 and 95); Deller (1999: 305). Crushed testicles constitute the most benign form of eunuchism and would allow some degree of sexual performance. See Ayalon (1999: 304–309) for castration procedures from complete removal of genitalia to removal of the testicles and their various results.
44 See Lanfranchi and Parpola (1990: 74); "Letter from Kumme. K 194."

Bibliography

Ackerman, Susan 2005 *When Heroes Love: The Ambiguity of Eros in the Stories of Gilgamesh and David*, Columbia University Press, New York.

Assante, Julia 1998 "The kar.kid/ *ḫarimtu*, Prostitute or Single Woman? A Reconsideration of the Evidence," *Ugarit-Forschungen* 30, 5–96.

———. 2000 *The Erotic Reliefs of Ancient Mesopotamia*, PhD dissertation, Columbia University, New York.

———. 2002 "Style and Replication in 'Old Babylonian' Terracotta Plaques: Strategies for Entrapping the Power of Images," *Ex Mesopotamia et Syria Lux; Festschrift für Manfried Dietrich zu seinem 65. Geburtstag*, Oswald Loretz, Kai Metzler and Hanspeter Schaudig, eds., Alter Orient und Altes Testament 281, Ugarit, Münster: 1–29.

———. 2003 "From Whores to Hierodules: The Historiographic Invention of Mesopotamian Female Sex Professionals," *Ancient Art and Its Historiography*, Alice A. Donohue and Mark. D. Fullerton, eds., Cambridge University Press, Cambridge: 13–47.

———. 2007 "The Lead Inlays of Tukulti-Ninurta I; Pornography as Imperial Strategy," *Ancient Near Eastern Art in Context: Studies in Honor of Irene J. Winter*, Jack Cheng and Marian Feldman, eds., Brill, Leiden: 369–407.

———. 2009 "Bad Girls and Kinky Boys? The Modern Prostituting of Ishtar, Her Clergy and Her Cults," *Tempelprostitution im Altertum: Facten und Fiktionen*, Tanja Scheer and Martin Lindner, eds., Verlag Antike, Berlin: 23–54.

———. 2010 "Inside and Out: Extra-Dimensional Aspects of the Mesopotamian Body, with Egyptian Parallels," *Religion und Menschenbild*, Manfried Dietrich, Wilhelm Dupre, Ansgar Häußling, Annemarie Mertens, and Rüdiger Schmittt, eds., Mitteillungen fur Anthropologie und Religionsgeschichte 20, Ugarit, Münster: 3–18.

Ayalon, David 1999 *Eunuchs, Caliphs and Sultans: A Study of Power Relationships*, The Hebrew University Magnes Press, Jerusalem.

Biggs, R. D. 1967 ŠÀ.ZI.GA. *Ancient Mesopotamian Potency Incantations*, Texts from Cuneiform Sources 2, Augustin, Locust Valley, NY.

———. 2002 "The Babylonian Sexual Potency Texts," *Sex and Gender in the Ancient Near East*, Simo Parpola and Robert M. Whiting, eds., Proceedings of the 47th Rencontre assyriologique internationale, Helsinki: 71–78.

Bottéro, J. and Petschow, H. 1972/1975 "Homosexualität," *Reallexicon der Assyriologie* IV, 459–468.

Cantarella, Eva 1992 *Bisexuality in the Ancient World*, Cormac Ó. Cuilleanáin, trans., Yale University Press, New Haven and London.

Cifarelli, Megan 1995 *Enmity, Alienation and Assimilation: The Role of Cultural Difference in the Visual and Verbal Expression of Assyrian Ideology in the Reign of Ashurnasirpal II (883–859, B.C.)*. PhD dissertation, Columbia University.

———. 1998 "Gesture and Alterity in the Art of Ashurnasirpal II of Assyria," *Art Bulletin* 80, 210–228.

Cooper, Jerrold 1977 "Gilgamesh Dreams of Enkidu," *Essays on the Ancient Near Eastern Studies in Memory of Jacob Joel Finkelstein*, Maria de Jong Ellis, ed., Memoirs of the Connecticut Academy of Arts and Sciences 19; Archon Books, Hamden, CT: 39–44.

———. 2002 "Buddies in Babylonia: Gilgamesh, Enkidu, and Mesopotamian Homosexuality," *Riches Hidden in Secret Places: Ancient Near Eastern Studies in Memory of Thorkild Jacobsen*, Tzvi Abusch, ed., Eisenbrauns, Winona Lake, IN: 73–85.

Deller, Karheinz 1999 "The Assyrian Eunuchs and Their Predecessors," *Priest and Officials in the Ancient Near East*, Kazuko Watanabe, ed., Universitätsverlag Winter, Heidelberg: 303–312.

DeVoto, James 1992 "The Theban Sacred Band," *The Ancient World* 23.2, 3–19.

Dover, Kenneth J. 1978 *Greek Homosexuality*, Harvard University Press, Cambridge and London.

Dynes, Wayne R., and Donaldson, Stephen 1992 *Homosexuality in the Ancient World*, W. R. Dynes and S. Donaldson, eds., Routledge, London and New York.

Fantham, Elaine 1991 "*Stuprum*: Public Attitudes and Penalties for Sexual Offenses in Republican Rome," *Échos du monde classique* 35, 267–291.

Foucault, Michel 1976 *The History of Sexuality, Volume I: An Introduction*, Robert Hurley, tr., Pantheon Books, New York.

———. 1985 *The Use of Pleasure: The History of Sexuality, Volume II*, Robert Hurley, tr., Pantheon Books, New York.

Golden, Mark 1991 "Thirteen Years of Homosexuality and Other Recent Works on Sex, Gender and the Body in Ancient Greece," *Échos du monde classique* 35, 327–340.

Grayson, A. Kirk 1987 "Assyrian Rulers of the Third and Second Millennium BC (to 1115 B.C.), RIMA," *Journal of Cuneiform Studies* 41.1, 117–126.

———. 1991 *Assyrian Rulers of the Early First Millennium BC I [1114–859 BC], RIMA* 2, Toronto: University of Toronto Press.

———. 1995 "Eunuchs in Power: Their Role in the Assyrian Bureaucracy," *Vom alten Orient zum alten Testament: Festschrift für Wolfram Freiherrn von Soden zum 85. Geburtstag*, Manfried Dietrich and Oswald Loretz, eds., Alter Orient und Altes Testament 240, Ugarit, Münster: 85–98.

———. 1999 "The Struggle for Power in Assyria: Challenge to Absolute Monarchy in the Ninth and Eighth Centuries B.C.," *Priests and Officials in the Ancient Near East: Papers of the Second Colloquium on the Ancient Near East – The City and Its Life, Held at the Middle Eastern Culture Center in Japan*, Mitaka, Tokyo, March 22–24, 1996, Kazuko Watanabe, ed., Universitätsverlag C. Winter, Heidelberg: 253–270.

Güterbock, Hans Gustav. 1954 "Authority and law in the Hittite kingdom." *Journal of the American Oriental Society*, Supplement 17, 16–24.

Hallett, Judith and Skinner, Marylin 1997 *Roman Sexualities*, Judith P. Hallett and Marilyn B. Skinner, eds., Princeton University Press, Princeton, NJ.

Halperin, David M. 1990 *One Hundred Years of Homosexuality*, Routledge, New York and London.

Halperin, David M., Winkler, John J., and Zeitlin, Froma I. 1990 *Before Sexuality: The Construction of Erotic Experience in the Ancient Greek World*, D. M. Halperin, J. J. Winkler and F. I. Zeitlin, eds., Princeton University Press, Princeton, NJ.

Hammond, Dorothy and Jablow, Alta 1987 "Gilgamesh and the Sundance Kid: The Myth of Male Friendship," *The Making of Masculinities: The New Men's Studies*, Harry Brod, ed., Unwin Hyman, Winchester, MA: 241–258.

Hawkins, J. David 2002 "Eunuchs among the Hittites," *Sex and Gender in the Ancient Near East*, Simo Parpola and Robert M. Whiting, eds., Proceedings of the 47th Rencontre assyriologique internationale, Neo-Assyrian Text Corpus Project, Helsinki: 217–234.

Kinnier Wilson, J. V. 1972 *The Nimrud Wine Lists: A Study of Men and Administration at the Assyrian Capital in the Eighth Century, B.C.*, British School of Archaeology, London.

Lanfranchi, Giovanni B. and Parpola, Simo 1990 *The Correspondence of Sargon II, Part II: Letters from the Northern and Northeastern Provinces*, Vol. V, State Archives of Assyria: Helsinki.

Lilja, Saara 1983 *Homosexuality in Republican and Augustan Rome*, Commentationes Humanarum Litterarum 74: Helsinki.

Marcus, Michelle 1993 "Incorporating the Body: Adornment, Gender, and Social Identity in Ancient Iran," *Cambridge Archaeological Journal* 3.2, 157–178.

Mayer, Walter 1995 *Politik und Kriegskunst der Assyrer*, Abhandlungen zur Literatur Alt-Syrien- Palästinas und Mesopotamiens 9, Ugarit, Münster.

———. 2004 "Gedanken zur Deportation im Alten Orient," *Macht und Herrschaft*, Christian Sigrist, ed., Alter Orient und Altes Testament 316, Ugarit, Münster: 215–233.

McCaffrey, Kathleen 2002 "Reconsidering Gender Ambiguity in Mesopotamia: Is a Beard Just a Beard?" *Sex and Gender in the Ancient Near East*, Simo Parpola and Robert M. Whiting, eds., Proceedings of the 47th Rencontre assyriologique internationale, Neo-Assyrian Text Corpus Project, Helsinki: 379–391.

Nissinen, Martti 1998 *Homoeroticism in the Biblical World*, Fortress Press, Minneapolis.

Oppenheim, Leo 1973 "A Note on *ša rēši*," *Journal of the Ancient Near Eastern Society* 5, 325–334.

Ornan, Tallay 2007 "The Godlike Semblance of a King: The Case of Sennacherib's Rock Reliefs," *Ancient Near Eastern Art in Context: Studies in Honor of Irene J. Winter*, Jack Cheng and Marian Feldman, eds., Brill, Leiden: 161–175.

Parpola, Simo 1980 "The Murderer of Sennacherib," *Death in Mesopotamia*, Bendt Alster, ed., Proceedings of the 26th Rencontre assyriologique internationale, Mesopotamia 8, Akademisk Forlag, Copenhagen: 171–182.

Parpola, Simo and Watanabe, Kazuko 1988 *Neo-Assyrian Treaties and Loyalty Oaths*. State Archives of Assyria 2, Eisebrauns, Warsaw, IN.

Paul, Shalom M. 2002 "The Shared Legacy of Sexual Metaphors and Euphemisms in Mesopotamian and Biblical Literature," *Sex and Gender in the Ancient Near East*, Simo Parpola and Robert M. Whiting, eds., Proceedings of the 47th Rencontre assyriologique internationale, Neo-Assyrian Text Corpus Project, Helsinki: 489–498.

Reade, Julian 1972 "The Neo-Assyrian Court and Army: Evidence from the Sculptures," *Iraq* 34.II, 87–112.

———. 1975 "Aššurnasirpal I and the White Obelisk," *Iraq* 37, 129–150.

Reed, Stephanie 2007 "Blurring the Edges: A Reconsideration of the Treatment of Enemies in Ashurbanipal's Reliefs," *Ancient Near Eastern Art in Context: Studies in Honor of Irene J. Winter*, Jack Cheng and Marian Feldman, eds., Brill, Leiden: 101–130.

Richlin, Amy 1993 "Not Before Homosexuality: The Materiality of the *Cinaedus* and the Roman Law Against Love Between Men," *Journal of the History of Sexuality* 3.4, 523–573.

Roth, Martha 1995 *Law Collections from Mesopotamia and Asia Minor*, Writings from the Ancient World, Society of Biblical Literature 6, Scholars Press, Atlanta.

Sedgewick, Eve Kosofsky 1990 *Epistemology of the Closet*, University of California Press, Berkeley and Los Angeles.

Shafter, Ann 2007 "Assyrian Royal Monuments on the Periphery: Ritual and the Making of Imperial Space," *Ancient Near Eastern Art in Context: Studies in Honor of Irene J. Winter*, Jack Cheng and Marian Feldman, eds., Brill, Leiden: 133–160.

Tadmor, Hayim 2002 "The Role of the Chief Eunuch and the Place of Eunuchs in the Assyrian Empire," *Sex and Gender in the Ancient Near East*, Simo Parpola and Robert M. Whiting, eds., Proceedings of the 47th Rencontre assyriologique internationale, Neo-Assyrian Text Corpus Project, Helsinki: 603–612.

Tigay, Jeffrey 1982 *The Evolution of the Gilgamesh Epic*, Bolchazy-Carducci Publishers, Philadelphia.

Walters, Jonathan 1997 "Invading the Roman Body: Manliness and Impenetrability in Roman Thought," *Roman Sexualities*, Judith Hallett and Marilyn B. Skinner, eds., Princeton University Press, Princeton, NJ: 29–43.

Watanabe, Kazuko 1999 "Seals of Neo-Assyrian Officials," *Priest and Officials in the Ancient Near East*, Kazuko Watanabe, ed., Universitätsverlag Winter, Heidelberg: 313–366.

Westenholz, Joan 2000 "The King, the Emperor, and the Empire: Continuity and Discontinuity of Royal Representation in Text and Image," *The Heirs of Assyria (melammu symposia I)*, Sanna Aro and Robert M. Whiting, eds., Neo-Assyrian Text Corpus Project: Helsinki: 99–125.

Williams, Craig 1999 *Roman Homosexuality: Ideologies of Masculinity in Classical Antiquity*, Oxford University Press, Oxford and New York.

Winter, Irene 1989 "The Body of the Able Ruler: Toward an Understanding of the Statues of Gudea," *Dumu-E$_2$-dub-ba-a: Studies in Honor of Åke Sjöberg*, Hermann Behrens, Darlene Loding and Martha Roth, eds., Occasional Publications of the Samuel Noah Kramer Fund 11: Philadelphia: 573–583.

———. 1995 "Aesthetics in Ancient Mesopotamian Art," *Civilizations of the Ancient Near East*, Jack Sasson, John Baines, Gary Beckman and Karen S. Rubinson eds., Oxford: 2569–2580.

———. 1996 "Sex, Rhetoric, and the Public Monument: The Alluring Body of Naram-Sîn of Agade," *Sexuality in Ancient Art*, Natalie B. Kampen, ed., Cambridge University Press, Cambridge: 11–26.

———. 1997 "Art *in* Empire: The Royal Image and the Visual Dimensions of Assyrian Ideology," *Assyria 1995: Proceedings of the 10th Symposium of the Neo-Assyrian Text Corpus Project Helsinki*, September 7–11, 1995. Simo Parpola and Robert M. Whiting, eds., Neo-Assyrian Text Corpus Project, Helsinki: 359–381.

3 Wisdom of former days

The manly Hittite king and foolish Kumarbi, father of the gods

Mary R. Bachvarova

Introduction

I explore here some aspects of how masculinity was constructed in Late Bronze Age Anatolia, focusing specifically on the masculine identity of the Hittite king and using the insights provided by two sets of texts coming from the Hittite capital of Hattuša, Old and Middle Hittite ritual and admonitory texts, and Hurro-Hittite narrative song. In so doing, I take advantage of the fact that the materials available to us are focused almost exclusively on the top stratum of human society. All of the texts found at Hattuša were written down and preserved in order to maintain and exalt the hegemony of the Hittite king, either directly or indirectly;[1] for example, while the rituals do give us a lucky glimpse into the activities of a class of illiterate performers – although mediated by the redactive activities of scribes – and they can be presumed to draw on "folk beliefs," they were written down because they were used to maintain the health and well-being of the royal family and other privileged people. In addition, much of the most interesting material available to us actually speaks of the doings of gods. But, my assumption – a safe one I hope – is that the gods' behavior and concerns are based more or less on the human world, although their powers are much greater. I will therefore read the Hurro-Hittite mythical material as addressing the Hittite king and his concerns.[2] I will concentrate specifically on a set of normative views that help us to understand the transgression of masculine ideals in the Hurro-Hittite Kumarbi cycle, the story of how the Storm-god ascended to kingship in heaven and consolidated his power against a series of adversaries; whereas the Storm-god provided an example for the king, the actions of his rivals provided a series of negative examples.

I begin by outlining the role of the king as foremost male among the Hittites, and I show how he used the Storm-god as a role model. Then, with this background in place, I move on to a discussion of the Kumarbi cycle, explaining how it relates to the values embodied in the manly role of the king as expressed in Hittite ritual, historical, and admonitory texts. I show that both sets of texts laid stress on regulating "male" impulses. In addition, the opposition of continent, rational, and powerful versus impulsive, foolish, and weak was not constructed as masculine versus feminine, but man versus child. Finally, the life cycle of the male human had two phases in adulthood: in the first physical power predominated, while in the second mental power came to the fore. Both age classes needed to work together to best ensure the prosperity of their society; honesty, justice, and mercy were cultivated in men through mentoring care and punishment, the latter sometimes emasculatingly humiliating, by their elders and betters.

The masculine role of the Hittite king

The king's masculine authority was derived from controlling his environment, social and physical, and from his relations with his predecessors, the royal ancestors, and with his superiors, the gods. In turn, when fully in control of himself, his family, and his kingdom, the king ensured the peaceful prosperity of his land and his subjects. However, the king's position, and therefore the safety of his entire kingdom, was always under threat, not only from external enemies, but also from those with whom he was most intimate, members of his family, who served as his top administrators, and the king's concern to protect himself and his designated heir against power-hungry and treacherous subordinates shaped much of the Hittite discourse on masculinity available to us, including the Kumarbi cycle. The texts examined here also provide the context necessary to understand the cultural constructs that gave meaning to key images and themes of the Kumarbi cycle for its Hittite audience: violation of bodily borders, the sea, living rock, sexual humiliation, the phallus as weapon, and the connection between immature lack of self-control and the inability to rule.

The spatial component of the king's relations with the world

The male social role was conceived as enmeshed in a set of relations stretching in all directions, horizontally across space, up to the heavenly gods, down into the earth to the former kings and Former Gods, and across time as families were sustained by proper relations between father and son, and as masters trained apprentices. Hittite territory, the civilized world, can be seen as rings within rings, each with its own male authority figure: the farm (with its *paterfamilias*), the village (with its council of elders), districts with governors appointed by the king, the entire land with its king (who was judge). The king's relation with the gods was conceived within this scheme of horizontal relations as administrating for them a part of the whole cosmos (Bryce 2002: 18–19). The Storm-god thus delegated the rule of the land to him as the king would to a district governor, as we can see in this ritual recitation of the king's rights and obligations:

> When the [ki]ng bows to the gods, the *gudu*-priest recites as follows: "May the [*t*]*abarna*, the king, be dear to the gods. The land is the Storm-god's alone, heaven and earth and the people are the Storm-god's alone. He made the *tabarna*, the king, his gov[er]nor. He gave him all the land

> of Hattusa. May the *labarna* go[v]ern the whole land by his hand. Who has assaulted (*šaliga*) the body and territory of the *labarn*[*a*, the kin]g, let the Storm-god destroy [hi]m."[3]

Here, the cross-culturally common construct of the impenetrable/inviolable masculine body is equated with the king's land, the borders of which must be protected from assault.[4] In fact, the boundaries of the land were further equated with parts of the body of the Storm-god himself, as shown by a fragment of a ritual that explicitly equates boundaries with the knees of the Storm-god, and a road with his chest, warning that he who breaks (*paršzi*) them, that is, removes them as a marker, wears out (*dariyanuzi*) the equivalent body part of the Storm-god.[5]

The Hittite funerary rituals show that demarcating the borders of the area that belonged to the king was essential in defining his masculine role of property owner, owner of land and livestock. In the literal way typical of Hittite rituals, the boundaries of the land he would possess in the afterlife were physically marked off:[6] A piece of turf is cut with a hoe and spade and laid on top of a loaf of bread, and the Sun-god is adjured, "this meadow, Sun-god, hold it as made properly for him (*āra iyan hark*), let no one divide it (or) get judgment against him. On this meadow, let oxen and sheep, horses and mules graze."[7]

Just as in the afterlife, in the "real world" the edges of the king's territory, the zones within which civilization prevailed and the king held sway, both large scale and small scale, were carefully demarcated with monumental stone works, and inscriptions and reliefs proclaiming his ownership were carved into the living rock, which, as I will argue in more detail later, itself represented dynastic continuity and masculine power. Thus, Hattusa was ringed with a high stone wall pierced by gates that give one the sensation of peering through a keyhole at the vast landscape beyond, an architecture that emphasized the difference between inside and outside.[8] The gates themselves were flanked by masculine protective images: a pair of lions, a warrior. The homology of lion and warrior symbolized the harnessing of masculine wild power to guard the domestic space. Similarly, important junctures in the larger landscape, such as passes at the borders between territories, presented the traveler with a portrait of the king or tutelary god as warrior carved into a rock face, as at the Karabel pass in southwestern Anatolia, which separated the land of Mira from the Seha River Land.[9] The upper edge of the king's territory was the mountaintop, and here too we find images of the king, as on the peak of Kizildag, where the king on his throne was carved into the mountain's highest peak. Here there is an implicit homology of king and god, because mountains were thought of as thrones for the gods, especially the Storm-god.[10]

The paternal role of the king

As *paterfamilias*, the king's social role was also patterned on the reciprocal relation between father and son. As some Old and Middle Hittite texts show, he was expected to exhibit the paternal qualities of mercy and justness. Self-control, which showed he was an adult, not a child, was required to assert the right to rule. The fatherly duty to pass down wisdom along the chain of biological descent meant a father was expected to guide and discipline his son, and the king did the same with his immediate subordinates, his family, and his assembly.

A father should mold his son into an object of praise and the son owed him a reciprocal obligation. This is nicely elucidated in one of the parables associated with the Middle Hittite *Song of Release*, which belonged to the same genre of Hurro-Hittite narrative song as the Kumarbi cycle:

> (KBo 32.14 ii 42–51) A smith cast a cup for glory; he cast it and stood it up. He set it with ornamentation. He engraved it. He made it shine with brilliance. But, the one who cast it, him the foolish (*marlanza*) copper beg[an] to curse in return, "If only he who cast me, his han[d] would break off, and his right tendon would wither away!" When the smith heard, his heart was sickened inside him.
>
> (ii 52–60) The smith began to speak before his heart, "Why does the copper which I poured curse me in return?" The smith said a curse against the cup. "Let Tarhun also strike it, the cup, <let> him wrench off its ornaments. Let the cup fall into the canal, and let the ornaments fall into the river."
>
> (iii 1–5) It is not a cup. That one is a man, a son who is an enemy before his father. He grew up, and he reached maturity, and he was no longer paying attention to his father, (he is one) whom the gods of his father have cursed.[11]

The parable describes how a smith created a beautiful cup, but the idiotic copper artifact – the same adjective *marlanza* is used to describe a mentally handicapped child in an omen text[12] – cursed its maker, who cursed it in return, destroying it. In case we might miss the point, the narrator explains the meaning: the cup is a boy who turned on his father once grown, and no longer paid any attention to him. The "gods of his father" duly punish him. This is one of the stock plot lines of the parables.

The king had an equally strong obligation to oversee and discipline his administrators. Thus, the other stock plot of the parables is about a greedy administrator punished by his superiors:

> (KBo 32.14 iii 9–12) A dog pulled out a *kugulla*-bread from an oven. He dragged it forth from the oven, and he drenched it in oil. He drenched it in oil, and he sat down, and he began to eat it.
>
> (iii 13–19) It is not a dog. He is a man whom his lord makes district commander. He increased the collecting of taxes in that city afterwards,

> and he became very rebellious, and he was no longer paying attention to the city. They were able to report him before his lord, and the taxes that he had swallowed he began to pour out before his lord.[13]

Such a message was not confined to the world of fable; this parable and its point are matched by an exemplary story from the Old Hittite *Palace Chronicles*, a series of disconnected brief vignettes describing the failings of various officials, who were not careful in their duties, were fearful in the face of the enemy, or cheated the king or the people of the town they governed, and how "the father of the king," probably the first great Hittite king, Hattusili I,[14] dealt with them:

> In Arzawa Nunnu was the man of Hurma, a[nd] he did not bring the silver and [gol]d. What he finds, that one also carries to his house. The man of Huntara informed on him. The father of the king sent (for him).[15]

A failure to administrate effectively and honestly was considered to be a failure of manhood, and was dealt with by humiliating punishments that not only caused physical harm but a loss of face and masculinity. Often the punishments of the *Palace Chronicles* are picturesque, even humorous, while others seem horribly cruel, as in the case of the man who was forced to blind his in-law, and then show the blood on his garment as proof.[16] In some cases, the victim is humiliated sexually, such as the loser of an archery contest, who is forced to parade himself naked.[17] Another story tells how the lord in Hurma, Askaliya, "a man in every way," had his status taken from him:

> (CTH 8.A, §14, ii 8–14) Askaliya was lord in Hurmi. And he was in every way a man (*kuwatta kuwatta pešneš*). They denounced him to my father. They led him to Ankuwa. He made him AGRIG (an agricultural administrator) in Ankuwa itself. He was a powerful (*šarkuiš*) man, but he died in disgrace. He hunted partridges (*kakkapaš*) in Kuzru. The partridges in Ankuwa were skinny.
>
> (§15, A ii 15–20) Ispudas-Inara was a potter. Askaliya, the man of Hurma took him. He made him administrator in Utahzuma. When Askaliya tried to kill him, he put him in prison. But the words with regard to Askaliya arrived, and they sent for Ispudas-Inara, they let him out of prison. He mentioned about Askaliya in particular: "You are deceitful!"[18]

I do not understand what appears to be a witticism at Askaliya's expense about the condition of the partridges, but the key point for us is that his optimal situation was one in which he was "a man in every way." I take this as treated respectfully and obeyed as a "real man" (according to the Hittites) should be. But, when he was shown to lack the qualities a man should have – he falsely imprisoned and tried to have executed a man whom he had previously favored with an administrative post in the town of Utahzuma (or Ullama) – he was publically tried and humiliated with a demotion.

In another fragmentary passage there is talk of something the brother of the king did to two men. Someone comes before the king, and he speaks of something done to "the nipples [of] the chest of my brother," and then something about, "I was the lord of the staff (an administrative title) . . ."[19] What is preserved suggests that we are hearing someone of high station complaining about being humiliated. I am tempted to speculate that we have the first extant mention of a titty-twister! In any case, it is clear from the *Palace Chronicles* that masculinity must be performed in a certain way by high-status males, or they will face a punishment that directly impinges on their masculinity.

Hattusili's Testament shows that in raising up a young man properly the father or father-figure should seek to inculcate the same values as a king should enforce in his administrators: besides mercy and loyalty, transparency and fairness in judgments – this is wisdom, *ḫattatar* – and eventually, when the child is old enough, heroism in battle. The text appears to be a death-bed proclamation of Hattusili I, enjoining his subordinates, the men of the assembly (those who are wise) and the army (those with the military might) to care for and raise to maturity his young heir, his grandson and adopted son Mursili. The king opens by complaining about the previous heir:

> (CTH 6.A, §1 = KUB 40.65+ i/ii 1–16) The [Great] King, *tabarna*, to the whole army and the notables, spoke: I am now ill. I had named to you the young *labarna*, "Let that one sit (on the throne)." And, I, the king, named him my son. I constantly instructed him. I raised him. I ran after him constantly. But he was not a son (fit) to be seen. He did not shed tears. He did not show mercy. He was ice. He was not merciful (*genzuwalaš*).[20]

Thus, Hattusili was forced to banish the merciless young man and bring in a new heir, who had not yet reached maturity: "The god elevates another lion in the place of the lion" (§7, A i/ii 39).

Another key value is temperance and self-restraint, expressed as keeping to a strict diet of bread and water (unlike the greedy dog from the parable, who soaked his bread in oil), and not eating too often. Because of the self-mastery of its leaders, the land of the Hittites will "stand tall" and be in a state of peaceful rest, rather than in a tumult of internecine conflict, afflicted by enemy invasions:

> (§19', A iii 26–32) (Until) now no one [of my family] has accepted my will (*ištanzanan*). [But you, m]y [son] Mursili, you take it. Guard [the wor]ds [of your father]. If you guard the word, you will eat bread and you will drink water. When manly vi[go]r (^{LÚ}*maya*[*nda*]*tar*) is in your [heart], eat two times, three times a day. Ta[ke ca]re of yourself. And

[when] old age (^{LÚ}ŠU.GI-*tar*) is in your heart, ge[t] drunk, and toss aside the word [of your father].

(§20', A iii 33–6) You are my [fore]most servants. [Guar]d my w[or]ds, those of the king. Eat bread, and drink water, and [Hatt]usa will stand tall (*šarā artari*), and my land will be [rest]ed ([*waršīy*]*an*). . . .

The lust for power that drove dynastic conflict is thus implicitly constructed as another carnal appetite that must be kept in check.

In the end, Hattusili's admonitions were not effective. Mursili was assassinated by his brother-in-law and cupbearer Hantili, as described in the *Telipinu Edict*, and the assassinations continued until Telipinu, the brother-in-law of king Huzziya, seized power and united the kingdom again so it could prosper and dominate its enemies.[21] But, certainly such threats did carry some weight even after death, for the king depended on his royal ancestors for support. Offerings for the former kings were a standard part of Hittite festivals, and they played a role in substitution rituals meant to rid the king of pollution and in other sorts of purification rituals.[22]

The permanence and stability that the royal ancestors' approval offered was expressed through monumental constructions, often carved into the living rock (neut. *peru*, or common gender *perunaš*) sticking through the crust of the earth. Thus, one type of funerary monument, the "eternal rocky peak" (*ukturi*/SAG.UŠ ^{NA_4}*ḫekur*), was made from the living rock.[23] Living rock also physically expressed the power of the king, "[whose r]oots reach to the bottom of the sea, while (his) branches [reac]h to heaven," according to the Hittite version of the Hattic *Words of the Goddess Zintuhi in the Temple of the Sun-goddess*,[24] and the security he offered his people. In one section of the Old Hittite *Benedictions for Labarna*, the practitioner makes quite explicit the metaphor of the king as fortress, and his dynasty as a house (*per*/*parnaš*) whose foundations are the unmoving living rock emerging from the earth, taking advantage of the pun created by the juxtaposition of *per* and *peruni*:

(CTH 820.1, §1' = KUB 36.110 rev. 5–7) . . . w[e] eat his bread, (that) of the king. And we drink his [wate]r. We repeatedly drink his pure [wi]ne, [of] the golden cup.

(§2', rev. 8–10) Let [the *laba*]*rna*, king of Hatti, be ou[r] fortress, and le[t] the whole land hold their backs supporting Hattusa (*iškiš=šmet anda* ^{URU}*Ḫattuša lagan ḫard*[*u*]).

(§3', rev. 11–12) The *labarna*, the king, is full of vigor (*inarauwanza*), and the whole land is vital (*innaraḫḫi*) like him.

(§4', rev. 13–14) Of the *labarna*, his house (*per*) is of joy, for his children, for his descendants, and it is built on rock (^{NA_4}*peruni*).

> (§5', rev. 15–16) But, of an ambusher/traitor (*appaliyallaš*), [his] house is b[uilt] in front of a flood. The flood flo[ws], and it covers it up, and it brings i[t] to the sea.[25]

The manly vigor of the king, proven by the progeny he has sired, causes his land to be vital and prosperous. The people of the land, in turn, are imagined as supporting the king on their backs, just as mountain gods are depicted supporting the Storm-god.[26] The term *inarauwanza* 'vigorous, strong, manly' is perhaps cognate with Greek *anēr*, male human. Certainly it has the connotation of male potency.[27] The house of the *appaliyalla*, on the other hand, will be washed away. The threat that lying will lead to the destruction of a man's household is typical for the conditional curses of oaths, and the chaos caused by lying is represented here by the turbulent sea.

Another ritual draws on the same rock imagery to combat the divisive internecine slander and curses of Ziplandawiya, the sister of Middle Hittite king Tudhaliya I/II:

> We brought the sta[tue]s to ex[actly thei]r [place]. They lined them up on another rock/cliff (*p*[*er*]*uni*). The container of dough where [the honey] was poured, she sets it on the rock/cliff (*peruni*). She breaks up 3 thick [br]eads. She libates wine. She speaks as follows, "As this rock (*pēru*) is everlasting, may the lord (i.e., client of the ritual), his wife, and his children likewise be everlasting. Let his weapon be pointing forth." They offer a *tūruppa*-bread with wine.[28]

The reference to the king's "weapon pointing forth" (TUKUL-*ŠU parā neanza*) has an obvious double meaning, as weapon and vigorous phallus producing progeny. It is exploited more clearly in other blessing formulas, for example, in the New Hittite *Daily Prayer to Telipinu*, which segues from fertility to martial prowess via the "powerful divine weapon of a man pointed straight ahead" (LÚ-*aš tarḫūilin parā neya*[*nt*]*a*[*n*] $^{\text{d.GIŠ}}$TUKUL-*in*):

> Keep giving [to the]m male [chil]dren, female children, grandchildren, and great-grandchildren. Keep giving them assent and obedience. Keep giving them flourishing of grain, grapes, cattle, sheep, and people. Keep giving them the powerful divine weapon of a man poi[nte]d straight ahead. Keep placing the lands of the enemy under their feet for them. [Let them destroy] them a[t will].[29]

The king and the Storm-god

The two powers of what was considered to be the ideal masculine body, might and ability to father children, were thus inextricably connected in the Hittite construction of male potency, and the divine embodiment of both sides of male potency was the Storm-god. The thunderstorms he unleashed represented the king's martial prowess, while the rain his storms brought fostered the fertility that the king's orderly rule should promote. His emblem of the bull also combined both, with his thunderous roar and potency.

Because the expectations of the Hittite king's social role were based on the expectations for a *paterfamilias*, the master of a farming household, key themes were domination and production, control and domestication of natural resources, and an opposition of wild/chaotic vs. cultivated/cultured/ordered. The Hittite king was deeply concerned with separating the one from the other, and turning the former into the latter, and this was a duty he shared with the Storm-god.[30] Indeed, as we saw in the funerary ritual, the king's only superior, the one who can adjudicate his cases, was a god.[31] Therefore, the most apt masculine entity for the king to pattern his adult behavior on was a god, and when the king worked at removing or keeping at bay the chaotic from the world of humans, he explicitly followed the example set by the Storm-god. Festivals celebrated the Storm-god vanquishing chaos, associating his activities with those of the king. Thus, the *(ḫ)išuwa* festival, a Syrian-derived festival coming from Kizzuwatna (Plain Cilicia), empowered the king by having harpists engage in battle dance in the name of the Storm-god.[32] In addition, the Syrian Storm-god of Aleppo, known to the Hittites by his Hurrian name Teššub, was particularly popular throughout the Near East because he legitimated kingship through the exemplary myth of how he dominated and controlled chaos, represented by the turbulent sea, as in the *Benedictions for Labarna*, or by a monstrous being.[33] Finally, from the indigenous Hattic culture came the *purulli* festival, which was linked to the story of the Storm-god's overcoming the snake Illuyanka. Although the end of the first version of the story is fragmentary, it is clear that it justified the king's rule and connected it with control over water:[34]

> Inara [went] to the town Kiskil[ussa]. As she se[t] her house [and] the [course] of the flood [in] the hand of the king, therefore we enact the f[i]rst *purull*[*i*], and the hand [of the king does X to the house] of Inara and the course of the flood.[35]

The Kumarbi cycle

We turn now to the Kumarbi cycle, a set of songs that tell of the birth of the Storm-god, in Hurrian Teššub, in Hittite Tarhun, and how he vanquishes a series of rivals put against him by his progenitor, the chthonic god Kumarbi. The first in the cycle is the *Song of Birth*; after that would have come the now lost *Song of the Sea*, then the *Song of Hedammu*, and finally the *Song of Ullikummi*. I focus here only on the Hittite versions of the songs.[36]

I argue that Kumarbi, Tarhun's "mother" and older rival, in his excessive striving for power reveals himself to be a failure as a man and thus unfit to rule: he first sexually assaults his superior, Anu, but ends up pregnant and forced to give birth in agony, creating the perfect rival that will drive him from power; then, not having learned his lesson, to fight the Storm-god he produces two misbegotten, malformed children, nothing but phalluses, that represent his destructive sexual incontinence and immaturity. Thus, his transgressions help to define for us what the Hittites considered to be normative masculinity. Furthermore, the Kumarbi cycle reveals to us the same "deep interior division" David Glover and Cora Kaplan (2009: 105–106) describe for 19th-century Englishmen:

> between the need for mastery or control that will create order out of chaos and a fear of the potentially untameable flows of energy within . . . a splitting of gendered identity, in which the instability of what for the early Victorians constituted "maleness," the potent physical powers that were thought to be of the basic essence of man, begins to sabotage the "manliness" or self-discipline with which an individual conducts himself.[37]

Finally, whereas in the equivalent stories in Sumerian, Akkadian, and Greek, female entities (Ninmah, Tiamat, and Hera) give birth on their own to misshapen monsters, representing the failure of the female principle, despite its special ability to gestate progeny, to procreate on its own, here the failure is transferred to the male realm. The change, I think, was quite pointed and would have been noticed by the original audience. I do not believe, however, that Kumarbi's incontinence was therefore constructed as feminizing; rather, he was meant to be seen as fatally immature in wanting to "have it all."

The *Song of Birth* begins by calling on the Former Gods to listen to how they lost their power and Tarhun came to be their king:[38]

> (CTH 344.A, §1 = KUB 33.130+ i 1–4) [I sing of Kumarbi, father of the gods.] Let them who are the [F]o[r]mer Gods, [. . .], the powerful [Form]er Gods listen. Let Na[ra, Napšara, Mink]i, Ammunki listen, let Amme[z]zadu, [Alulu,] father (and) mother of [X], listen.
>
> (§2, A i 5–11) Let [Enlil (and) Abad]u, father (and) mother of Iš[h]ara, listen. Let Enlil [(and) Ninli]l, who are powerful (and) ete[r]nal gods [below] and [ab]ove, [. . .] and [the S]hining One listen. Long ago, i[n f]ormer years, Alalu was king in heaven. Alalu was on the throne, and Powerful Anu, their foremost, (that) of the gods, stood before hi[m], and he kept bow[i]ng down at his feet, and he kept putting drinking cups in his hand.
>
> (§3, A i 12–17) As just nine years were counted off, Alalu was king in heaven, and in the ninth year Anu [w]ent in batt[le] against Alalu. He defeated him, Alalu, and he ran away before him, and he went down

> into the dark earth. He went down into the dark earth, while Anu seated himself on the throne. Anu was sitting on the throne, and powerful Kumarbi kept giving him to drink. He kept bowing down at his feet and putting drinking cups in his hand.

The story starts off like an episode of the bloody dynastic conflict that wreaked such havoc within the Hittite ruling house. Just as the harvest god Alalu was deposed by his cupbearer Anu ("Heaven") and Anu in turn by his cupbearer Kumarbi, the aggrieved son of Alalu, in the generations following Hattusili, ungrateful usurper after ungrateful usurper seized the throne, operating from high posts such as Cupbearer, Chief of the Bodyguards, and Man of the Golden Spear.[39]

Then, Kumarbi, the seed of Alalu, goes into battle against Anu:

> (§4, A i 18–24) As just nine years were counted off Anu was king in heaven, and in the ninth year Anu went in battle against Kumarbi.[40] Kumarbi, the seed of Alalu, went in battle against Anu, and Anu was no longer able to withstand the eyes of Kumarbi. He broke away from Kumarbi and from his hands. He ran, Anu, and he set off for heaven. Kumarbi assaulted (*šaliga*) him from behind, and he grabbed Anu (by) the feet, and he dragged him down from heaven.

The glaring eyes of Kumarbi are what cause Anu to flee. In the Hittite view the eyes seem to be highly important for masculine power. Thus, Hattusili I boasts in his *Annals* that among his "manly deeds" ([LÚ]*pešnatar*, lit. "manliness"),[41] he glared at the town Hahhu like a lion, which seems to cause the town to capitulate.[42] In addition, in the *Myth of Illuyanka*, the snake renders the Storm-god helpless by stealing his eyes, along with his heart.[43] This may help us to understand the punishment of blinding inflicted upon the in-law of one of the men punished in the *Palace Chronicles*. It is a symbolic destruction of his manhood. I offer the speculative suggestion that the eyes are stand-ins for the testicles, as with Oedipus. Hattusili, I suggest, is in effect boasting about his big balls, and Anu is left without any balls.

At this point in the story Kumarbi appears to be the epitome of virility, and his assault on Anu begins like a humiliating anal rape, the stereotypical stuff of dominating male fantasy, of which the Roman poet Catullus wrote so pithily,[44] and which is still used as a tool of wartime terror today. Note that the term *šaliga*, which I translate as "assaulted," was also used in the passage quoted earlier concerning the Old Hittite king's rights and obligations, to refer to the unlawful crossing of boundaries, whether territorial or bodily. This kind of sexual humiliation is an extreme variation of the insulting punishments the Hittite king would inflict on his subordinate that we saw in the *Palace Chronicles*, but here it is a subordinates inflicting it on his ruler, a serious violation of norms.

Moreover, Kumarbi in fact gets it all wrong! He is successful in emasculating his older rival, yes, but in the process of appropriating his power he in effect fellates him:

> (§5, A i 25–29) He bit his butt-cheeks and his manliness fused with Kumarbi's heart like bronze. When Kumarbi swallowed down the manliness of Anu, he rejoiced, and he laughed. Anu turned back to him and began to say <to> Kumarbi, "Did you rejoice before [yo]ur heart because you swallowed my manliness?"

Kumarbi's act of putting Anu's penis in his mouth was surely not viewed as anything but humiliating, although until recently scholars of Hittite society had believed that homosexual relations, male or female, were not a concern among Hittites (Hoffner 1973: 83, 85). The *Hittite Laws* cover all sorts of bestiality and improper sexual relations,[45] and the *Instructions to Priests and Temple Officials* worry about pollution brought on by heterosexual sex,[46] but there is no sense from these documents that homosexual sex was abhorrent enough to merit special mention. However, two recently published articles have suggested that two Luwian-influenced rituals by the women Anniwiyani and Paskuwatti, which had been interpreted as cures for male impotence, were actually meant to inspire men who suffered from the desire to be penetrated like a woman to stop being "a man of piss and shit" and to "become a yoke" for a woman.[47] Thus, the Hittites can now be included among the many societies that worried about men when they willingly took on the receptive role of women, and we can read this scene through that lens.

Secondly, the description of Anu's manliness fusing with Kumarbi's "heart" (ŠÀ) like bronze refers to the combining of white tin and red copper, mapping on to the dichotomy of white semen and red menstrual blood, often considered in traditional cultures to be the female equivalent of semen. That the Hittites thought so is shown by suggestive rites performed before the king and queen engage in ritual intercourse, in which red and white wool is twined together, then tied to the belt at the loins, or placed in a wool basket, a symbol of the womb.[48]

Anu then mocks Kumarbi, taunting him with the knowledge that he is pregnant with his rival's offspring:

> (§6, A i 30–36) "Don't rejoice before your heart. I have put a burden inside your heart. First, I have impregnated you with Tarhun, the august one. Secondly, I have also impregnated you with the River Aran[z]ah, not to be resisted. Thirdly, I have also impregnated you with august Tašmišu. I have also placed three terrifying gods as burdens inside your heart.[49] You will go and finish (the pregnancy?) by smashing the cliffs of Mt. Tassa with your head."

> (§7, A i 37–41) When Anu finished speaking, he we[nt] up to heaven and he concealed himself. [K]um[arbi], the wise king, spat forth from his mouth, he spat forth from his mouth s[pit and manliness (*pešnatar*)][50] mixed together. What Kumarbi s[pat] forth, [M]t. Kanzura acce[pted] as a fearsome god.

Thus, Kumarbi does in fact display the female ability to gestate a child, symbolic of his wrong-headed fantasy to be all powerful, even controlling that which is not "naturally" his realm, but the poet dwells on the humiliation of taking on the feminine role and physical problems that arise. Kumarbi has violated in the most violent and intimate way the boundaries of Anu's body, and now his own body is inhabited by a hostile being, who can only emerge by violently breaking the container of his gestating parent. The union creates a son that is the perfect blend of heaven and earth,[51] sure to eclipse Kumarbi when mature, and soon enough, as with the Sumerian myth of *Enki and Ninhursag*,[52] in the *Song of Birth* the pregnant male is faced with the dilemma of where the baby will emerge from. The unborn Tarhun is loath to pollute himself by emerging from an unclean orifice:

> (§13', A ii 29–38) He began to speak to Kumarbi in his heart, "[. . .] they stand . . . the place. If I [come f]orth [from X,] he will break [the X thing]s like a reed. I[f] I come [f]orth [from] the 'good place' I will defile myself by that way also. In heaven, on earth [. . .]. I will defile myself inside by means of the ear. But, if I come forth from the 'good place' [. . .] l[ike] a woman (subj.) [. . .] he will cry out (with birth pangs) for my sake. When I/me, Tarhun of Heaven, withi[n . . .] he decreed it/them within. S/he broke him, Kumarbi, [li]ke a stone, (at) his skull, and s/he came up from him by means of his skull, Powerful One, the heroic king."[53]

In the end, Tarhun comes forth from the "good place," either some part of the skull from which other gods are also emerging or a different location.[54] Kumarbi attempts to eat the child, is fed a rock instead, breaks his teeth and weeps, and then has his head sewn up by the Fate-goddesses, possibly tracing the mark of the sutures in a human skull.

There is more to the story, but it is quite fragmentary, and the assumed accession of Tarhun is not preserved. The *Song of the Sea*, which apparently told of a battle between the Storm-god and the Sea, as Baal fights Yam in Ugaritic myth, could fit in after this episode, explaining why the Sea is an ally of Kumarbi in the *Song of Hedammu*.[55] The latter song is only preserved in disjointed fragments,[56] and we do not know how the story started, but when we pick it up in the second(?) tablet, Kumarbi, "father of the gods," is negotiating with the Sea for the hand of his daughter, whose chief virtue appears to be her gigantic size.[57] We are missing what happens next, but we can assume that the child, Hedammu, is a product of their union.

He is a sea serpent with a voracious appetite who gulps down all manner of livestock and water creatures. It is the Storm-god's sister Anzili who takes action against the creature, using her special powers of seduction.[58]

She dresses herself up and goes to the seaside to dance alluringly before the monster, accompanied by drums and cymbals:

> (KBo 26.72+ iv 3'-10', KUB 36.56+ 1'-8') [. . .] in [heave]n the clouds [. . .] from the [powe]rful waters [. . .] s/he did. Whe[n Anzil]i, the queen of Nineveh thought it good, she sprinkled love, *šaḫi*, and [*parnull*]*i*[59] in the powerful waters, and the love, *š*[*aḫi*], (and) *parnulli* dissolved in the waters. When Hedammu tasted the sc[e]nt, the beer, [a sweet] dream seized victorious Hedammu, h[is] mental powers (ZI.ḪI.A). He was dreaming like an ox or an ass. [. . .] he recognized [no]thing, and he was eating his fill of frogs and lizards.

> (KBo 26.72+ iv 10'-19', KUB 36.56+ 9'-10') [Anzil]i began to speak to Hedammu, "C[ome] up again, fr[om] the powerful [water]s [. . .] come straight up, and cutting through the middle." 90,000 [. . .] pulls . . . the place from the earth, and Anzili holds forth [before Hedammu her naked limb]s. Hedammu (subj.) [. . .] his manliness (*pešnatar*) springs forth. His manline[ss . . .]. He impregnates repeatedly [(pl. object) . . .] 130 towns [. . . he] did [X]. And, with his belly/embryo(s) . . . 70 towns [. . .] in . . . he finished off [(pl. object) . . .] heaps of heads he [h]eap[ed] up.

The goddess reveals her naked body to Hedammu, and manages to get him to consume a love potion she has prepared. At the first taste of the beer-based drink he falls asleep, but then we find that he is ready for action, and his manliness repeatedly springs forth. It seems he sprays his semen indiscriminately, because there is mention here of him impregnating (something), then mention of 130 cities. Or is that when he crawls out on dry land he crushes cities left and right? – because then we read "with his big belly" or "with the fetus/embryo" (depending how ^{UZU}*šarḫuwantit* is translated) he did something to 70 cities. I can imagine a variety of scenarios, but the one I like best is his spawn covering the surface of the earth like frog eggs. In the next two paragraphs he and Anzili engage in some kind of action punctuated by dialogue.[60] Although we do not know how the scene ends, we presume that the goddess takes full advantage of Hedammu's uncontrolled sexual appetite to trick him in some way.

Where other fragments of the song fit into the overall narrative is subject to interpretation, but it is clear that the conflict among the gods is wreaking havoc among humankind:

> (KUB 33.103 ii 9–16, KUB 33.100+ ii/iii 17'-26') [E]a, king of wisdom, began to speak to Kumarbi, "What is the reason why [y]ou, Kumarbi, purs[ue] mankind for evil? Doesn't mankind make pile(s) of

grain, and don't [the]y pr[om]ptly off[er] (it) to you, Kumarbi? Also, inside the temple, in joy, to you alone, Kumarbi, father of the gods, they promptly made offerings. Don't they make offerings to Tarhun, the canal inspector of ma[nk]ind? And, don't they mention me, Ea the king, by name? [. . .] you put the wisdom of all after [. . .] the blood (and) tears of mankind [. . . K]umarb[i . . .]"

Another fragment humorously describes the suffering of humans:

(KUB 33.103 iii 1'-7') [. . . ". . .] strikin[g . . . . B]ut, the lightni[ng] and [th]under of Tarhun and Anzili, with the water, is not going away from us yet, s[o] we are not able to go yet. Our knees keep [s]haking, and our heads spin like the [whe]el of a potter, and our cocks are limp!"[61]

According to my interpretation, the internecine strife between the gods, which is patterned on the dynastic strife that was such an issue for the Hittite court, makes the humans who are the gods' subjects suffer, just as Hattusili I insisted that internecine conflict could destroy his country.

The sea-snake rival that Kumarbi has created to battle Tarhun is a monstrous combination of phallus and misborn child, a fetus still swimming in the amniotic fluid of his mother, the daughter of the Sea. (In Mesopotamian texts, the baby in labor is often visualized as a boat in a stormy sea – a cross-culturally common conception. In addition, among the Hittites, semen was thought of as water.[62]) With his voracious appetite for food and superabundant semen Hedammu represents the fatal incontinence of Kumarbi, who is simultaneously father of the gods and too immature to rule.

Kumarbi continues in his wrong-headed quest to produce a son more powerful than Tarhun in the *Song of Ullikummi*.[63] This time he mates with a huge rock in a cool lake (*ikunta lūli*), which Itamar Singer (2002a) has proposed is the Great Rock in Lake Van.

(1, §1, B = KUB 33.98+ i 1–8, A = KUB 33.96+ i 1–8) [I shall] s[ing of X], in whose [mi]nd [is X], and he takes wisdom in his mind, the head (and) father of all the gods, Kumarbi. Kumarbi takes wisdom with his mind, he who raises up an evil day. He takes evil for himself against Tarhun, and he raises a rival against Tarhun.

(1, §2, B i 9–20, A i 9–19) Kumarbi [takes] wisdom with his mind, and he lines it up like jewel bead(s). When Kumarbi took wisdom before his mind, he promptly rose up from his throne. He took his staff with his hand, [and] he put o[n his feet] the swift wind[s] as shoes. He set off from Urkeš, the city, and he arrived at the Cool Lake, and when Kumarb[i . . . . I]n the Cool La[ke] a great cliff (*perunaš*) [l]ies. In length it is three miles, [and] in width [it is . . . miles] and half a mile. What it holds below, his desire (ZI) sprang forth [to sleep with it]. He slept with

> the r[ock] (*p*[*eruni*]). To it [. . .] his manliness withi[n]. He took it five times, [again] he took it ten times.

Whereas in the *Song of Hedammu* it is the snake who responds uncontrollably, here it is Kumarbi himself who is completely unable to contain himself when he looks at "what the cliff held below." His *ištananza* springs forth and he sleeps with the rock, "taking" the rock multiple times.

The rock has been treated as female by translators, but in fact the Hittite does not specify the gender, and it is best to assume that the rock is male, since mountains are always depicted as male in the Hittite iconography.[64] Indeed the neuter noun *peru* serves as the base both for the common gender noun *perunaš* and the name of the Hittite god Pirwa, who is attested at the head of the pantheon already in the Old Assyrian colony of Kanesh, where he was paired with Hassusara ('queen'). Pirwa was also a very common man's name. The god was associated with horses and with high cliffs, where his temple was placed.[65] This Hittite context helps to explain the connotations of Kumarbi's interest in the rock for the song's Hittite audience, although the setting is in the Caucasus, and the motif of ejaculating on a rock has good Caucasian parallels.[66] That is, Kumarbi is interested in creating a more perfect contender for kingship than Tarhun, so he turns to an entity associated with kingship to create a new child, and the rock's maleness is an asset, rather than a liability, since it would give the child the same extra dose of masculinity that Tarhun has.

Lacunae prevent us from understanding how the fetus gestated or exactly how he was born, but the process of mountain formation is explicitly metaphorized as an erection, for Kumarbi describes him springing out from Kumarbi's body like a spear (^{GIŠ}*šiyatal*):

> (1, §8", A iii 10'-25', E = KBo 26.60 1'-7') . . . Kumarbi began to [sp]eak before [his] mi[nd], "What name [shall I give] him? Which child the Fate-goddesses, the Great Goddesses, gave to me, [he] sprang from my body like a spear. Com[e], let his name be Ullikummi. Let him go up to [kingsh]ip in heaven, let him crush flat Kummi, [the beau]tiful city, and let him strike Tarhun. Let him grind [him] up like [c]haff, and let him pulverize him with his foot [like] an ant, and let him shred apart Tašmišu like a britt[le re]ed, and let him scatter all the gods down from [heaven] like birds, let him sha[t]ter them [like] empty vessels."

In Kumarbi's vision of the destruction that his son will wreak, he will grow tall enough to reach heaven, and he will use his stony body to grind and break the city Kummi and the gods, and to knock them from the sky like birds struck down by a nasty boy throwing rocks. Indeed, later on in the third tablet, when Ullikummi takes on the gods in battle, the stone, now grown to an immense 9,000 miles tall, stands before the gates of the Storm-god's city like a spear (*šiyatal*), blocking Hebat, the Storm-god's consort, from having access to him and filling her with fear that he has been killed.[67] I take this as a perversion of the spear (ŠUKUR) that stood before the Hittite palace gate, the phallic symbol of royal power and potency, the theft of which received the death penalty.[68]

Kumarbi's phallic fantasy of an erection big enough to reach the sky and hard enough to crush the other gods like reeds not only oversteps the bounds of propriety, but can only lead to misery for all, divine and human. When the child is placed on the knees of Enlil, in the gesture that expects the god to welcome the child as a father would, he immediately exclaims:

> (1, §15", A iv 14'-17', D = KUB 33.92+ iii 1'-4') "Who is this child? Wh[om] have the Fate-goddesses, the Great Goddesses, raised again? Who will look [again] on the weighty battle[s] of the great gods? Of no one else, of Kumarbi alone is i[t], an [evi]l thing."

And, the all-seeing Sun-god, when he catches sight of the rapidly growing monster emerging from the sea, rushes in such agitation to the Storm-god, that Tašmišu says to Tarhun, "Why is he coming, Istanu of Heaven, [king of] the land[s], and for what matter is he coming? It is an [important] matte[r]. It is [n]ot one to be cast aside. The struggle is weighty, [and] the battle is weighty. And, it is a ferment of heaven, and it is famine of the land and death."[69] Clearly the gods understand the effects that their constant internecine strife can have upon humans.

Indeed, the entire narrative is a meditation on the stupidity of Kumarbi, although he presumes that he is wise (*ḫattanza*), and it connects his foolish and incontinent behavior seeking power with sexual incontinence through the Hittite noun *ištanza*(*na*) (Sumerogram ZI), which refers to that which makes a person a thinking, sentient being. It covers the semantic space: "life, soul, mind, desire, will,"[70] and was used by Hattusili in his *Testament* to refer to his good intentions and advice that was flouted by his failure of a son. It is used in the Ullikummi myth to refer both to the mind, the ability to plan and carry out plans, and to the uncontrollable desire Kumarbi feels when he lays his eyes on the lower part of the rock, a sight that he has deliberately sought out. In the opening lines of the song the poet prepares his audience for his point by using the word *ištanzana* three times in the repeated expression, "Kumarbi repeatedly takes wisdom (*ḫattātar*/GALGA-*tar*) in his mind (ZI-*ni*)."

In fact, the child Kumarbi produces is profoundly disabled, deaf, and blind, as one would expect from a rock, and as an ancient auditor would expect from such an improper conception; according to Babylonian omen texts, at least, parents were blamed for their children's disabilities, which were supposed to be caused because they had engaged in improper coitus (Stol 2000: 2–3). Indeed, we might use the standard image of intercourse as a man plowing a fertile field[71] to infer that Kumarbi should have realized spilling seed on a rock was the height of futility, and it may be that among the Hittites and Hurrians spilling seed on the ground was seen as an improper act, as in the story of Onan in the Hebrew Bible,[72] and as opposed to Enki ejaculating to fill the Tigris with water in *Enki and the World Order*,[73] where it seems to be completely positive.

It is true that Kumarbi needed a child hard enough to withstand Tarhun's thunderbolts and to be impervious to the wiles of Anzili, as the goddess finds out he is when she goes down to the seashore to attempt to seduce him as she had Hedammu:

> (2.A, §9''' = KUB 33.87+ ii 15'-25') There is a great wav[e] from the sea. The great wave says to Anzili, "Before whom are you singing, and before whom are you filling your mouth with wi[nd]? The man is deaf, so he doe[s not] hear. He is blind in his [ey]es, so he does not see. He h[as] no graciousness (*kariyašḫaš*). Go away, Anzili, and [r]each your brother, while he is not yet bone-hard (*ḫaštališzi*), while the skull of his head has not yet become terrifying."

The Hittite verb I translate literally as "become bone-hard," *ḫaštališzi*, also means "to become heroic"; the monster seems to be conceived of as getting harder and more powerful as he gets older, as molten rock or metal hardens as it cools.

Such a being, however, as Anzili tells her brother, "does not know even a little *mal*, although bone-hardness/heroism (UR.SAG-*tar*/*ḫaštaliyatar*) has been given him tenfold."[74] *Mal* is a quality expected of men, grouped with *tarḫuilatar*, the ability to overcome, and *ḫaddulatar* "good health." Thus, the *Chicago Hittite Dictionary* (L-N 124) defines it as "a quality desirable for men in combat, such as boldness, ferocity, skill." Indeed, the term connects intelligence and manliness.[75] One wonders whether the Hittites believed, as people in many traditional cultures do, that the brain and semen are made of the same substance.[76]

In addition, the wave asserts that the stone monster has no graciousness. The Hittite term *kariyašḫaš* 'mercy, graciousness' is related to the Greek noun *kharis*, the feeling of pleasure one gets when giving or receiving a favor, which in Greek is also used to describe the (sexual) appeal of one person to another. For the Hittites it is another manly quality, one that gods were supposed to exhibit to their worshippers and kings also were supposed to exhibit, especially towards women,[77] as seen in Hittite historiographical works. Thus, in the *Deeds of Suppiluliuma I* the king responds to the plea of Tutankhamen's widow, left with no son to carry on the royal line, by giving her one of his sons in marriage. His son Mursili II says, "Because my father was merciful (*genzuwallaš*), he presented graciousness (*kāri*) to the matter of the woman and sent (someone with regard to the matter) of his son."[78] And, Mursili II describes how he himself exhibited this quality to the womenfolk of one of his treacherous vassals, king Manapa-Tarhunta of the Seha River Land. When Mursili moved in to his territory on a punitive expedition, the king, who had taken sides with his enemy, begged for mercy, but Mursili refused until the king's mother came and groveled before him. The Hittite king explicitly refers to her gender to explain his subsequent actions: "Because women groveled at my feet, I willingly presented graciousness (*kāri*) [to the women] and I did [not] go any further into the Seha River Land."[79]

Thus, the English metaphor "heart of stone" applies perfectly to Ullikummi. Hard as a bone, full of the manly trait of heroism, but born of an unnatural union in which no woman took part, he is unable to respond to a woman as a man should, whether in love or in sympathy. Thus, he will never be able to produce the progeny that was the hallmark of the successful man. He may be a "weapon pointed forth," but he can only carry out one of its two functions.

Whereas Tarhun was able to defeat his watery opponent Hedammu because he combined in himself earth and heaven, now, to defeat the dumb but hard Ullikummi, he will need to combine a young man's martial power with an old man's wisdom. The new generation of gods turns to a god more ancient than Kumarbi, Ea, who stands outside and earlier than the line begun by Alalu, to find the wisdom that defeats Ullikummi. The Storm-god and Tašmišu go to the Abzu, the place of the primordial waters, here conceived of as a city, and bow repeatedly to Ea, asking him for help and advice:

> (3, §24"", A = KBo 26.65+ iii 48'-55a', B = KBo 26.67 1'-8') Ea began to speak in turn to the Former (*karūiliyaš*) Gods, "[L]isten to my words, Former Gods, the ancient (*karūili*) words which you [k]now: Open it up, the ancient fatherly, grandfatherly (*annalla addalla ḫūḫadalla*) storehouse. Let them bring the seal of the ancestors (lit. "former fathers," *karūiliyaš addaš*), [and] let them unseal [i]t. Let them take [for]th the ancient (*karūiliya*) copper saw, with which they cut apart heaven and earth. [We will] cut off Ullikummi, the basalt, at his feet, at the bottom, whom [K]umarbi rai[sed] as a r[i]v[a]l against the gods.

Here the Storm-god makes use of the advice and care of the Former Gods just as the king depends on the support of his divinized ancestors, the former kings. The primeval tool, dating to the time before the invention of bronze, used to cut apart heaven and earth – the two parents of Tarhun, in a sense – is the only thing that can defeat the stone monster. Thus, Kumarbi is left with no authority whatsoever. He is unable to conceive a rival to the Storm-god and unable to battle him himself. His wisdom as father of the gods is bested by the wisdom that antedates even his creation, symbolized by a monumental administrative structure, the ancient storehouse, guarded by scribes and accountants, which safeguarded the prosperity of a kingdom by storing the grain the king in his wisdom had the foresight to collect from his subjects to use in times of scarcity.

Although the close of the tablet is very damaged, we can see that the monster makes a reference to the invincibility of vigorous manliness and elderly wisdom combined:

> (3, §30''''', A iv 23'-24', C = KBo 26.68 5') The basalt began to speak in turn to Tarhun, "What shall I say to you, Tarhun? Strike and carry out (that) of your desire (ZI-*aš=šaš*)! Ea, king of wisdom, stands with you."
>
> . . .
>
> (3, §32''''', A iv 29'-36') Ullikummi bega[n] to speak in [t]urn t[o Tarhun], "[Stri]ke over and over a[gai]n like a man (LÚ-*nili*), and carry out [(that) of your desire!] Ea, king [of] wisdom, stan[ds] with you.

Thus, the story ends with the misborn creature acknowledging he has been defeated by the perfect combination of Tarhun's might and Ea's knowledge.[80]

Conclusion

Hittite texts from every layer of Bronze Age Anatolian culture and every genre are united in their message about the proper values for a good man: sexual restraint; curbing greed, including the outward manifestations of ambition; and mutual care and loyalty across generations. Kumarbi, whose rebellion represents the greatest fear of a Hittite king, has failed on every front: his drive to attain power caused him to engage in an act of – literally – voracious sexual congress, which he intended as a violent removal of his opponent's masculinity, an extreme example of the humiliating punishments described in the *Palace Chronicles*, but the violation of Anu's intimate boundaries proves to be symbolically humiliating to Kumarbi, showing him to be unfit for rule. When defeated by his hypermasculine son Tarhun, created from two "fathers" and combining heaven and earth, Kumarbi unites sea and earth in his next son Hedammu, but Hedammu carries the trait of his father's fatal incontinence, which leads to his defeat at the hands of a female. Kumarbi next tries to create a son whose masculinity is equal to Tarhun's, but the stone Ullikummi embodies his father's other failings, stupidity and lack of feeling. Kumarbi is willing to create sons and sacrifice them one after another solely to kill another of his sons. He thus embodies the most dangerous failing of a father, a selfish and misguided refusal to accede power once his son has grown to maturity, the opposite of Hattusili I's careful concern with his successor's moral upbringing in *Hattusili's Testament* and the inverse of the crime of the ungrateful son whose story is told in the cup parable associated with the *Song of Release*. To contrast with the failings of Kumarbi that are the theme of the *Song of Ullikummi*, the poet highlights the cooperation among the generations of gods in coming up with a plan to defeat Ullikummi, with the older generations, represented by Ea and Enlil, providing the knowledge and administrative resources, and the younger gods the martial power to destroy the monster, a communal response that *Hattusili's Testament*, which addresses both the assembly and the army, shows to represent the Hittite ideal. In addition, Hittite magical and mythical texts show that the cliff with which Kumarbi mates does not only represent masculine hardness, but also connotes the link across generations, extending from the remote past to future progeny, the stability of the household grounded firmly in domestic cooperation, upon which the Hittite kingdom as a whole rests, and which Kumarbi refuses to acknowledge.

Notes

1 As a whole the texts found in the libraries and archives of Hattusa cover a range of genres, including annalistic histories, treaties, diplomatic letters, admonitions by the Hittite kings to their underlings, descendants, and other Great Kings, the Hittite legal code, native Hattic rituals, Hittite rituals, Luwian-influenced rituals, Hurrian-derived rituals, festival descriptions, and Hurro-Hittite narrative songs. We can define the full extent of the geographic area covered in the texts discussed here as Anatolia and north Syria, with some connections as far north as the Caucasus. In this area there was a mix of ethnic groups, and the time period ranges from the beginning of Hittite rule to the end of the empire, some 500 years, but for the most part I will not be attempting to tease out from the sources diverse attitudes towards masculinity. Given that there has been little research on the topic as of yet, it is appropriate at this point to define some commonly held ways of constructing Hittite manhood as revealed in the textual sources. I use the following abbreviations: CHD = *Chicago Hittite Dictionary* (Güterbock, Hoffner, and van den Hout, 1989 ff.), CTH = *Catalogue des textes hittites* (Laroche, 1974), ETCSL = Electronic Text Corpus of Sumerian Literature (http://etcsl.orinst.ox.ac.uk/), HED = *Hittite Etymological Dictionary* (Puhvel, 1984 ff.), HEG = *Hethitisches etymologisches Glossar* (Tischler, 1983 ff.), IBoT = *Istanbul Arkeoloji Müzelerinde Bulunan Boğazköy Tableteri(nden Seçme Metinler)*, KBo = *Keilschrifttexten aus Boghazköi*, KhT = Konkordanz der hethitischen Texten (http://www.hethport.uni-wuerzburg.de/hetkonk), KUB = *Keilschrifturkunden aus Boghazköy*, RlA = *Reallexikon der Assyriologie*. Further bibliography on any of the Hittite texts named here can be found at KhT, searching by the CTH number or publication number.

2 Some may object that I should not be using Hittite sources to elucidate a Hurrian story, but I have argued in a pair of publications that there are extensive connections between the concerns and themes of Hurro-Hittite myth and Hittite royal concerns, using Old and Middle Hittite texts (Bachvarova, 2005, 2010). There are two possible reasons for this: the two peoples shared much in common, and Hurro-Hittite narratives were adapted to the concerns of a Hittite audience.

3 *Kingship and Holy Law*: CTH 821.A = IBoT 1.30 1–8 (translit. Archi, 1979: 31–32). Archi (1979) discusses other examples of such requests prefaced by a statement of the Hittite king's position as a legitimate appointee of the Stormgod. Also see Güterbock (1954), Hutter (2014: 146), and Singer (2002b: 302).

4 On the inviolable body of high-status males in classical Roman culture, for example, see Walters (1997).

5 CTH 470.96: *Ritual Fragments* = KUB 17.29 ii 8–13. See translations and discussions of Hoffner (1998: 319–321) and Hutter (2014: 145–146).

6 The *Hittite Laws* have quite detailed provisions about property rights and disputes over livestock (Bryce, 2002: 84 ff.), and careful records were kept of boundaries. See further Hoffner (1998).
7 *Funerary Ritual. Days 8–9*: CTH 450.1.1.2.A, §15" = KUB 30.24+ ii 1–4 (translit. and trans. Kapełus, 2011, on KhT). The king also owned agricultural fields in the afterlife. On the tenth day, they plough the ground with several furrows, then burn the plough, representing the duties of the farmer (*Funerary Ritual. Days 10–11*: CTH 450.1.1.3.A, §§2'-3' = KBo 40.178+ i 4'-17').
8 On the significance of boundaries separating civilized and uncivilized space at Hattusa, see Hutter (2014: 138–141).
9 See Hawkins (1998), viewing the image as royal. Simon (2012) argues these boundary images are of the tutelary deity. It should be noted that whether all the images were actually boundary markers has come under dispute. See Ullmann (2014), who suggests that at least some of them mark stopping points along the Hittite army's seasonal itineraries.
10 For the throne at Kizildag, see Plate 236 in Hawkins (2000). Hittite *šarpa-* 'throne' was the name of more than one mountain. Cf. DEUS.MONS.THRONUS = Mt. Sarpa (Forlanini, 1987: CHD Š: 288). One Mt. Sarpa is at Emirgazi, close to Ikona in Lycaonia, another is at Karakuyu (Forlanini, 1987). See Ehringhaus (2005: 49–50) for a description of the monument and the Hieroglyphic Luwian inscription on the latter mountain.
11 The edition of the *Song of Release* (CTH 789) used here is by Neu (1996); trans. Bachvarova in López-Ruiz (2013: 297–298).
12 See CHD (L-N: 191), referring to CTH 540.II.5 = KBo 13.34 iv 17–19 (translit. and trans. Riemschneider, 1970: 28–29, 31, 38).
13 Trans. Bachvarova in López-Ruiz (2013: 298).
14 Forlanini (2010: 118–121), on the other hand, argues that the "father of the king" was Hattusili's uncle by marriage, Labarna I.
15 CTH 8.A = KBo 3.34, §2, i 11–13 (translit. Dardano, 1997: 33). See Bachvarova (2010: 75), comparing the two texts.
16 CTH 8.A, §3, i 11–18 (translit. and trans. Dardano, 1997: 32–33).
17 CTH 8.A, §18, ii 33–35 (translit. and trans. Dardano, 1997: 52–55).
18 Translit. Dardano (1997: 46–49).
19 *AḪI-YA takkaniaš=šaš parḫuš=šuš* (CTH 8.B, §7' = KBo 3.35 8'-9', translit. Dardano, 1997: 38–39), see CHD (P: 147).
20 I use the edition of Sommer and Falkenstein (1938) for *Hattusili's Testament*. I fill in the Hittite with the Akkadian, not marking the lacunae.
21 CTH 19: *Telipinu Edict*, see the trans. of van den Hout in Hallo and Younger (1997: 194–198).
22 In one case, the Hurrian-derived *Ritual of Allaiturahhi*, the dead kings intervene from the underworld to rid the client from fear of lions and snakes and to restore his lordliness, that is, to restore his masculine pride and courage (KBo 12.85+ ii 16–36, iii 34–39, translit. and trans. Haas and Wegner, 1988: 133–134, 139); see Bachvarova (2013: 33–37). Also see *King Lists*: CTH 661.5 = KUB 11.8 + 9 iv 20'-5' (translit. and trans. Nakamura, 2002: 272–273) and Nakamura (1994); Middle Hittite *Ritual for the Sun-goddess of the Earth*: CTH 448.4.1.b.A = KUB 42.94 iv? 15'-20', with D = KUB 7.10 i 9-10 (translit. and trans. Taracha, 2000: 50–53, 70); New Hittite *Substitution Ritual for the King*: CTH 419.A = KUB 24.5 + 9.13 obv. 6' (translit. and trans. García Trabazo, 2010: 32–33)
23 Van den Hout (2002).
24 CTH 736.2 = KUB 28.9 (+) KBo 37.48 rev. r. col. 9'-11' (translit. Klinger, 2000: 158).
25 CTH 820.1.A = KUB 36.110 (translit. and discussion in Hoffner, 2010). Hoffner (2007: 126–128) links this passage to the *Myth of Illuyanka*, in which the goddess

Inara, daughter of the Storm-god, builds herself a house on a cliff (*peruni*) in which she places Hupasiya, her human helper, whom he sees as representing the Hittite king in his relations with the divine protectress (CTH 321.C, §11 = KUB 17.6, i 14–15, translit. Rieken et al. (2010) on KhT; trans Bachvarova in López-Ruiz, 2013: 137). However, Gilan (2013) argues against much of the standard interpretation of the text in which the two versions of the myth are embedded, including that the myth was focused on legitimizing kingship.

26 On the iconography of mountain gods holding up the Storm-god on their bent backs, see Danrey (2006: 209–212).

27 Cf. CTH 393: *Anniwiyani's Ritual* (translit. and trans. Bawanypeck on KhT *sub* CTH 393), in which a man's *lulumi* ('effeminate' or 'feminine') lack of interest or ability to have sexual relations with a woman is to be replaced with the ability to engage in sex with a woman, construed as *innarauwanza*; see Peled (2010: 73–74). It is a standard good thing included in lists of blessings; Puhvel (HED: A, E/I 65–72) argues against a gendered meaning. Tischler (*HEG*: I-K: 360–362) and Kloekhorst (2008: 387) are unsure of the etymology.

28 *Propitiation Ritual for the King's Sister Ziplantawiya*: CTH 443.A, §8" = KBo 15.10+ ii 1–7 (translit. Görke, 2011 on KhT).

29 CTH 377.A, §12' = KUB 24.1+ iii 9'-15' (translit. Kassian and Yakubovich, 2007: 431).

30 The productivity of the land was a particular concern among the Hittites for two reasons: lack of manpower, in part due to the competing demands of military and agriculture (Bryce, 2002: 77–78), and the fact that the central Anatolian plateau was such an unforgiving landscape. Thus, "the state seems to have given much attention to ensuring, through a mixture of sticks and carrots, that all land capable of cultivation was worked to its maximum capacity" (Bryce, 2002: 76).

31 Also see Bachvarova (2006: 126–127) on Hittite kings bringing their cases to the gods for judgment.

32 CTH 628.A = KBo 15.52 + KUB 34.116, with duplicate KBo 20.60; see Bachvarova (2016: 261–262).

33 Bachvarova (2009: 34–35; 2016: 258–262). On the Storm-god of Aleppo dominating the sea, see Bunnens (2006).

34 Hoffner (2007: 124, 126, 136).

35 CTH 321.A, §15 = KBo 3.7 ii 15'-20' (translit. Rieken et al., 2010 on KhT; trans. Bachvarova in López-Ruiz, 2013: 138).

36 Although each of the songs presupposes the action of the previous one, we should be careful not to assume that the cycle was treated as a book with fixed chapters, rather than a flexible text from which episodes could be drawn to be elaborated in a particular performance (Polvani, 2008). Indeed, it is fairly clear that different poets must have been responsible for the different songs, because of differences in style and vocabulary, and various versions of the respective songs differ enough for us to infer that this was an oral-derived genre preserved for us in multiple textualizations (Bachvarova, 2014a).

37 The Hittites also present a precursor to Foucault's notion of *askesis*, self-improvement through self-examination and cultivation of moderation (*sophrosyne*) and self-control (*enkrateia*) (Foucault, 1985: 25–37).

38 Translit. Rieken et al. (2009) on KhT. Also see Beckman (2011) and Bernabé (2009).

39 *Telipinu Proclamation*, CTH 19.II.A, §§9, 21 = KBo 3.1+ i 31, ii 5, 6 (translit. Hoffman, 1984: 18, 26; trans. van den Hout in Hallo and Younger, 1997: 195, 196).

40 Has the scribe slipped here, switching the two gods?

41 *Annals of Hattusili I*, CTH 4.II.A = KBo 10.2 iv 2 (translit. de Martino, 2003: 78). *Pešnatar* is an abstract noun derived from *pešna-* 'penis,' which is etymologically related to Eng. "penis," cf. Kloekhorst (2008: 670).

42 UR.MAḪ *maḫḫan arḫa tarkuwalliškinun* (CTH 4.II.A = KBo 10.2 iii 2, translit. de Martino, 2003: 64).
43 CTH 321.A, §19 = KBo 3.7+ iii 2'; see §21, iii 11'.
44 See Manwell (2007).
45 *Laws*, CTH 292, §§188–200a/*86a (translit. and trans. Hoffner, 1997: 148–158).
46 CTH 264.A, §14 = KUB 13.4 iii 68–83 (translit. and trans. Taggar-Cohen, 2005: 62–63, 81).
47 *Paškuwatti's Ritual*, CTH 406, §§5, 6 = KUB 7.8+, i 35–6, iii 6' (translit. and trans. Mouton, 2011 on KhT). See Peled (2010) on *Anniwiyani's Ritual* (cf. note 27 here) and Miller (2010) on *Paškuwatti's Ritual.*
48 The ritual (CTH 669.9.A, B = KUB 11.20 i 5–21, KUB 11.25 iii 2–30) is discussed by Melchert (2001); on menstrual blood nourishing the fetus see Stol (2000: 14).
49 On the identity of the three other gods, see Bernabé (2009).
50 The reconstruction follows García Trabazo (2002: 168).
51 This insight comes from Campbell (2013).
52 Translit. and trans. on ETCSL, 1.1.1.
53 The Powerful One may be the bigendered Šawuška, whose name means "powerful one" in Hurrian; see Bernabé (2009: 25–26), who, however, translates dKA.ZAL as "Shining-Faced one." Corti and Pecchioli Daddi (2012: 613–616) show that KA.ZAL corresponds to Hittite *walliura-* in a lexical list, and note that the related *walliwalli-* is an epithet of Shawushka/Anzili. Beckman (2011: 28–29) argues that the god is Teššub/Tarhun, but note that the birth of this divinity is referred to in the past tense, so it has already taken place.
54 Corti and Pecchioli Daddi (2012: 615) consider the good place to be a different location, citing §16, A ii 71–5 (trans. Bachvarova in López-Ruiz, 2013: 143), which they argue shows the skull was sewed up again by the Fate-goddesses before the Storm-god is born.
55 A description of a festival for Mt. Hazzi, the location of the Baal's fight against Yam in Ugaritic myth, mentions the Hurrian *Song of the Sea*. Although we know only its title and incipit, it was synopsized in a separate Hurro-Hittite narrative. See Rutherford (2001), discussing KUB 44.7 obv. 11–12; the Hurrian version of the *Song of the Sea*, KUB 45.63; and the synopsis in KUB 33.108.
56 I use the transliteration of Rieken et al. (2009 ff.) *sub* CTH 348. Since my own numbering of the fragments differs from theirs, I cite the passages here by the publication numbers of the fragments. For my analysis of the story see my translation in López-Ruiz (2013: 144–153).
57 KBo 26.70+ i 7–8.
58 The name of his sister is written in the Hittite texts with the Akkadogram *IŠTAR*, but it hides the name of the Hittite goddess Anzili, who corresponds to the Hurrian Šawuška (Wilhelm, 2010; Bachvarova, 2013: 25–29).
59 Two fragrant plant-based substances.
60 KBo 26.72+ iv 20'-30'.
61 See Stefanini (2004: 629).
62 As in Mesopotamia (Stol, 2000: 4–5); cf. CHD (L-N: 315–316, *sub muwa-*), discussing the Hittite use of the Sumerogram A.A.UR 'manliness, virility,' with A here corresponding to Akkadian *mû* 'water.'
63 Translit. by Rieken et al. (2009) on KhT, *sub* CTH 345.
64 For the depictions see Haas (1982: 49–54). Spring goddesses are the consorts of mountain gods (Taracha, 2009: 56). I plan to address apparent exceptions such as Mt. Wasitta (see *Fragments of the Kumarbi Myth*: CTH 346.5.A = KUB 33.118, translit. Rieken et al., 2009ff.; trans. Bachvarova (2014b: 283–284) and Mt. Išhara, discussed by Haas (1982: 99–101) as an example of a mountain

goddess, elsewhere. Danrey (2006) considers the Sumerian goddess Ninhursag to be the exception, but she herself is not a mountain.

65 Some scholars claim Pirwa is called Queen; they are dismissed in RlA *sub Pirwa* by Pecchioli Daddi; cf. *Fragments Naming Pirwa*: CTH 337.1.A = KUB 48.99 (translit. and trans. Rieken et al., 2009 on KhT). Also see Lebrun (1983: 145) on Pirwa as the personification of *peru*.

66 See Gadjimuradov (2004), and cf. the Circassian *Birth of Sawseruquo* (trans. Colarusso, 2002: 52–54), and equivalent tales in other Caucasian languages.

67 CTH 345.3.A, §§2'-3' = KBo 26.65+ i 21'-29'.

68 *Laws*, §126/*23 (translit. Hoffner, 1997: 114–116; see Singer, 1983: 91). On the symbolic importance of the city gate as boundary marker see Miller (2012).

69 CTH 345.1, §21", A iv 44'-48', C = KBo 26.61+ iv 3'-10', D iii 31'-36'.

70 Puhvel in his etymological dictionary compares the two meanings of the Greek term *mēdea*, "mental deliberations, genitals" (HED A, E-I: 468).

71 Discussed by Stol (2000: 1–3).

72 Stol (2000: 5, 38), Gen. 38:10.

73 ETCSL 1.1.13, ll. 250 ff.

74 CTH 345.2, §6" A = KUB 33.87 i 35'-36'.

75 Watkins (1985) has argued that it means "mental force," and is related to Greek *menos*, **men* 'mental operations.' Although other scholars follow a different etymology (**mel*, cf. Gr. *melein* 'to be a care,' HED M: 20–1, HEG L-M: 100, Kloekhorst, 2008: 546), they all agree that the word encompasses both intelligence and a quality proper to men.

76 See Katz (1998: 211–212, with earlier references).

77 See citations in HED (K: 80–1).

78 *CTH* 40.IV.1.A = KBo 5.6. iv 13–15 (translit. del Monte, 2009: 122–123), see Bryce (2005: 178–179).

79 *Annals of Mursili II*: CTH 61.I.A = KBo 3.4 iii 16–17, and cf. KUB 14.15 (translit. Götze, 1933: 70).

80 Del Monte (2010) has shown that this version at least of the *Song of Ullikummi* ends with this tablet.

Bibliography

Archi, A. (1979) "Auguri per il labarna," in *Piero Meriggi dicata*, ed. O. Carruba. Studia Mediterranea 1. Pavia. 27–51.

Bachvarova, M. R. (2005) "Relations between god and man in the Hurro-Hittite Song of Release." *Journal of the American Oriental Society* 125: 45–58.

——— (2006) "Divine justice across the Mediterranean: Hittite arkuwars and the trial scene in Aeschylus' Eumenides." *Journal of Ancient Near Eastern Religions* 6: 123–154.

——— (2009) "Hittite and Greek perspectives on travelling poets, festivals and texts," in *Wandering Poets in Ancient Greek Culture: Travel, Locality and Pan-Hellenism*, eds. R. Hunter and I. C. Rutherford. Cambridge. 23–45.

——— (2010) "The manly deeds of Hattusili I: Hittite admonitory history and didactic epic," in *Epic and History*, eds. K. Raaflaub and D. Konstan. Waltham, MA. 66–85.

——— (2013) "Adapting Mesopotamian myth in Hurro-Hittite rituals at Hattuša: IŠTAR, the underworld, and the legendary kings," in *Beyond Hatti: A Tribute to Gary Beckman*, eds. B. J. Collins and P. Michalowski. Atlanta, GA. 23–44.

——— (2014a) "Hurro-Hittite narrative song as a bilingual oral-derived genre," in *Proceedings of the Eighth International Congress of Hittitology*, Warsaw, 5–9 September 2011, eds. P. Taracha and M. Kapełus. Warsaw. 77–109.

——— (2014b) "Hurro-Hittite stories and Hittite pregnancy and birth rituals," in *Women in the Ancient Near East: A Sourcebook*, ed. M. W. Chavalas London and New York. 272–306.

——— (2016) *From Hittite to Homer: The Anatolian Background of Ancient Greek Epic*. Cambridge.

Beckman, G. (2011) "Primordial obstetrics: 'The Song of Emergence' (CTH 344)," in *Hethitische Literatur: Überlieferungsprozesse, Textstrukturen, Ausdrucksformen und Nachwirken. Akten des Symposiums vom 18. bis 20. February 2010 in Bonn*, eds. M. Hutter and S. Hutter-Braunsar. Alter Orient und Altes Testament 391. Münster. 25–33.

Bernabé, A. (2009) "El extraordinario embarazo de Kumarbi," in *Reconstruyendo el Pasado Remoto: Estudios sobré el Proximo Oriente Antiguo en homenaje a Jorge R. Silva Castillo*, eds. D. A. Barreyra Fracaroli and G. del Olmo Lete. Aula Oreintalis – Supplementa 25. Barcelona. 23–30.

Bryce, T. R. (2002) *Life and Society in the Hittite World*. Oxford and New York.

——— (2005) *The Kingdom of the Hittites*. New edn. Oxford and New York.

Bunnens, G. (2006) *A New Luwian Stele and the Cult of the Storm-god at Til Barsip-Masuwari. Tell Ahmar 2. Leuven*, Paris and Dudley, MA.

Campbell, D. R. M. (2013) "On the theogonies of Hesiod and the Hurrians: An exploration of the dual natures of Teššub and Kumarbi," in *Creation and Chaos: A Reconsideration of Hermann Gunkel's Chaoskampf Hypothesis*, eds. J. Scurlock and R. Beal.Winona Lake, IN. 26–43.

Colarusso, J. (2002) *Nart Sagas from the Caucasus: Myths and Legends from the Circassians, Abazas, Abkhaz, and Ubykhs*. Princeton, NJ.

Corti, C. (2007) "The so-called 'Theogony' or 'Kingship in Heaven': The name of the song." *Studi Micenei ed Egeo-Anatolici* 49: 109–121.

Corti, C. and F. Pecchioli Daddi (2012) "The power in heaven: Remarks on the so-called Kumarbi cycle," in *Organization, Representation, and Symbols of Power in the Ancient Near East: Proceedings of the 54th Rencontre Assyriologique Internationale*, Würzburg, 20–25 July 2008, ed. G. Wilhelm. Winona Lake, IN. 611–618.

Danrey, V. (2006) "L'homme-montagen ou l'itinéraire d'un motif iconographique." *Res Antiquae* 3: 209–217.

Dardano, P. (1997) *L'aneddoto e il racconto in etá antico-Hittita: La cosiddetta "Cronaca di Palazzo."* Rome.

de Martino, S. (2003) *Annali e res gestae antico ittiti*. Studia Mediterranea 12. Pavia.

del Monte, G. F. (2009) *L'opera storiografica di Mursili II re di Hattusa. Vol. I: Le gesta di Suppiluliuma*. Pisa.

——— (2010) "La fine del Canto di Ullikummi." *Orientalia* 79: 140–151.

Ehringhaus, H. (2005) *Götter, Herrscher, Inschriften: Die Felsrelifs der hethitischen Grossreichszeit in der Türkei*. Mainz am Rhein.

Forlanini, M. (1987) "Le mont Šarpa." *Hethitica* 7: 73–87.

——— (2010) "An attempt at recontructing the branches of the Hittite royal family of the Early Kingdom period," in *Pax Hethitica: Studies on the Hittites and Their Neighbours in Honour of Itamar Singer*, eds. Y. Cohen, A. Gilan and J. L. Miller. Studien zu den Boğazköy-Texten 51. Wiesbaden. 115–135.

Foucault, M. (1985) *The Use of Pleasure: Volume 2 of the History of Sexuality*. trans. by R. Hurley. New York.

Gadjimuradov, I. (2004) "Die vulkanische Urheimat der altanatolischen Sukzessions- und Steingeburtsmythen." *Altorientalische Forschungen* 31: 340–357.

García Trabazo, J. V. (2002) *Textos religiosos hititas: Mitos, plegarias y rituales: Edición bilingue*. Madrid.

——— (2010) "CTH 419, Ritual de sustitución real: edicíon crítica y traducción." *Historiae* 7: 27–49.

Gilan, A. (2013) "Once upon a time in Kiškiluša: The dragon-slayer myth in central Anatolia," in *Creation and Chaos: A Reconsideration of Hermann Gunkel's Chaoskampf Hypothesis*, eds. J. Scurlock and R. Beal. Winona Lake, IN. 98–111.

Glover, D. and C. Kaplan (2009) *Genders*. London and New York.

Götze, A. (1933) *Die Annalen des Muršiliš*. Mitteilungen der Vorderasiatisch-Ägyptischen Gesellschaft 38. Darmstadt, reprinted 1967.

Haas, V. (1982) *Hethitische Berggötter und hurritische Steindämonen. Riten, Kulte und Mythen. Eine Einführung in die altkleinasiatischen religiösen Vorstellungen*. Mainz am Rhein.

Haas, V. and I. Wegner (1988) *Die Rituale der Beschwörerinnen* [SAL]*ŠU.GI*. Corpus der hurritischen Sprachdenkmäler I/5. Rome.

Hallo, W. W. and K. L. Younger, Jr. (eds.) (1997) *The Context of Scripture: Vol. I. Canonical Compositions from the Biblical World*. Leiden, New York and Cologne.

Hawkins, J. D. (1998) "Tarkasnawa king of Mira: 'Tarkondemos,' Boğazköy sealings and Karabel." *Anatolian Studies* 48: 1–31.

——— (2000) *Corpus of Hieroglyphic Luwian Inscriptions. Volume I. Inscriptions of the Iron Age*. Untersuchungen zur indogermanischen Sprach- und Kulturwissenschaft 8.1. Berlin and New York.

Hoffman, I. (1984) *Der Erlaß Telipinus*. Texte der Hethiter 11. Heidelberg.

Hoffner, H. A., Jr. (1973) "Incest, sodomy, and bestiality in the ancient Near East," in *Orient and Occident: Essays Presented to Cyrus H. Gordon on the Occasion of His Sixty-Fifth Birthday*, ed. H. A. Hoffner, Jr. Alter Orient und Altes Testament 22. Kevelaer, Neukirchen-Vluyn. 81–90.

——— (1997) *The Laws of the Hittites: A Critical Edition*. Documenta et Monumenta Orientis Antiqui 23. Leiden, New York and Cologne.

——— (1998) "Agricultural perspectives on Hittite laws §167–169," in *III. Uluslararası Hititoloji Kongresi Bildirileri: Çorum 16–22 Eylül 1996 – Acts of the IIIrd International Congress of Hittitology: Çorum, 16–22 September 1996*, eds. S. Alp and A. Süel. Ankara. 319–330.

——— (2007) "A brief commentary on the Hittite Illuyanka myth," in *Studies Presented to Robert D. Biggs*, eds. M. T. Roth, W. Farber, M. Stolper and P. von Bechtolsheim. Assyriological Studies 27. Chicago. 119–140.

——— (2010) "The political antithesis and foil of the Labarna in an Old Hittite text," in *Ipamati kistamati pari tumatimis: Luwian and Hittite Studies Presented to J. David Hawkins on the Occasion of His 70th Birthday*, ed. I. Singer. Tel Aviv. 131–139.

Hutter, M. (2014) "Grenzziehung und Raumbeherrschung in der hethitischen Religion," in *Raumkonzeptionen in antiken Religionen: Beiträge des internationalen Symposiums in Göttingen, 28. und 29. Juni 2012*, ed. K. Rezania. Wiebaden. 135–152.

Kassian, A. and I. Yakubovich (2007) "Muršili II's prayer to Telipinu (CTH 377)," in *Tabularia Hethaeorum: Hethitologische Beiträge Silvin Košak zum 65. Geburtstag*, eds. D. Groddek and M. Zorman. Dresdener Beiträge zur Hethitologie 25. Wiesbaden. 423–455.

Katz, J. T. (1998) "Testimonia ritus Italici: Male genitalia, solemn declarations, and a new Latin sound law." *Harvard Studies in Classical Philology* 98: 183–217.

Klinger, J. (2000) "'So Weit und breit wie das Meer. . .' – das Meer in Texten hattischer Provenienz," in *The Asia Minor Connexion: Studies on the Pre-Greek Languages in Memory of Charles Carter*, ed. Y. L. Arbeitman. Leuven. 151–172.

Kloekhorst, A. (2008) *Etymological Dictionary of the Hittite Inherited Lexicon*. Leiden and Boston.

Lebrun, R. (1983) "Réflexions relatives à la complémentarité entre l'archéologie et la philologie hittites," in *Archéologie et religions de l'Anatolie ancienne. Melanges en l'honneur du professeur Paul Naster*, eds. R. Donceel and R. Lebrun. Homo Religiosus 10. Louvain-la-Neuve. 135–156.

López-Ruiz, C. (2013) *Gods, Heroes, and Monsters: A Sourcebook of Greek, Roman, and Near Eastern Myths in Translation*. New York and Oxford.

Manwell, E. (2007) "Gender and masculinity," in *A Companion to Catullus*, ed. M. B. Skinner. Malden, MA. 111–128.

Melchert, H. C. (2001) "A Hittite fertility rite?," in *Akten des IV. Internationalen Kongresses für Hethitologie. Würzburg, 4.–8. Oktober 1999*, ed. G. Wilhelm. Studien zu den Boğazköy-Texten 45. Wiesbaden. 404–409.

Miller, J. L. (2010) "Paskuwatti's Ritual: Remedy for impotence or antidote to homosexuality?" *Journal of Ancient Near Eastern Religions* 10: 83–89.

——— (2012) "The (city-)gate and the projection of royal power in Ḫatti," in *Organization, Representation, and Symbols of Power in the Ancient Near East: Proceedings of the 54th Rencontre Assyriologique Internationale, Würzburg, 20–25 July 2008*, ed. G. Wilhelm. Winona Lake, IN. 675–685.

Nakamura, M. (1994) "The cult of deceased kings in the New Hittite kingdom: Some comments on the 'sacrifice lists for the deceased kings.'" *Oriento* 37: 35–51.

——— (2002) *Das hethitische nuntarriyašḫa-Fest*. Leiden.

Neu, E. (1996) *Das hurritische Epos der Freilassung I. Untersuchungen zu einem hurritisch-hethitischen Textensemble aus Hattuša*. Studien zu den Boğazköy-Texten 32. Wiesbaden.

Peled, I. (2010) "Expelling the demon of effeminacy: Anniwiyani's ritual and the question of homosexuality in Hittite thought." *Journal of Ancient Near Eastern Religions* 10: 69–81.

Polvani, A. M. (2008) "The god Eltara and the Theogony." *Studi Micenei ed Egeo-Anatolici* 50: 617–624.

Riemschneider, K. K. (1970) *Babylonische Geburtsomina in hethitischer Übersetzung*. Studien zu den Boğazköy-Texten 9. Wiesbaden.

Rutherford, I. C. (2001) "The Song of the Sea (ŠA A.AB.BA SÌR): Thoughts on KUB 45.63," in *Akten des IV. Internationalen Kongresses für Hethitologie. Würzburg, 4–8. Oktober 1999*, ed. G. Wilhelm. Studien zu den Boğazköy-Texten 45. Wiesbaden. 598–609.

Simon, Z. (2012) "Hethitische Felsreliefs als Repräsentation der Macht: Einige ikonographische Bemerkungen," in *Organization, Representation, and Symbols of Power in the Ancient Near East: Proceedings of the 54th Rencontre Assyriologique Internationale, Würzburg, 20–25 July 2008*, ed. G. Wilhelm. Winona Lake, IN. 687–697.

Singer, I. (1983) *The Hittite KI.LAM Festival: Part I*. Studien zu den Boğazköy-Texten 27. Wiesbaden.

——— (2002a) "The Cold Lake and Its Great Rock," in *Gregor Giorgadze von Kollegen und ehemaligen Studenten zum 75. Geburtstag gewidmet*, ed. L. Gordesiani. Tblisi. 128–132.

——— (2002b) "'Kantuzili the priest and the birth of personal prayer," in Piotr Taracha (ed.), *Silva Anatolica: Anatolian Studies Presented to Maciej Popko on the Occasion of his 65th Birthday*. Warsaw, pp. 301–313.

Sommer, F. and A. Falkenstein (1938) *Die hethitisch-akkadishe Bilingue des Ḫattušili I. (Labarna II.)*. Abhandlungen der Bayerischen Akademie der Wissenschaften, N. F. 16. Munich.

Stefanini, R. (2004) "The catch line of Ḫedammu 10 (KUB 33.103, Rs.)," in *Šarnikzel: Hethitologische Studien zum Gedenken an Emil Orgetorix Forrer (19.02.1894–10.01.1986)*, eds. D. Groddek and S. Rößle. Dresdner Beiträge zur Hethitologie 10. Dresden. 627–630.

Stol, M. (2000) *Birth in Babylonia and the Bible: Its Mediterranean Setting*. Cuneiform Monographs 14. Groningen.

Taggar-Cohen, A. (2005) *Hittite Priesthood*. Texte der Hethiter 26. Heidelberg.

Taracha, P. (2000) *Ersetzen und Entsühnen: Das mittelhethitische Ersatzritual für den Großkönig Tuthalija (CTH *448.4) und verwandte Texte*. Culture and History of the Ancient Near East 5. Leiden, Boston, Cologne.

——— (2009) *Religions of Second Millennium Anatolia*. Dresdner Beiträge zur Hethitologie 27. Wiesbaden.

Ullmann, L. Z. (2014) "The significance of place: Rethinking Hittite rock reliefs in relation to the topography of the land of Hatti," in *Of Rocks and Water: Towards an Archaeology of Place*, ed. Ö. Harmanşah. Oxford and Philadelphia. 101–127.

van den Hout, T. P. J. (2002) "Tombs and memorials: The (Divine) Stone-House and Ḫegur reconsidered," in *Recent Developments in Hittite Archaeology and History: Papers in Memory of Hans G. Güterbock*, eds. K. A. Yener and H. A. Hoffner, Jr. Winona Lake, IN. 73–92.

Walters, J. (1997) "Invading the Roman body: Manliness and impenetrability in Roman thought," in *Roman Sexualities*, eds. J. P. Hallett and M. B. Skinner. Princeton, NJ. 29–43.

Watkins, C. (1985) "Greek menoināai: A dead metaphor." *International Journal of American Linguistics* 51: 614–618.

Wilhelm, G. (2010) "Die Lesung des Namens der Göttin *IŠTAR-li*," in *Investigationes Anatolicae: Gedenkschrift für Erich Neu*, eds. J. Klinger, E. Rieken and C. Rüster. Studien zu den Boğazöy-Texten 52. Wiesbaden. 337–344.

4 Female trouble and troubled males

Roiled seas, decadent royals, and Mesopotamian masculinities in myth and practice

J. S. Cooper

A discussion of masculinity in ancient Mesopotamia risks becoming very large indeed.[1] For societies as determinedly patriarchal as those documented in Mesopotamia from earliest times, reams could be filled, and have been, discussing, for example, the virtues of the ideal king. (Rulership, it should be noted here, was never exercised by women, unless one accepts the single and surely fictional example of the tapstress who reigned in Early Dynastic Kish according to the so-called Sumerian King List).[2] An early Sumerian royal epithet makes the identification of kingship and masculinity explicit: nita kal-ga, "mighty male." Interestingly, this first gets translated into Akkadian as just *dannum*, "mighty," not, I think, because Akkadian was less androcentric in its usage, but because unlike Sumerian, Akkadian has grammatical gender, and *dannum* alone signifies the masculinity of the ruler to whom it is applied.[3]

Rather than focus on the virtues of males in authority in general, whether public or domestic, I would like to examine some instances where masculinity is implicitly or explicitly called into question. In doing so, I will not consider the special case of Inana/Ishtar, warrior goddess who is able to change masculinity to femininity, nor the various marginal and cult personages who to varying degrees are so afflicted. Finally, my subject will be idealized masculinity, not simply valorized modes of male behavior. The loyalty and obedience of a male slave, for example, is not the kind of masculinity I will pursue.

First, however, it is probably necessary to recall that sexual difference, male and female, was recognized in the earliest artifacts from Babylonia,[4] and birth incantations going back to the middle of the third millennium impose gendered destinies on the newborn: boy babies are given or shown weapons, while girl babies are presented with spindles and pins.[5] Such gendered destinies are well documented both textually and artifactually. When, in the Sumerian myth "Enki and the World Order," Enki reminds the ever dissatisfied Inana that she can change male warriors into women, one part of that transformation occurs when she puts spindle and pin into a warrior's hands.[6] And a Pseudepigraphic letter of a high Ur III official to king Shulgi includes the following description of the pastoral peoples in the peripheral provinces: "As for their men and women, their men go wherever they please, and their women, holding spindle and pin, travel wherever they please."[7]

Before continuing, I should disclose my own predilections on the fraught questions of sexual and gender differences. I have grown more willing to acknowledge the power of nature and recognize the limits of nurture. The similarity of distinct basic gender roles in the vast majority of known cultures must to a large extent be determined by biological universals: women give birth and nurse, and men are, on average, somewhat larger and more muscular than women, giving them significant advantages in wielding weapons for the hunt and war. This is not intended either to justify or to apologize for the horrors of patriarchy, only to try to understand how those horrors may have developed out of a very early gendered division of labor based on sexual difference.

It all began, of course, "when on high heaven had not been designated, down below terra firma[8] had not been named," with the initial couple, Tiamat and Apsu. Tiamat, female, is at once the ocean, a somewhat anthropomorphic wife and mother, and a terrible dragon. Apsu, male, is fresh water, and a cranky husband and father. *Enuma Elish*, the so-called Babylonian Creation Epic, begins by presenting the forebears of the god Marduk, who descend from this initial couple, culminating in Marduk's father Ea.[9] Unmentioned other deities also came into being, some of whom were associated with Marduk's ancestors, while others lived within or alongside the first couple. The gods on the side of Marduk's line were boisterous, roiling Tiamat and disturbing the sleep of the gods on her side. Apsu and his sidekick approached Tiamat with a plan to do away with the offenders, but Tiamat was horrified: "What? Shall we put an end to what we created? Their behavior may be most noisome, but we should bear it in good part" (I 45f.). The good mother, indulging her brats, resists their father's desire to inflict the ultimate punishment.[10]

Apsu and his buddy proceeded in spite of her objections, but Ea – god of magic, after all – put Apsu to sleep with a spell, killed him and founded his own dwelling on Apsu's carcass. Ea then begot Marduk, "a hero at birth . . . a mighty one from the beginning" (I 88), made more perfect and mighty by his grandfather Anu, who also made the four winds as a toy for him. Playing with his new toy, Marduk agitated Tiamat's insides, and again the gods therein were disturbed and unable to sleep. The sleepless gods confronted Tiamat and chastised her for standing by earlier when her husband, Apsu, was killed: "As for us . . . you do not love us! . . . Lift this unremitting yoke, let us sleep! . . . give them" – the boisterous gods – "what they deserve!" (I 120, 123)

This time, Tiamat agreed, and prepared for battle, deploying "serpents, dragons, hairy hero-men, lion monsters, lion men, scorpion men, mighty demons, fish men, bull men, bearing unsparing arms, fearing no battle" (I 141–144). Hearing of these preparations, a frightened Ea approached his grandfather Anshar: "Tiamat our mother has grown angry with us" (II 11), and he described hostile Tiamat and her fearsome host. Anshar blamed it all on Ea for killing Apsu, but Ea promised to subdue the new threat as he did the old. Yet, when he sought out Tiamat, "he stopped, horror-stricken, then turned back" (II 106), reporting to Anshar that his spell was impotent against her. "Her strength is enormous, she is utterly terrifying, she is reinforced with a host, none can come out against her." But then, oddly, he added, "My father, do not despair, send another to her, a woman's force may be very great, but it cannot match a man's" (II 115f.).[11] This, after admitting that she was more than a match for *him*!

Anshar was furious, and summoned Anu, who was likewise unsuccessful, and repeated Ea's words about a woman being no match for a man. Anshar and the gods reacted to Anu's failure with stunned silence, and the stage was set for the advent of their savior, Marduk. Anshar was overjoyed to see him, and Marduk declared his readiness to battle Tiamat. Again, there is a curious reference to her gender: "What man is it who has sent forth his battle against you? Why, Tiamat, a woman, comes out against you to arms!" (II 143f.).[12] Despite this macho deprecation of Tiamat's martial abilities, Marduk immediately demanded and got the assembly of gods to make him their supreme leader, and they gave him "unopposable weaponry" (IV 30) for his task. Marduk fashioned and armed himself with bow and arrow, adding mace, thunderbolts, fire, battle net, and the four winds that Anu had given him, plus seven more winds of his own making. Armored and holding his great Deluge-bow (see below), he rode forth on his storm-demon chariot pulled by four fierce steeds. Just in case, he, too, had prepared a magic spell and was carrying an antidote to Tiamat's venom.

Like his father and grandfather before him, he panicked when confronted by Tiamat and her host. Tiamat tried to rattle him even more, the text tells us, with "falsehood" and "lies" (IV 72; feminine wiles!); she suggested that the gods accompanying Marduk did not really support him. Marduk accused her of deceit, and of being an unnatural mother, willing to kill her own children. Then, he suggested that they engage in one-on-one combat. At that, "She was beside herself, she turned into a maniac, Tiamat shrieked aloud, in a passion, her frame shook all over, down to the ground" (IV 88f.), and she recited incantations and spells. Marduk defeated and killed her, using not spells as his father and grandfather had attempted to do, but rather weapons: battle net, winds, bow and arrow.

All this has been to demonstrate the very odd discourse on masculinity that permeates the story of the conflict with and defeat of Tiamat, the dragon lady cum oceanic chaos monster. Why, after describing the ferocious terror of Tiamat and her host, and admitting their own impotence when confronting her, why do Ea and then Anu predict that some other god will defeat her, because "a woman's force may be very great, but it cannot match a man's"? What kind of masculinity might Ea and Anu be invoking, masculinity that by their own admission they lack? Was there anything about

Tiamat's womanhood that made her vulnerable despite her ferocity and her monstrous host? Was there something that Ea and Anu knew they lacked, but some other male possessed, that was certain to defeat Tiamat?

I cannot agree with Harris (2000: chap. 5), who attributes the failure of Ea and Anu to old age (although I can certainly sympathize),[13] nor with Metzler (2002), who sees these passages as constitutive of the power relationships between the sexes. Rather, *Enuma Elish*, more than most Mesopotamian myth, is shot through with gender norms from the patriarchal society of the author that seem to work against the story being told. When Ea returned to tell Anshar that Tiamat's "strength is enormous, she is utterly terrifying, reinforced with a host, none can come out against her" (II 87f.), followed by the remark that a woman was no match for a man, and he should send someone else, Anshar turned to Anu. But he did not tell Anu to act forcefully; rather, as if responding to a hysterical female, he told Anu to "soothe her feelings, let her heart be eased . . . say something by way of entreaty to her, so that she be pacified" (II 100, 102).[14] It is as if Anshar, once he has been reassured that the threat is female, thinks she can be disarmed by a little sweet talk from Anu. Even Anshar's initial response to Marduk vastly underestimates what will be needed: "Go, son, knower of all wisdom, bring Tiamat to rest with your sacral spell!" (II 149f.).

The failures of Ea and Anu are designed to build up to Marduk's ultimate triumph over Tiamat, but the reassurance that Tiamat, a woman, is no match for a man, an assertion supported even by Marduk himself, seems to diminish Marduk's accomplishment. Yet Marduk was fully aware of what would be necessary to subdue Tiamat. Although he too was armed with spells, he also had, unlike his predecessors, a battle chariot and real weapons, especially his bow. And it is with these weapons, not with spells, that he slew Tiamat. Real men, men who are more than a match for the woman Tiamat, the text seems to tell us, use real weapons in battle, and the battlefield, as we know from Sumerian texts, was the ki nam-nita, "the locus of masculinity."[15]

That Marduk's masculinity derived from his weapons, equipment that neither Ea nor Anu possessed, is supported by a late Assyrian ritual commentary, explaining that "The king, who opens the vat in the race, is Marduk, who [defeat]ed Tiamat with his penis."[16] *Enuma Elish* is very clear about the defeat of Tiamat: Marduk forced her mouth open with wind and shot an arrow into it; the arrow penetrated her insides and pierced her heart (IV 95–103). The arrow was shot from the bow that Marduk himself made just prior to setting out against Tiamat: "He made the bow, appointed it his weapon" (IV 35). The epithet "his weapon" is used only of the bow and the Deluge in *Enuma Elish*, the latter called "his great weapon," and once simply "his weapon." Context strongly implies that the Deluge (*abūbu*) is a name for Marduk's bow: In IV 49 he carries the Deluge-weapon into his battle chariot, and in IV 75 he raised it as he taunted Tiamat. In VI 125 the Deluge is Marduk's signature weapon, which he used to defeat (*kamû*) his forefathers' enemies, using the same verb (*kamû*) used to describe the ultimate effect of Marduk's bowshot on Tiamat in IV 103.[17] The centrality of the bow to Marduk's identity in *Enuma Elish* is made explicit when Anu praises it before the assembled gods and transforms it into a heavenly body (VI 82–91).[18]

As discussed in Chapter 2 of this volume, the bow is a well-known metaphor for the penis,[19] and thus the Assyrian ritual commentary was concretizing the metaphor, but by so doing it was acknowledging the primary importance of Marduk's masculinity in his defeat of Tiamat.[20] Unlike Ea and Anu, Marduk fought not just with cleverness and spells, but with real weapons, which made him masculine, able to vanquish Tiamat and overcome "a woman's strength," which "cannot match a man's."

The fateful confrontation between Marduk and Tiamat (IV 65–104) began with Tiamat casting a spell and trying to shake Marduk's confidence. Marduk responded by holding aloft his mighty Deluge-bow in what seems like both an apotropaic and admonitory gesture. He taunted her with accusations that speak directly to her femininity: She is deceitful, she is an unnatural mother, and she has married inappropriately. Gender played a role, too, in her hysterical and quasi-orgasmic reaction to Marduk: "She was beside herself, she turned into a maniac, Tiamat shrieked aloud, in a passion, her frame shook all over down to the ground" (IV 88–90).[21] And the only thing she did in self-defense was to recite spells, exactly what Ea and Anu – both lacking Marduk's masculinity – had done to no effect. Then Marduk attacked, shooting an arrow into her mouth and penetrating her insides. If we keep in mind the phallic symbolism of bow and arrow, and the homology of mouth and vagina,[22] the sexuality of the scene is unmistakable. Marduk's subjugation of Tiamat (whom he later uses for his own purposes) is both martial and sexual.[23]

Thus, the image of Tiamat as only a woman enhances the portrayal of Marduk as mighty male, even as it subverts the image of Tiamat as a chaos monster whom only Marduk, made king of the gods, is able to subdue. Yet, we never see the valor of Ishtar, the woman warrior of the Mesopotamian pantheon, diminished because she is female, nor the demon Lamashtu's terror ameliorated by referring to her gender.[24] The emphasis on Tiamat's gender and the strange portrayal of major deities impugning their own masculinity are artifacts of *Enuma Elish*'s peculiar patriarchal perspective, peculiar because it doesn't impose itself on other Mesopotamian mythological texts, even if it may accurately reflect contemporary social norms. As others have noted, this same perspective is seen further on in the story, where Marduk and Ea manage to create humankind without the benefit of a mother-goddess. Indeed, except for Tiamat and the briefest mention of Ea's spouse Damkina, *Enuma Elish* is entirely bereft of identifiable females. The awkward presence of the gender issue in *Enuma Elish* may well be an artifact of a western origin of the motif of god vs. sea: The sea is masculine in the west, and it is only in Mesopotamia, where the sea in Akkadian is feminine, that the motif would present opponents of opposite sexes.

Marduk, heroic warrior, used his victory to persuade the gods to build him a great city, Babylon, and a grand dwelling, his temple Esagila (V 117–155; VI 45–65). If the battlefield was "the locus of masculinity," the ideal Mesopotamian man returned from battle to his urban home and family, without diminishing that masculinity in any way. However, in "City Bread and Bread Baked in Ashes," a short article written in 1967, Reiner pointed out that although cuneiform literature tends to see as superior "high-level urban culture, there runs an opposite trend, which exalts the freedom of the wandering nomad and despises the effeminate life of the Mesopotamian cities. . . . This way of life seeks its virtues in the manly occupations of wars and raids; it boasts of hardships, and finds its rewards in the free and unfettered life of the highway."[25] Her prime example comes from the *Erra Epic*, which I cite from Foster's translation:[26]

> . . . Up, do your duty!
> Why have you been sitting in the city like a feeble old man,
> Why sitting at home like a helpless child?
> Shall we eat woman food, like non-combatants?
> Have we turned timorous and trembling, as if we can't fight?
> Going to the field for the young and vigorous is like to a very feast,
> But the noble who stays in the city can never eat enough.
> His people will hold him in low esteem, he will command no respect,
> How could he threaten a campaigner?
> However well developed is the strength of the city dweller,
> How could he possibly best a campaigner?[27]
> However toothsome city bread, it holds nothing to the campfire loaf,
> However sweet fine beer, it holds nothing to water from a skin,
> The terraced palace holds nothing to the wayside sleeping spot.

This topos of the superiority of life on campaign and the salutary effects of roughing it is well known from Mari, and Reiner could have cited the letter from Shamshi-Adad (eighteenth century BC) to his son and viceroy at Mari, Yasmakh-Adad, in which the former berated the latter: "Your brother has been victorious here, while you lie around there among the women. Now then, when you go to Qatna with the army, be a man! (*awīlāt*) Just as your brother has made a great name for himself, so you, too, make a great name for yourself in the campaign against Qatna!"[28] To be a man meant to be successful on the battlefield, and more particularly, to prefer life on campaign to staying at home, lying around the harem. J.-M. Durand doesn't think that Shamshi-Adad was accusing his son of debauchery,[29] but rather of staying at home and being inactive, living the life of a woman. Yet Shamshi-Adad in another letter characterized Yasmakh-Adad's court as a place of "debauchery, taverns and entertainment,"[30] and in one letter implied that his son is too fond of alcohol and fine food.[31] Yasmakh-Adad endeavored to acquire musicians of a sort that even his father didn't have,[32] and musicians actually seemed to prefer the posh working conditions at Mari to the those of the more austere court of Shamshi-Adad. This all suggests that Yasmakh-Adad was an esthete who decidedly did not measure up to his father's standard of masculinity. So refined was Yasmakh-Adad's taste that he even wanted his father to send him a scribe who knew some Sumerian, but his father – ever pointing out the hapless son's inadequacies – told him to learn Amorite first![33]

In 1992, Marello reprised Reiner's theme (without mentioning her treatment) in his "Vie nomade," as part of a discussion of a remarkable letter he published there. One Amorite sheikh was criticizing another for not joining him to campaign with Zimrilim of Mari:[34]

> You prefer eating, drinking and sleeping to going with me. Staying inactive and not getting tan! As for me, I assure you that I've never stayed at home for a whole day without moving around! Until I go out for some air, I feel smothered . . . Tell me, why would I need to put you down? Perhaps because neither hot nor cold wind has battered your face. You're unworthy of your race![35] At the very place where your father and mother first saw your face when you dropped from her vagina, vaginas have received you, and you know of nothing else!

The writer then held himself up as a positive example: he is so valiant and has escaped death so often that, in his escapes from death, he's like the god Dumuzi! This letter is much more explicit than Shamshi-Adad's letters. It is not just women who are evoked in criticism, but vaginas! Twice! The recipient's masculinity is thereby questioned unambiguously.

In his discussion of the letter, Marello referred to the Erra passage central to Reiner's article, and also cited a wonderful passage from the then still unpublished *Epic of Zimrilim*:[36]

> Until the king attained his goal,
> And made the land of Idamaraṣ kneel at his feet,
> He drank only water from waterskins.
> Ranging among the troops, he experiences every care.
> Their sorties are like those of great hunters,
> As the onager eats straw on the plains,
> His men ate (raw) flesh,
> They took heart and grew in strength.
> Zimrilim goes at their head, like a battle standard,
> Turning 'round, he gives courage to those who have none:
> "Be strong, press forward!
> The enemy will see how well trained you are!"

According to Marello, "l'idéal nomade est . . . une conception virile de l'existence. L'aspect sauvage et inconfortable de l'existence est la marque de l'homme d'action, du guerrier,"[37] and Durand, also seemingly not cognizant of Reiner's article, suggested that it is exactly this "idéal de vie de l'homme amorrite" that one finds echoed in the much later *Erra Epic*.[38]

But if an Amorite sheikh could define himself as man solely in terms of combat skills and outdoorsiness, much more was expected of Yasmakh-Adad, son of the great monarch of all Northern Mesopotamia. In fact, most of the criticism from his father had to do with the son's apparent inability to administer properly both his realm and his own estate. His masculinity was questioned most frequently not in terms of masculine vs. feminine, but rather in terms of mature vs. immature.

> For how long must we continue to give you directions? Are you a child, aren't you an adult (*eṭlēt*)? Don't you have hair on your cheek? For how long will you still not manage your household? Don't you see your brother, who manages vast armies? So you should manage your palace and your household![39]

Another time, his father complains:

> Are you a child? Don't you have hair on your cheek? Despite being physically mature (*ina lalīka*), you still haven't set up a household! You're behaving like a pauper! Your households in Shubat-Enlil and Ekallatum are abandoned! . . . Besides your household at Shubat-Enlil, the one at Mari is certainly shaky.[40]

For his part, Yasmakh-Adad always replied that his father's animosity toward him was being provoked by certain courtiers who disliked him and had undermined his father's trust in him. After all, his father, he wrote, "installed me in my position, and by his orders determined my duties."[41] Yet, Yasmakh-Adad did own up to one of his alleged shortcomings: "I'm learning to speak Amorite, really!"[42]

We see then, that masculinity, as defined by Shamshi-Adad, was to behave in a manner befitting an adult male royal: exhibiting skills on the battlefield and in governance, keeping one's own estates in order, and not being too enamored of the arts, fine living, and the enticements of the harem. Being a man was not to be womanly or too attached to women, but most often it was not to be a child, as Durand has emphasized.[43] The two deficient conditions – associating with women and being immature – overlap, since children grew up in the harem, surrounded by females. But it is interesting to note that women were evoked in the Mari material only in contrast to battlefield prowess, when Yasmah-Adad was encouraged to make a name for himself in the campaign against Qatna, or the Amorite sheikh was castigated for preferring his comfortable life at home to the rough life of a soldier. Similarly, the *Enuma Elish* material revolved around assumed male superiority in battle, an assumption that underlies certain curses on Assyrian monuments and treaties of the eighth–seventh centuries BC:

> If Mati'-ilu sins against this treaty with Aššur-nerari, king of Assyria, may Mati'-ilu become a prostitute, his soldiers women, may they receive [a gift] in the square of their cities like any prostitute . . . may Mati'-ilu's (sex) life be that of a mule, his wives extremely old; may Ištar, the goddess of men, the mistress of women, take away their bow, bring them to shame.[44]

> May they (the gods) spin you around like a spindle-whorl, may they make you like a woman before your enemy.[45]

> Whoever removes this stele from its place, erases my name and writes his name . . . May Ištar, mistress of battle and combat, make his masculinity (*zikrūssu*) womanly (*sinnišāniš*) and make him sit bound at his enemy's feet.[46]

To be a man, in contrast to a woman, meant, above all, to be a competent warrior.[47]

In fact, there is relatively little explicit discourse on masculinity as such in Mesopotamia, whether in terms of gender appropriate or age appropriate behavior, perhaps because patriarchal norms were so well defined and well entrenched that explicit statements were unnecessary, except in the cases of the marginal figures that are discussed in this volume by Marti Nissinen. That such discourse appears in *Enuma Elish* in ways that subvert the narrative and intention of the composition perhaps reveals the mythographer's discomfort with the gender of the hero Marduk's opponent, yet, in other compositions, the martial Ishtar never seems to provoke such discomfort. Shamshi-Adad's treatment of his son is the rare example in writing of what must have certainly been said orally to many sons, as it still is.

Let me close by noting that despite the dominance of patriarchy, there is not a lot of evidence for misogyny in ancient Mesopotamia. The most blatant examples come from Early Dynastic Sumerian proverbs (Alster 1991–92) and later Sumerian women's dialogues, and the much later Akkadian ritual texts ironically referred to as "Love Lyrics" (Foster 2005 IV.28). Sexual prowess and sexual aggression were never components of Mesopotamian masculinity; neither male deities nor kings are praised for their sexual performance.[48] Examples of rape in Sumerian literature – I can't think of any in Akkadian – always end badly for the rapist. Sexual punishments in law are always for sexual offenses only, and rape is never mentioned among the grisly punishments meted out by Assyrian conquerors.[49] If we could generalize at all, we might say that Mesopotamian men were terribly patriarchal, but not especially phallocentric.

Notes

1 I would like to thank P. Jones, P. Michalowski, B. Pongratz-Leisten, G. Rubio, K. Sonik, and I. Zsolnay for their comments.
2 Glassner (2004: 123). Note, too, that omens of this woman ruler are always negative (e.g. Leichty (1970: 8); Nougayrol (1966: 91).
3 The literal Akkadian translation of nita kal-ga, *zikaru dannu*, is used mainly by later Assyrian kings, as is *zikaru qardu*, "valiant male," and, rarely, *zikrāku*, "I am virile" (Seux 1967: 377f.).
4 E.g. Strommenger (1964: 10–12).
5 E.g. Krebernik (1984: 36 and 44f). (Fara with OB parallels); see Stol (2000: 63).
6 Contra Black et al. (2004: 224); see my forthcoming edition.
7 Michalowski (2011: 294) (my translation).
8 "Terra firma" is an attempt to render the rare *ammatu*, equated with *dannatu* and glossed *kīma erṣeti* (CAD s.v. *ammatu* B). How nice to discover that the much missed and fondly remembered J. Bottéro had resorted to a similar solution! (Bottéro and Kramer 1989: 604).
9 For everything *Enuma Elish* see Lambert (2013); Kämmerer and Metzler (2012); also Talon (2005). The English translation is cited after Foster (2005), except for my translation of I 1f. above.
10 On the image here of good mother but stern father, see Metzler (2002: 401).
11 *abī ē tuštāniḫ tūr šupurši / emūq sinništi lu dunnuna ul māla ša zikri.*
12 *ayyu zikri tāḫazašu ušēṣika / u Tiāmat ša sinnišat i'ârka ina kakki.*
13 Their failure is a narrative necessity, emphasizing the uniqueness of Marduk among all the other gods.
14 *šupšiḫ kabtatušma libbuš lippuš / . . . / amāt unnīni atmešimma šī lippašḫa.*
15 Most explicitly in *Gilgamesh, Enkidu and the Netherworld* 228 and 236: ki nam-nita-a-ke$_4$ mè-a nu-un-šub "He did not fall in battle, at the locus of masculinity" (Gadotti 2014).
16 Livingstone (1989: No. 37:18).
17 In Sennacherib's description of the scene on the akitu-building doors, Assur (= Marduk) is depicted setting out to fight Tiamat "as he carries the bow, riding in a chariot, the Deluge that he [assig]ned?" (Pongratz-Leisten 1994: 207–209; Frahm 1997: 222–224). Despite the ambiguous syntax, the Deluge can't be the chariot, so must be the bow that Marduk in *Enuma Elish* "appointed" as his weapon.
18 Ninurta, on whom the Marduk of *Enuma Elish* is modeled, carries his Deluge-bow (OB giš.ban a-ma-ru; NA giš.ban a-má-uru$_5$ = *qaštu [abūbi]*) in *Angim* 142, although in *Angim* 141, "Deluge of battle" is the name of his 50-headed mace (Cooper 1978).
19 Hoffner (1966); Hillers (1973); Zsolnay (2010: 393); Hepner (2010: 142–155). The penis in the ritual commentary was identified as Marduk's bow already by V. Horowitz (2005: 53 n.8), and is to be preferred to the interpretation in Pomponio (1997: 70 n. 2), following Livingstone (1991) (penis = seeder plow).
20 Metzler (2002: 400) notes that the slaying of Tiamat by Marduk becomes a mythological image of the discourse on masculinity in *Enuma Elish*.
21 *maḫḫūtiš ītemi ušanni ṭēnša / issima Tiāmat šitmuriš elīta / šuršiš malmališ itrura išdāšu.* The same word, *šitmuriš* ("in a passion") is used to describe Nergal and Ereshkigal when they jump into bed (Gurney 1960: 126:36). Note Inana's orgasm in a Sumerian love song: lú si-ga-gin$_7$ mu-na-dè-gub / ki-ta tuk$_4$-e-da si-a mu-na-ni-gar "As if dumb struck I moved toward him, trembling below, I pushed quietly to him" (Sefati 1998: 152:15f.; Cooper 1997: 94).
22 Malul (2002: 248–249).
23 See Malul (2002) Chap. 7, "Carnal Knowledge: Controlling the Unknown in Woman."

24 The threat of Tiamat and her ultimate defeat by Marduk is based upon the earlier Anzu myth, in which the mythical eagle Anzu is defeated by Ninurta. Nowhere there do the other gods who refuse to confront Anzu suggest that all will be well in the end because "a bird is no match for a god."
25 Reiner (1967: 118–119).
26 Foster (2005: 883f).
27 Note the similarity to *Enuma Elish*: "A woman's strength may be very great, but it cannot match a man's."
28 ARM 1 69+ = Durand (1998) (LAPO 17) No. 452.
29 Durand (1997) (LAPO 16) 137f.
30 ARM 1 28 = Durand (1997) (LAPO 16) No. 2.
31 ARM 1 52 = Durand (1997) (LAPO 16) No. 1. See also an Old Assyrian merchant's reproof of a subordinate: "Amurili should know how to show respect! He should not always be thinking of food and drink! He should be a man!" (Michel 2001 [LAPO 19] No. 354).
32 ARM 5 76 = Durand (1997) (LAPO 16) No. 10 = Ziegler (2007: 33).
33 Ziegler and Charpin (2007).
34 A. 1146 (Marello 1992 115–125) = Durand 1997 (LAPO 16) No. 38.
35 Alternative translation: Are you wearing someone else's balls? See the discussions of Marello and Durand ad loc.
36 Marello (1992: 121f.); now published in Guichard (2014: 19–20, iii, 7–18).
37 Marello (1992: 121).
38 Durand (1997): (LAPO 16) 138.
39 ARM 1 73, 108 = Durand (1997): (LAPO 16) Nos. 29, 34.
40 ARM 1 61 = Durand (1997) (LAPO 16) No. 35.
41 ARM 1 108 = Durand (1997) (LAPO 16) No. 34.
42 Charpin and Ziegler (2007): 61:10.
43 Durand (1997) (LAPO 16) 137f.
44 Parpola and Watanabe (1988: 12: 8–14).
45 Ibid. 56: 616A–617. For similar curses already in MA royal inscriptions, and the problem of *sinnišānu* here, see Zsolnay (2010: 394–401).
46 Leichty (2011: No. 98: 53–56).
47 Cf. the Babylonian and Assyrian royal epithet *zikaru qardu* "valiant male," cited in n. 3.
48 In Sumerian royal hymns, kings are praised for doing their marital duty to the goddess Inana, in the probably metaphorical "sacred marriage" (Cooper 2013), but the only claim to extraordinary sexual ability is for a goddess, found in an Akkadian hymn to Ishtar (Foster 2005 III.43.e "Ishtar Will Not Tire").
49 That rape was a fact of ancient Mesopotamian warfare can be assumed from the following NA treaty curse: "May Venus . . . before your eyes make your wives lie in the lap of your enemy!" (Parpola and Watanabe 1988: 46, 428) See also J. Reade's proposed illustration of the curse with a scene on an Assyrian palace relief, Ibid. 47 fig. 13.

References

Alster, B. 1991–92 "Early Dynastic Proverbs and Other Contributions to the Study of Literary Texts from Abū Ṣalābīkh." *Archiv für Orientforschung* 28–29, 1–51.

Black, J., G. Cunningham, E. Robson and G. Zólyomi 2004 *The Literature of Ancient Sumer*. Oxford: Oxford University Press.

Bottéro, J. and S. Kramer 1989 *Lorsque les dieux faisaient l'homme: Mythologie mésopotamienne*. Paris: Gallimard.

Charpin, D. and N. Ziegler 2007 "Amurritisch lernen." *Festschrift für H. Hunger = WZKM* 97, 55–77.

Cooper, J. 1978 *The Return of Ninurta to Nippur. an-gim dím-ma*. Analecta Orientalia 52. Rome: Pontifical Biblical Institute.

Cooper, J. 1997 "Gendered Sexuality in Sumerian Love Poetry." *Sumerian Gods and Their Representations*, ed. I. Finkel and M. Geller. Groningen: Styx, 85–97.

Cooper, J. 2013 "Sex and the Temple." *Tempel im Alten Orient*, eds. K. Kaniuth, A. Löhnert, J. Miller, A. Otto, M. Roaf and W. Sallaberger. ICDOG 7. Wiesbaden: Harrassowitz, 49–57.

Durand, J.-M. 1997 *Documents épistolaires du palais de Mari* I. LAPO 16. Paris: Éditions du Cerf.

Durand, J.-M. 1998 *Documents épistolaires du palais de Mari* II. LAPO 17. Paris: Éditions du Cerf.

Foster, B. 2005 *Before the Muses: An Anthology of Akkadian Literature*. 3rd edition. Bethesda: CDL Press.

Frahm, E. 1997 *Einleitung in die Sanherib-Inschriften*. Archiv für Orientforschung Beiheft 26.

Gadotti, A. 2014 '*Gilgameš, Enkidu and the Netherworld*' *and the Sumerian Gilgamesh Cycle*. Untersuchungen zur Assyriologie und Vorderasiatischen Archäologie 10. Berlin: De Gruyter.

Glassner, J.-J. 2004 *Mesopotamian Chronicles*. Writings from the Ancient World 19. Atlanta: Society for Biblical Literature.

Guichard, M. 2014 *L'Épopée de Zimrī-Lîm*. Florilegium marianum 14. Mémoires de N.A.B.U. 16. Paris: SÉPOA.

Gurney, O. 1960 "The Sultantepe Tablets VII: The Myth of Nergal and Ereshkigal." *Anatolian Studies* 10, 105–131.

Harris, R. 2000 *Gender and Aging in Mesopotamia*. Norman: University of Oklahoma Press.

Hepner, G. 2010 *Legal Friction: Law, Narrative, and Identity Politics in Biblical Israel*. New York: Peter Lang.

Hillers, D. 1973 "The Bow of Aqhat: The Meaning of a Mythological Theme." *Orient and Occident: Essays Presented to C. H. Gordon*, ed. H. Hoffner. AOAT 22. Neukirchen-Vluyn: Neukirchener Verlag, 71–80.

Hoffner, H. 1966 "Symbols for Masculinity and Femininity." *Journal of Biblical Literature* 85, 326–334.

Horowitz, V. 2005 "Genesis." *Bible Review* 21/1, 37–54.

Kämmerer, T. and K. Metzler 2012 *Das babylonische Weltschöpfungsepos* Enūma elîš. Münster: Ugarit-Verlag.

Krebernik, M. 1984 *Die Beschwörungen aus Fara und Ebla*. Texte und Studien zur Orientalistik 2. Hildesheim: Georg Olms.

Lambert, W. 2013 *Babylonian Creation Myths*. Mesopotamian Civilizations 16. Winona Lake: Eisenbrauns.

Leichty, E. 1970 *The Omen Series Šumma Izbu*. Texts from Cuneiform Sources 4. Locust Valley: J. J. Augustin.

Leichty, E. 2011 *The Royal Inscriptions of Esarhaddon, King of Assyria (680–669 BC)*. The Royal Inscriptions of the Neo-Assyrian Period 4. Winona Lake: Eisenbrauns.

Livingstone, A. 1989 *Court Poetry and Literary Miscellanea*. State Archives of Assyria 3. Helsinki: Helsinki University Press.

Livingstone, A. 1991 "An Enigmatic Line in a Mystical / Mythological Explanatory Work as Agriculture Myth." *N.A.B.U.* 1, 5–6.
Malul, M. 2002 *Knowledge, Control and Sex*. Tel Aviv-Jaffa: Archaeological Center.
Marello, P. 1992 "Vie nomade." *Florilegium marianum*. Mémoires de N.A.B.U. 1. Paris: SÉPOA, 115–125.
Metzler, K. 2002 "Tod, Weiblichkeit und Ästhetik im mesopotamischen Welschöpfungsepos *Enūma eliš*." *Sex and Gender in the Ancient Near East* (RAI 47), eds. S. Parpola and R. Whiting. Helsinki: State Archives of Assyria, 393–411.
Michalowski, P. 2011 *The Correspondence of the Kings of Ur*. Mesopotamian Civilizations 12. Winona Lake: Eisenbrauns.
Michel, C. 2001 *Correspondance des marchands de Kanish*. LAPO 19. Paris: Éditions du Cerf.
Nougayrol, J. 1966 "BM 75224." *Revue d'Assyriologie* 60, 90–91.
Parpola, S. and K. Watanabe 1988 *Neo-Assyrian Treaties and Loyalty Oaths*. State Archives of Assyria 2. Helsinki: Helsinki University Press.
Pomponio, F. 1997 "Cuori strappati e *Quisling* babilonesi." *Studi Epigrafici e Linguistici* 14, 69–89.
Pongratz-Leisten, B. 1994 *Ina Šulmi Īrub*. Baghdader Forschungen 16. Mainz: Von Zabern.
Reiner, E. 1967 "City Bread and Bread Baked in Ashes." *Language and Area Studies Presented to G. V. Bobrinskoy*. Chicago: Division of the Humanities, 116–120.
Sefati, Y. 1998 *Love Songs in Sumerian Literature*. Ramat Gan: Bar-Ilan University Press.
Seux, M.-J. 1967 *Épithètes royales akkadiennes et sumériennes*. Paris: Letouzey.
Stol, M. 2000 *Birth in Babylonia and the Bible*. Cuneiform Monographs 14. Groningen: Styx.
Strommenger, E. 1964 *5000 Years of the Art of Mesopotamia*. New York: Abrams.
Talon, P. 2005 *The Standard Babylonian Creation Myth*. State Archives of Assyria Cuneiform Texts 4. Helsinki: The Neo-Assyrian Text Corpus Project.
Ziegler, N. 2007 *Florilegium marianum IX. Les Musiciens et la musique d'après les archives de Mari*. Mémoires de N.A.B.U. 10. Paris: SÉPOA.
Zsolnay, I. 2010 "Ištar, Goddess of War, Pacifier of Kings: An Analysis of Ištar's Martial Role in the Maledictory Sections of the Assyrian Royal Inscriptions." *Language and City Administration in the Ancient Near East* (RAI 53), eds. L. Kogan, N. Koslova, S. Loesov, and S. Tischenko. Winona Lake: Eisenbrauns, 389–402.

5 Mapping masculinities in the Sanskrit *Mahābhārata* and *Rāmāyaṇa*

Simon Brodbeck

Introduction

The *Mahābhārata* and *Rāmāyaṇa* are India's most popular tales.[1] I concentrate here on the Sanskrit versions of the *Mahābhārata* and *Rāmāyaṇa*, which are the earliest surviving versions.[2] Scholars often date these Sanskrit texts to an extended period, from about 500 BCE to 500 CE, and for various adventitious reasons assume – there is no direct evidence for it – that they developed gradually, with significant dependence upon oral versions. Much of the secondary literature on these texts involves text-historical speculation, and until recently they have rarely been studied as unitary works of literature. Taking them as units could imply more unitary dates of composition.

These texts are immensely influential across South (and to some extent also Southeast) Asia. Many versions have been and still are produced in other languages and media; stories from these two texts form the basis for much of classical Sanskrit literature (Brockington 1998: 484–91); medieval kings from all over India presented themselves in their inscriptions in terms of the heroes of these texts (Hegarty 2012: 164–70); and in recent times the religio-political wrangling over the Ayodhyā mosque – allegedly the birthplace of Rāma – has shown the power of these tales to speak to current affairs (Nandy, Trivedy, Mayaram, and Yagnik 1995; Pollock 1993).

The two texts are similarly structured. They are stories of royal houses, and depict succession problems. In the *Mahābhārata* the conflict is between two sets of paternal cousins, the Pāṇḍavas and the Kauravas. The Kauravas, led by Duryodhana, beat the Pāṇḍavas at dice, abuse their wife Draupadī, and exile them; but the Pāṇḍavas later return, and there is a devastating war which, with Kṛṣṇa's assistance, the Pāṇḍavas win, but at great cost. In the *Rāmāyaṇa*, Rāma, the eldest prince of Ayodhyā, is exiled due to the schemings of the king's youngest wife, who wants the throne for *her* son. That son refuses it, but while Rāma is in exile his wife Sītā is abducted by Rāvaṇa, and he has to fight a great war to get her back; and although, with Hanumat's assistance, he does so, and although he becomes king when he returns to Ayodhyā, again it is at great cost.

One traditional Indian view is that the events that these texts portray really occurred – those of the *Rāmāyaṇa* before those of the *Mahābhārata*. Historical readings can extend beyond the precise plots, to the culture the texts depict; thus, for example, there is a book titled *India in the Rāmāyaṇa Age* (Vyas 1967). I read the texts as fictions, partly because so many of the events they portray seem unrealistic to me, but mostly because I think that a 'true story' is a contradiction in terms. A story is a human creation, a tool carefully fashioned by a complex agent for a complex purpose, and the suggestion that it could be 'true' works as a confidence trick by tending to hide this aspect, as if the teller were a passive conduit for something that already existed. In this regard, it should be appreciated that almost all the events portrayed in these texts are contained within reported speech. In principle, the text may say that so-and-so said such-and-such, and may even expect us to believe that, without implying that we should also believe what was said.

In what follows I try to take these two texts seriously as a pair; but just as with the two sides of a record or the two acts of a play, one wants really to know which of the pair one is to take as the first, and which of the pair one is to see in light of the other. And it is hard to tell.[3] So I take them as if they are simultaneous, and of one piece with each other.

The *Mahābhārata* and *Rāmāyaṇa* portray many male characters, and thus provide rich material for study of masculinities. This chapter focuses on the multiple constructions of masculinity in these texts.[4] These masculinities are to a large degree relational – that is, they are constructed in relation to other masculinities and/or in relation to particular characters or groups. The paper has four main sections. The first section discusses how the construction of masculinities for a diverse audience seems to be an explicit concern of the texts, as signalled in several different ways. The second section explores the texts' most salient constructions of masculinity – those that concern members of the *kṣatriya* class of rulers and warriors, from which the main characters are drawn. The third section shows how aspects of *kṣatriya* masculinity are generalised for application to audience members of all classes, but also shows how *kṣatriya* masculinity is problematised by the narratives. The fourth section discusses various masculinities associated with the brahman class, whose roles and social functions are distinct from those of the *kṣatriya*. Included among these brahmin masculinities is the yogic masculinity of the renouncer. I show how the texts devise a new, non-renunciative yogic masculinity incorporating aspects of *kṣatriya* and brahmin masculinities; by implication, this is the masculinity constructed for the male audience member.

Masculinity and textual purpose

When we say that these texts construct various different masculinities, what does the verb 'construct' indicate in this context? Perhaps it indicates that the idioms in which the texts' audiences think and speak of masculinity are in some sense related to their exposure to the texts – that is, that in terms of masculinity at least, the audiences *learn from* the texts. But even if we set aside the question of how the textual construction of masculinities relates to the authors' construction of the texts (a question which would take us into the vexed issue of how the texts might have come to be the way they are), the problem remains that most of the texts' historical audiences are largely inaccessible; so perhaps the best way to think about the audience is to read the texts, thus becoming part of the audience, and then (or simultaneously) to think about oneself thinking about them.

The texts encourage this approach. Both texts contain verses detailing the benefits of exposure to the texts or to specific subsections thereof. For example:

> A man who reads this *Rāmāyaṇa* story, which leads to long life, will after death rejoice in heaven together with his sons, grandsons, and attendants. A brahman who reads it becomes eloquent, a kshatriya becomes a lord of the earth, a *vaiśya* acquires profit from his goods, and even a lowly *śūdra* achieves greatness.
>
> (*Rāmāyaṇa* 1.1.78–79, tr. Goldman 1984: 126)

I will return to the patrilineal aspect mentioned here. The first of these sentences has a long reach, since there would presumably be quite a gap between the man's death and the deaths of his grandsons. More immediately, the male reader understands that the text is intended to be transformative for him in important ways.[5] By collating such verses, one could build details of a paradigmatic masculinity that the texts construct and coerce in their male audience. The 'man who reads this *Rāmāyaṇa* story' is in the first place an imaginary character within the text; but he models the text's paradigmatic masculinity for, and mediates it to, the actual male audience member outside the text. That masculinity is formatted here as one basic model with four subvarieties, one for each social class.

The dialogical structure of the texts demonstrates this transformative effect within the narrative, and shows us that even the characters must learn the dominant construction of masculinity for their class; it doesn't necessarily come naturally. For example: at many points in the *Mahābhārata*'s narrative, Yudhiṣṭhira, the eldest Pāṇḍava brother and eventual king, is told stories about men whose lives have much in common with his; and his character develops (and his masculinity is constructed) through his hearing those stories. And the story of the Pāṇḍavas is framed by the story of its being told to King Janamejaya, descendant of the Pāṇḍavas, at an important juncture in *his* life; and hearing it helps *his* character to develop, and prompts him to make a good decision. And the story of Janamejaya is framed by the story of its being told to the brahmin Śaunaka; and that story is framed by the story of its being told to a group of sages; and at the edge of the text, by implication, that story is framed by the fact of its being told to us. So the promised transformation of the reader is not merely hypothetical; it is illustrated within the narrative. We are shown – in practice, as it were – how the process of textual construction of masculinities works through the various audiences and thus through us.

That the construction of masculinity is a primary purpose of the text is made clear at the very beginning of the *Rāmāyaṇa*. The text's author is allegedly Vālmīki, and the preamble describes how he came to compose it. Vālmīki asks a divine sage:

> Is there a man in the world today who is truly virtuous? Who is there who is mighty and yet knows both what is right and how to act upon it? Who always speaks the truth and holds firmly to his vows? Who exemplifies proper conduct and is benevolent to all creatures? Who is learned, capable, and a pleasure to behold? Who is self-controlled, having subdued his anger? Who is both judicious and free from envy? Who, when his fury is aroused in battle, is feared even by the gods? This is what I want to hear, for my desire to know is very strong. Great seer, you must know of such a man.
>
> (*Rāmāyaṇa* 1.1.2–5, tr. Goldman 1984: 121)

Vālmīki is then told, in brief, the story of Rāma; and thereafter, presumably convinced that Rāma does indeed performatively instantiate this ideal construct of masculinity, he composes the more detailed version (i.e., the majority of the *Rāmāyaṇa* text). If we juxtapose Vālmīki's summary description of the ideal man with the promised transformation of the male audience member, the implication would be that the 'man who reads this *Rāmāyaṇa* story' becomes more like Rāma in these listed ways – most of which are not specific to any particular social class.

Kṣatriya models of masculinity

The most obvious generic masculinity constructed by the texts is presented as specific to the social class of the *kṣatriya*s; that is, the ruling and warrior class (Hiltebeitel 2004), of which Rāma is a member. The texts contain recurring catalogues of paradigmatic *kṣatriya* behaviour, the best known of which is found in the *Bhagavadgītā*:

> [V]alor, vigor, resolve, skill, generosity, mastery, and not fleeing from a battle are the natural activities of the kshatriya . . .
>
> (*Mahābhārata* 6.40.43, tr. Cherniak 2008: 297)

They also contain recurring discussions of the role of the principal *kṣatriya*, the king.

The masculinity of the regal role is ramified in the mythology and symbolism of kingship. The king is the husband of the Earth,[6] and fulfils a protective, fertilising, and nurturing role with respect to her (Brodbeck 2009b; Derrett 1959; Hara 1973). The Earth represents the land which the king controls, and extends by implication to the population he must organise, which is symbolically female. The king's protective function requires him to use the rod of punishment to prevent the strong abusing the weak (Fitzgerald 2004: 128–42; Glucklich 1988). The judicious use of the rod of punishment is the hallmark of royal propriety, and ensures the Earth's felicity and productivity; in this respect and others (not least in the idea that the king is the *enjoyer* of the Earth), the rod has phallic overtones. The reproductive symbolism extends, by analogy, to natural forces: if there is no king, or if the king is absent or disfunctional, it will not rain.[7]

The *kṣatriya*'s negotiation of his duty to use violence is a recurring topic, often explored in discussions between brothers who have contrasting personalities and attitudes, and who thus embody different constructions of masculinity. As the opening speech of the *Rāmāyaṇa* suggests, such discussions emphasise that the *kṣatriya* must retain his self-control, heed good advice and the example of distinguished forebears, subdue his passions, but be merciless if necessary. The texts do not shy away from the existential burden that the duty to use violence involves. In the *Mahābhārata*, the fact that the Pāṇḍavas must kill their own cousins and teachers causes them great distress: just before battle, in the text's most famous scene, the *Bhagavadgītā*, Arjuna Pāṇḍava breaks down and declares that he will not fight, but Lord Kṛṣṇa, his charioteer, explains that he must set aside his personal feelings and do his duty (*Mbh* 6.23–40). To opt for a simpler life would be negligent, the act of a coward, a eunuch, or a fool – three abjected constructs of masculinity which occur repeatedly and are used as limit cases to contrast with the dutiful *kṣatriya*. Nonetheless, *kṣatriya*s often lament their specific duty; 'Damn the duty of *kṣatriya*s!' is a repeated refrain.[8]

The *Mahābhārata* and *Rāmāyaṇa* both include important preliminary passages that explain the central events in a cosmic perspective, in terms of the antagonism between gods and demons (*Mbh* 1.58–61; *Hv* 44; *Rām* 1.14–16). These framing passages illustrate the regal-heroic role. Demons have taken refuge on Earth, and as a result, the Earth and/or the sages suffer. This suffering is the marker of evil; by implication, anyone about whom the Earth or the sages would have cause to complain is a demon. So, the diagnosis having been made, gods descend into (usually unknowing) human beings, to destroy the demons. The great wars in both texts are thus instigated and won by secret agency from a context transcending the motives and interests of most of the human participants; Rāma and Yudhiṣṭhira are gods, but they do not know it. Nonetheless, though they think they are simply involved in human business, the Earth is rescued from great evil through their deeds. The disparity in awareness is presented vertically, as a matter of humanity compared to divinity, the terrestrial compared to the cosmic.

The myth is the same in both cases, and is replicated in both texts also at the mundane level: the damsel's distress (that of Earth, Draupadī, and Sītā) compels and is assuaged by heroic action.

If the king's relationship with Earth represents one aspect of his stance towards the feminine, another aspect is signalled by the mythology of Śrī (Hara 1996–97). She is the personification of the king's glory, his fortune, his success. His queen is sometimes said to represent this goddess; and sometimes when the king is defeated and replaced, his wife transfers to the victor (see e.g., *Rām* 4.2–28). Earth is a dependent, but Śrī is fickle and faithless. She transfers her affections almost whimsically, on some pretext; whoever the king happens to be, a medley of rivals is implied. And the king may be his own worst enemy, for the four famous vices of kings are hunting, gambling, drinking, and womanising, any of which may cause disaster.[9] Indulgence in these activities is associated with an abjected construction of kingship which is proverbial within the text but ultimately aberrant, the ideal king being constructed in contrast to it.

The king manages the economy; he extracts tribute from his subjects, and from subordinate kings, and redistributes it. He is the paradigmatic bestower of gifts; it is a matter of principle, constitutive of their social position, that *kṣatriya*s do not accept gifts. Amongst other things, this constrains the ways in which they may contract marriages (Hara 1974). A *kṣatriya* can give his daughters away, but he cannot receive the gift of anyone else's daughter as his wife; he must take her by force, either by defeating his rivals in a competition where she is the prize (Brockington 2006), or by abducting her from her natal family (McGrath 2009: 51–62).

When redistributing wealth, the *kṣatriya* must in particular ensure the prosperity of the brahmins. Brahmins are specialists in ritual and knowledge. The king depends upon them, for they are custodians of discourse, including discourse about him and his propriety – and from their perspective, the primary indicator of his propriety is their welfare. Brahmins will be discussed in more detail below; but here it should be noted that the *kṣatriya* role is constructed as a role in relation to others, and that brahmins often occupy the space of those others, either on their own behalf, or as solicitors. To that extent, a *kṣatriya* is doing his duty if and only if the brahmins say he is.

Kṣatriya masculinity is premised on the acquisition and preservation of reputation, primarily through generosity and heroism. It is performative, and always in need of redemonstration. Heroism is physical and martial; the *kṣatriya* must be wholehearted in battle, fighting without concern for his survival. When Arjuna refuses to fight, Kṛṣṇa says:

> You should attend to your own duty and stand firm, for there is nothing better for a warrior [*kṣatriya*] than a legitimate battle. Happy the warriors who find such a battle, Partha [Arjuna] – an open door to heaven, arrived at by chance.

But if you won't wage this legitimate war, then, forsaking your duty and your fame, you will have committed a sin. For people will tell of your lasting disgrace; and to an honored man, disgrace is worse than death. The great warriors will think you withdrew from the battle out of fear, and though highly regarded by them before, you will be slighted. Your enemies too will say many unseemly things, disparaging your ability; and what could be more painful than that? Get up, son of Kunti, and resolve to fight! For you will either be killed and attain heaven, or you will prevail and enjoy the earth.

(*Mahābhārata* 6.24.31–37, tr. Cherniak 2008: 187)

Another marker of the constructed masculinity of the *kṣatriya*s is bold speaking, the assertion of superiority over their opponents in advance of battle. Hence their reputation also depends on their ability to make good on their boasts, as if the boast itself sets the context against which the character's martial heroism must be judged. In the *Mahābhārata*, Karṇa, the Pāṇḍavas' unknown elder brother who fights for the Kauravas, is one of the finest warriors on either side, but he is nonetheless criticised for his idle boasting.[10] Sometimes, especially in moments of high passion, advance boasts take the form of vows, the keeping of which is then especially crucial. The fulfilment of Bhīma Pāṇḍava's vow to kill all 100 Kaurava brothers is facilitated by his allies, who spare opponents they might otherwise have killed, in order that Bhīma may kill them himself later on.[11] With Bhīma's two other salient vows – to break Duryodhana's thigh, and to drink Duḥśāsana's blood – the requirement to fulfil the vow is used, with mixed success, as a mitigating circumstance to help justify actions which would ordinarily be contrary to martial etiquette.[12]

Elsewhere there is mention of constraints on behaviour that do not result from passionate public utterances, but that seem almost to be constitutive of the individual *kṣatriya*'s self-definition (Ernest 2007, chapter 3). Here we deal with masculinity as something that is partially self-constructed and thus inherently plural; though the basic building-blocks of *kṣatriya* masculinity are non-negotiable, there is room for individuality in nuances that vary from person to person, and these nuances are often held very dear by the individual concerned. Thus Yudhiṣṭhira Pāṇḍava will never refuse a challenge (*Mbh* 2.52.16); Karṇa will never refuse any brahmin's request (*Mbh* 3.284.24–29); Bhīma will kill anyone who insults him (*Mbh* 7.123.4–6); Arjuna will kill anyone who tells him to give his famous bow, Gāṇḍīva, to another (*Mbh* 8.49.9); and Arjuna will also kill anyone who causes Yudhiṣṭhira's blood to flow anywhere but on the battlefield (*Mbh* 4.63.44–64.10). Such life-rules bear on individual interactions in terms of honour and ongoing reputation.

Slightly different are the various instances where a king rejects a woman who was his but who, whether voluntarily or not, has been with another man – and rejects her regardless of the precise sense of 'being with him' that would in truth apply. Śālva rejects Ambā after she has been with Bhīṣma (*Mbh* 5.172), and Rāma rejects Sītā after she has been with Rāvaṇa (*Rāmāyaṇa* 6.102–106; 7.42–44); the circumstances of the two rejections differ, in that Śālva was beaten in battle by his rival but Rāma was not, but in both cases the character explains the rejection by appealing to his royal position, the need to safeguard the reputation upon which it rests, and the need to set an appropriate example for his subjects to follow. Here it seems to be a matter not of personal choice or even of *kṣatriya* masculinity, but of the standards required in a holder of royal office – that is, of a specifically *regal* construction of masculinity.

The battles described by the texts proceed largely through episodes of single combat between prominent warriors mounted on chariots. One aspect that comes through strongly, as it does in generic action films today, is the ability of heroes to sustain massive injuries in battle and yet fight on ably through the pain. The action tends to feature standard deeds in combination: the piercing of the opponent's body with arrows, the deflection of the opponent's arrows in mid-flight, the breaking of the opponent's bow with a well-aimed arrow, the incapacitation of the opponent's chariot by killing his charioteer and/or horses (after which the duel may continue on foot with maces or swords). There is some scope for viewing such deeds in terms of the metaphorical resexing (or desexing) of the opponent, for example by likening the wound to the vagina, the broken bow to the opponent's phallus, and/or the charioteer and horses to the dependents he is powerless to protect; but the texts do not go out of their way to encourage such interpretations.

In physical terms, *kṣatriya* masculinity is generally marked by bodily size and strength – *kṣatriya*s are often compared to bulls, or to tigers. Beyond this, masculinity is rarely associated with hair or clothing; but there are incidents that suggest such an association. When Draupadī is briefly kidnapped by Jayadratha, the Pāṇḍavas rescue her, and Bhīma, forbidden by Yudhiṣṭhira to kill Jayadratha, instead partially shaves his head in order to humiliate him (*Mbh* 3.255.39–256.23). A similar instance is found after King Bāhu is ousted from his kingdom: Bāhu's son Sagara, born in exile, in time returns to reclaim it, but his prime minister forbids the execution of the usurpers; so Sagara's chosen punishment includes shaving many of their heads, either partially or wholly (*Hv* 10.30–46). As regards clothing, it is significant that at the nadir of the Pāṇḍavas' fortunes, after Yudhiṣṭhira has gambled and lost himself and his brothers to his cousin Duryodhana in a dicing match, they are ordered to strip down to their underwear – an order which they cannot disobey, for they are now slaves (*Mbh* 2.61.38–39). It would seem that although those who undergo it retain their masculinity, the forced removal of a man's hair or clothing is a marker of his disempowerment by (and subordination to) another.[13] And in the case of clothing, it can be so for women too, as the (failed) attempt to strip Draupadī is an attempt to subordinate her to her new 'owners' (*Mbh* 2.61).

The wider sense of the patrilineal *kṣatriya* model

The royal model requires one king per generation. Heredity is the facilitating principle; the king is typically the previous king's eldest son. This invokes a line of kings from the distant past into the future; and it is these kings with whom the present king has most in common, and in terms of whom he conducts himself (Brodbeck 2009a; Jay 1992). The king plays on his forefathers' behalf, and after death he joins them, and his descendants play on; and he is remembered. Being remembered is being in heaven – in this case, the ancestral heaven.

This is the patrilineal theory of salvation. It is precarious salvation, since any line of ancestors might tumble at any point because of political or genetic developments or bad management; but it is salvation nonetheless. What it lacks in permanency it makes up in applicability; our texts, and various Sanskrit texts from the same period, give details of the *śrāddha* ritual, prescribed for regular performance by all men, in which patrilineal ancestors are fed with food offerings to keep them alive in heaven.[14]

The line requires a good son every generation. In this respect men are at a disadvantage; they cannot produce children. Here there is a biological component which operates as a constraint on the social construction of masculinities. The patrilineal texts describe how wives should be chosen, obtained, guarded, and treated.[15] Many old stories depict men falling madly in love (usually while out hunting), with various complications (Brodbeck 2009a); and although the hero sometimes manages to produce a good heir nonetheless, these are cautionary tales. More usually the production of children is presented not as a result of romantic love and/or sexual attraction, but as one aspect of the responsible discharging of one's debt to one's patrilineal ancestors (Olivelle 1993: 46–53). To this end the children should be sons in particular, and should not merely be produced but also made and kept loyal to their patriline;[16] which would tend to imply a long-term, carefully negotiated and managed relationship between the parents. The texts thus construct an ideal masculinity whereby sensual desire is acknowledged as powerful and dangerous and as something to be mastered and controlled – as are the women who would prompt it. The man who pays his ancestral debt is the man who can resist temptation, who can privilege prudence over passion.

Negotiating reproductive facts within a patrilineal framework is not just the business of kings. And the technology of kingship as described in the *Mahābhārata* and *Rāmāyaṇa* is applicable by analogy to those involved in patrilineal family businesses of whatever kind, those with ongoing custody of whatever patrimonial estate. Patrilineal inheritance is the norm in the texts, which means patrilocy: brides, 'given away' in marriage, typically move to live with their in-laws. As Sulabhā tells King Janaka:

> Every man is a king in his own house; every man is a head of household in his own house – meting out punishments and bestowing rewards,

> Janaka, he is the equal of kings. Sons, wife, and likewise his own self; treasury, allies, and supplies – these are common to them both [i.e., to both householders and kings], along with other things that also move him to act.
>
> (*Mbh* 12.308.147–148, tr. Fitzgerald 2002: 665)

In consonance with this analogy, although in the innermost frame-stories of the *Mahābhārata* and *Rāmāyaṇa* a story about kings is told to a king, also listening are many non-kings, and women; and at the outer edge the texts are presented to an audience of all classes. By contrast, Vedic Sanskrit literature – generally thought to be the only Sanskrit literature to precede these texts – was forbidden to women and lower-class men.[17]

This switch of audience, from the fictional *kṣatriya* within the text to the real and open audience, means that the material is presented not just to but also *for* all. Although only *kṣatriya* audience members could possibly act out the constructed *kṣatriya* masculinity in its entirety, the analogy and the mode of presentation by implication generalise some approximation of *kṣatriya* masculinity as appropriate for males of all social classes. In a similar fashion, if we say 'an Englishman's home is his castle',[18] we imply that the type of behaviour typically or mythically demonstrated by those who live in castles (i.e., presumably, the landed and military aristocracy) is a paradigm generalisable across all social classes of Englishmen as regards the attitude of each to their own private residential domain. In the *Mahābhārata* and *Rāmāyaṇa* we find explicit statements asserting that the king's behaviour is imitated across the population. Having heard that Rāma has taken Sītā back even after she was resident with Rāvaṇa, Rāma's subjects are reported as saying:

> We shall now have to countenance the same state of affairs regarding our own wives, since what a king does, his subjects follow!
>
> (*Rām* 7.42.19, tr. Shastri 1952–59, 3: 522)[19]

It is because of this that Rāma abandons Sītā; and the same reasoning underlies Śālva's abandonment of Ambā (*Mbh* 5.172.7). There is no suggestion that only *kṣatriya* subjects would follow the king's example.

When the Sanskrit texts function in the way I am suggesting, the notion of the *kṣatriya* is opened up from being a group in any possible or actual society, to being a mythic or paradigmatic mode of relation for any patrilineal householder. This is the promised transformation that the male audience member is told to expect as a result of his exposure to the text. And although in this chapter I am not concerned with constructions of femininity, it is clear that they would often have relations of mutual reinforcement with constructions of masculinity – so both the mother and the wife of the five Pāṇḍava brothers tell them to (and how to) discharge their responsibilities (*Mbh* 3.28–29; 5.130–135; 10.11), and the text is then seeking to make the women in its audience (*kṣatriya* women, brahmin women, and so on) complicit in the appropriation of some degree of the male *kṣatriya* model by their close male relations.

However, the fact that the *kṣatriya* masculinity constructed within the texts is largely to be applied outside the texts by non-*kṣatriya*s, and therefore in an attenuated or renegotiated form, means that the *kṣatriya* construct that the texts present can be a caricature from the start – it stands as a tragic regal nonsense, an ideology deconstructed in the telling, and as a source of entertainment, however bleak. In the *Rāmāyaṇa*, Rāma becomes king; but because Sītā was meanwhile compromised, he rejects her and lives his days out in misery, and there is no good son to be king of Ayodhyā after him. In the *Mahābhārata*, the Pāṇḍavas win the war, but all five of the brothers lose sons in the process and mourn them, sometimes with great pathos; Yudhiṣṭhira, who reigns thereafter, is scarred for life; and the Pāṇḍava story as a whole is framed by the abject lamentations of Dhṛtarāṣṭra for his 100 dead sons (*Mbh* 1.1).

Although, as mentioned earlier, there is a cosmic justification for the bloodshed in both tales, giving the impression that these military events – and thus the violent *kṣatriya* masculinities through which they are facilitated – are exceptionally and unfortunately necessary for the ongoing greater good, nonetheless there is in fact little evidence to suggest that things are going to be qualitatively better thereafter. In the *Mahābhārata* the *kaliyuga*, the worst of all epochs, is said to begin around the time of the war (González-Reimann 2010: 62–63), thus giving the lie to the idea of cosmic regeneration; and a frame story depicts further conflicts and massive bloodshed a few generations later, when King Janamejaya, Arjuna Pāṇḍava's great-grandson, begins a major massacre in order to avenge his father's assassination. And in the *Rāmāyaṇa*, despite the allegedly cosmic problem, it is not clear that Rāvaṇa was really much of a nuisance at all (Goldman and Masson 1969). If Rāma had had the courage of his convictions and had left Sītā safe at home when he went into exile (*Rām* 2.23–27), or if he had managed not to arouse Rāvaṇa's enmity by being so cruel to Rāvaṇa's sister Śūrpaṇakhā (*Rām* 3.16–17),[20] then it is not clear that there would have been any problem with Rāvaṇa. So both texts deconstruct their cosmic contexts, disrupting the dominant mythic paradigm even as they present it; and one is thus invited to wonder about the ultimate value of the *kṣatriya* model and, by implication, about the value of its partial extension across all classes of men.

These tales are horror stories. If what there is of masculinity for patrilineal male householders of all classes is by way of approximation towards the *kṣatriya* ideal that these texts present, then that is enough to make one want to go and live in the woods – as the protagonists dutifully do, albeit temporarily. Are the texts designed to make men behave like *kṣatriya*s? That way lies slaughter and woe. Though these texts are generally viewed as orthodox productions, they might alternatively be viewed as satirising an orthopraxy that they place within inverted commas and fictionalise. This satirised orthopraxy would include by implication the system and contents of orthodoxy within the fiction – that is, the ramifications of the patrilineal model, and even the success within it that the male audience member is promised. At the centre of the *Mahābhārata* we find the character of Bhīṣma, who, though he is the eldest son of a king, renounces kingship and vows celibacy as a young man, and keeps his vow. Vālmīki, author of the *Rāmāyaṇa*, seems to have no wife or family. Vyāsa, author of the *Mahābhārata*, was produced from a brief affair, fathers sons in another man's family, never marries, but miraculously has one son of his own – Śuka, who as a young man renounces the world and seeks higher salvation (*Mbh* 12.309–320). The texts' dominant construction of masculinity is subverted by these characters, and is also severely problematised by the dismal outcomes met with by those *kṣatriya* characters who do manage to live up to the ideal.

The stance of the texts is thus paradoxical, opaque, and/or extraordinarily sophisticated; while from one perspective the patriarchal *kṣatriya* construct is seemingly a prescription, on further reflection it seems to be set up as part of a meditation or a puzzle. One thus begins to wonder to what extent the *kṣatriya* model can really be said to constitute the texts' *dominant* construction of masculinity. In the following section we will thus explore brahmin masculinity as constructed within the texts. The brahmin class is heavily represented, through the compositional status of Vyāsa and Vālmīki, the narratorial status of Vaiśaṃpāyana, the patronial status of Śaunaka, and the fact that the *kṣatriya* is constructed largely in relation to the brahmin. As with *kṣatriya* masculinity, we would expect to find brahmin masculinity constructed in broad outline as a masculinity common to brahmins, and in plural detail through the various individual brahmin characters explored situationally within the narrative.

Brahmin and yogic masculinities

In some stories, where brahmins are depicted competing for patronage and reputation just as *kṣatriya*s compete for Śrī (see, e.g., *Mbh* 3.135–139), brahmin masculinity seems to be comparable with *kṣatriya* masculinity. But in principle there should be royal patronage for all good brahmins; and while *kṣatriya*s are supposed to strive for public supremacy, brahmins should make do with what they get, or emigrate in search of better and thus more generous kings (*Mbh* 12.90.3–6).

The mutual dependence of brahmins and *kṣatriya*s is often stressed, particularly in the *Mahābhārata*. *Kṣatriya*s rely on brahmins as ministers and advisors, as ritual specialists, and for their public relations; and brahmins rely on *kṣatriya*s to protect them and sponsor their way of life (Biardeau 1981; Fitzgerald 2006). It certainly seems that the relationship between the naturalised categories of brahmin and *kṣatriya* is a central concern of the texts. But I would like to suggest a comparison between brahmins and women. Though these categories differ in gender,[21] both play a similar role as indispensable 'others' to the *kṣatriya* stereotype. Here brahmins and women of all classes are defined largely in terms of their differing from *kṣatriya* men; yet they are necessary to them. A *kṣatriya*'s ongoing success depends crucially upon his relationship with them.

Brahmins and women are similarly constructed in their comparative physical helplessness, in contrast to which *kṣatriya* masculinity is defined;[22] the main stories of *kṣatriya*s rescuing Earth, or Sītā, or Draupadī, contain many sub-stories of *kṣatriya*s rescuing brahmins from situations of peril. But we also have stories of women and brahmins cornered without recourse, having to rely on their own resources; and as it turns out, in both cases these are deep resources of fearsome and mysterious power. Relying on the existential charge of their suffering and dedication in the name of truth and their own duty, brahmins and women can work miracles and cast curses.[23] And because the male *kṣatriya* is in their service, when he is in receptive evidence they direct him in his proper duty to their advantage. Indeed, just as their suffering is supposedly his business, so his suffering, which follows from his supposed business, is fashioned by them, and they are complicit in it. And so his suffering is not something that the carefully constructed and largely non-*kṣatriya* audience can stand apart from or blame him for.

Something interesting seems to be implied by the descriptions of the origins of three brahmins who fight in the *Mahābhārata* war on the side of the (supposedly demonic) Kauravas, and who are therefore, in brahmin terms, aberrant. These are Droṇa and Kṛpa, both of whom are martial arts instructors in Kaurava service, and Aśvatthāman. Droṇa was born when his brahmin father ejaculated into a pot, and the pot gave birth; and Kṛpa was born when *his* brahmin father ejaculated into a clump of reeds, and the reeds gave birth (*Mbh* 1.120–121). In Kṛpa's case there was also a twin sister, Kṛpī. Whereas most human children are made from both male and female human parents and have a mother and a father, these children were not and did not. Then Kṛpī married Droṇa and they had Aśvatthāman, as if further to distil the male essence; though Aśvatthāman had a mother, he had no grandmothers. Aśvatthāman was a very dangerous man: driven to bloodcraze after the underhand killing of his father Droṇa, he (or through him his supernatural puppet-master) was responsible for particularly shocking deeds after the end of the battlefield action – the murder of barracks of soldiers (including the sons of the Pāṇḍavas) in their sleep by stealth attack, and the discharging of a magical weapon against unborn and future descendants of the Pāṇḍavas (*Mbh* 10).

What do these examples imply about brahmin as compared to *kṣatriya* masculinities? Is it that normative brahmin masculinity would somehow be constructed as less masculine than normative *kṣatriya* masculinity, since the brahmins who behave like *kṣatriya*s are precisely those whose maternal input is compromised? Perhaps these examples are also intended as a comment upon the salient patrilineal myth of procreation, whereby the son is simply a replica of the father (*Mbh* 1.68.36, 47–48). If so, then the suggestion would be that this myth would fit the production of *kṣatriya*-style offspring more than it would fit the production of brahmin-style offspring.

It seems from the strange birth stories that brahmin masculinity, though patrilineal, would be less intense than *kṣatriya* masculinity.[24] Presumably it would also vary in tone from brahmin to brahmin, just as *kṣatriya* masculinity does for the three eldest Pāṇḍava brothers, Yudhiṣṭhira, Bhīma, and Arjuna, three sons of Kuntī, whose distinct constructs are also traceable to their celestial fathers, Dharma (Propriety), Vāyu (the Wind), and Indra (the chief of the gods).[25] Yudhiṣṭhira is rather standoffish about his *kṣatriya* duty; he does not want war, and he does not want to be king (Brodbeck 2007: 150–162); Bhīma is passionate, impetuous, and particularly physically powerful; and Arjuna is a phlegmatic virtuoso and their supreme warrior, as if lying somewhere between and beyond the other two. In the *Rāmāyaṇa*, Rāma and Lakṣmaṇa (Goldman 1980), who are often present as a pair (since Lakṣmaṇa accompanies Rāma on his exile and fights with him in the battle against Rāvaṇa), sometimes play a double-act comparable to that of Yudhiṣṭhira and Bhīma, but without the transcendent median present; Bharata is back in Ayodhyā holding the fort.

On the basis of these different constructions of *kṣatriya* masculinity, one might imagine comparably different constructions of brahmin masculinity, and expect some extreme characters within the text. But while the various *kṣatriya* characters can give the impression of a *kṣatriya* continuum based on one variable, the brahmin case seems to be more complex. One construct would be the 'martial brahmin' type mentioned above; but the brahmin who takes on another class's role in anything other than the direst extremity is reprehensible (and a bad reflection upon the king). Another construct would be represented by the wandering brahmin Durvāsas, who is famous for being an extremely demanding, irascible, and even abusive guest, with a hair-trigger in the matter of curses but also, if well served beyond any reasonable point of endurance, with a good stock of boons to bestow.[26] Though he is a comedy character to some extent, he certainly seems to take unfair advantage of his powers and status. Other extreme brahmin characters would include the ungrateful (and stupid) brahmin of *Mahābhārata* 12.162–167, who gets rich through the connections of his generous host (a crane), and then kills him casually for food (Bowles 2007: 391–404). On the other hand, behavioural extremity seems to be quite common for brahmins, since many of them undertake extraordinary deprivations apparently by choice.

There are occupations particularly associated with brahminhood – ministerial collaboration and ritual officiation for rulers, teaching, and study – but it is a broad church. A resounding trend in ancient India deems brahminhood to be dependent on personal qualities irrespective of birth, and although the *Mahābhārata*'s dominant view seems to be that class is inherited, the text repeatedly refers to brahmins who are brahmins in name only (i.e., born in brahmin families but wanting in brahmin qualities), and implies that brahmins can be brahmins regardless of their parents.[27] Thus the dominant construction of brahmin masculinity can be performed by people not born into brahmin families. In the *Bhagavadgītā* Kṛṣṇa describes brahmins as follows:

> [C]almness, self-restraint, austerity, purity, patience, honesty, knowledge, insight, and piety are the brahmin's activities as determined by his own intrinsic nature . . .
>
> (*Mahābhārata* 6.40.42, tr. Cherniak 2008: 297)

On the face of it, these are virtues that we would also hope the most powerful *kṣatriya*s to have. But in the Sanskrit tradition they evoke a specific soteriological path – the 'path of the gods,' contrasted with the patrilineal 'path of the fathers' – that is based not on deeds but on knowledge, and on the yogic orientation that follows from that knowledge.[28] This knowledge, as described in the *Mahābhārata* (particularly within 6.23–40, the *Bhagavadgītā*, and 12.168–353, the *Mokṣadharmaparvan*), is knowledge of the pervasiveness of suffering, of its origin in the misapprehension of the nature of the self (and thus also of the phenomenal world-process), and of the possibility of its eradication through the conquest of desire, success in which will ensure the end of a karmic chain of lives.

Duryodhana argues that a *kṣatriya* should be dissatisfied, since it is this that will spur him to heroic action and fortune (*Mbh* 2.50.18). But the texts showcase not so much *kṣatriya* dissatisfaction as *kṣatriya* desolation, suffering on a grand and pitiful scale, suffering that cries out for a systematic solution – and suffering most particularly in terms of the loss of loved ones (especially sons, but also a brother in the case of Karṇa, and a wife in the case of Sītā). Though it might seem that in such situations suffering is natural, the suggestion is repeatedly made that suffering is not just situational but results from the individual's dependence, attachment, and ignorance. In part this is because in the patrilineal soteriology one can never do enough oneself to remain saved; one only remains in heaven if the patriline keeps on extending itself even long after one has died. In contrast, the path of the gods is a path of self-reliance and independence, associated with a distinct construction of masculinity: the masculinity performed by the *yogin*.

The one who travels the path of the gods is often presented – as for example in early Jainism and Buddhism – as the one who renounces the performance of the role of the patrilineal householder. The renouncer's life is presented in romantic terms by Yudhiṣṭhira when, traumatised by recent events, he plans to adopt it after the *Mahābhārata* war:

> Covered with dust, taking refuge in empty houses or dwelling at the foot of a tree, having let go of everything pleasant or irritable, neither grieving nor delighting, holding praise and blame to be of equal value, having no wishes, free of possessiveness, beyond the pairs of

> opposites, having no holdings, delighting in myself alone, completely at peace, seeming to be blind, deaf, and dumb, making no agreements with others, not with anyone at all, doing no harm to any of the four orders of animate or inanimate beings, being the same toward all living creatures as they observe their proper Laws, ridiculing no one, frowning at nothing, my face always cheery, all my faculties thoroughly restrained, questioning no one about the road, traveling by any way whatsoever, not seeking to go in any particular direction, nor to any particular place, paying no heed to my going, not looking back, straight and steady as I go, but careful to avoid creatures moving and still – so will I be.
>
> (*Mahābhārata* 12.9.13–19, tr. Fitzgerald 2004: 185)

Rāma may seem to view forest life in similar terms; he is not unhappy to go into exile after his stepmother's coup, and his initial plans are to go alone (*Rām* 2.16–33).

The aloofness of the forest wanderer is a paradigm of masculinity radically at odds with the *kṣatriya* paradigm of the man circumscribed by (and directed in accordance with) his heavy responsibility to his citizens, family, and domain. And the renouncer's lifestyle has an analogical resonance on the metaphysical plane, for according to a common understanding it goes together with the realisation that the soul in its relationship with the phenomenal world is similarly aloof. Even while embodied during life (or during a karmically connected series of lives), the soul is changeless, intrinsically impervious to any and all physical and mental circumstances, and also gendered masculine, while the bodymind and the consubstantial universe are gendered feminine (as *prakṛti*; Brodbeck 2007). In realising the distinction between the soul and the not-soul, one identifies more and more with the former, and less and less with the latter; and thus in these terms one effectively becomes more and more masculine, before eventually abiding – after one's last life – in splendid and permanent removal from the feminine. Accordingly, in this paradigm the business of soteriology is presented in terms of masculinity and heroism, with the truth-knowing *yogin* being the ultimate. The discourse of renunciation which Yudhiṣṭhira evokes in the passage just quoted tends to stress a masculine role performed, for example, by Mahāvīra the Jina and Gotama the Buddha ('the victorious one' and 'the awakened one' respectively), whose renunciation was all the more drastic – and whose (soteriological) heroism was all the more appropriate – because they were born into royal families.

However, the abandonment of the conventional responsibilities of the householder, which is presented in renunciative discourse as a marker of detachment, can also be presented as a marker of attachment to the renunciant lifestyle and of aversion to responsibility; and this presentation marks our texts, which intervene in order to set up a new construction of yogic masculinity. When Yudhiṣṭhira muses about wandering in the woods and demonstrating his detachment, he does so precisely because he is *not* detached; if he were, he would be able to be king in a responsible but detached manner, rather than wanting to avoid kingship. This view of the renunciative option is used to good effect by Kṛṣṇa in the *Bhagavadgītā* in response to Arjuna's plan to renounce his *kṣatriya* duty: Kṛṣṇa insists that Arjuna should fight as a good *kṣatriya*, but should do so in a spirit of detachment. In order to bring this suggestion into line with the soteriology of the soul escaping rebirth, all that is required is a small adjustment to the mechanism of *karman*: so Kṛṣṇa explains that it is not action per se that generates *karman* and binds the soul to further rebirth, but rather it is only action performed under the influence of desire and aversion which does so – and this could include the actions of the renouncer (*Mbh* 6.25.4–9). This being the case, in principle it is possible for Arjuna and Yudhiṣṭhira to eschew the renunciant lifestyle and yet attain the goal of the renouncers.[29] The renunciative impulse is thus shown to depend upon an aberrant and extreme brahmin masculinity, based on a misapprehension of the karmic process; and if Kṛṣṇa's proposals are taken seriously, the masculinity of aloofness can be preserved on the metaphysical and affective levels while the masculinity of responsible action is preserved on the conventional level. The resulting yogic hybrid combines elements of what I have called brahmin and *kṣatriya* masculinities, but would be available for all men, since it would be compatible with performance of the duties associated with any conventional class role.

Conclusion

The *Mahābhārata* and *Rāmāyaṇa* narratively experiment with various constructs of masculinity. One basic taxonomy which the texts affirm is the taxonomy of social class, which results in four distinct masculinities defined in broad terms by occupation, one for each class. Though there are subconstructs with varying emphases within each class, there is a scale of value defined by one's level of focus on one's proper class duties and one's consequent success in terms of eloquence, lordship, profit, and greatness, as the case may be (see again the quotation on p. 127).

In addition to occupational masculinities, the texts' self-presentation to an audience of all classes implies the construction of masculinities that are not specific to any particular class. But because every literary character is of a particular class, such masculinities tend to be based on virtues and preoccupations that are otherwise associated with one class in particular. Thus the presentation of Rāma as the ideal man, the concentration of these texts upon royal families, and the idea that the king sets an example for men as a whole, allow *kṣatriya* masculinity to stand as a general paradigm. In this regard the emphasis is upon responsible custodianship of an ongoing patrilineal inheritance, and salvation through one's descendants – which is a concern for members of all classes. But by serving as a paradigm for the patrilineal soteriology (the 'path of the fathers'), the *kṣatriya* class is the locus wherein the problems of that soteriology – the competition, violence, and great sufferings that it spawns, and the precarious nature of its rewards – are narratively demonstrated.

The soteriology of escape from rebirth, which is the main alternative to the patrilineal soteriology, is typically proposed in association with the masculinity of the brahmin class, whose characteristic virtues and preoccupations (austerity, knowledge, etc.) are thereby generalised – via the discourse of the 'true brahmin' – across those born in any and all classes. Specifically, the soteriology of escape (the 'path of the gods') is associated with a yogic masculinity of disciplined renunciation, which is constructed to a large degree as the movement of a heroic individual beyond the conventional patrilineal duties of whatever class. One soteriology seems thus to imply a rejection of the other, and two masculinities, both of which apply beyond class boundaries, are in conflict.

One of the texts' responses is to combine the two masculinities into one, while preserving and discarding elements of each. The newly emergent yogic masculinity championed by Kṛṣṇa in the *Bhagavadgītā* involves the responsible discharging of class duties and the responsible preservation of the patriline, but remedies the deficiencies of patrilineal salvation by contextualising it within the frame of escape from rebirth. It obviates physical renunciation while preserving yogic aloofness in affective terms. The resulting construct of masculinity – which, by his own admission, is performed by Kṛṣṇa – combines a public-spirited interest in the 'holding-together of the world'[30] with the prospect of individual progress beyond the sphere of rebirth. However, this new hybrid masculinity has the curious distinction of not being behaviourally marked, since the difference between the dutiful man and the yogically dutiful man lies in his *internal attitude* to his actions; so we cannot tell whether Rāma, Yudhiṣṭhira, Arjuna, or any other character(s) performed this ideal construct of yogic masculinity. Thus the performance of ideal masculinity is not a performance for an audience of other human beings; rather, it is a performance for oneself, and for Kṛṣṇa Almighty.

I hope this chapter has demonstrated that where the business of salvation is presented in terms of the salvation of males – and this tends to be the case in ancient India, at least as witnessed by the surviving texts – then there is a close and non-accidental relationship between soteriology and masculinity, and a good argument for pursuing religious studies under the broader umbrella of gender studies. But in this respect it seems that Kṛṣṇa's hybrid soteriology, which implies a yogic masculinity radically different from, but also conventionally indistinguishable from, the masculinity of patrilineal responsibility, has nowhere to go. How can human discourse include an unmarked soteriology? That would undermine the semiotics of performative masculinity and lead to chronic ambiguity. Hence it makes sense that a renouncer, in a flat contradiction of Kṛṣṇa's basic premise, tells King Janaka, an alleged exponent of Kṛṣṇa's yogic masculinity (cf. *Mbh*

6.25.20), that it is impossible to be a non-attached householder (*Mbh* 12.308.133–166), because non-attachment must be accompanied by conventional indications:

> O lord of the earth, what indication is there that one is Freed when . . . ? What indication is there that one is Freed when . . . ? What indication is there that one is Freed when . . . ? So you are not Freed . . .
> (*Mahābhārata* 12.308.128–131, tr. Fitzgerald 2002: 664)

In this perspective, the hybrid yogic masculinity is just the old patrilineal masculinity rebranded. And thus it may seem that the soteriological aspect of masculinity cannot achieve independence from the sociological.

Notes

1 I would like to thank: Ilona Zsolnay for arranging and managing the Pennsylvania conference, for inviting me to participate, and for her written comments on previous versions of this chapter; the conference sponsors for their generosity; the other participants for their papers and comments; and the UK Arts and Humanities Research Council for funding the research.

2 I include the *Harivaṃśa* (*Hv*), as it completes the *Mahābhārata* (*Mbh*). For *Mahābhārata* translations, see Smith 2009 (books 1–18, abridged); Ganguli 1993 (books 1–18); Debroy 2015 (books 1–18); van Buitenen 1973–78 (books 1–5); Cherniak 2008–09 (book 6, including the *Bhagavadgītā*); Pilikian 2006–09 (part of book 7); Bowles 2006–08 (book 8); Meiland 2005–07 (book 9); Johnson 2008 (book 10); Fitzgerald 2004 (book 11 and part of book 12); Wynne 2009 (the next part of book 12); Fitzgerald 2002 (chapter 308 of book 12); Dutt 1897 (*Harivaṃśa*); Saindon 1998 (*Harivaṃśa* chapters 11–19); Couture 1991 (*Harivaṃśa* chapters 30–78). For *Rāmāyaṇa* (*Rām*) translations, see Shastri 1952–59 (books 1–7, complete); Goldman et al. 1984–2009 (books 1–6). The Sanskrit texts cited in this chapter are the critical editions, but many of the translations are of other editions, and thus may have different chapter and verse numbers.

3 For arguments for the priority of the *Mahābhārata* and references to most of the relevant scholarship on this issue, see Hiltebeitel 2009, esp. pp. 170–171 and n. 5. I suspect that the existence of views on this matter is more to do with the desire to know than with the ability to find out.

4 Studies directly addressing the topic of masculinity in ancient Indian literature are few and far between. Monti 2002 includes some useful essays on this topic in the *Mahābhārata*, as does Brodbeck and Black 2007. For the masculinity of the Buddha, see Powers 2009; for masculinity in the Vedas, Whitaker 2011; for masculinity in the Purāṇas, Taylor 2013.

5 The Sanskrit word *nara*, here translated 'man,' frequently has the sense not just of 'person' but of 'male person' – a sense which I tend to assume 'man' has in English, since there are any number of ways of stipulating the inclusion of women if that is what one intends. Though the texts' audience includes women, and though women are involved in the encouragement of masculine performance and are sometimes explicitly included in benefit verses of this type, the promised reward is here being held out specifically for the *male* reader.

6 Heterosexuality is normative in these texts, in consonance with the procreative imperative; though there are close male friendships, notably that between Arjuna Pāṇḍava and Kṛṣṇa. The latter relationship has been studied in terms of 'same-sex

love' (Vanita 2001: 3–7; cf. Shah 2009: 327–328); but although the *Mahābhārata* clearly sees this relationship as more than a natural friendship between cousins and in-laws, it is presented as being extraordinary in theological terms, rather than in romantic or sexual ones. Notwithstanding Shah's claims (Shah 2013: 232, 236), the closest thing to an explicit mention of homosexuality that I know of in these texts is at *Harivaṃśa* 23.117, where, as if to explain his non-succession to his father's throne (which is explained in other ways elsewhere in the *Mahābhārata*), Devāpi, who a few verses earlier was described as a great warrior (*mahāratha*), is said to have chosen Kṛtaka, the son of the brahmin Cyavana (*cyavanasya putraḥ kṛtaka iṣṭaś cāsīn mahātmanaḥ*). More important to the *Mahābhārata* plot are several instances of transsexuality and/or gender bending: Arjuna pretends to be emasculated for a year, as a disguise (Custodi 2007; Pelissero 2002); Śikhaṇḍinī becomes Śikhaṇḍin through the gift of a phallus, and is thus able to fight in the war and take Ambā's revenge upon Bhīṣma (Custodi 2007); and Sāmba pretends to be a woman as a practical joke (von Simson 2007). These episodes, though obviously intriguing, are not discussed further in this chapter. For an overview of 'third-sex constructs in ancient India,' see Zwilling and Sweet 2000.

7 See *Mbh* 1.89.32; 1.163.14–19; 12.67.31; 12.68.10, 21, 29; 12.70.23–24; *Hv* 29.30–33; *Rām* 2.61.8 (here almost the whole chapter is a description of the kingless state).

8 See *Mbh* 5.137.5; 5.180.36–38; 6.48.37; 6.92.9; 6.103.49; 7.122.16; 7.164.23; 7.169.4; 12.7.5; 12.192.110; 15.46.8. Cf. also *Mbh* 8.64.20; *Rām* 2.93.35. A similar sentiment is implied on the part of *kṣatriya* women (here Gāndhārī) at *Mbh* 11.26.5 (Brodbeck 2009b: 45).

9 See *Mbh* 2.61.20–21; 3.14.7; 3.125.8; 5.33.74; 5.88.5; 12.28.31; 12.59.59–61; 12.138.26; 12.277.26; 13.141.28–29; cf. *Manusmṛti* 7.47, 50; *Arthaśāstra* 8.3.5–22, 38. The chequered reputation of these activities is due to their close relationship with desire (*kāma*), and thus their tendency to encourage immoderation and the neglect of royal duties. The dangers of gambling are starkly illustrated in *Mbh* 2.

10 *Mbh* 5.48.33–41; 5.61.7–17; 5.165.3–8; cf. the boasting of the coward Uttara, *Mbh* 4.33–41.

11 See e.g., *Mbh* 6.80.40; 7.99.26; 7.122.68–69; 8.*179.

12 *Mbh* 9.57.4–8; 9.59.14–15; 11.14.12–19. The observation of martial etiquette is itself a matter of honour and constitutive of reputation; Duryodhana, though in many ways a villain, is a respectable one because of his decent behaviour on the battlefield (*Mbh* 9.60, 63–64).

13 For head-shaving as a punishment, see Kane 1973: 396–97. Olivelle's theorisation of hair in South Asia derives the 'root meaning' of hair to be sexual maturity (1998: 37); hence its enforced removal would be a demonstration and a marker of impotence.

14 See *Mbh* 13.23–24; 13.87–92; *Hv* 11–13; *Rām* 1.71.18–20; *Manusmṛti* 3.122–285.

15 See *Mbh* 13.38–46; *Manusmṛti* 5.146–169; 8.371–373; 9.1–102.

16 The lineal ritual aspect is clear in Olivelle's translation of *Śatapatha Brāhmaṇa* 1.7.2.4 (Olivelle 1993: 48): 'Because he has to desire offspring . . . he is born as a debt to the fathers; and he pays it to them when he has children that provide the continuity of their lineage.'

17 For the general principle, see *Manusmṛti* 2.109–16; for lower-class men, 3.156; 4.99; 10.127; for women, 9.18.

18 The phrase is derived from Blackstone 1769: 223 ('. . . the law of England has so particular and tender a regard to the immunity of a man's house, that it stiles it his castle . . .'). For the general legal principle, Blackstone refers to Cicero's *De Domo Sua*, 41.

19 Cf. *Rām* 2.101.9–10; 3.48.8–9; *Mbh* 6.25.21; 12.59.10.

20 Śūrpaṇakhā comes across Rāma and his brother Lakṣmaṇa in the wilderness, falls in love immediately, and proposes first to Rāma and then to Lakṣmaṇa. The brothers make fun of her; and when she then makes to attack Sītā out of jealousy, Rāma has Lakṣmaṇa cut off her ears and nose. In a way, then, the *Rāmāyaṇa* tragedy is a result of Rāma's response to female sexual desire. By contrast, in the *Mahābhārata*, the standard – and proper – male response when a woman requests sex is simply to give her what she wants (see, e.g., the encounter of Arjuna and Ulūpī at *Mbh* 1.206).

21 This would seem to be the reason why a masculinity can be constructed for one and not the other.

22 See *Mbh* 13.8.27–28: 'As the herdsman, stick in hand, protects the herd, even so should the Kshatriya always protect the Vedas and the Brahmanas. Indeed, the Kshatriya should protect all righteous Brahmanas even as a sire protects his sons' (tr. Ganguli 1993: 22–23). The non-appearance of wives in these similes is perhaps to be explained by their appearance earlier in the same chapter: 'As the husband is to the wife, even so are the Brahmanas unto Kshatriyas' (*Mbh* 13.8.19, tr. Ganguli 1993: 22). The husband–wife relationship is seemingly multivalent.

23 See, e.g., *Mbh* 3.122 for Cyavana's constipation spell; *Mbh* 3.60.31–38 for Damayantī's disposing of a lustful hunter. Examples could easily be multiplied.

24 Bhīṣma, who is the firstborn son of a king but opts out of both kingship and sexuality, is once called a brahmin (*Mbh* 5.21.9), with the implication of negligence. When the young Pāṇḍavas are forced into hiding in fear of their lives, they present themselves as brahmins – a subdued *kṣatriya* presence that comes back into its own at the competition to win Draupadī. Arjuna in his brahmin disguise defeats all other suitors (to their strenuous objection, since this is a *kṣatriya* event) and, with in-laws now on their side, the disguise is lifted (*Mbh* 1.144–91).

25 Pāṇḍu was cursed (by a brahmin whom he shot, mistaking him for a deer, while that brahmin was copulating with a deer), to die instantly should he ever again have sex; so Kuntī invited gods to impregnate her on his behalf (*Mbh* 1.109–14).

26 It was Durvāsas who, pleased with her unfailingly diligent services, gave young Kuntī the boon of being able to summon gods for sex (*Mbh* 1.104.4–7). For the time when Durvāsas came to stay with Kṛṣṇa, see *Mbh* 13.143–45; for how Durvāsas's inopportune arrival effectively caused Lakṣmaṇa's death, see *Rām* 7.93–96.

27 For discussion and examples, see Brodbeck 2009c: 138–43, esp. n. 16.

28 For descriptions of the two postmortem paths, see *Mbh* 6.30.23–28; *Bṛhadāraṇyaka Upaniṣad* 6.2.9–16; *Chāndogya Upaniṣad* 5.4–10. Fitzgerald has expressed misgivings about the applicability of the word 'soteriology' to some ancient Indian contexts, since as he sees it, '"soteriology" implies a *sōtēr*, a "savior"' (Fitzgerald 2015: 128). But despite the word's etymology, I don't think it necessarily implies that; I use the word as per the *Oxford English Dictionary* definition, to mean 'doctrine of salvation.'

29 Similarly, it is possible for a man to have children and yet not be soteriologically invested in them or subject to desire. Several *Mahābhārata* brahmins only reproduce because they are begged to do so by their endangered ancestors in heaven (*Mbh* 1.41; 3.94.11–15).

30 That is, *lokasaṃgraha*; see *Mbh* 5.50.54; 6.25.20, 25; 12.122.14; 12.156.16; 12.251.25; 12.252.9. *Mbh* 14.46.37 mentions *lokasaṃgraha* from the renouncer's perspective, in negative terms. *Mbh* 12.58.19 seems to use the compound in a slightly different sense (with *loka* meaning 'people').

References

Arthaśāstra. R. P. Kangle (ed., tr.), *The Kauṭilīya Arthaśāstra*, 2nd edn. 3 vols. Delhi: Motilal Banarsidass, 1986 [1965–72].

Biardeau, Madeleine. 1981. 'The Salvation of the King in the *Mahābhārata*.' *Contributions to Indian Sociology* (new series) 15: 75–97.

Blackstone, William. 1769. *Commentaries on the Laws of England: Book the Fourth*. Oxford: Clarendon. Reprint, London: Dawsons, 1966.

Bowles, Adam (tr.). 2006–08. *Mahābhārata Book Eight: Karṇa*. 2 vols. New York: New York University Press/John and Jennifer Clay Foundation.

———. 2007. *Dharma, Disorder and the Political in Ancient India: The Āpaddharmaparvan of the Mahābhārata*. Leiden: Brill.

Bṛhadāraṇyaka Upaniṣad, Valerie J. Roebuck (tr.), *The Upaniṣads*: 11–105. London: Penguin, 2003.

Brockington, John L. 1998. *The Sanskrit Epics*. Leiden: Brill.

———. 2006. 'Epic Svayaṁvaras.' In Raghunath Panda and Madhusudan Mishra (eds), *Voice of the Orient: A Tribute to Prof. Upendranath Dhal*: 35–42. Delhi: Eastern Book Linkers.

Brodbeck, Simon P. 2007. 'Gendered Soteriology: Marriage and the *Karmayoga*.' In Simon Brodbeck and Brian Black (eds), *Gender and Narrative in the Mahābhārata*: 144–75. London: Routledge.

———. 2009a. *The Mahābhārata Patriline: Gender, Culture, and the Royal Hereditary*. Farnham, Surrey: Ashgate.

———. 2009b. 'Husbands of Earth: *Kṣatriyas*, Females, and Female *Kṣatriyas* in the *Strīparvan* of the *Mahābhārata*.' In Robert P. Goldman and Muneo Tokunaga (eds), *Epic Undertakings: Papers of the 12th World Sanskrit Conference, Vol. 2*: 33–63. Delhi: Motilal Banarsidass.

———. 2009c. 'The Bhāradvāja Pattern in the *Mahābhārata*.' In Petteri Koskikallio (ed.), *Parallels and Comparisons: Proceedings of the Fourth Dubrovnik International Conference on the Sanskrit Epics and Purāṇas*: 137–79. Zagreb: Croatian Academy of Sciences and Arts.

Brodbeck, Simon, and Brian Black (eds). 2007. *Gender and Narrative in the Mahābhārata*. London: Routledge.

van Buitenen, J. A. B. (tr.). 1973–78. *The Mahābhārata*, vols 1–3. Chicago: University of Chicago Press.

Chāndogya Upaniṣad, Valerie J. Roebuck (tr.), *The Upaniṣads*: 107–204. London: Penguin, 2003.

Cherniak, Alex (tr.). 2008–09. *Mahābhārata Book Six: Bhīṣma*. 2 vols. New York: New York University Press/John and Jennifer Clay Foundation.

Couture, André (tr.). 1991. *L'enfance de Krishna: Traduction des chapitres 30 à 78 (éd. cr.)*. Quebec: Presses de l'Université Laval / Paris: Éditions du Cerf.

Custodi, Andrea. 2007. '"Show You Are a Man!" Transsexuality and Gender Bending in the Characters of Arjuna/Bṛhannaḍā and Ambā/Śikhaṇḍin.' In Simon Brodbeck and Brian Black (eds), *Gender and Narrative in the Mahābhārata*: 208–29. London: Routledge.

De Domo Sua. N. H. Watts. (ed., tr.), *Cicero: The Speeches, with an English Translation*: 132–311. London: William Heinemann, 1923.

Debroy, Bibek (tr.). 2015 [2010–14]. *The Mahabharata*. 10 vols. Delhi: Penguin Books India.

Derrett, J. Duncan M. 1959. '*Bhū-Bharaṇa, Bhū-Pālana, Bhū-Bhojana*: An Indian Conundrum.' *Bulletin of the School of Oriental and African Studies* 22.1: 108–23.

Dutt, Manmatha Nath (tr.). 1897. *A Prose English Translation of Harivamsha: Translated Literally into English Prose*. Calcutta: Elysium Press.

Ernest, Phillip A. 2007. 'History and the Individual in the Sanskrit *Mahābhārata*.' PhD thesis, University of Cambridge.

Fitzgerald, James L. (tr.). 2002. 'Nun Befuddles King, Shows *Karmayoga* Does Not Work: Sulabhā's Refutation of King Janaka at MBh 12.308.' *Journal of Indian Philosophy* 30.6: 641–77.

——— (tr.). 2004. *The Mahābhārata*, vol. 7. Chicago: University of Chicago Press.

———. 2006. 'Negotiating the Shape of "Scripture": New Perspectives on the Development and Growth of the *Mahābhārata* between the Empires.' In Patrick Olivelle (ed.), *Between the Empires: Society in India 300 BCE to 400 CE*: 257–86. New York: Oxford University Press.

———. 2015. '"Saving *Buddhis*" in Epic *Mokṣadharma*.' *International Journal of Hindu Studies* 19.1–2: 97–137.

Ganguli, Kisari Mohan (tr.). 1993 [1883–96]. *The Mahabharata of Krishna-Dwaipayana Vyasa Translated into English Prose from the Original Sanskrit Text*. 4 vols. Delhi: Munshiram Manoharlal. Online at http://www.sacred-texts.com/hin/maha/.

Glucklich, Ariel. 1988. 'The Royal Sceptre (*Daṇḍa*) as Legal Punishment and Sacred Symbol.' *History of Religions* 28.2: 97–122.

Goldman, Robert P. 1980. 'Rāmaḥ Sahalakṣmaṇaḥ: Psychological and Literary Aspects of the Composite Hero of Vālmīki's *Rāmāyaṇa*.' *Journal of Indian Philosophy* 8.2: 149–89.

——— (tr.). 1984. *The Rāmāyaṇa of Vālmīki: An Epic of Ancient India. Volume I: Bālakāṇḍa*. Princeton, NJ: Princeton University Press. Vol. 1 of Goldman et al. 1984–2009.

Goldman, Robert P., and Jeffrey M. Masson. 1969. 'Who Knows Rāvaṇa? A Narrative Difficulty in the *Vālmīki Rāmāyaṇa*.' *Annals of the Bhandarkar Oriental Research Institute* 50: 95–100.

Goldman, Robert P., Sheldon I. Pollock, Rosalind Lefeber, Sally J. Sutherland Goldman, and Barend A. van Nooten (trs). 1984–2009. *The Rāmāyaṇa of Vālmīki: An Epic of Ancient India*, vols 1–6. Princeton, NJ: Princeton University Press.

González-Reimann, Luis. 2010. 'Time in the *Mahābhārata* and the Time of the *Mahābhārata*.' In Sheldon Pollock (ed.), *Epic and Argument in Sanskrit Literary History: Essays in Honor of Robert P. Goldman*: 61–73. Delhi: Manohar.

Hara, Minoru. 1973. 'The King as a Husband of the Earth (*Mahī-Pati*).' *Asiatische Studien/Études Asiatiques* 27.2: 97–114.

———. 1974. 'A Note on the *Rākṣasa* Form of Marriage.' *Journal of the American Oriental Society* 94.3: 296–306.

———. 1996–97. 'Śrī: Mistress of a King.' *Orientalia Suecana* 45–46: 33–61.

[*Hv*] *Harivaṃśa*. Parashuram Lakshman Vaidya (ed.), *The Harivaṁśa: Being the Khila or Supplement to the Mahābhārata, for the First Time Critically Edited*. 2 vols. Poona: Bhandarkar Oriental Research Institute, 1969–71.

Hegarty, James M. 2012. *Religion, Narrative and Public Imagination in South Asia: Past and Place in the Sanskrit Mahābhārata*. London: Routledge.

Hiltebeitel, Alf. 2004. 'Role, Role Model, and Function: The Sanskrit Epic Warrior in Comparison and Theory.' In Jacqueline Suthren Hirst and Lynn Thomas (eds), *Playing for Real: Hindu Role Models, Religion, and Gender*: 27–50. Delhi: Oxford University Press.

———. 2009. 'Authorial Paths through the Two Sanskrit Epics, via the *Rāmopākhyāna*.' In Robert P. Goldman and Muneo Tokunaga (eds), *Epic Undertakings: Papers of the 12th World Sanskrit Conference, Vol. 2*: 169–214. Delhi: Motilal Banarsidass.

Jay, Nancy. 1992. *Throughout Your Generations Forever: Sacrifice, Religion, and Paternity*. Chicago: University of Chicago Press.

Johnson, W. J. (tr.). 2008 [1998]. *The Sauptikaparvan of the Mahābhārata: The Massacre at Night*. Oxford: Oxford University Press.

Kane, Pandurang Vaman. 1973. *History of Dharmaśāstra: Ancient and Mediæval Religious and Civil Law*, 2nd edn. Vol. 3. Poona: Bhandarkar Oriental Research Institute.

McGrath, Kevin. 2009. *Strī: Women in Epic Mahābhārata*. Boston, MA: Ilex Foundation / Washington, DC: Center for Hellenic Studies, trustees for Harvard University.

[*Mbh*] *Mahābhārata*. Vishnu S. Sukthankar, Franklin Edgerton, Raghu Vira, Sushil Kumar De, Shripad Krishna Belvalkar, Parashuram Lakshman Vaidya, Ramachandra Narayan Dandekar, Hari Damodar Velankar, Vasudev Gopal Paranjpe, and Raghunath Damodar Karmarkar (eds), *The Mahābhārata for the First Time Critically Edited*. 19 vols. Poona: Bhandarkar Oriental Research Institute, 1933–66.

Manusmṛti. Patrick Olivelle (ed., tr.) with Suman Olivelle, *Manu's Code of Law: A Critical Edition and Translation of the Mānava-Dharmaśāstra*. New York: Oxford University Press, 2005.

Meiland, Justin (tr.). 2005–07. *Mahābhārata Book Nine: Śalya*. 2 vols. New York: New York University Press/John and Jennifer Clay Foundation.

Monti, Alessandro (ed.). 2002. *Hindu Masculinities Across the Ages: Updating the Past*. Turin: L'Harmattan Italia.

Nandy, Ashis, Shikha Trivedy, Shail Mayaram, and Achyut Yagnik. 1995. *Creating a Nationality: The Ramjanmabhumi Movement and Fear of the Self*. Delhi: Oxford University Press.

Olivelle, Patrick. 1993. *The Āśrama System: The History and Hermeneutics of a Religious Institution*. New York: Oxford University Press.

———. 1998. 'Hair and Society: Social Significance of Hair in South Asian Traditions.' In Alf Hiltebeitel and Barbara D. Miller (eds), *Hair: Its Power and Meaning in Asian Cultures*: 11–49. Albany: State University of New York Press.

Oxford English Dictionary. Online edition, August 2015. http://www.oed.com/.

Pelissero, Alberto. 2002. 'A Sexual Masquerade: Arjuna as a Eunuch in the *Mahābhārata*.' In Alessandro Monti (ed.), *Hindu Masculinities Across the Ages: Updating the Past*: 123–55. Turin: L'Harmattan Italia.

Pilikian, Vaughan (tr.). 2006–09. *Mahābhārata Book Seven: Droṇa*. 2 vols. New York: New York University Press/John and Jennifer Clay Foundation.

Pollock, Sheldon. 1993. 'Rāmāyaṇa and Political Imagination in India.' *Journal of Asian Studies* 52.2: 261–97.

Powers, John. 2009. *A Bull of a Man: Images of Masculinity, Sex, and the Body in Indian Buddhism*. Cambridge, MA: Harvard University Press.

[*Rām*] *Rāmāyaṇa*. G. H. Bhatt, P. L. Vaidya, P. C. Divanji, D. R. Mankad, G. C. Jhala, and U. P. Shah (eds), *The Vālmīki-Rāmāyaṇa Critically Edited for the First Time*. 7 vols. Baroda: Oriental Institute, 1958–75.

Saindon, Marcelle (tr.). 1998. *Le Pitrikalpa du Harivamsha: Traduction, analyse, interprétation*. Quebec: Presses de l'Université Laval.

Śatapatha Brāhmaṇa. Julius Eggeling (tr.), *The Śatapatha-Brāhmaṇa According to the Text of the Mādhyandina School*. 5 vols. Delhi: Motilal Banarsidass, 1972 [1882–1900].

Shah, Shalini. 2009. 'The Principle of *Kāma Puruṣārtha* in the Mahābhārata: Its Conception and Variations.' In Kalyan Kumar Chakravarty (ed.), *Text and Variations of the Mahābhārata: Contextual, Regional and Performative Traditions*: 321–29. Delhi: National Mission for Manuscripts/Munshiram Manoharlal.

———. 2013. 'Homosexuality in Ancient Indian Literature.' In D. N. Jha (ed.), *Contesting Symbols and Stereotypes: Essays on Indian History and Culture*: 226–43. Delhi: Aakar.

Shastri, Hari Prasad (tr.). 1952–59. *The Ramayana of Valmiki*. 3 vols. London: Shanti Sadan.

von Simson, Georg. 2007. 'Kṛṣṇa's son Sāmba: Faked Gender and Other Ambiguities on the Background of Lunar and Solar Myth.' In Simon Brodbeck and Brian Black (eds), *Gender and Narrative in the Mahābhārata*: 230–57. London: Routledge.

Smith, John D. (tr.). 2009. *The Mahābhārata: An Abridged Translation*. London: Penguin.

Taylor, McComas. 2013. 'Purāṇic Masculinities and Transgender Adventures in the Garden of the Goddess.' *International Journal of Hindu Studies* 17.2: 153–79.

Vanita, Ruth. 2001. 'Introduction: Ancient Indian Materials.' In Ruth Vanita and Saleem Kidwai (eds), *Same-Sex Love in India: Readings from Literature and History*: 1–30. New York: Palgrave.

Vyas, Shantikumar Nanooram. 1967. *India in the Rāmāyaṇa Age: A Study of the Social and Cultural Conditions in Ancient India as Described in Vālmīki's Rāmāyaṇa*. Delhi: Atma Ram.

Whitaker, Jarrod L. 2011. *Strong Arms and Drinking Strength: Masculinity, Violence, and the Body in Ancient India*. New York: Oxford University Press.

Wynne, Alexander (tr.). 2009. *Mahābhārata Book Twelve: Peace. Volume Three: 'The Book of Liberation.'* New York: New York University Press/John and Jennifer Clay Foundation.

Zwilling, Leonard, and Michael J. Sweet. 2000. 'The Evolution of Third-Sex Constructs in Ancient India: A Study in Ambiguity.' In Julia Leslie and Mary McGee (eds), *Invented Identities: The Interplay of Gender, Religion and Politics in India*: 99–132. Delhi: Oxford University Press.

6 Mesopotamia before and after Sodom

Colleagues, crack troops, comrades-in-arms

Ann K. Guinan and Peter Morris

Introduction

Sex between men is not a salient or celebrated feature of the Mesopotamian erotic repertoire, but it is still surprising that the texts referring explicitly to sexual relations between men are so sparse. Direct references to the topic are limited to two Middle Assyrian laws concerning acts that one man commits against another, and four omens from one tablet of the first-millennium compendium of omens, *šumma ālu*.[1] What is equally surprising is that the vocabulary of these two legal texts and one of these omens makes anal penetration and the men's equality of status explicit. The other three omens from *šumma ālu* are recorded in a topical set, the subject of which is male sex partners of differing social status, thereby highlighting by contrast the focus on equal status in the fourth omen which is placed separately in the text.[2] In addition to these explicit references, the erotically evocative language that is used to portray the relationship between Gilgamesh and Enkidu in the opening tablets of the Standard Babylonian *Epic of Gilgamesh* consistently emphasizes their equality of status, while being altogether more reticent about the subject of sexual relations. Taken together, these sources overall preserve a judicial, literary, and divinatory perspective on a single topic – the erotics of male equals in Mesopotamia – with the omens existing midway between criminal acts and the idealized poetic love of comrades.

It is to this body of evidence that Assyriologists have returned again and again – it has not changed or expanded since Thorkild Jacobsen published "How Did Gilgamesh Oppress Uruk?" in 1930.[3] While the history of Assyriological discussion reflects the pursuit of the same sources across a changing cultural and theoretical landscape, the study of sex between men has itself undergone a vast shift in the intervening decades: when Jacobsen published his article, the English word "homosexual" had only been in use for 38 years.[4] In this chapter, we approach the same body of evidence, to reconsider it in light of Queer Theory, which presents a more fully developed and coherent picture of a subject often occluded by silences. This approach suggests the possibility of exploring latent content below the surface of the

Mesopotamian sources: Queer Theory, we argue, can suggest interpretive strategies that may allow us to connect the dots, as it were, between the seemingly isolated but charged Mesopotamian texts.

Mesopotamia before Sodom

The two Middle Assyrian laws are the centerpiece and linchpin of the small set of textual sources that deal with homosexual sex in Mesopotamia. The 11th-century text, which comes from the Assyrian capital Aššur, claims to be a copy of a 14th-century original; whether the laws originate with Aššur-uballiṭ (1363–1328 BCE) or Tiglath-pilesar I (1114–1076 BCE), they date to the rise of the Middle Assyrian empire. There is no parallel to these laws in any of the other Mesopotamian legal formulations; they make their appearance within a narrow temporal and cultural moment and then vanish.

> MAL¶19 If a man furtively spreads rumors about his comrade, saying, "Everyone sodomizes him," or in a quarrel in public says to him, "Everyone sodomizes you," and further, "I can prove the charges against you," but he is unable to prove the charges and does not prove the charges, they shall strike that man 50 blows with rods; he shall perform the king's service for one full month; they shall cut off his hair; moreover, he shall pay 3,600 shekels of lead.
>
> MAL¶20 If a man sodomizes his comrade and they prove the charges against him and find him guilty, they shall sodomize him and turn him into a eunuch.[5]

The subject of both MAL¶19 and MAL¶20 is a *tappā'u*. The word refers to a close associate with mutual business interests, shared danger, or adjacent property: these are crimes committed by one social equal against another. The first of these laws deals with slander, but slander of a specific kind: the accusation of repeated passive homosexual receptivity. Implicit, however, in the demand for proof of the slanderous accusation is the idea that such behavior could or did occur. What, in the mind of its formulators, does MAL¶20 deal with? Scholarly opinion varies, but it would appear to be a rape law. The penalty mandates gang rape of the convicted offender. That the crime and the punishment are virtually the same is significant, and should not be dismissed as simply a strategy of power or an example of *lex talionis* taken to its contradictory extreme – the act also has to be sexual, or the punishment couldn't be accomplished.

"Sodomy" remains the standard modern legal term to refer to anal sex between men, historically employed to refer to other proscribed sexual activities as well. In a note to the translation, Roth clarifies that in MAL¶19 and MAL¶20 "the implication of sodomy is obtained from the context, and not from the verb *nâku*, which refers to fornication."[6] The use of the word in Martha Roth's translation is not intended as anachronistic reference to the Biblical narrative of Sodom, the composition of which postdates the cuneiform sources. MAL¶20 with its lavish punishment of just one man seems puzzling when considered alongside well-known Biblical parallels: sexual acts between two male partners are proscribed in two verses of Leviticus (18:22, 20:13) and the latter mandates the death penalty for both men. Gerstenberger quotes MAL¶20 in his commentary on Leviticus, but admits: "It is unclear why only one man is condemned. In any event, the public nature of the court proceedings does become evident."[7] It is hard to read MAL¶20 and consider it lenient, but perhaps it is, if we take Leviticus to be normative as subsequent sodomy laws have often done.

In Mesopotamian jurisprudence, legal reasoning is never stated outright and can only be surmised through the way individual cases relate to one another. Barry L. Eichler has shown that "within a single topical grouping" of Mesopotamian laws, any interpreter must bear two principles in mind: first, the "principle of polar cases with maximal variation," and second, "the principle of the creation of a legal statement by juxtaposing individual legal cases with one another."[8] Eichler argues that these principles offer "the master key for elucidating the structure of the law collections," when "structurally it is neither the whole nor the elements that count but rather the relationships existing between and among the elements."[9] Mesopotamian legal discourse on a given topic stakes out polar positions that define the outer boundaries of any legal situation to construct "a large discretionary middle that is not addressed." What the formulators meant by the area enclosed is left to later interpreters (both ancient and modern) to infer.[10] These laws both involve anal sex between men of equal status; they presuppose an accuser, an accused, and a public forum for adjudication. In the first case, the victim has been publically identified as someone known to be the receptive partner, and in the polar case he has been placed in the same position through active violation. Either by word or deed, one close associate has subordinated another – it is an infringement of masculine position or agency in a community of men who share the prerogatives of power. It is not hard to detect a sense of masculinity under threat in these legal texts: their placement in MAL A, which deals with crimes against and committed by women, seems to highlight this fact. But there are no women in MAL¶19 or MAL¶20: subject and object here are each a *tappā'u*. This creates a sort of mirror-effect in considering the laws: every subject here can potentially switch to being an object. As soon as the interpreter does what the discourse demands – picture the sort of cases that are not explicitly covered, or imagine what possibilities might exist in the discretionary area – the text seems to generate contradictions.

According to the hermeneutic method outlined by Eichler, MAL¶19 needs to be considered in the context of the laws that immediately precede it as well as the law that follows it. Slander is also the subject of MAL¶18 – a *tappā'u* claims that the wife of another is persistently and constantly being penetrated by men who are not her husband:

> MAL¶18 If a man says to his comrade, either in private or in a public quarrel, "Everyone has sex (*ittinikku*) with your wife; I can prove the charges," but he is unable to prove the charges and does not prove the charges, they shall strike him 40 blows with rods; he shall perform the king's service one full month; they shall cut off his hair; and he shall pay 3,600 shekels of lead.[11]

The legal topic of both MAL¶18 and MAL¶19 is thus the unsubstantiated slanderous humiliation of a fellow *tappā'u*. We should note that the stated penalty for a slanderer convicted under MAL¶18 is all but identical to that of a slanderer convicted under MAL¶19; the only difference is slightly more corporal punishment in MAL¶19. It is a more serious slander, but not much more, if one is accused directly of being a persistent passive sodomite than if it is implied that one is constantly cuckolded. Implying that someone is a constant cuckold is couched immediately in terms of accusation both public and private; calling someone a persistent passive sodomite by contrast immediately conjures up the word "furtively." The differing styles of perpetration in the criminal speech acts here seem to reflect the content of those speech acts, almost as though slanderer and sodomite are engaged in similar activities – both "furtively" pursue contact with social equals where someone is shamed. The difference is that the laws criminalize the act of shaming another *tappā'u* by slander, but are silent on the *tappā'u* who shames another or himself by consensual anal sex. If sodomy laws ordinarily restrict the consensual sex act between two male equals, Middle Assyria has no proper sodomy law at all: consensual sex is not criminalized but unmentioned.[12]

Criminalization of sexual acts between male equals is concentrated in the single law MAL¶20. Yet the discretionary space between MAL¶19 and MAL¶20 permits a wide latitude of inference for interpreters. Jacobsen in 1930 understood the laws to prohibit all "paederasty" (i.e., homosexuality).[13] W. G. Lambert argues MAL¶20 is not a rape law but a general prohibition of homosexuality, consensual or otherwise, because a rape law would specify that force was used.[14] Neither addresses why penalty is imposed only on one. Jean Bottéro and Petschow read MAL¶20 as a rape law, arguing consensual homosexual sex was seen as "perfectly natural and in no way condemned."[15] If Bottéro and Petschow and Lambert all understand the laws to address the same outer poles of violation – persistent receptivity on one hand, and using a *tappā'u* as a passive partner on the other – they read contradictory meanings into the discretionary space. For Bottéro and Petschow, the extremes of MAL¶19 and MAL¶20 are defined by a *tappā'u* who prefers and is known to be the passive partner and a *tappā'u* who is a rapist: accordingly, any act that falls between those polar cases is licit. Lambert by contrast reads all acts that fall in the same space as illicit. Jerry Cooper tries to harmonize these previous readings: he refutes Lambert's complaint about force not being specified in the text (noting it is not specified in other rape laws), but argues that – regardless of whether MAL¶20 means "that the victim was forced or constrained in some way to submit to anal penetration" or indicates only "that using another citizen as a passive partner, whatever the circumstances, was gravely offensive" – the level of shame inherent when one *tappā'u* buggers another means that (*contra* Bottéro and Petschow) "there was no free love in ancient Mesopotamia."[16]

The issue of proof, as specified in both MAL ¶19 and MAL ¶20, and the way it has been analyzed in each of the laws also reveals contradictory logic. Raymond Westbrook examines MAL¶20 through its use of the "dual phrase" of proof (the formula translated "they prove the charges against him, and they find him guilty"). In Westbrook's analysis of MAL¶20:

> [T]he evidence of the accuser himself is a statement against interest . . . [T]he offense is imposing on a free man the despicable passive role in intercourse. . . . For the victim to admit publicly that he had played the passive role, whether willingly or unwillingly, would be deeply shaming. Accordingly, the personal, uncorroborated evidence of the victim will cross a threshold of credibility.[17]

Westbrook understands the crime as something "impos[ed]" and therefore rape, but does not elaborate why no law criminalizes the "despicable passive role." Julia Assante focuses on the same demand for proof; she reads MAL¶20 as criminalizing all sex between men of equal status (not rape), but argues that the proof clause in MAL¶19 effectively serves as a sodomy law where "the circumstances of the clause tell us that a man who allows himself to be habitually sodomized . . . is punishable under the law."[18] This reading, however, does not explain why, if passive sodomy is "punishable under the law," no legal punishment for it is specified here. On the surface MAL¶19 criminalizes the false accusation that a *tappā'u* is a passive sodomite; but its demand for proof of such an assertion would effectively prevent anyone of whom the accusation is true from demanding satisfaction for being slandered.[19]

We would argue that the contradictions, both mutual and internal, inherent in these scholarly readings derive from the structure of the text. The structural problem in the text of MAL¶19 and MAL¶20 is that they focus solely on men. Ann Guinan has elsewhere noted one feature of reading the Middle Assyrian legal texts: "A single item in a text is related both to the one it follows and then to the next in line. At some point a sequence reaches its outer limit. This is only known when the next item in line crosses a boundary provoking, in the process, a new topic of inquiry."[20] This is precisely the dynamic that governs the order of laws in MAL A. Three subjects – husband, wife, and another man – govern a three-part judicial logic. In MAL¶19, this reduces to two subjects; in the penalty of MAL¶20 to a single subject. If the positionality that defines the relationship between two male equals – somatic obverse and inverse (penis and anus), agency (sexual subject or sexual object), social hierarchy (superior and inferior), or directional hierarchy (front and back) – can be occupied by one, or by everyone, the instability of reversible position is embodied in every man. The only thing that can arrest this mutually implicating process is an inflationary force; according to such somatic and cultural logic, the outlandish penalty of MAL¶20 seems almost inevitable.

For the 21st-century commentator, the penalty specified in MAL¶20 is both utterly alien and all-too-familiar. It is familiar because, in 2015, the activity described – gang rape imposed as a penalty for rape – is widespread in America's prison population (the largest in the world). Joe Loya, in a 2005 memoir of life in a California prison, notes that "in the hierarchy of criminals in prison, the child molester and rapist are the lowest caste. So the prison ethic has it that the other prisoners are allowed to rape the rapist without being rapists themselves."[21] A 2005 stage drama about the Abu Ghraib prison abuses during the Iraq War makes the same point: "They got a rule in here – it's okay to rape a rapist."[22] What makes MAL¶20 so alien is its status as law: prison rape is a social dynamic established by male equals, not juridical punishment. We would search in vain for a legal code today that enlists all citizens to rape a convicted criminal as a state-sanctioned penalty: it seems less a means to discipline and punish and more a primitive scapegoating mechanism out of René Girard.[23]

But one noteworthy element of reading MAL¶19 and MAL¶20 in sequence is the shadowy presence in both of the man who is repeatedly penetrated. In MAL¶19, it is defamatory to imply falsely that any *tappā'u* is such a man; in MAL¶20, it is mandatory that a *tappā'u* convicted of rape be made such a man. Perhaps, then, the concept lurking beneath the surface of MAL¶20 is one of an unlawfully independent phallic agency: if the rape of another male is an act that only the state itself can enact, then the crime punished so extravagantly in MAL¶20 is less sexuality than subversion.

Mesopotamia after Sodom

The history of sodomy – and its rigorous theoretical and historical examination by Queer Theory – shows that, of course, there does seem to be something inherently subversive about the subject in subsequent discourse, conceived of as the primally subversive crime against nature itself. Michael Foucault's famous statement about this "great sin against nature" is worth repeating in full:

> Silence and secrecy are a shelter for power, anchoring its prohibitions; but they also loosen its holds and provide for relatively obscure areas of tolerance. Consider for example the history of what was once "the" great sin against nature. The extreme discretion of these texts dealing

> with sodomy – that utterly confused category – and the nearly universal reticence in talking about it made possible a twofold operation: on one hand, there was an extreme severity (punishment by fire was meted out well into the eighteenth century, without there being any substantial protest expressed before the middle of the century), and on the other hand, a tolerance that must have been widespread (which can be deduced indirectly from the infrequency of judicial sentences, and which one glimpses more directly through certain statements concerning societies of men that were thought to exist in the army or in the courts).[24]

The contrast Foucault makes between "certain statements concerning societies of men" and the infrequency and severity of judicial sentences should seem similar to the way the two Middle Assyrian laws structure the issue. But Foucault's observations here contain, in embryonic form, many of the major themes upon which subsequent Queer Theory elaborates: the sense of subversion going far beyond mere sexual norms, the contradictory coexistence of tolerance with violent punishment, and the regime of silence that enforces this utterly confused cognitive structure.

In approaching the matter of silence, the first wave of Queer Theory to emerge after Foucault's death proves particularly useful. We might begin by considering Eve Kosofsky Sedgwick's emphasis on the signifying force of "silence . . . rendered as pointed and performative as speech," and the areas of ignorance and unknowing summed up in her phrase "the epistemology of the closet."[25] Across what Sedgwick describes as a "homosocial continuum," intense bonds and affiliations that men form with one another are all too similar to sexual bonds, and are moreover open to sexual shading and possibility.[26] For Sedgwick, the notion of the "closet" is defined simply as an "open secret" – readily available for reading yet circumscribed by silence. The possibility of being known or unknown creates willed ignorance on the one hand, and on the other a deep reservoir of potential violence. The displaced tensions of these contradictory demands are marked in discourse and are detectable in gaps, distortions of language, and signifying silences. The epistemological force of social and sexual dynamics can be employed as a critical tool of reading.

Other first-wave Queer Theorists observe a similar queasy instability of meaning, from which the potential for violence emerges. Alan Bray approaches the subject of male equals in "Homosexuality and the Signs of Friendship in Elizabethan England," where a cherished cultural ideal conjures up its own nightmarish congruent shadow or inverted mirror-image. Bray is looking here not only at social and sexual behavior, but also implicitly at the underlying ideologies of state formation. As Bray describes the vocabulary of the later 16th century in Britain:

> Two powerful images: One is the image of the masculine friend. The other is the figure called the sodomite. The reaction of these two images

> prompted was wildly different; the one was universally admired, the other execrated and feared: and yet in their uncompromising symmetry they paralleled each other in an uncanny way. . . . The distinction between the two was then apparently sharp and clearly marked: the one was expressed in orderly "civil" relations, the other in subversive behavior.[27]

Bray argues that "sodomy" cannot be collapsed into a synonym for homosexuality, but was instead primarily mobilized in the face of threats to the social order. Bray's point extends to other contexts where heretics or foreigners – in short, whatever a culture wishes to see as dangerously other – were the most likely sodomites. But the accusation of sexual misbehavior is seen to follow from the violation of the social order, and sodomy must remain unnamable and invisible, which (as Bray argues) allowed it to be tolerated within socially sanctioned relations of friendship or patronage where sexual acts that accompanied such relations went unnoticed.

In this connection we would like to employ one queer theoretical approach first suggested in the 1990s, and invoke Jonathan Goldberg's concept of "sodometry" – an obsolete word repurposed (or "queered") by Goldberg to represent the relational nature of the term and its contradictory double deployment. Sodomy is always the act that is performed or located elsewhere, yet the accusation has a way of returning in the direction from which it originated. Historically, sexual acts between men were subsumed into this shifting category of "sodomy," which could at various times and in different contexts include any number of stigmatized or nonprocreative acts (anal intercourse, masturbation, fellatio, bestiality). But sodomy in early modernity soon becomes a category with theological and political implications, a charge leveled against papists, traitors, heretics, spies, or foreigners. In the era before the advent of the "homosexual" individual, persons were accused or punished as sodomites in order to marginalize them, while the very same acts performed by those whose social position was secure passed without comment, recognition, or disturbance. Sodomy becomes something that one accuses others of but can never recognize in oneself, and the accusation "can be delivered only through what is said (or what is not), through slippages capable of being mobilized in more than one direction."[28] Goldberg's idea of "sodometry" trades on reversals of front and back, confusions, silences, and misrecognitions – it is a site of "the mutual implications of prohibition and production," lethal when applied in one direction, indifferent in the other.[29] Goldberg shows how accusations of sodomy only occurred where there was perceived to be a threat to the social order: the energy that fueled acts of annihilating violence directed at the sodomite comes in proportion to the threat perceived. The cost of this willed ignorance in homosocial structures is that all internal sense of threat is externalized, deflected out toward cultural boundaries that are vulnerable and in need of policing. What is at risk in addition to social or sexual prerogatives, Goldberg emphasizes, is the conceptual structure of the state, and its political and sexual order.

Goldberg's concept of "sodometry" follows Patricia Parker in examining how early modernity links the rhetorical trope of hysteron proteron – "inverted order," which reverses syntax for rhetorical effect, "putting the cart before the horse" – with more troubling challenges to the social order. This Greek rhetorical term of "hysteron proteron" translated into Latin yields the term "preposterous" – nowadays used as shorthand for something ridiculous or unbelievable, but representing for both Parker and Goldberg "a reversal of 'post' for 'pre,' behind for before, back for front, second for first, and end or sequel for beginning."[30] This trope becomes itself a signifier in the Renaissance for the imagination of apocalyptic social upheaval: after all, it is only a short step from putting the cart before the horse to putting down the mighty from their seats and exalting those of low degree. Goldberg's "sodometry" resembles the subversive structure of hysteron proteron, when "reversing before and behind could mean crossing over the boundary that separates licit from illicit behavior."[31] Sodomy – the sexual crime that cannot even be spoken of – thus becomes a dangerous threat to the social order, one that "spreads uncontrollably, violating borders and differences – upside down, inside out, animal/human."[32] But it does seem to be the preposterous logic of hysteron proteron that governs the discourse here. It hardly matters whether someone who engages in sodomy is accused of subverting the state, or whether the subversive is spuriously accused of sodomy. One way or the other, defamation and excessive punishment go hand in hand.

Colleagues

The texts, largely modern, examined by Queer Theorists are reticent and frequently cloaked in rhetoric that eludes definitional stability. The Mesopotamian texts are equally reticent in their way, but not rhetorically elusive. Direct in their terse formulation, the Middle Assyrian laws exhibit slippage only through the spaces left unaddressed. The interpretive strategy that the Middle Assyrian laws presuppose is one that also has a direct parallel in Queer Theory. In Eichler's account, interpretation of Mesopotamian legal texts demands attention to the "interplay" between "a pair of polar cases with maximal variation that leaves a large discretionary middle that is not addressed."[33] The text of MAL¶20 appears to handle the extreme polar case by positing that the criminal misdirection of the active and penetrative force against a fellow citizen results in forced submission to the same force that has been wrongfully employed. But to some degree, the text itself advertises the same phenomenon it is designed to protect against. Goldberg's "sodometry," with its emphasis on what the category of sodomy "enabled and disenabled" through "the mutual implications of prohibition and production," seems precisely apposite here.[34]

Queer Theory further permits us to read this "discretionary" space as similar to Sedgwick's "silence . . . rendered as pointed and performative as speech." As a result, the broad spectrum of scholarly opinion on what precisely is permissible within the discretionary space between MAL¶19 and MAL¶20 is comprehended in full by Queer Theory: the vast difference between Bottéro's "free love" and Lambert's idea of total prohibition recalls nothing so much as Foucault's "twofold operation" of sodomy, where excessive punishment somehow accompanies widespread tolerance. Queer Theory can also enable us to see how such succinct laws might govern a far larger cognitive realm than first may seem apparent. Sedgwick argues that, historically, even limited legal restrictions could ultimately have a much larger effect, especially within a "homosocial" paradigm: "not only must homosexual men be unable to ascertain whether they are to be the objects of 'random' homophobic violence, but no man must be able to ascertain that he is not (that his bonds are not) homosexual. In this way, a relatively small exertion of physical or legal compulsion potentially rules great reaches of behavior and filiation."[35] Sedgwick later argues that when homosexual men "could not know whether or not to expect to be an object of legal violence, the legal enforcement had a disproportionately wide effect. At the same time, however, an opening was made for a subtler strategy in response, a kind of ideological pincers-movement that would extend manyfold the impact of this theatrical enforcement."[36] Given the supremely "theatrical enforcement" of the law required by MAL¶20, it is not hard to suggest the discretionary space between the two laws is caught in the same sort of "ideological pincers-movement" Sedgwick describes, designed to discourage the same activities it declines to prohibit outright. Instead it curbs the activities by placing men in a "double bind," as Sedgwick observes:

> If such compulsory relationships as male friendship, mentorship, admiring identification, bureaucratic subordination, and heterosexual rivalry all involve forms of investment that force men into the arbitrarily mapped, self-contradictory, and anathema-riddled quicksands of the middle distance of male homosocial desire, then it appears that men enter into adult masculine entitlement only through acceding to the permanent threat that the small space they have cleared for themselves on this terrain may always, just as arbitrarily and with just as much justification, be foreclosed.[37]

In other words, the homosocial regime obliges men to police themselves, which results not only in men's "*manipulability*" but also "a reservoir of potential for *violence* caused by the self-ignorance this regime constituently enforces": Sedgwick notes that this is most readily observed in the military, "where both men's manipulability and their potential for violence are at the highest possible premium, the *pre*scription of the most intimate male bonding and the *pro*scription of (the remarkably cognate) 'homosexuality' are both stronger than in civilian society – are, in fact, close to absolute."[38] Sedgwick's analysis of this double bind, like Goldberg's concept of "sodometry," appears to offer some explanation not just for MAL¶20's violent penalty, but also for the silence of what occurs in the discretionary space between the two laws.

This is why the omen texts are crucial. The Mesopotamian law collections are drafted with the intent of producing a body of knowledge that is stable and knowable; legal inquiry examines the existing boundaries and obligations of the social world and seeks to clarify them. Divination, on the other hand, does not investigate the customary or conventional. It looks to an extraordinary source of knowledge in order to deal with aspects of life whose solutions lie outside range of ordinary vision and control. Omens don't have the same salience as the law; they are not part of the same order of knowledge. Many of the preserved on Tablet 104 of *šumma ālu* were formulated in direct conversation with the Middle Assyrian laws.[39] These omens address the spaces in the law, which are open to contradictory readings. The omens may address the circumstances that encompass legal norms; however, they have an opposing perspective. They probe the ambiguities, contradictions, and potential cultural instabilities that the laws evoke but do not resolve. Four omens regarding anal sex between men come from Tablet 104.[40] But only one of these four, Omen 13, approaches precisely the same subject as the laws – anal sex between male equals – and thus offers a divinatory rather than legal perspective:

> If a man has anal sex with his social peer, that man will become foremost among his brothers and colleagues.[41]

Omen 13 only states reversible position in a positive way. It also explicitly turns on the contradictory logic of rank and sexual position. The text of Omen 13 makes use of the rhetorical device, hysteron proteron, discussed above: the one standing behind as a penetrator finds himself standing foremost. The protasis of Omen 13 revolves around parity of status through the use of the term *meḫru*, a term for "equal" that carries implications of identity, symmetry, and reduplication. Similarly the paronomastic relationship between the words *qinnatu* (anus) and *kinātu* (colleagues) is more than a simple pun: if nothing else, it acknowledges the prospect that the collegiate relations between male equals could readily be sexual. But the apodosis reasserts the switch of positions from "behind" to "in front," resolving and rectifying any confusion that might exist between sexual and social position.

When the subject matter of the omens corresponds to the laws, their meanings offer a striking contrast and appear to play off and to invert the more explicitly articulated legal norms. We can note this elsewhere in Tablet 104, where an omen can be demonstrated to have an explicit connection to the Middle Assyrian laws. MAL¶2 is a law dealing with blasphemy. Tablet 104 contains an omen on precisely the same topic. MAL¶2 legislates that

> If a woman, either a man's wife or a man's daughter, should speak something disgraceful or utters a blasphemy, that woman alone bears

> the responsibility for her offense; they will have no claims against her husband, her sons, or her daughter.[42]

The corresponding omen text begins from a notably similar premise:

> If a man's first-ranking wife curses his god – he bears the punishment of the god. [If the man] bears the [punish]ment – discord will be imposed on his family.[43]

In terms of how this particular omen responds to the legal text, it is through an expression of "obverse statements of responsibility": the law ponders whether family members could be held accountable for the woman's blasphemy before assigning guilt to the woman alone, but the omen reveals that "in the divine world, the blasphemed god applies a different standard."[44] The chief fact to observe here is that blasphemy and sodomy are topics treated in the Middle Assyrian laws but nowhere else before or after in the cuneiform legal sources.[45] But the confluence of these two specific offenses is also noteworthy from the standpoint of Queer Theory: beyond Mesopotamia, there is a remarkable historical propensity to link sodomy and blasphemy conceptually. The two crimes seem primally, fundamentally subversive; each indicates a subjectivity so far from normative, but also so easily disguised, that it can provoke widespread suspicion regarding its extent, panic about its surreptitious contagion, and inquisitions to extirpate it. The Middle Assyrian laws are the first recorded instance of this conceptual linkage between blasphemy and sodomy. What is more unusual is that, for both, the omens seem to directly respond to the codified laws, probing the spaces left unaddressed by their text. Omen 13, in treating anal sex between men, certainly seems to overturn the underlying assumptions an interpreter might believe governs the two legal texts. The laws, after all, both demand proof and punishment; Omen 13 describes a consensual sex act between two men that goes unpunished, and that is deemed auspicious.

We may compare Omen 13 with a "mysterious" omen apodosis, recently described by Marten Stol, that comes from Emar, a roughly contemporaneous Late Bronze Age source.[46] Stol believes an omen text here depicts a consensual sex act between two men – one that also apparently goes unpunished. "Two men will be seized in their sin, they will not be beaten, they will be released" is Stol's translation of the apodosis.[47] The word he translates as "sin," *ḫīṭu*, can just as easily mean "offense." Stol records that the apodosis of the same omen in Tablet I of the later canonical series *Enūma Anu Enlil* specifies instead a penalty of being burnt alive: "The king will make the men go out for burning, and those men who have been summoned without being guilty will be saved."[48] Stol, arguing that both apodoses refer to homosexuality, with the apodosis of the earlier text offering an "unexpected" resolution that the later scribe is keen to reverse, writes "I think that the omen was still aware of its original intent; the 'being burnt alive' is suggestive."[49] In Stol's reading of these lunar omen texts, where the "offense" is assumed to be a homosexual one, both of the apodoses (the two men are set free, the two men are burnt alive) occupy the same divinatory space as Omen 13: they represent divination, not law. Stol claims of the earlier omen where the men walk away unharmed that "the forecasts of omens are often unexpected, and one may assume that normally the two men were not left alone unharmed"; this seems to imagine a legal statute under which both men were either freed or burnt.[50] If the two widely different apodoses of Stol's astrological omens suggest, in his reading, that sex between male equals could be a legal offense for both, this possibility is never openly addressed in any Mesopotamian laws. Such an emphasis on the equal culpability of both male partners is readily found in legislation elsewhere, from Leviticus on down, but is not found in Mesopotamia. Stol's reading assumes the perspective of Leviticus. But even if his reading is correct, the question nevertheless remains: are these two men equally implicated, or are they implicated because they are equals?

In both examples from Tablet 104 (Omen 13 and the blasphemy omen) the topics considered, and the structure of reversal in both cases, demonstrate that these particular omens represent ancient secondary readings of the laws. Returning to Omen 13, however, we should note that it has not invariably been read as a reversal of the law. Cooper, for example, reads Omen 13 as equivalent to the law, where both condemn using an equal as a passive partner; therefore he does not see the omen as auspicious and reads the switch of position differently. In Cooper's reading, the man who anally penetrates his equal, sexually shaming him, is put in the position of having to guard his own anus: he will "take the lead not because he has won their approval" but rather "his position in front is the result of the act, because nobody wants to be his next victim!"[51] While we suggest the meaning of Omen 13 is primarily propitious, its "tropologics" suggest that Cooper's reading may also be in play: the text itself of Omen 13 essentially forces his reading into the same structure of hysteron proteron, where what is in the back must be reimagined as being in the front.[52]

To a certain degree Cooper's reading sees a nervous joke in Omen 13 about the reversal of position in MAL¶20: the rhetorical structure of hysteron proteron, which generates preposterous reversals, has the propensity to generate wordplay. But as noted, the text of this omen already incorporates its own wordplay: the punning on *qinnatu* (anus) and *kinātu* (colleagues). Cooper's reading appears to suggest that this paronomasia is infused with anxiety: keeping a watchful eye on one's colleagues and guarding one's anus become the same thing. When phallic penetration is tied to hegemonic positionality, the anus becomes a site of anxiety and charged contradictions: Sophus Helle notes the Akkadian idiom for the anus, *bāb šuburri* – literally "the gate of the buttocks" – emphasizes liminality and anxiety over the possibility of penetration.[53] Even though Omen 13 links phallic agency with social supremacy, anxiety about social role-reversals through sexual acts is still lurking. We can see something similar in MAL¶20, too: the masculine ideology it is supposed to bolster suddenly finds itself at cross-purposes when it is forced to acknowledge such possible reversals, and the rape of one is punished with rape by all. Queer Theory would look at these texts and inquire whether they encourage a *tappā'u* to lead with his phallus, or to cover his anus. If Cooper's reading puts an emphasis on the latter, our reading emphasizes the former.

Crack troops

The reversal of front and back is not seen only in the Middle Assyrian laws and in Omen 13 of *šumma ālu*. It is central to the Gilgamesh epic as well, even employing the same vocabulary as Omen 13. The same phrasing exists in the Akkadian of both texts: *ašarēdūta illak* – to walk foremost, but also to do so in a military capacity, as the vanguard of armed aggression.[54] Outside of that phrase, the term *ašarēdūtu*, meaning "highest rank," refers above all else to military rank or echelon. The language of front and back in the omen may look like a mere reversal of physical position, but the usage of the same language of front and back in *the Epic of Gilgamesh* – with relation to the two loving comrades, Gilgamesh and Enkidu – indicates that what is at stake in this phrase is an ideology and vocabulary of military hierarchy.

The epic uses the language of both laws and of Omen 13 by employing the term *tappā'u* while also employing the term *meḫru*, the "social equal" – someone who is both the equal and mirror of another.[55] In Tablet I, lines 31–32, Gilgamesh is foremost in rank; his position of leadership makes him foremost in relation to those whom he leads. Gilgamesh is introduced by using the exact language of Omen 13:

> He goes in the front, he is a leader
> At the rear he goes also, the trust of his brothers.[56]

If there is a reversal here, it is not one in which Gilgamesh alters in status. In his position going at the vanguard (*illak . . . ašared*) and his position "going also at the rear," he is always the leader Gilgamesh. But to lead the charge is the vulnerable position, so it must be emphasized that Gilgamesh as foremost commander must necessarily be in the rear. He is "behind" in line 32 in the sense that "he has their backs"; his brothers and colleagues trust in his leadership to go forward and do battle.

Indeed when the same language recurs in Tablet III of *Gilgamesh*, the text quite clearly plays on the contradictions of positionality. The text of *Gilgamesh* emphasizes the hero's equality with Enkidu in every way, using not only the vocabulary of equal status between male citizens that is seen in the laws (*tappā'u*) but also the more abstract terminology of equality that is represented by the term *meḫru* – a term whose shades of meaning encompass geometric congruence, replication and copying, and counterparts or rivals. What is important for our purposes is to note that, in the narrative of the epic, Enkidu is the *meḫru* of Gilgamesh after being created as a direct response to Gilgamesh and his oppression of Uruk. If the pair attain perfect equality by Tablet III, it is because Gilgamesh was there first, and Enkidu was fashioned by the gods in response.

The perfect equality between Gilgamesh and Enkidu does exist by Tablet III, however; it is at this point that the issue of positionality asserts itself again in the text, now in terms of hierarchy. As Gilgamesh and Enkidu are about to leave for the forest, the elders of the city tell Gilgamesh not to overestimate himself. Enkidu should go in front because he knows the terrain of the cedar forest, and Gilgamesh does not:

> [Come back in safety] to [the quay of] Uruk!
> Do not trust, O Gilgameš, in the fullness of your strength
> let your eyes be satisfied, strike a blow to rely on!
> "He who goes in front saves (his) comrade,
> he who knew the road [protected] his friend."
> Let Enkidu go in front of you,
> he knows the way to the Forest of Cedar!
> He is tried in battles and experienced in combat,
> let Enkidu protect (his) friend and keep safe (his) comrade!
> let him bring his [person] back to his *wives*!
> In this our assembly we hereby give the king into your care:
> you will ensure (his) return and give the king into our care.[57]

The elders of the city make an attempt here to impose positionality on the pair, one that makes explicit reference to the military utility of these positions, even as they are based on the affective bonds of comrades and equals: "He who goes in front saves (his) comrade, he who knows the road should protect his friend."[58] We should note that it is Gilgamesh who is being persuaded here by the elders – "Let Enkidu go in front of you" – in the context of Gilgamesh's potential fecklessness, in which he might attempt to assert his own positionality by traveling in front despite the fact that Enkidu knows the terrain and Gilgamesh does not. What is being worked through here, in some sense, is the presence of potential conceptual contradictions in military hierarchy itself. The epic insists on the mutuality of their bond – employing language where every possible usage summons intimate human relationships free from the binary structure of power – they are friends, brothers, equals, loving comrades. Even so, Enkidu goes first because he is more experienced, and therefore less vulnerable in the more vulnerable position. So Enkidu's position in front is both positive and negative; in terms of relative ability and expertise he is undoubtedly ahead of Gilgamesh here, who is young and foolhardy. But going in front does, ultimately, place him in the weaker position militarily, a fact that is underscored when Enkidu ultimately dies in the narrative that ensues. This conception of being "foremost" in a military sense should not be understood as somehow referring to expendable cannon fodder. Indeed the use of "crack troops" in the title of this chapter is based on the translation offered in the CAD for an attested use of *ašarittu*: these would be troops preeminent in their excellence, whether they fight on the front line or not. The etymological relation between *ašarēdūtu* (meaning "foremost") and *ašarittu* (meaning "preeminence") as specifically military terminology reveals that the concept of martial excellence is never far off.

Of course the Gilgamesh epic as we have it does not ever make any direct reference to a sexual relationship between Gilgamesh and Enkidu – but no reader of the epic can deny this relationship is one suffused with a deep erotic connection. This eros that pervades the relationship between Gilgamesh and Enkidu – perhaps most apparent in Gilgamesh's lament for his dead comrade – seems intimately related to their status not only as male equals but as military comrades. But the militarily inflected language employed to describe their relation as traveling companions, and particularly the way in which that language directly overlaps with that of Omen 13, highlights the complex and troubling matter of reversible positions. We can note in all of these sources – legal, divinatory, epic – a focus on position, whether that position is imagined as social, spatial, sexual.

Comrades-in-arms

Anyone who has spent time reviewing the study of sexuality knows that theories, surveys, and observations all potentially have the shelf-life of a croissant; in the space of a few years, categories and concepts can change so rapidly that scholars make confident assertions or predictions at their own risk. But at the same time parallels, analogues, and suggestive likenesses can be found separated by a distance even of millennia. This is not a matter of claiming straightforward historiographical continuity in such connections. Instead, it is a theoretical approach – and, to a certain extent, a queer critique of conventional historiography. Some Queer Theorists have proposed the concept of "heterotemporality" – admittedly the kind of jargon that can make some readers wince (including both writers of this chapter) but that in this instance is useful. Heterotemporality, in the words of Madhavi Menon, is simply "the contemporary tendency to enshrine difference as the basis for all historiography"; critique begins with an acknowledgment that "conventional historians insist on seeing difference as the most prominent feature of our scholarly encounters with the past" and that "nowhere has the emphasis on difference been heavier than in the field of sexuality studies."[59]

When faced with a text like MAL¶20, it may seem impossible for a scholar in 2015 to move beyond a sense of profound difference with a culture that produces a law that demands the mandatory group rape of the man convicted under it. But there are analogues to be had even here. For example,

Jane Ward's 2015 study *Not Gay: Sex Between Straight White Men* looks at sexual acts that take place between men. Ward offers a queer theoretical approach to contemporary social phenomena rather than texts, but her insights can be used to shed light on the Middle Assyrian texts under examination. In Ward's account, "the line between straight men having sex with men and 'actual' homosexuality is under constant scrutiny, and for straight men, violence is a key element that imbues homosexuality with heterosexual meaning . . . reframing homosexual sex as an act that men do to build one another's strength."[60] If the Middle Assyrian Empire offers no precise analogue to what Ward describes as "actual" homosexuality, it does nonetheless offer the same "line . . . under constant scrutiny," which demarcates two distinct categories that evince a queasy similarity to each other. In the case of MAL¶20, it would seem that the line is indeed defined in precisely the way that Ward suggests – by the addition of violence, in this case sanctioned by the state, which does indeed take the same act and reframe it, imbue it with meaning, or indeed build up the strength of the state that requires its citizens to enact the penalty, and inoculate the circle of social equals against the action of a rogue individual by imitating his transgression en masse. The punishment specified in MAL¶20 is essentially a governmental mandate that all citizens demonstrate the ability to penetrate another male, under these circumstances – circumstances that sound like an uneasy combination of coercive sodomy and jury duty.

However, in Ward's analysis, we can understand this as less an expression of *eros* than essentially a function of statecraft. Ward notes, with regard to the sexualized hazing in the 21st-century American military:

> . . . [H]azing rituals involving anal penetration . . . are extreme, exciting, humiliating, and effective at building cohesion and establishing hierarchy among men precisely *because* the participants know that these acts have sexual meaning. They are designed to occupy or evoke the fine line between sex and humiliation or submission.[61]

If we step back and view the logic of MAL¶20 not in terms of the standard dyads regarding active and passive – familiar from viewing Middle Assyrian texts through the lens of Greek and Roman notions of active and passive – and instead view it as engaged primarily with the dynamics of consent and rape, we can understand that all male citizens are, in essence, willing or unwilling, compelled by the law to take part in homosexual activity. MAL¶20 does not punish male-on-male rape so much as it reclaims it as the privilege and prerogative of the state. The body politic becomes the active penetrative agent here; individual agency is what is being punished in the convicted rapist, and elided in all other citizens required to take part in punishing him.

In the context of the sexualized ideology of Middle Assyrian empire-building, what matters most is that the penetrative male acts as an agent of the militarized state. Visual arts in Mesopotamia offer many arresting examples of this sexualized military ideology. Julia Asher-Greve has noted that in Mesopotamian art:

> . . . dead or captured enemies about to be killed, blinded, or castrated, are stripped of all clothes. Fallen or captured enemies who are depicted naked are always men. In the context of war and captivity the bodies of enemies convey the message of victory and subjugation.[62]

Within this paradigm – in which the otherness of a military enemy is conceived of as something to be penetrated and humiliated, in which enemy captives are rendered into eunuchs in the same way that the convicted rapist is – we can begin to glimpse an underlying logic in the law's inflationary dynamic of coercive homosexual sex. The militarized sexuality explains the conflation between sexual performance in both senses of "performance" – every *tappā'u* has to get an erection to punish the rapist, and thus be "able to perform," but also the punitive act is conceived of here as a public spectacle. Group rape necessitates public performance. Karen Franklin, a forensic psychiatrist who studies the psychosocial conditions of group rape, argues that "antigay violence and group rape" are best understood as "participatory theater" or "hypermasculine performance art."[63] Franklin writes that by "demonstrating and/or celebrating masculinity, asserting or claiming power, and bolstering solidarity and cohesion in loosely knit social groups . . . rape in concert is a form of public theatre, performed for the consumption of both the immediate actors and a larger audience."[64]

It is informative to consider MAL¶20, then, as part of a larger culture of sexualized public performance of the sort that Assante (2007) in her reading of the lead inlays of Tukulti-Ninurta I terms "pornography as imperial strategy" and "sexual theatre."[65] The artistic representations Assante examines pornographically depict an empire's fantasies of the ultimate sexualized otherness: the enemy who has succumbed to sexualized military conquest. The sexualized public performance implicit in MAL¶20 is admittedly different; the text's vision of the execution of justice is, by contrast, a communal act in which the transgressing *tappā'u* is publically and ritually transformed into the other, and effectively removed from the circle of equals by an act that combines military discipline with the ideology of state-sanctioned sexual aggression. That is why the punishment of MAL¶20 concludes with castration, an act normally reserved for enemy captives. In this case the enemy captive is a male equal whose errant and violent sexuality threatens to destabilize the social order – this is why the convicted male rapist of MAL¶20, though operating in a historical context that predates the Genesis account of Sodom, is best understood according to the logic and mythology that for centuries adhered to the sodomite. What better way to construct an "utterly confused category" than to confess – as the logic of MAL¶20 seems to – that we have met the enemy and he is us?

Conclusion

An inexorable, almost geometric logic governs Mesopotamian imaginings of sex between male social equals. Any possibility of mutuality and eroticism instantly is collapsed into positionality, and reinscribed with hierarchy and power. Someone takes his colleague from behind, in an act of sexual violation – the law requires everyone else to commit an act of sexual violation upon him in reply, where he is placed foremost to his own permanent disadvantage. If individual agency threatens to invert the social order, the social order responds in kind, with preposterously logical excess, demanding equivalent inflationary reinversion. To escape this trap one would have to escape from society itself: this is, after all, what Queer Theory means by the social construction of sexuality.

Somebody has to go in front, by this Mesopotamian logic, and somebody has to go behind. The language of the opening tablets of the *Gilgamesh* epic employs all available vocabulary to insist upon the mutuality of the bond between Gilgamesh and Enkidu – they are friends, equals, brothers, loving comrades. But they cannot in the end be lovers, because they are equals: if the word *meḫru* hints at the possibility of mutual relations, the possibility is instantly quashed. Similar mutuality is suggested in the paronomasia in Omen 13: the word for equal, *meḫru*, occurs there too. But we note the emergence in the omen's text of a fundamentally poetic language – more than a simple pun, the paronomastic relationship between the words *qinnatu* (anus) and *kinātu* (colleagues) is in itself a secret meaning to be discovered, perhaps even a hidden confirmation of mutuality and desire. But if the protasis of Omen 13 somehow hints that such things might be possible, the apodosis reasserts the switch of positions from "behind" to "in front," ending any confusion that might exist between sexual and social position, and with it ending erotic possibility. Likewise as Enkidu and Gilgamesh are about to escape into the forest from the city, perhaps to explore the erotic possibilities of their mutual bond, the elders of the city reimpose equivalent positional hierarchies upon them. The elders declare Enkidu goes first in knowledge and experience, and instruct Gilgamesh to willingly take the rear. Are the rich circumlocutions and equivocal language of the poem a response to tensions within the culture itself? Or was the poet trying to suggest something known to all that could not be named? These may be reasonable questions to ask, but they can never find an answer. Somebody has to be behind, and somebody has to be in front.

One goes first, another is left behind. This is not only the logic of military hierarchy and social position, it is the logic of life and death. (Queer Theory has known this from the start: its own historical emergence in the 1980s was occasioned by mass deaths – largely unmourned by the dominant culture – in a plague that claimed, among so many others, Michel Foucault himself.) When Enkidu dies, Gilgamesh lives to chant one of the most haunting laments in poetic history for his lost comrade; it is the world's first elegy, sung to bewail a loss of the match made for Gilgamesh by the gods themselves. Death is, after all, the surest way to escape the social construction of sexuality itself:

> He covered (his) friend, (veiling) his face like a bride,
> circling around him like an eagle.
> Like a lioness who is deprived of her cubs,
> he kept turning about . . . before him and behind him.[66]

The words in the last line here are identical to the words that announced Gilgamesh at the poem's beginning: "going at the fore he was the leader, / going also at the rear, the trust of his brothers." What is gone is social construction; what is present is profound love. "Veiling his face like a bride": normally the commencement of lawful and socially sanctioned sexual possibility, now a queer signifier for love's irretrievable loss and absence. Social position vanishes: similes maintain Gilgamesh's status as a preeminent warrior, but the apex predators to which he is likened are at a loss as well, traveling in circles, hunting for a lost futurity. There is only one man standing, with no men to lead or brothers to trust, but still the inexorable logic of hierarchy and positionality does not relent. Instead it only results in the aimless wandering, back and forth, of a subjectivity in search of its lost love. But this is the moment that the silence ends; in loss, this love of comrade for comrade must finally begin to speak.

Notes

1 See Martti Nissinen. "Are There Homosexuals in Mesopotamian Literature?," *Journal of the American Oriental Society* 130, no. 1 (2010), 73; also *Homoeroticism in the Biblical World* (Minneapolis: Fortress, 2001), 26. Another reference on a tablet cataloguing astrological incantations dates to the Hellenistic period: we agree with Nissinen 1998) that it "can scarcely be interpreted as referring to mutual love between two equal and consenting male citizens," 35.

2 In addition to the *šumma ālu* omens, Stol has identified two lunar omens whose apodoses may make oblique reference to homosexuality. See Marten Stol. "Remarks on Some Sumerograms and Akkadian Words." In *Studies Presented to Robert D. Biggs*, ed. Martha Roth, Walter Farber, Matthew W. Stopler, and Paula von Bechtolsheim (Chicago: Oriental Institute, 2007), 236.

3 Thorkild Jacobsen. "How Did Gilgamesh Oppress Uruk?" *Acta Orientalia* 8 (1930), 74.

4 David Halperin. *One Hundred Years of Homosexuality* (New York: Routledge, 1990), 15.

5 Martha Roth. *Law Collections from Mesopotamia and Asia Minor* (Atlanta: Scholars, 1997), 159–160. MAL¶19 (ii 82–92) *šumma a'īlu ina puzre ina muḫḫi tappā'išu abata iškun mā ittinikkuš lu ina ṣalte ana pani ṣābē iqbiaššu mā ittinikkuka mā ubârka ba'ura la ila'e la uba'er a'īla šuātu 50 ina ḫaṭṭāte imaḫḫuṣuš iltēn uraḫ ūmāte šipar šarre eppaš igaddimuš u* 1 *bilat annaka iddan*. MAL¶20 (ii.93–97) *šumma a'īlu tappâšu inīk ubta'eruš ukta'inuš inikkuš ana ša rēšēn utarruš*.

6 Roth, *Law Collections*, 192.

7 Erhard Gerstenberger. *Leviticus: A Commentary* (Louisville: Knox, 1996), 298.
8 Barry L. Eichler. "Literary Structure in the Laws of Eshunna." In *Language Literature and History*, ed. Francesca Rochberg-Halton (New Haven: AOS, 1987), 72.
9 Ibid., 72–73.
10 Barry L. Eichler. "Examples of Restatement in the Laws of Hammurabi." In *Mishneh Todah*, ed. Nili Sacher Fox, David Glatt-Gilad, and Michael Williams (Winona Lake, IN: Eisenbrauns, 2009), 368.
11 Roth, *Law Collections*, 159. MAL¶18 (ii.72–81) *šumma a'īlu ana tappā'išu lu ina puzre lu ina ṣalte iqbi mā aššatka ittinikkku mā anāku ubâr ba'ura la ila'e la uba'er a'īla suātu 40 ina ḫaṭṭāte imaḫḫuṣuš iltēn uraḫ ūmāte šipar šarre eppaš igaddimuš u 1 bilat annaka iddan.*
12 It can certainly be argued that what is unmentioned here is also what is unmentionable, if one purpose of MAL¶19 is to render the consensual sex act between men something that cannot be spoken about.
13 Jacobsen. "How Did Gilgamesh Oppress Uruk?," 74.
14 W. G. Lambert. "Prostitution." In *Aussenseiter und Randgruppen*, ed. Volkert Haas (Konstanz: University Press, 1992), 146–147.
15 Jean Bottéro and Herbert Petschow. "Homosexualität." In *Reallexikon der Assyriologie und vorderasiatischen Archaologie*, 4th ed., ed. Erich Ebeling and Bruno Meissner (Berlin: De Gruyter, 1975), 462.
16 Jerrold Cooper. "Buddies in Babylonia." In *Riches Hidden in Secret Places: Ancient Near Eastern Studies in Memory of Thorkild Jacobsen*, ed. Tzvi Abusch (Winona Lake, IN: Eisenbrauns, 2002), 84.
17 Raymond Westbrook. "Evidentiary Procedure in the Middle Assyrian Laws." In *Law from the Tigris to the Tiber*, Volume 2, ed. Bruce Wells and F. Rachel Magdalene (Winona Lake, IN: Eisenbrauns, 2009), 223.
18 Julia Assante. "Men Looking at Men: The Homoerotics of Power in the State Arts of Assyria." (Chapter 2, this volume; personal communication.)
19 The modern legal history of homosexuality suggests an obvious parallel with Oscar Wilde's lawsuit against the Marquess of Queensberry over the defamatory charge that Wilde was a "somdomite" [sic]. Wilde's suit for libel failed because Queensberry could prove the truth of his accusation (even if he could not spell "sodomite"). Wilde was then himself prosecuted for "gross indecency" (i.e., sodomy) and convicted. The Middle Assyrian equivalent of Wilde's libel suit against Queensberry would be conducted under the provisions of MAL19 – but oddly, the legal texts do not appear to offer any equivalent to the sodomy law under which Wilde himself was convicted. See Richard Ellmann. *Oscar Wilde* (New York: Vintage, 1987), 423.
20 Ann K. Guinan. "Laws and Omens: Obverse and Inverse." In *Divination in the Ancient Near East*, ed. Jeanette C. Fincke (Winona Lake, IN: Eisenbrauns, 2014), 115.
21 Joe Loya. *The Man Who Outgrew His Prison Cell* (New York: Harper Collins, 2005), 249.
22 Peter Morris. *Guardians* (London: Oberon Books, 2005), 25.
23 Girard posits a concept of "mimetic desire," i.e., individuals desire something based on seeing another desire it first, but the process builds up the potential for violence based on competition. Violence of all-against-all is then prevented by permitting a violence of all-against one, as "societies unify themselves by focussing their imitative desires on a scapegoat," a single individual who is blamed for the initial "mimetic pathogen." If the sexually penetrative homosexual desire of the rapist in MAL¶20 is seen as the initial "pathogen" according to this theoretical model, the consequence – where all citizens are required to imitate the desire in a ritualized act of punitive violence – follows. See René Girard. *Violence and the Sacred* (Baltimore: Johns Hopkins University Press, 1977).

24 Ibid., 27.
25 Eve Kosofksy Sedgwick. *The Epistemology of the Closet* (Berkeley: University of California, 1990), 4.
26 Eve Kosofsky Sedgwick. *Between Men: English Literature and Male Homosocial Desire* (New York: Columbia, 1985), 201–202.
27 Alan Bray. "Homosexuality and the Signs of Friendship in Elizabethan England," *History Workshop Journal* 29, no. 1 (1990), 1–8.
28 Jonathan Goldberg. *Sodometries: Renaissance Texts, Modern Sexualities* (Palo Alto: Stanford University Press, 1992), xv–xvi.
29 Goldberg. *Sodometries*, 20.
30 Patricia Parker. "Hysteron-Proteron, or the Preposterous." In *Renaissance Figures of Speech*, ed. Sylvia Adamson, Gavin Alexander, and Katrin Ettenhuber (Cambridge: Cambridge University Press, 2007), 133.
31 Goldberg, *Sodometries*, 4.
32 Ibid., xv–xvi.
33 Eichler, "Examples of Restatement," 368.
34 Goldberg, *Sodometries*, 20.
35 Sedgwick, *Between Men*, 88.
36 Sedgwick, *Epistemology of the Closet*, 185.
37 Ibid., 186.
38 Ibid., 186 (Italics in original).
39 See Guinan, "Laws and Omens: Obverse and Inverse," for a fuller discussion.
40 Three omens, grouped together in isolation from the fourth, describe a man homosexually penetrating partners intrinsically defined as lower status, specified as an *assinnu*, a *gerseqqû*, and a *dušmu* – respectively a religious functionary of Ištar, a courtier, and a house slave. The first of these omens is plainly auspicious, the second ambiguously auspicious; only the third, with the partner of lowest status, is a bad omen. All of them depict queer sexual encounters. Their texts are in C. J. Gadd. *Cuneiform Texts from Babylonian Tablets in the British Museum*, Volume 39 (London: British Museum Publications, 1926), Tablet 104, Plate 45:32–34.
41 Gadd, *Cuneiform Texts*, Tablet 104, Plate 44:13. DIŠ NA *ana* GU.DU (*qinnati*) *me-eḫ-ri-šú* TE NA.BI *ina* ŠEŠ.MEŠ-*šú ù ki-na-ti-šú a-šá-re-du-tam* DU-*ak*.
42 Roth, *Law Collections*, 155. MAL¶2 (a i 14–22 b 5–7) *šumma sinniltu lu aššat a'īle u lu mārat a'īle šillata taqṭibi lu miqit pê tartiši sinniltu šīt aranša tanašši ana mutiša mārēša mārāteša la iqarribu*.
43 Gadd, *Cuneiform Texts*, 39:46, lines 64–65. [DIŠ NA] ⌜ *ḫir* ⌝ *-ta-šú* DINGIR-*šú iz-zu-ur* NAM.TAG.GA DINGIR-*šú na-ši* [DIŠ NA *ar*]-*na iš-ši* É.BI NU ŠE.GA GAR-*šú*.
44 Guinan, "Laws and Omens: Obverse and Inverse," 111.
45 The regulatory concern for blasphemy that emerges in the historical moment of the Middle Assyrian Empire is also seen in the Middle Assyrian Palace. See Roth, *Law Collections*, 202–203; and Sophie Lafont. *Femmes, Droit et Justice dans l'Antiquité* (Göttingen: Vanderhoeck and Ruprecht, 1999), 445–450.
46 Daniel Arnaud. *Recherches au Pays d'Aštata. Emar VI: Les textes sumériens et accadiens* Volume 4 (Paris: Recherche sur les Civilisations, 1986), 650. The later Standard Babylonian version is found in Lorenzo Verderame. *Le Tavole I–VI della Serie Astrologica Enūma Anu Enlil* (Rome: Dipartimento di Science dell'Antichità, 2002), 26.
47 Stol, "Remarks," 236.
48 Ibid.
49 Ibid.
50 Ibid.
51 Cooper, "Buddies in Babylonia," 85.
52 For discussion of the "tropologics of the reversible statement," see Goldberg, *Sodometries*, 2.

53 Sophus Helle. "Putting the Anal Back in Analysis: Some Notes on Anal Sex in Babylonian Scholarship." Conference Paper, Oxford Postgraduate Conference in Assyriology, 2015. Wolfson College, Oxford. April 24–25.
54 Gadd, *Cuneiform Texts*, 39:44 l.13; A. R. George. *The Babylonian Gilgamesh Epic* (Oxford: Oxford University Press, 2003), 538. The apodosis of the omen reads: *a-šá-re-du-tam* DU-*ak*. The use of the same idiom in Gilgamesh I.31 reads: [*i*]*l-lak . . . a-šá-red.*
55 The Standard Babylonian version of the Gilgamesh epic employs the spelling *tappû.*
56 George, *Babylonian Gilgamesh Epic*, 538, lines 31–32. The text reads: "[*i*]*l-lak ina pa-ni a-šá-red* / [*a*]*r-ka il-lak-ma tukul-ti aḫḫē* (šeš)[meš]*-šú*." George's translation of these lines is "Going at the fore he was the leader / Going also at the rear, the trust of his brothers!"
57 George, *Babylonian Gilgamesh Epic*, 574–575, lines 1–12. [*a*]*-na* [*ka-a-ri šá*] ⌜ *uruk ki* ⌝ [*ṭi-ḫa-a ina šul-mi*] / [*l*]*a ta-tak-kil* GIŠ-*gím-maš a-na* ⌜ *gi-mir* ⌝ *e*-⌜ *mu-qi-ka* ⌝ / [*i*]*-na-ka liš-ba-a mi-ḫi-iṣ-ka tuk-k*[*il*] / ⌜ *a* ⌝*-lik maḫ–ri tappâ* (tab.ba) *ú-še-ez-z*[*eb*] / *šá ṭú-du i-du-ú i-bir-šú iṣ-ṣu*[*r*] / [*l*]*il-lik en-ki-dù i-na pa-ni-ka* / ⌜ *i* ⌝*-de ḫarrāna*(kaskal)[*min*] *šá*[*giš*] *qišti*(tir) [*giš*]*erēni*(eren) / [*t*]*a-ḫa-zi a-mir-ma qab-lu kul-lu*[*m*] / *en-ki-dù ib-ri li-iṣ-ṣur tap-pa-a li-šal-lim* / *a-na ṣēr*(edin) *ḫi-ra-a-ti pa-gar-šú lib-la* / *i-na pu-uḫ-ri-ni-ma ni-ip-qí-dak-ka šarra*(lugal) / *tu-tar-ram-ma ta-paq-qí-dan-na-ši šarra*(lugal).
58 A. R. George understands this couplet as a bit of proverbial wisdom, based on the Yale OB version of Tablet III (Col. IV, lines 255–256); George, *Babylonian Gilgamesh Epic*, 204, 214, 810.
59 Stephen Guy-Bray, Vin Nardizzi, and Will Stockton. *Queer Renaissance Historiography* (Burlington: Ashgate, 2009), 3.
60 Jane Ward. *Not Gay: Sex Between Straight White Men* (New York: NYU, 2015), 43.
61 Ibid., 38.
62 Julia Asher-Greve. "The Essential Body: Mesopotamian Conceptions of the Gendered Body." In *Gender and the Body in the Ancient Mediterranean*, ed. Maria Wyke (Oxford: Blackwell, 1998), 20.
63 Karen Franklin, "Enacting Masculinity: Antigay Violence and Group Rape as Participatory Theater" In *Sexuality Research and Social Policy* 1 (2004): 25–40.
64 Karen Franklin. "Masculinity, Status, and Power: Implicit Messages in Western Media Discourse on High-Profile Cases of Multiple Perpetrator Rape." In *Handbook on the Study of Multiple Perpetrator Rape*, ed. Miranda Horvath and Jessica Woodhams (New York: Routledge, 2013), 52.
65 Julia Assante "The Lead Inlays of Tikulti-Ninurta I: Pornography as Imperial Strategy." In *Ancient Near Eastern Art in Context*, ed. Jack Cheng and Marian Feldman (Leiden: Brill, 2007), 371.
66 George, *The Babylonian Gilgamesh Epic*, 654–657. Tablet VIII, RV2 [Nineveh], lines 59–62. *ik-tùm-ma ib-ri kīma*(gim) *kal-la-ti* [*pānīšu*] / *kīma*(*gim*) *a-re-ê i-sa-a*[*r eli- šú*] / *kīma*(gim) *neš-ti* [*š*]*á šu-ud-da-at me-ra-*[*ni-šá*] / *it-ta-n*[*a*]*-as-ḫur a-na pa-ni-*[*šú u arkīšu*].

Bibliography

Ackerman, Susan. *When Heroes Love: The Ambiguity of Eros in the Stories of Gilgamesh and David.* New York: Columbia University Press, 2005.

Arnaud, Daniel. *Recherches au Pays d'Aštata. Emar VI: Les textes sumériens et accadiens*, Volumes I–IV. Paris: Recherche sur les Civilisations, 1985–1987.

Asher-Greve, Julia M. "The Essential Body: Mesopotamian Conceptions of the Gendered Body." In *Gender and the Body in the Ancient Mediterranean*, edited by Maria Wyke, 8–37. Oxford: Blackwell, 1998.

Assante, Julia. "The Lead Inlays of Tikulti-Ninurta I: Pornography as Imperial Strategy." In *Ancient Near Eastern Art in Context: Studies in Honor of Irene J. Winter*, edited by Jack Cheng and Marian Feldman, 369–407. Leiden: Brill, 2007.

Boone, Marc. "State Power and Illicit Sexuality: The Persecution of Sodomy in Late Medieval Bruges." *Journal of Medieval History* 22 (1996): 135–153.

Bottéro, Jean and Petschow, Herbert. "Homosexualität." In *Reallexikon der Assyriologie und Vorderasiatischen Archäologie* 4, edited by Erich Ebeling and Bruno Meissner, 459–468. Berlin: De Gruyter, 1975.

Bray, Alan. "Homosexuality and the Signs of Friendship in Elizabethan England." *History Workshop Journal* 29 (1990): 1–19.

Bredbeck, Gregory W. *Sodomy and Interpretation: Marlowe to Milton*. Ithaca: Cornell University Press, 1991.

Chicago Assyrian Dictionary. Edited by Martha T. Roth. Chicago: Oriental Institute, 2011.

Cooper, Jerrold. "Buddies in Babylonia." In *Riches Hidden in Secret Places: Ancient Near Eastern Studies in Memory of Thorkild Jacobsen*, edited by Tzvi Abusch, 73–85. Winona Lake, Indiana: Eisenbrauns, 2002.

Eichler, Barry. "Examples of Restatement in the Laws of Hammurabi." In *Mishneh Todah: Studies in Deuteronomy and Its Cultural Environment, in Honor of Jeffrey H. Tigay*, edited by Nili Sacher Fox, David A. Glatt-Gilad, and Michael J. Williams, 365–400. Winona Lake, IN: Eisenbrauns, 2009.

Eichler, Barry. "Literary Structure in the Laws of Eshnunna." In *Language, Literature, and History: Philological and Historical Studies Presented to Erica Reiner*, edited by Francesca Rochberg, 71–84. New Haven: American Oriental Society, 1987.

Foucault, Michel. *The History of Sexuality*. New York: Penguin, 1990.

Franklin, Karen. "Masculinity, Status, and Power: Implicit Messages in Western Media Discourse on High-Profile Cases of Multiple Perpetrator Rape." In *Handbook on the Study of Multiple Perpetrator Rape: A Multidisciplinary Response to an International Problem*, edited by Miranda Horvath and Jessica Woodhams, 37–66. New York: Routledge, 2013.

Gadd, C. J. *Cuneiform Texts from Babylonian Tablets in the British Museum*, Volume 39. London: British Museum Publications, 1926.

George, A. R. *The Babylonian Gilgamesh Epic*. New York: Oxford University Press, 2003.

Gerstenberger, Erhard. *Leviticus: A Commentary*. Louisville: John Knox Press, 1996.

Girard, René. *Violence and the Sacred*. Baltimore: Johns Hopkins University Press, 1977.

Goldberg, Jonathan. *Sodometries: Renaissance Texts, Modern Sexualities*. Palo Alto: Stanford University Press, 1992.

Guinan, Ann Kessler. "Auguries of Hegemony: The Sex Omens of Mesopotamia." In *Gender and the Body in the Ancient Mediterranean*, edited by Maria Wyke, 38–55. Oxford: Blackwell, 1998.

Guinan, Ann Kessler. "Laws and Omens: Obverse and Inverse." In *Divination in the Ancient Near East*, edited by Jeanette C. Fincke, 105–121. Winona Lake, IN: Eisenbrauns, 2014.

Guy-Bray, Stephen, Nardizzi, Vin, and Stockton, Will. *Queer Renaissance Historiography: Backward Gaze*. Burlington, VT: Ashgate, 2009.

Haas, Volkert. *Babylonischer Liebesgarten: Erotik und Sexualität im Alten Orient.* Munich: Beck, 1999.

Halperin, David M. *One Hundred Years of Homosexuality*. New York: Routledge, 1990.

Helle, Sophus Umberto. "Putting the Anal Back in Analysis: Some Notes on Anal Sex in Babylonian Scholarship." Conference Paper, Oxford Postgraduate Conference in Assyriology, 2015. Wolfson College, Oxford. April 24–25.

Jacobsen, Thorkild. "How Did Gilgamesh Oppress Uruk?" *Acta Orientalia* 8 (1930): 62–74.

Jacobsen, Thorkild. *The Treasures of Darkness: A History of Mesopotamian Religion*. New Haven: Yale University Press, 1976.

Jordan, Mark. *The Invention of Sodomy in Christian Theology*. Chicago: University of Chicago Press, 1997.

Lafont, Sophie. *Femmes, Droit et Justice dans l'Antiquité: Contribution à l'Étude du Droit Penal au Proche-Orient Ancien*. Orbis Biblicus et Orientalis, 165. Göttingen: Vanderhoeck and Ruprecht, 1999.

Lambert, W. G. "Prostitution." In *Aussenseiter und Randgruppen*, edited by Volkert Haas, 127–157. Konstanz: Konstanz University Press, 1992.

Loya, Joe. *The Man Who Outgrew His Prison Cell: Confessions of a Bank Robber.* New York: Harper Collins, 2005.

Mills, Robert. *Seeing Sodomy in the Middle Ages*. Chicago: University of Chicago Press, 2015.

Morris, Peter. *Guardians*. London: Oberon Books, 2005.

Nissinen, Martti. *Homoeroticism in the Biblical World: A Historical Perspective.* Minneapolis: Fortress Press, 1998.

Nissinen, Martti. "Are There Homosexuals in Mesopotamian Literature?" *Journal of the American Oriental Society* 130 (2010): 73–77.

Olsen, Glenn. *Of Sodomites, Effeminates, Hermaphrodites, and Androgynes: Sodomy in the Age of Peter Damian*. Toronto: Pontifical Institute of Mediaeval Studies, 2011.

Parker, Patricia. "Hysteron-Proteron, or the Preposterous." In *Renaissance Figures of Speech*, edited by Sylvia Adamson, Gavin Alexander, and Katrin Ettenhuber, 133–145. Cambridge: Cambridge University Press, 2007.

Philips, Kim and Reay. Barry. *Sex Before Sexuality: A Premodern History.* Cambridge: Polity, 2011.

Puff, Helmut. *Sodomy in Reformation Germany and Switzerland, 1400–1600*. Chicago: University of Chicago Press, 2003.

Rocke, Michael. *Forbidden Friendships: Homosexuality and Male Culture in Renaissance Florence*. New York: Oxford University Press, 1998.

Roth, Martha. *Law Collections from Mesopotamia and Asia Minor*. Atlanta: Scholars Press, 1997.

Sedgwick, Eve Kosofsky. *Between Men: English Literature and Male Homosocial Desire*. New York: Columbia University Press, 1985.

Sedgwick, Eve Kosofksy. *The Epistemology of the Closet*. Berkeley: University of California Press, 1990.

Stol, Marten. "Remarks on Some Sumerograms and Akkadian Words." In *Studies Presented to Robert D. Biggs*, edited by Martha Roth, Walter Farber, Matthew W. Stolper, and Paula von Bechtolsheim, 233–242. Chicago: Oriental Institute, 2007.

Verderame, Lorenzo. *Le Tavole I-VI della Serie Astrologica Enūma Anu Enlil.* Rome: Dipartimento di Science dell'Antichità, 2002.

Walls, Neal. *Desire, Discord and Death: Approaches to Ancient Near Eastern Myth.* Boston: American School of Oriental Research, 2001.

Ward, Jane. *Not Gay: Sex Between Straight White Men.* New York: NYU Press, 2015.

Westbrook, Raymond. "Evidentiary Procedure in the Middle Assyrian Laws." In *Law from the Tigris to the Tiber: The Writings of Raymond Westbrook, Volume 2, Cuneiform and Biblical Sources*, edited by Bruce Wells and F. Rachel Magdalene, 211–229. Winona Lake, IN: Eisenbrauns, 2009.

Wiggerman, Frans. "Sexualität." In *Reallexikon der Assyriologie und Vorderasiatischen Archäologie* 12 5/6, edited by M. P. Streck, 410–426. Berlin: De Gruyter, 2010.

7 Shaved beards and bared buttocks

Shame and the undermining of masculine performance in biblical texts

Hilary Lipka

Introduction

2 Samuel 10:1–5[1] and 1 Chronicles 19:1–5 tell of an incident between David, king of Israel, and Hanun, the newly crowned king of the Ammonites. David, who had been on good terms with Hanun's father, and most likely had been in a covenant relationship with him, sent some emissaries[2] to express David's condolences to Hanun over the loss of his father, which was what a treaty partner was expected to do.[3] However, Hanun, suspecting that David's emissaries were actually spies, responded as follows, according to 2 Samuel 10:4: "Hanun took David's emissaries, shaved half of their beards[4] and cut their garments in half up to their buttocks,[5] and sent them away." The narrator tells of David's response in v.5: "When David was told, he sent men to meet them, for the men were very ashamed.[6] And the king said: 'Stay in Jericho until your beards grow back; and then return.' " The result of this breech in diplomacy, described in the rest of the chapter, was a war between David and the Ammonites.

To the modern reader, this passage may raise several questions. Why would shaving off half a man's beard, or, if one follows the nearly identical version in 1 Chronicles 19, all of a man's beard, and cutting his garment in half up to his buttocks and then sending him off on his way be seen as an appropriate response when you believe that the man is a spy? Why were David's emissaries so humiliated by this treatment? Why did David tell them to stay in Jericho until their beards grew back? Why was this incident seen as so grave that it resulted in a war between the Israelites and the Ammonites, even though the emissaries suffered no serious physical harm?

In order to understand Hanun's intent in cutting beards and baring buttocks, and the response that this act inspired in both the emissaries and David, we must consider the ancient Israelite construction of masculinity, focusing on what attributes are associated with the hegemonic masculine ideal that permeates many biblical texts. We will then consider situations in which men are depicted as having their performance of hegemonic masculinity undermined through various circumstances or actions, and the relationship between shame and performance of alternative constructions of masculinity in some of these texts.[7] We will see through this examination that both Hanun's and David's actions make complete sense within their original sociocultural context.

Hegemonic masculinity in biblical texts: An overview

By now there is widespread scholarly consensus that when we talk about the construction of masculinity within a given culture, we are really talking about multiple masculinities and, in fact, a whole spectrum of relative masculinities. At one end of the spectrum is what is termed hegemonic masculinity, the predominant cultural ideal, and then there is something of a sliding scale of other masculinities whose relationship with the hegemonic model can generally be characterized as one of complicity, subordination, or marginalization.[8] The relationship between hegemonic masculinity and other masculinities on the spectrum is not fixed, and the continuing predominance of the current hegemonic ideal at any given point is never a given. In order to retain dominance, the hegemonic ideal will often have to evolve over time, changing as society changes, reflecting evolving societal norms and mores, the effects of shifting politics, and changes in socioeconomic conditions, sometimes incorporating aspects of other, relative masculinities in order to do so effectively.[9]

The Biblical evidence indicates that ancient Israel was no exception in its construction of masculinity,[10] and in fact there was a rather wide spectrum of relative masculinities whose relationship with the hegemonic model spanned the entire range from complicity to subordination to marginalization.[11] While fully acknowledging the wide variety of masculinities present in the Hebrew Bible, and that what was considered hegemonic was to an extent fluid and likely evolved over time, one particular masculine ideal appears to be predominant in the majority of biblical texts.[12]

Hegemonic masculinity in biblical texts is tied to the notion of strength, as expressed by terms such as כך, זרוע, חיל, גבורה, and עז, all of which denote strength, almost exclusively male strength.[13] In order to perform the ideal masculine role, an Israelite man needed to demonstrate several different kinds of strength, including physical strength, virility, and power in sexual matters, and inner strength (explained below). A man's physical strength was often perceived as tied to his ability and courage in warfare; a man who epitomized this masculine ideal was expected to be strong, brave, and skilled in battle.[14] In terms of sexual virility and power, he was supposed to produce many children as evidence of his potency.[15] He was also supposed to always be the active and dominant partner, who had control over both his wife and his household, in addition to, of course, sexual control over his own body.[16] A man's inner strength was demonstrated by virtues such as perseverance, self-control, fortitude, endurance, integrity, and dignity.[17] The epitome of hegemonic masculinity was the גבור,[18] who was noteworthy for his exceptional strength, usually exhibited on the battlefield and/or through his leadership ability, and for his ability to produce many offspring.[19] One of the results of a successful performance of hegemonic masculinity[20] in each of these areas was honor within the community, which in the biblical construction of masculinity is very highly prized.[21]

Throughout the Hebrew Bible, masculinity tends to be depicted in contrast to femininity.[22] There are clearly delineated gender specific roles, spaces, behaviors, attire, tasks, and tools.[23] Even when terms of strength are used to describe women, they have a different or much more limited meaning than when used in the context of men. For example, while an איש חיל is a man who possesses strength in every sense, the אשת חיל is a woman of strong character who has the makings of an excellent wife. She is industrious, capable, efficient, and virtuous, and thus worthy of respect, as is the husband who is lucky enough to have her.[24] Nowhere is an אשת חיל described as possessing much in the way of physical strength, much less ability in warfare or sexual vigor.[25] This emphasis on maintaining a distinction between the genders and their respective roles is reflected in the aversion to the blurring of gender boundaries that we see in Deuteronomy 22:5, where men are prohibited from wearing women's garments, and women from using men's implements, כלי גבר, which likely refers to weapons or other items associated exclusively with men.[26] Such gender-bending behavior is labeled by the author as a תועבה, an abomination.[27] In Leviticus 18:22 and 20:13, men are commanded not to lie with a man "as one lies with a woman." Such behavior is likewise labeled a תועבה. While there has been quite a lot of debate as to the reasoning behind this prohibition, Martti Nissinen, noting that no such prohibition is made against women lying with women, convincingly suggests that the issue is not one of homosexual activity, but of putting one of the men in the passive sexual position, which should only be reserved for women.[28]

Physical attributes associated with hegemonic masculinity in biblical texts

In addition to being tied to the notion of strength, hegemonic masculinity in biblical texts is also associated with several physical attributes. The first is a biological marker: facial hair, which marked an adult (mature) male. A beard marked a man as a man, in contrast to a boy or a woman.[29]

The second physical attribute associated with hegemonic masculinity is also a biological marker: the penis, as well as the whole male genital area. One of the biblical terms for penis, שפכה,[30] is derived from the verb שפך, which means "to pour out," as in the part of the male anatomy that pours out sperm, which, after all, was a good part of what male sexual potency in ancient Israel was all about. There are several terms used euphemistically for the male genitalia.[31] בשר, literally "flesh," is used as a euphemism for the penis in several texts (Lev 15:2, 3, 7; Ezek 16:26; 23:20; and 44:7, 9).

Ezekiel twice, in 16:26 and 23:20, uses בשר in his description of the Egyptians as having huge penises. In the latter text, he compares their "flesh" to those of asses, and their ejaculations[32] to that of horses. Size, at least to Ezekiel, apparently did matter.

The term ירך, "thigh," is also used on several occasions to refer to the male genitals, in which case it is usually translated as "loins," also a euphemism. Whenever ירך is used in this sense, it is always in the context of a man's great procreative power, the producing of lots and lots of offspring.[33] Not surprisingly in a culture in which the hegemonic ideal of masculinity was largely tied up with the ability to produce numerous offspring, one way of taking an oath in biblical texts was for a man to put his hand under his ירך, "thigh," in this usage probably best translated "loins," so that he is swearing by his procreative power.[34] Other euphemisms for male genitalia include רגלים, "feet,"[35] and מבושים, perhaps best translated "male privates."[36]

The third physical attribute associated with hegemonic masculinity is weaponry. The ability to successfully wield a weapon epitomized a man's strength and bravery, especially in battle, which was perceived as a crucial aspect of the performance of hegemonic masculinity. Being able to wield and use a weapon separated men from boys and women. In Judges 8:20, Gideon commands his oldest son to kill two captive kings, but, as the narrator describes "the boy did not draw his sword, for he was afraid, still being a boy." Gideon ends up having to kill the captives himself, after they tell him in v. 21: "Come, you kill us, for strength comes with being a man."[37]

It is no great shock that none of the physical attributes associated with masculinity are associated with women in biblical texts. While the absence of the first two attributes speaks for itself, it is noteworthy that the few times a woman is described as killing a man in biblical texts, she does so using nontraditional weapons. The anonymous woman from Tevetz (Judg 9:50–57) throws a piece of millstone down on Abimelech's head, and Yael (Judg 4:17–22; 5:24–30) uses a tent peg to impale Sisera's temple after he has fallen asleep. Traditional weapons are the exclusive domain of males.[38]

Ways of undermining masculine performance in biblical texts

In the world of the Hebrew Bible, masculinity was hardly a given. Rather, it had to be accomplished and achieved. Once a man did succeed in achieving hegemonic masculinity, there was always the fear that something or someone could come along and undermine his masculine performance. In the biblical construction of masculinity, those who don't perform the hegemonic masculine ideal satisfactorily are viewed as being associated with lesser, sometimes subordinate masculinities on the spectrum, which means in practical terms a loss in social power and prestige.[39] While men who achieve a successful performance of hegemonic masculinity are rewarded with honor, those who cannot maintain their performance risk being subject to shame.[40]

Performance of hegemonic masculinity could be undermined several different ways in biblical texts. First, it could happen as the result of a natural process, such as growing old or being hampered by illness or a physical handicap. Second, this construct could be undermined through one's own actions, such as cowardice at the prospect of battle, succumbing to overwhelming fear when confronting the enemy face-to-face, or losing self-control when facing a devastating military loss.[41] Third, another party could undermine a man's performance of the ideal masculinity, by removing or altering physical attributes associated with masculinity or by forcing him into a position of passivity and powerlessness. All of these result in the inability to maintain the performance of hegemonic masculinity, which results in a performance associated with lesser masculinities on the spectrum. We will now consider each of these ways of undermining performance of masculinity in biblical texts.

The first way that a man's performance of hegemonic masculinity could be undermined in biblical texts was as the result of a natural process. A prime example of this is growing old, which results in the loss of strength in several areas and the loss of control over one's own body, with the result that the performance of masculinity associated with a man in his prime cannot be sustained. In 1 Kings 1:1–4, King David is described as now quite old, and always feeling cold, so his attendants (עבדים) decide on a solution, which is to find a beautiful young woman[42] to be a companion to David and to share his bed, thereby keeping him warm. After searching the entire territory of Israel, they find a young woman named Abishag who is described as being יפה עד מאד, exceedingly beautiful. Verse 4 describes how Abishag became the king's companion, and presumably shared his bed, והמלך לא ידעה, "but the king was not sexually intimate with her." Apparently, the king's servants went on this search to find the most beautiful young woman in the land to be the king's bedmate because they were concerned that in addition to the weakness that comes with old age, the loss of sexual potency on David's part would be highly problematic in terms of how he was perceived by others who might want to challenge his claim to the throne. And, as it turns out, immediately after this incident there is a description of how one of David's sons, Adonijah, apparently seeing David weakened and enfeebled by age and now sexually disempowered, took him to be weak and disempowered in other areas associated with masculinity, as well. Since David seemed to be no longer capable of performing the construct of masculinity that a king must perform, Adonijah decided to declare himself the new king, without notifying David.[43]

Now, when a man's performance of hegemonic masculinity is undermined by natural processes such as age, illness, and physical handicap, resulting in a performance associated with lesser masculinities on the spectrum, it is generally not depicted in biblical texts as shaming. However, the same is not true of the two other forms of undermining masculine performance, both of which are associated frequently with the language of shame.

The next category is those whose performance of hegemonic masculinity is undermined through their own behavior. Not surprisingly, this theme comes up frequently in biblical texts, largely in the form of descriptions of men who demonstrate an alternate construct of masculinity either by displaying cowardice at the prospect of battle, being overcome by fear in the face of battle, or loss of self-control at the prospect of a devastating military loss. Once a man demonstrates cowardice, being overwhelmed by fear, or total loss of self-control, he is no longer performing the socially ideal, hegemonic construct of masculinity, and so must be shamed.

There are those men who are afraid to fight in the first place, who display fear even at the prospect of battle. In Deuteronomy 20:5–8, instructions are given for battle with the enemy, including questioning the men to see if some should be excused from the fighting. Those who have just built a house and have not yet dedicated it, those who have planted the harvest and not yet harvested it, and those who have paid the bride price for a wife but have not yet married her are all excused from battle, the logic being that they might die, and another man will reap the benefits of their labor, or, in the last case, bed the wife for whom they have already paid the bride price. The last category is in verse 8: "The officials shall go on addressing the troops and say, 'Is there any man who is afraid and faint-hearted? Let him go and return to his house, lest he cause the hearts of his comrades to melt like his.' " The last category is the man who is afraid to fight. He lacks the courage and inner strength, and thus is a liability to the rest of the men, lest his fear prove contagious.[44] Judges 7:3 presents a similar scenario. God instructs Gideon to winnow down the number of his troops by announcing "Let anyone who is afraid and fearful turn back as a bird flies from Mount Gilead."

Then there are those men who succumb to overwhelming fear when confronting the enemy face-to-face, who as a result can no longer perform the hegemonic masculine ideal successfully. In some texts, men who become overwhelmed by fear in the face of battle are even described as turning into women. The image of men turning into women is used several times by Israelite prophets making pronouncements against the enemy. Jeremiah 50:36–37 tells of how Yahweh's might will instill such fear in the Babylonian troops, even its mightiest warriors (גבוריה) will become women.[45] Jeremiah 51:30 similarly describes the mightiest warriors among the Babylonian army (גבורי בבל) becoming women after they give up fighting and their strength (גבורתם) is "dried up" in the face of Yahweh's vengeance.[46] The implication is that the soldiers, giving in to their fear, will lose their masculine strength and demonstrate behavior that is associated with the feminine, thus becoming like women (at least as women are constructed in these particular texts): terrified, weak, powerless, and vulnerable. And of course conquered nations, including Israel and Judah, are likened to women throughout the prophetic texts of the Bible, often depicted as subjected to forced stripping, rape, and other humiliating forms of sexual abuse (See, for example, Isa 47:1–4; Jer 13:22–26; Ezek 16:35–39; and Nah 3:5–6).[47]

Lastly, there are those men who lose self-control in panic, terror and despair when facing a devastating military loss. These men, overwhelmed by emotion, rather than being described as turned into women, are likened in their terror and distress to women in the throes of labor or writhing in the unbearable agony of childbirth. Men who successfully perform hegemonic masculinity in biblical texts are supposed to maintain their dignity and self-control at all times, no matter what adversity and devastation they are facing. In contrast, these men give into overwhelming emotion and thus perform an alternative, and, presumably, less desirable masculinity that, according to these biblical authors, make them like women at their most vulnerable and out of control. Jeremiah 48:41 states that "On that day," meaning the day the Yahweh utterly destroys Moab, "the heart of Moab's warriors (גבורי מואב) shall be like the heart of a woman in travail," that is, in the grip of childbirth.[48] Isaiah, in an oracle of doom against Babylon (Isa 13:7–8), describes what the warriors of Babylon will experience when faced with Yahweh's wrath on the Day of YHWH: "Therefore all hands will grow limp, and every man's heart will grow faint; they will be terrified; pangs and throes will seize them, they will writhe like a woman in travail. They will gaze stupefied at each other, their faces feverish."[49] Such language is not only used to describe the reaction of the enemy. Jeremiah, for example, also uses such language to mock his own people. In a pronouncement against both Israel and Judah in Jeremiah 30:6, the prophet states: "Can a man bear children? Why then do I see every man with his hands on his loins like a woman in labor, and every face turned pale?"[50]

The last category is those whose performance of hegemonic masculinity is undermined by another party. This can be achieved either by removing or altering physical attributes associated with hegemonic masculinity or by forcing men into a performance of passivity and powerlessness, qualities not associated with the hegemonic ideal. One effective means of undermining masculine performance in biblical texts was by destroying, altering, or otherwise tampering with biological markers that served as attributes of masculine identity. In the introduction to this chapter, I referred to 2 Samuel 10:4–5 and 1 Chronicles 19:4–5, in which Hanun shaves the beards of David's envoys and cuts their garments up to "their seat," meaning that their buttocks, as well as possibly the rest of their genitalia, were showing. Whether half the beards were shaven or all the beards, the psychological effect on the men may have been virtually the same. The removal of a man's facial hair was seen as a means of depriving him of one of the essential attributes of hegemonic masculinity, and thus taking away his masculine identity, since the beard was one of the primary ways that a man was differentiated from women and boys. Removing or tampering with a man's beard thus resulted in an undermining of his ability to perform this construct. That is the first part of the reason that the men are ashamed, and why David tells them to remain in Jericho until their beards grow back. New clothes can readily be obtained, but the men cannot show their faces in Jerusalem until they once again have the proper gender and maturity marker, namely their beards.[51]

In addition to the shaving of the beards, the exposure of the men's buttocks and/or genitalia was also deeply shaming, a form of sexual humiliation that greatly undermined successful performance of the masculine ideal. In Isaiah 7:20, Isaiah tells of a day of reckoning, either for Samaria or Judah (the text is not clear), when Yahweh will borrow a razor from the king of Assyria and shave the head and what is termed the "hair of the feet" (שער הרגלים), which appears to refer to pubic hair, given the context and the euphemistic usage of רגלים, "feet," that sometimes occurs in biblical texts. Yahweh will also sweep away the beard, presumably after a razor has been taken to it.[52] The verse is in the context of an oracle of doom, in which Isaiah predicts disaster at the hands of Assyria, which here functions as God's tool of vengeance against his own people. While it is not clear whether Samaria or Judah was the intended object of God's wrath in this oracle, the intent of the punishment is clear: the shaving of the heads, the pubic hair, and the beards of the captives was intended to humiliate them, to make them feel exposed, vulnerable, and without dignity. Similarly, in Isaiah 20:3–5, the prophet describes how the defeated captives of Egypt and Nubia will be driven off by the Assyrians (v. 4) "naked and barefoot and with bared buttocks – to the shame of Egypt!"

We know from the biblical evidence that in ancient Israel men were supposed to keep their genitals covered, and that is was a very shameful thing if they were exposed. While it is quite unclear what Ham did to Noah in Genesis 9:20–27, if he simply saw his father naked or did something to Noah while he was drunkenly passed out, we do know that his two other sons had to engage in some complicated maneuvering to cover up their father while avoiding the sight of their father's nakedness.[53] In 2 Samuel 6:20, Michal sarcastically comments that David surely honored himself that day when he exposed himself before the gathered crowds while dancing before the ark. The narrator's earlier comment in 2 Samuel 6:14 that David was wearing only a simple linen loincloth, and was thus rather scantily clad, supports this interpretation.[54] Thus it is not surprising that a way to humiliate prisoners of war, in addition to shaving off their hair and beards, was to expose their private parts through forced stripping and exposure.[55]

Another way of undermining hegemonic masculine performance was by forcing a man into a performance of passivity and powerlessness by taking unauthorized sexual control of the women within his household. It was considered deeply shaming for a man to fail to prevent sexual access of others to his wives, sisters, and/or daughters without his consent, and was sometimes seen as reflecting a man's powerlessness in other areas, as well.[56] We can see a classic example of this in the way that Absalom, King David's oldest (living) son, challenges his father's claim to the throne in 2 Samuel 15–16. When he is told of Absalom's challenge and approach toward Jerusalem, David, performing qualities distinctly not associated with the hegemonic masculine ideal, flees Jerusalem, leaving ten of his secondary wives (פלגשים)[57] to watch over the palace. In 2 Samuel 16:20–23, Absalom, as a declaration of his claim and as an illustration of his father's personal and political weakness, has sex with all ten of his father's secondary wives on the palace rooftop, in a very intentional public display.[58] The importance of retaining control over the women of one's household is also reflected in Deuteronomy 22:20–21, where a young wife found guilty of her husband's accusation that she did not remain chaste before marriage is sentenced to be stoned in front of her father's house, "because she committed an outrage (נבלה)[59] against Israel by acting promiscuously in her father's house." Generally, stoning took place at the town gate. The fact that she is stoned in front of her father's house is a shaming act that places blame on him for failing to properly guard his daughter's virginity.[60]

Perhaps the most devastating way of undermining hegemonic masculine performance, even worse than baring a man's buttocks and exposing his nakedness and/or undermining the sexual control he exerts over the women in his household, was to force a man into a submissive sexual position by forcibly penetrating him. There are no successful male-on-male sexual assaults in biblical texts, but there are two incidents of attempted male-on-male sexual assault, in both cases intended solely to humiliate the victims. In both Genesis 19:4–9 and Judges 19:22–25, all of the males in a town demand that a male stranger who is spending the night be handed over to them for the purpose of sexual assault, in a show of complete contempt for the rules of hospitality.[61] In both Genesis 19 and Judges 19, the host attempts to stave off the sexual advances of the men of the town by offering what he sees as a suitable substitute as far as humiliating the household is concerned: his virgin daughters, and, in the latter case, the Levite's secondary wife.[62]

When a man was forced into a position of sexual submission by others, it put him into the position of a woman, that of a passive sexual partner, utterly humiliating him through his sense of powerlessness.[63] This was viewed as something that was to be avoided at all costs.

Shame and the undermining of masculine performance in biblical texts

In both cases where hegemonic masculine performance is undermined by the behavior of the men themselves, and cases where performance of masculinity is undermined by the actions of others, the result is shame. The notions of honor and shame were integral to ancient Israelite culture, and the construction of honor and shame was in large part determined by gender role expectations – certain behavior was expected of men and certain behavior was expected of women. A man had a strong sense of honor when his behavior, both as perceived by himself and by others, was seen as conforming to the hegemonic masculine ideal, which focused largely on the possession of virility, strength, and power, demonstrated through performances of skill and courage in battle, dominance over one's wife and household, the production of multiple children, and complete mastery over one's own body, appetites, and emotions. This performance required the avoidance of any behavior that was associated with alternative constructions of masculinity that were considered lower on the spectrum. As we have seen in this study, when a man's sense of masculinity is undermined, either by the altering of one of the markers of masculinity or by being rendered weak and powerless, whether through his own actions or the actions of others, he no longer lives up to the hegemonic masculine ideal, and the result is a deep sense of shame.

The answer to the questions, then, posed at the beginning of this chapter, is that Hanun, by shaving the beards and baring the buttocks of the emissaries sent by David, was sending the message to David that he was disinterested in maintaining a covenant relationship in the most insulting way possible. By sabotaging the masculine performance of David's emissaries, and possibly also mocking the common gesture of mourning that involves clipping part of the beard, Hanun was also sabotaging David's performance of masculinity. David, in response to this challenge to his honor, really had no choice but to go to war with Ammon, since, given the dynamic of honor and shame that was predominant in ancient Israel at that time, that was the only way that honor in a situation such as this could be restored, and the importance of honor for David as a leader of his people was fundamental. If David had not taken action to restore his honor, the result would likely have been challenges to his claim to royal authority similar to the ones his sons later posed when his masculine performance did start to visibly falter. Thus David was forced to start a war, the ultimate result being the defeat and humiliation of the Ammonites, and the restoration of the honor of David and the Israelites.

By looking at biblical texts through the lens of expectations regarding masculine performance and the negative consequences that result when performance of masculinity is undermined, we can better understand accounts of male behavior in biblical texts that might otherwise strike a modern reader as odd, unusual, or even baffling. Because of the integral connection between masculine performance and the dynamic of honor and shame in ancient Israelite culture, men felt a great deal of pressure to conform to the hegemonic masculine ideal. Under these circumstances, it should come as no surprise that men as they are depicted in biblical texts often appear to be preoccupied with asserting, maintaining, and/or defending their masculine performance, sometimes by taking actions that undermine the masculine performance of another.

Notes

1 1 Chr 19:1–5 has the same narrative, with one exception, which will be mentioned below. For issues dealing with the historicity of this narrative and questions regarding the order of events in 2 Samuel (neither of which are of concern for us here), see McCarter (1984: 273–276).

2 Literally עבדים, servants.
3 For a discussion about whether David's feelings of loyalty toward Nahash reflected a formal covenant relationship, see Lemos (2006: 232–233). Lemos contends that the use of חסד does reflect a formal covenant relationship, and thus David, by sending some of his men to mourn with the family, was simply fulfilling one of his obligations as a treaty partner. Similarly, Olyan (1996: 212). McCarter (1984: 273–274) suggests that the relationship was more informal.
4 This is the point where the narratives in 2 Samuel and 1 Chronicles are slightly different. In 1 Chr 19:4, Hanun shaves off the beards of the envoys, rather than half of their beards. The *LXX* of 2 Sam 1:4 agrees with the 1 Chronicles account. For the purposes of this study, the difference between the versions will have no impact – whether the whole beard or half of the beard was shaven, the impact on David's envoys was the same
5 The Hebrew is שתותיהם, which seems to refer to the seat of the body (from שית), and thus the buttocks, the part of the body with which one sits. See Isa 20:4 for a similar usage.
6 The verb used to denote the humiliation felt by the men is כלם.
7 This study will be limited to texts in the Hebrew Bible. The construction of masculinity is in some ways quite different in the Apocrypha and the New Testament.
8 While hegemonic masculinity at one end of the spectrum is the form that embodies the current, predominant cultural ideal of masculinity, complicit masculinities include those who cannot quite perform at the level of hegemonic ideal, but support the ideal and benefit from its predominance. Subordinated masculinities are those that are stigmatized and sometimes oppressed by those who support and benefit from the hegemonic ideal. Men whose masculinity falls into this part of the spectrum are sometimes viewed as having qualities associated with femininity. At the far end of the spectrum are marginalized masculinities, which are often associated with certain racial or ethnic minorities within a particular culture, those with severe physical disabilities, or those possessing a stigmatized sexuality. Marginalized masculinities are subverted and delegitimized by the socially dominant masculinities, and thus those who fall at this end of the spectrum often have the least authority and social status. On the idea that each culture has multiple masculinities and for a discussion on the interrelationships between them, see Carrigan, Connell, and Lee (1997: 63–100); Connell (2005: 36–37 and 76–81); Connell and Messerschmidt (2005: 829–859); and Howson (2006: 55–79). Synnott (2009: 11–24) expands upon the idea of multiple masculinities, contending that the construction of masculinity within a given culture should be viewed as a continuum. Burrus (2006: 1–8) makes a similar assertion about masculinities in the ancient Mediterranean world, contending that they should be seen as comprising a dynamic spectrum of relative masculinities. As we shall see, the same can also be said for ancient Israel.
9 Connell (2005: 37–39 and 76–81) and Synnott (2009: 12).
10 A similar, somewhat longer version of this discussion of the hegemonic masculine ideal in ancient Israel appears in Lipka (2014: 87–91).
11 Several excellent studies have examined different aspect of the masculinities spectrum to be found in biblical texts. Nissinen, in his paper in this volume, "Relative Masculinities in the Hebrew Bible" focuses on some of these relative masculinities that comprise other parts of the spectrum of the biblical construction of masculinity, namely the סריסים and the קדשים, demonstrating how complex and multifaceted the spectrum of masculinities was in ancient Israel. Several articles in Creangă (2010a) also address the wide range of masculinities on the spectrum. Haddox (2010: 15–16) compares how Abraham, Isaac, Ishmael, Jacob and Esau stack up in terms of hegemonic standards of masculinity, and finds that the those favored by God in the Genesis narratives often were not

exemplars of the hegemonic masculine ideal. George (2010: 81) discusses representations in Deuteronomy of several lesser masculinities in addition to the hegemonic ideal. Creangă (2010b: 101–103) discusses the depiction of marginalized and subordinated masculinities in Joshua 1–12. See also Kirova (2014) and Măcelaru (2014) in Creangă's follow-up volume (2014).

12 There are exceptions, of course. One of the models of masculinity provided in the book of Proverbs, for example, de-emphasizes physical strength in favor of qualities that relate to what I above term inner strength, presenting an alternative (and perhaps a challenge) to the hegemonic ideal. See Lipka (2014) for a discussion of this alternative model of manhood found in Proverbs.

13 There are also several verbs that mean "to be strong," in biblical Hebrew, including חזק and אמץ, in addition to the verbal forms of the nouns listed above. There are also other terms that are part of what could be called the vocabulary of masculinity. און can mean either sexual vigor or physical strength, depending on the context, and in both usages, always refers to male vigor or strength.

14 See, for example, the usage of חיל in Deut 3:18; Judg 21:10; 1 Sam 16:18; 18:17; 2 Sam 2:7; 1 Chr 5:24; 8:40; 11:22; זרוע in Ezek 22:6; 31:17; Prov 31:17; Jer 17:5; Ps 44:4 and Job 22:8; כך in Judg 16:5, 6, 9, 15, 17; Isa 44:12; Lev 26:20; and גבורה in Judg 8:21; Isa 3:25; 28:6; Jer 9:22; 49:35; 51:30; Ezek 32:29; 32:30; Mic 7:16.

15 See, for example, the use of חיל in Prov 31:3: "Do not give your strength (חילך) to women," meaning don't waste your semen on women other than your wife; the use of און in Deut 21:17, in which a man's son is referred to as ראשית און, "the first (fruit) of his vigor"; and the use of both און and זרוע in Gen 49:3 in reference to a firstborn son. In Ps 127:3–5, the connection between masculinity and male fertility is made when the poet compares a man surrounded by multiple offspring to a גבור with a bow full of quivers, and "happy is the man who has his quiver full of them" (v. 5).

16 See Stone (1996: 41–46); Brenner (1997: 136–139); Matthews (1998: 102–112); Frymer-Kensky (1998: 84–86); and the discussion below.

17 See, for example, the use of גבורה in Isa 11:2; 30:15; Mic 3:8; and Prov 8:14.The term חיל is used to denote qualities related to inner strength in Exod 18:21; 1 Kgs 1:42 and 52; and Hab 3:19.

18 גבור, which occurs 159 times in biblical texts, is an intensive form of גבר and denotes, as Kosmala (1975: 373) puts it "a particularly strong or mighty person who carries out, can carry out, or has carried out great deeds, and surpasses others in doing so." גבור often refers to experienced and skilled soldiers (e.g. Joel 4:9, where גבורים is parallel to אנשי מלחמה; 2 Chr 13:3; and 2 Chr 25:6) elite troops (e.g. 2 Sam 20:7; 1 Kgs 1:8; Isa 21:17; Jer 26:21; and Cant 3:7–8) or a man who has distinguished himself in military service through brave deeds, exceptional fighting skills, or exemplary leadership (e.g. Judg 6:12; 11:1; and 2 Sam 23:8–9, 16–17). God is referred to as a *גבור* several times (see, for example, Deut 10:17; Jer 32:18; and Neh 9:32). גבור appears several times in construct with חיל, usually (though see below) denoting a man of great strength and courage either in regard to fighting in the military or generally, as in 1 Kgs 11:28, Neh 11:14; and 1 Chr 5:24; 7:2, 5, 7, 9, 11. Josh 8:3 and 10:7 draw a distinction between regular men brought into military service and גבורי החיל, mighty men of valor, who he chooses for a special mission. While the vast majority of the uses of גבור have to do with strength and might, as Kosmala notes, the span of the term is broader than that, also encompassing those who have a heightened degree of physical strength or authority, a very high station or position, or have demonstrated excellence in a particular area, usually one associated with masculine virtues (for examples of these usages of גבור, see Gen 10:8–9; 1 Kgs 15:20; Ruth 2:1; 1 Chr 9:13; Ezra 7:28). In Isa 5:22, there is an ironic use of גבור, in that

men who distinguish themselves in drinking are termed "mighty (גבורים) at drinking wine and valorous (אנשי חיל) at mixing strong drink."

19 In 1 Chron 8:40, a direct connection is made between the might and valor of גבורי חיל and their ability to produce many offspring. In Cant 3:7–8, a looser connection seems to be made between גבורים and fertility. The Solomon of the Song of Songs is the lover of many women, and in this passage his bed, perfumed with spices and presumably ready for love, is guarded by sixty גבורים. On various aspects of hegemonic masculinity in biblical texts, see Hoffner (1966: 326–334); Haddox (2010: 36–39); George (2010: 67–81); and Creangă (2010b: 87–88). David J. A. Clines (1995, 2002, 2010) has been the most prolific author so far on this topic. Clines in his articles identifies several components of masculinity in the Hebrew Bible based on a combination of character studies of iconic figures such as David, Job, and Moses and more general studies on the construction of masculinity in the Book of Psalms and the prophets. In these studies he has included qualities such as strength, violence, male bonding, detachment from women, powerful and persuasive speech, honor, and beauty as attributes of masculinity in biblical texts. While I do see some of these qualities as attributes of hegemonic masculinity in biblical texts, others are more questionable. Clines seems to be making broad generalizations from only a few pieces of evidence for beauty as a quality associated with the hegemonic masculine ideal (in fact, see Macwilliam [2009: 265–287] on the ambivalence of several biblical authors towards male beauty). I also see little biblical evidence that powerful and persuasive speech is an attribute of the general masculine ideal. While there is evidence that persuasive speech was important for leaders, military and otherwise, there is little evidence that is was a quality expected of the general male population aspiring towards a successful performance of masculinity; it was more important that they performed well in battle. As for violence as a trait of masculinity, while males certainly commit a lot of violent acts in the Bible, that does not necessarily mean that it was considered an attribute of hegemonic masculinity. In fact, biblical texts often depict male violence negatively, especially when it is committed outside of the context of legitimate warfare. For a similar critique of Clines, see Creangă (2010b: 87–88).

20 There also seems to be a particular age range associated with being able to fulfill the necessary requirements of hegemonic masculinity. Men in their prime are most likely to be able to perform masculinity successfully, considering the demonstration of physical strength and sexual virility that was required. We will see later in the discussion that some biblical texts contrast men who perform hegemonic masculinity successfully with those who are considered too young or too old to do so.

21 While several scholars include honor among the attributes of masculinity, I think it is more that successful performance of hegemonic masculinity results in honor. Clines (2002: 316–318) discusses the relationship between honor and successful performance of masculinity in similar terms, contending that honor is the recognition by the group of a status of a male. On the nature of various aspects of honor in ancient Israel and how it was considered to be achieved and maintained, see also Olyan (1996: 202–218); Stansell (1996: 55–79); and Stone (1996: 37–49).

22 Much literature has been written on the nature of gender and the way that masculinity and femininity are generally constructed in relation, often in contrast, to one another, in societies that possess such constructions. For example, see Connell (2005: 67–76); Gilmore (1990: 9–29); Synnott (2009: 21); and West and Zimmerman (1991: 22–32).

23 Hoffner (1996: 328–329) discusses the differences in symbols associated with males and females in biblical texts. Women are associated with the spindle,

distaff, and feminine garments (see Prov 31:19; 2 Sam 3:29; Deut 22:5), while men are associated with weapons, especially the bow and/or its arrows (2 Sam 1:22; 22:35; 2 Kgs 13:15 ff; Hos 1:5; Ps 127:4–5). In both cases, these symbols reflect the cultural ideal for each gender. Vedeler (2008: 461–475) discusses the prohibition against men wearing women's garments and women handling a כל'גבר in Deut 22:5 within this context of strict delineation of gender roles, specifically regarding gender specific attire and objects. Haddox (2010: 4) discusses the importance of distinguishing men's space from women's space in biblical texts. There are of course depictions of men and women in biblical texts that are exceptions to the rules, but the fact that they stand out as exceptions rather makes the point that gender expectations were pretty fixed.

24 Yoder (2003: 427, note 1) makes a strong case for translating אשת חיל as "a woman of substance," since this expression conveys all of the qualities associated with the אשת חיל. See also E. F. Campbell (1975: 90), who uses the same translation of חיל in Ruth 2:1.

25 In Prov 31:10–31, the qualities of an אשת חיל are enumerated: she is industrious and hard-working, she treats her husband well and takes good care of her family and household, and she is generous and wise. In other words, the אשת חיל is the perfect housewife, the female equivalent of the איש חיל, since capability and efficiency in domestic matters is the strength of a woman. Terms of strength are used several times in these verses. In v. 17, two terms from the vocabulary of strength are applied to her: "she girds her loins with strength" (בעוז), which appears to be a reference to her enthusiastic industriousness, and "and she strengthens her arms" (ותאמץ זרעותיה). There are several ways one could interpret the second half of the verse. אמץ could in this context refer to a literal strengthening of the arms, which would be a logical result of performing all of those household duties. However, a more likely, option, given the first half of the verse is that אמץ, like עוז, is intended metaphorically, and refers to the vigorous energy with which she approaches her household tasks. An intriguing third option, provided by Novick (2009: 107–113), is that the entire verse should be translated literally as "Strongly she girds her loins, and binds her arms." The industrious wife binds both the lower half of the garment and the upper half so that she will not be encumbered by her garment; her arms and legs are free to do work. עוז appears again in v. 25a, where the term of strength is used metaphorically: "Her garment is strength and dignity (הדר)". In v. 29, חיל occurs again: "Many women have acted with strength, but you ascend over all." Prov 12:4 contrasts an אשת חיל with a מבישה, a woman acting shamefully: "The woman of substance is the crown of her husband, and the one acting shamefully is like rot in his bones." In Ruth 3:11, חיל is similarly used to denote a woman's strength of character.

26 On this interpretation of כלי גבר, see Hoffner (1966: 332–334) and Vedeler (2008: 459–476). See also Driver (1902: 250–251).

27 The term "abomination" (תועבה) is used in several different biblical traditions to designate a thing or an action that is considered abhorrent to Yahweh, though there is some variation in the way that different biblical traditions use the term. For a general discussion of the term "abomination" (תועבה), See Humbert (1960: 217–237); Paschen (1970: 28–30); Weinfeld (1977: 230–237); van der Toorn (1985: 44); Hallo (1985: 35–38); Preuss (1995: 582–591); and Milgrom (2000: 1569–1570). On the concept of תועבה specifically in Deuteronomy, see L'Hour (1964: 481–503) and Weinfeld (1972: 267–269 and 323).

28 Nissinen (1998: 43–44). Similarly, Bigger (1979: 202–203); Brenner (1997: 140–141); Olyan (1994: 183–186); and Stone (1996: 77–78).

29 See Conrad (1981: 122–131) on the connection between זָקָן, the Hebrew word for beard, and זָקֵן, which denotes maturity. If one looks at the texts in Leviticus regarding skin diseases (Lev 13:29–30 and Lev 14:9) and texts involving the

cutting or shaving off all or of part of the beard in the context of mourning rites (Lev 19:27 and 21:5 prohibit Israelite men from engaging in this kind of mourning ritual, while Isa 15:2 and Jer 48:37 depict it among the Moabites and Jer 41:5 depicts it among Israelites from Shiloh, Shechem, and Samaria; Ezra in Ezra 9:3 tears out the hair on his head and beard as an expression of grief), the assumption appears to be that men have beards. See also Chapman (2004: 26 and 39) and Lemos (2006: 233).

30 This term appears only once, in Deut 23:2, but from the context its meaning is clear.

31 While the term מתנים, generally translated as "loins," usually refers to the middle of the body, in one text, 1 Kgs 12:10–11 (=2 Chr 10:10–11), it appears to be used euphemistically to refer to the penis, when Reheboam is advised, not judiciously, as it turn out, to respond to a delegation of northerners led by Jeroboam, who request that he lighten the work burden that his father Solomon imposed on them: "My little finger is thicker than my father's מתנים. My father imposed a heavy yoke on you, and I will increase your yoke; my father disciplined you with whips, but I will discipline you with scorpions."

32 זרמה, which comes from the stem זרם, which means to pour fourth or flood.

33 See, for example, Gen 46:26 and Exod 1:5, and Judg 8:30. See also the usage of חלצים, generally translated as "loins," in Gen 35:11; I Kgs 8:19; and 2 Chron 6:9, where offspring are referred to as those coming forth (יצא) from the "loins."

34 See, for example, Gen 24:2, 9 and Gen 47:29.

35 See, for example, Exod 4:25; Isa 6:2; and Isa 7:20.

36 This term occurs only once, in Deut 25:11, and appears to derive from the term בוש, "to be ashamed." In this text, a woman who tries to help her husband out in a fight with another man by seizing the other man's genitals is sentenced to have her hand (כף) cut off. This is likely because by grabbing his genitals she threatened the man's procreative abilities, though it has also been suggested that her actions violated a societal taboo or were deemed as deeply shaming either to the man or to herself. See Cortez (2006: 431–447); Elliott (2006: 171–172); Mayes (1979: 328); Phillips (1973: 170); and Tigay (1996: 485–486). For a different approach, see Eslinger (1981: 269–291), who makes the interesting but not particularly convincing argument that the usage of כף in this passage, a common term for the hand in the Bible, here indicates that the woman's punishment is actually genital mutilation. For a detailed discussion of euphemisms used for both male and female genitalia in the Hebrew Bible, see Elliott (2006: 167–174).

37 Hebrew: כי כאיש גבורתו, literally "for as the man [is], [so is] his strength." In 1 Sam 17, David, described as still a youth (נער), defies expectations by rejecting traditional weaponry, which, being still a youth, he may not yet be accustomed to and perhaps cannot efficiently wield. Instead, he faces Goliath only with a sling and a rock with which he is ironically able to kill the heavily clad and very experienced warrior. It is noteworthy that in 1 Kgs 12:8–11 (see note 31), the men who give Reheboam such disastrous advice are referred to as ילדים, in contrast to the זקנים whose advice he didn't take in 1 Kgs 12:6–8. Here youth is associated with inexperience, lack of wisdom, and quite possibly a lack of strength of character. On the association of weaponry (and being able to handle weapons) with the hegemonic masculine ideal, see Hoffner (1966: 328–329) and Vedeler (2008: 470).

38 Similarly, Vedeler (2008: 474–475). While this discussion is limited to texts in the Hebrew Bible, it should be pointed out that in the Apocryphal Book of Judith, the heroine kills Holofernes with his own sword. However, Judith still uses the rather unorthodox means of getting the Assyrian general drunk in order to perform her task. The Book of Judith may also reflect evolving mores regarding women and weapons.

39 On the notion of masculinity as a tenuous achievement, see Gilmore (1990: 9–29) and Synnott (2009: 22–24).

40 There is both a social dimension and a psychological dimension to shame. The social dimension entails a person's concern over how others in society perceive him or her, while the psychological dimension entails how the individual esteems him or herself. Both aspects come into play when considering the notion of shame in biblical texts. On the general nature of shame, see Cairns (1993: 5–47); Lewis (1992: 2 and 71–76); and Miller (1985: 32). On the dynamic of shame in biblical texts, see Bechtel (1991: 47–76); Lemos (2006: 227–241); Olyan (1996: 201–218); and Stiebert (2002: 3–75).

41 Also in this category would fall men who fail to live up to the hegemonic ideal of masculinity in biblical texts by losing control of their physical appetites and being labeled a glutton or a drunkard (see Deut 21:20). See George (2010: 69–70, 81).

42 נערה בתולה, which does not necessarily mean a virgin.

43 When David is informed of Adonijah's actions, he responds by declaring Solomon as his successor (1 Kings 1:15–40). Later, after David's death, Adonijah, in an attempt to challenge his brother's claim to the throne, tries to arrange to marry Abishag, which Solomon takes as such a direct threat that he arranges to have Adonijah killed (2 Kings 2:13–25). Adonijah's actions were actually the second challenge to David 's royal authority by one of his sons. His half-brother Absolom's earlier challenge to David's claim to the throne will be discussed below.

44 George (2010: 72–73) contends that it is out of humanitarian concern that such men are excused from fighting, just as is the case for the other categories. However, since the reason given for excusing this last category of men from battle is that their fear might prove contagious, it seems more a concern that a coward has to potential to have a negative effect on other soldiers, rather than any humanitarian concern for the coward himself, that is the motivating factor.

45 Expressed by והיו לנשים.

46 A similar sentiment is expressed in the first part of Nah 3:13, a pronouncement against Assyria: "Your people are women (עמך נשים). The gates of your land have completely opened themselves to your enemies." See also Isa 19:16, where in the face of Yahweh's vengeance, Isaiah describes how the Egyptians will "be like women, trembling and quaking."

47 In each of these cases, it is Yahweh doing the actual punishing, using the nation's enemies as his tools of vengeance. See Chapman (2004: 64–65); Kamionkowski (2003: 89–91); Magdalene (1995: 327–352); and Washington (1997: 346).

48 Hebrew מצרה. The verb צרר used here (which *BDB*, 865, identifies as צרר II, an intensive form of what it identifies as צרר I) is explicitly tied with the travail experienced by woman in the throes of childbirth in Jer 4:31. Jer 49:22 makes an identical pronouncement against Edom.

49 We don't know much about childbirth practices in ancient Israel, nor do we know if men were ever present when a woman was giving birth. These verses may well reflect a construction of childbirth by men who never witnessed it. It is difficult to know what to make of להבים at the end of verse 8. להב appears to refer to a flame, or something burning. My translation reflects the notion that a burning face in this context could be feverish. Kamionkowski (2003: 86–87) points out that the pains expressed by the words צירים and חבלים are specific to the contraction pains of a woman in labor, which makes sense given the simile that immediately follows.

50 Some other examples of prophetic texts employing this motif include Isa 21:3–4; and Jer 6:24 and 50:43. For a discussion of prophetic use of this motif, see Kamionkowski (2003: 85–90).

51 Cutting one's beard as part of the rites of mourning is a different matter, since under the circumstances of mourning, humbling oneself through shaving off one's beard appears to have been the norm, though it was at times discouraged in Israel. On cutting the beard as part of mourning rites, see Jer 41:5 (practiced by men from Shechem, Shiloh, and Samaria – all northern Israel); Isa 15:2 and Jer 48:37 (both as parts of prophetic pronouncements against Moab). One could argue that shaving the beard as a mourning rite was a symbolic act of humiliation, but that is still very different from the psychological impact of someone else forcibly removing your beard.

52 This last part is phrased in the passive: וגם את הזקן תספה. I reversed it for a smoother translation.

53 Several scholars have contended that the author is using euphemistic language to express that Ham raped Noah. See, for example, Basset (1971: 233–234); Brenner (1997: 139–144); Nissinen (1998: 52–53); and Wold (1998: 65–107). However, in favor of the interpretation that Ham's crime was voyeuristic in nature, see Embry (2011: 417–433). Regardless of whether Ham's crime was looking at his father's nakedness or something more, the author makes a point of contrasting Ham's actions with that of his brothers, who take a great deal of care not to see their father's nudity in any way. Similarly, Nissinen (1998: 53).

54 See also Exodus 20:26, which instructs the Israelites to avoid building steps to the altar and Exodus 28:42–43, which instructs priests to wear linen undergarments extending from the hips (מתנים, usually translated as "loins"; see note 31) to the thigh when performing their duties, both as precautions against inadvertent exposure of genitalia.

55 Kamionkowski (2003: 61–65) cites evidence that in the ancient Near East, those captured in military defeat were often subject to mutilation, shaving, and stripping – all threats to the symbols of masculinity. See also Lemos (2006: 232–235).

56 On the relationship between a man's honor and successfully guarding the sexuality of his female kin, and the shame that resulted if he failed to do so, see Brenner (1997: 137–138); Carden (1999: 85–86); Frymer-Kensky (1998: 84–85); and Haddox (2010: 5–6); Matthews (1998: 102–112); and Stone (1996: 41–46).

57 On this translation of פלגש, see Exum (1993: 177).

58 Haddox (2010: 5–6) notes that Absalom's public sexual act displayed both his own potency and also demonstrated David's inability to protect his own wives. 2 Sam 20:3 notes that when David returned to the palace, he put the ten secondary wives in seclusion, and never had sexual relations with them again. Absalom's rebellion in part sprang from frustration at the weakness his father displayed in failing to protect Absalom's sister Tamar from sexual assault by their half-brother Amnon, and his father's subsequent failure to punish Amnon for what he did. Instead, Absalom takes matters into his own hands and kills Amnon (2 Samuel 13). This incident no doubt led to Absalom's perception of David's weakness, not only as a father who let his daughter be sexually violated and did nothing to avenge her, but also as a king who is too weak to properly rule his people. Similarly, in Gen 34:25–29, Dinah's enraged brothers avenge their sister's sexual "defilement" by Shechem themselves after Jacob fails to take what they view as proper action. Their response to Jacob in v. 31 when he confronts them about their actions and the possible repercussions is "Should he treat our sister like a whore (כזונה)?" The brothers' response to Jacob highlights the fact that in their eyes Shechem, by having sex with Dinah without the sanction of her family, treated her like a common whore, thus ruining both her honor and her family's honor. Since they felt that the damage to both Dinah's honor and the honor of the family was so great, blood vengeance was for them the only reasonable response. On these issues in Genesis 34, see Fewell and Gunn (1991:

198–199 and 206–207); Lipka (2006: 184–198) and Tikva Frymer-Kensky (1989: 89–102: 298 and 1998: 86–91).

59 On the meaning of נבלה, see Marböck (1998: 167–170); Phillips (1975: 238–241); and Roth (1960: 401–409).

60 The Deuteronomist appears to be treating this case as one of adultery, asserting that the husband's claim to ownership of his wife's sexuality is retroactive, extending to the period even before their betrothal. This idea that if a woman enters a first marriage without her virginity intact, it is a capital offense, regardless of when or how she lost her virginity, is most likely an innovation on D's part. For a discussion of these verses, see Frymer-Kensky (1998: 93–94); Lipka (2006: 97–101); Matthews (1998: 108–112); Pressler (1993: 25–31); and Rofé (1987: 137–142). Other texts that reflect a societal concern with women losing their virginity out of wedlock include Exod 22:15–16, Lev 21:9; Deut 22:23–29; Genesis 34, and 2 Samuel 13.

61 Most scholars agree that male-on-male sexual assault is in fact the intent of the men of the town in both narratives, for the purpose of sexually humiliating the strangers. However, not everyone has understood the intent of the men of the cities in these texts as attempted rape. See, e.g., Doyle (2004: 431–448) and Morschauser (2003: 461–485), who contend that ידע in this context has another, nonsexual meaning. In response, Nissinen (1998: 46) points out that Lot tries to appease the troublemakers by offering them his daughters who "have not known (לא ידעו) a man," that is, they are still virgins (Gen 19:8). In this context the meaning of the verb ידע is explicitly sexual, only a few lines after the men of the town demanded to "know" Lot's guests. See also Letelliler (1995: 146–157).

62 In the Genesis 19 story, the offer is rejected. In the Judges 19 story, the offer is rejected at first, but once the Levite pushes his secondary wife out the door, his offer is accepted, and she is viciously raped throughout the night. The Levite's wife is likely considered an acceptable substitute because the men of the town are still humiliating the Levite by taking sexual control of his wife. See Carden (1999: 91–92); Nissinen (1998: 49–52); and Stone (1996: 81–82 and 100).

63 Similarly, Brenner (1997: 138); Carden (1999: 84–92); Loader (1990: 37–38); Nissinen (1998: 48); and Stone (1996: 76–79).

Bibliography

Bassett, F. W. "Noah's Nakedness and the Curse of Canaan: A Case of Incest?" *VT* 21 (1971): 232–237.

Bechtel, L. "Shame as a Sanction of Social Control in Biblical Israel: Judicial, Political, and Social Shaming." *JSOT* 49 (1991): 47–76.

Bigger, Stephen F. "The Family Laws of Leviticus 18 in Their Setting." *JBL* 98 (1979): 187–203.

Brenner, Athalya. *The Intercourse of Knowledge: On Gendering Desire and 'Sexuality' in the Hebrew Bible*. Biblical Interpretation Series 26. Leiden: E.J. Brill, 1997.

Burrus, Virginia. "Mapping as Metamorphosis: Initial Reflections on Gender and Ancient Religious Discourses." In *Mapping Gender in Ancient Religious Discourse*, edited by Todd Penner and Caroline Vander Stichele, 1–10. Leidon: E.J. Brill, 2006.

Cairns, Douglas L. *Aidōs: The Psychology and Ethics of Honour and Shame in Ancient Greek Literature*. Oxford: Clarendon Press, 1993.

Campbell, E. F. *Ruth: A New Translation with Introduction and Commentary*. AB 7. Garden City, NY: Doubleday, 1975.

Carden, Michael. "Homophobia and Rape in Sodom and Gibeah: A Response to Ken Stone." *JSOT* 82 (1999): 83–96.

Carrigan, Tim, Bob Connell, and John Lee. "Toward a New Sociology of Masculinity." In *The Making of Masculinities: The New Men's Studies*, edited by Harry Brod, 63–100. Boston: Allen & Unwin, 1997.

Chapman, Cynthia. *The Gendered Language of Warfare in the Israelite-Assyrian Encounter*. HSM 62. Winona Lake: Eisenbrauns, 2004.

Clines, David J. A. "Dancing and Shining at Sinai: Playing the Man in Exodus 32–34." In *Men and Masculinity in the Hebrew Bible and Beyond*, edited by Ovidiu Creangă, 54–63. Sheffield: Sheffield Phoenix Press, 2010.

Clines, David J. A. "David the Man: The Construction of Masculinity in the Hebrew Bible." In *Interested Parties: The Ideology of Writers and Readers Hebrew Bible*, edited by David J. A. Clines, 212–243. JSOTSup, 205. Gender, Culture, Theory, 1. Sheffield: Sheffield Academic Press, 1995.

Clines, David J. A. "He-Prophets: Masculinity as a Problem for the Hebrew Prophets and Their Interpreters." In *Sense and Sensitivity: Essays on Reading the Bible in Memory of Robert Carroll*, edited by Alastair G. Hunter and Philip R. Davies, 311–328. JSOTSup 348. Sheffield: Sheffield Academic Press, 2002.

Connell, R. W. *Masculinities*. 2nd Ed. Berkeley: University of California Press, 2005.

Connell, R. W. and James W. Messerschmidt. "Hegemonic Masculinity: Rethinking the Concept." *Gender and Society* 19 (2005): 829–859.

Conrad, J. "זקן." In *Theological Dictionary of the Old Testament*, edited by G. Johannes Botterweck, Helmer Ringgren, and Heinz-Josef Fabry, translated by David E. Green and Douglass W. Stott, vol. 4: 122–131. Grand Rapids: Eerdmans, 1981.

Cortez, Marc. "The Law on Violent Intervention: Deuteronomy 25.11–12 Revisited." *JSOT* 30 (2006): 431–447.

Creangă, Ovidiu, ed. *Men and Masculinity in the Hebrew Bible and Beyond*. Sheffield: Sheffield Phoenix Press, 2010a.

Creangă, Ovidiu. "Variations of the Theme of Masculinity: Joshua's Gender In/stability in the Conquest Narrative (Josh. 1–12)." In *Men and Masculinity in the Hebrew Bible and Beyond*, edited by Ovidiu Creangă, 83–109. Sheffield: Sheffield Phoenix Press, 2010b.

Creangă, Ovidiu, and Peter-Ben Smit, eds. *Biblical Masculinities Foregrounded*. Hebrew Bible Monographs 62. Sheffield: Sheffield Phoenix Press, 2014.

DiPalma, Brian Charles. "De/constructing the masculinity in Exodus 1–4." In *Men and Masculinity in the Hebrew Bible and Beyond*, edited by Ovidiu Creangă, 36–53. Sheffield: Sheffield Phoenix Press, 2010.

Doyle, Bryan. "'Knock, Knock, Knockin' on Sodom's Door': The Function of dlt/ptch in Genesis 18–19." *JSOT* 28 (2004): 431–448.

Driver, Samuel Rolles. *A Critical and Exegetical Commentary on Deuteronomy*. ICC. Edinburgh: T & T Clark, 1902.

Elliott, John H. "Deuteronomy – Shameful Encroachment on Shameful Parts: Deuteronomy 25:11–12 and Biblical Euphemism." In *Ancient Israel: The Old Testament in Its Social Context*, edited by Philip F. Esler, 161–176. Minneapolis: Fortress, 2006.

Embry, Brad. "The 'Naked Narrative' from Noah to Leviticus: Reassessing Voyeurism in the Account of Noah's Nakedness in Genesis 9.22–24." *JSOT* 35 (2011): 417–433.

Eslinger, Lyle. "The Case of an Immodest Lady Wrestler in Deuteronomy XXV 11–12." *VT* 31 (1981): 269–291.

Exum, J. C. *Fragmented Women: Feminist (Sub)Versions of Biblical Narratives.* JSOTSup 163. Sheffield: JSOT Press, 1993.

Fewell, Danna Nolan and David M. Gunn. "Tipping the Balance: Sternberg's Reader and the Rape of Dinah." *JBL* 110 (1991): 193–211.

Frymer-Kensky, Tikva. "Law and Philosophy: The Case of Sex in the Bible." *Semeia* 45 (1989): 89–102. Reprinted *Women in the Hebrew Bible: A Reader*, edited by Alice Bach, 293–304. New York: Routledge, 1999.

Frymer-Kensky, Tikva. "Virginity in the Bible." In *Gender and Law in the Hebrew Bible and the Ancient Near East*, edited by Victor H. Matthews, Bernard M. Levinson, and Tikva Frymer-Kensky, 79–96. JSOTSup 262. Sheffield: Sheffield Academic Press, 1998.

George, Mark K. "Masculinity and Its Regimentation in Deuteronomy." In *Men and Masculinity in the Hebrew Bible and Beyond*, edited by Ovidiu Creangă, 64–82. Sheffield: Sheffield Phoenix Press, 2010.

Gilmore, David D. *Manhood in the Making: Cultural Concepts of Masculinity.* New Haven: Yale University Press, 1990.

Haddox, Susan E. "Favoured Sons and Subordinate Masculinites." In *Men and Masculinity in the Hebrew Bible and Beyond*, edited by Ovidiu Creangă, 2–19. Sheffield: Sheffield Phoenix Press, 2010.

Hallo, William H. "Biblical Abominations and Sumerian Taboos." *JQR* 76 (1985): 21–40.

Hoffner, Jr., Harry A. "Symbols for Masculinity and Femininity: Their Use in Ancient Near East Sympathetic Magic Rituals." *JBL* 85 (1966): 326–334.

Howson, Richard. *Challenging Hegemonic Masculinity.* London: Routledge, 2006.

Humbert, Paul. "Le substantif *to'eba* et le verb *t'b* dans l'Ancien Testament." *ZAW* 72 (1960): 217–237.

Kamionkowski, Tamar. *Gender Reversal and Cosmic Chaos: A Study on the Book of Ezekiel.* JSOTSup 368. London: Sheffield Academic Press, 2003.

Kirova, Milena. "When Real Men Cry: The Symbolism of Weeping in the Torah and the Deuteronomistic History." In *Biblical Masculinities Foregrounded*, edited by Ovidiu Creangă and Peter-Ben Smit, 35–50. Hebrew Bible Monographs 62. Sheffield: Sheffield Phoenix Press, 2014.

Kosmala, Hans. "גבר." In *Theological Dictionary of the Old Testament*, edited by G. Johannes Botterweck, Helmer Ringgren, and Heinz-Josef Fabry, translated by David E. Green and Douglass W. Stott, vol. 2: 367–382. Grand Rapids: Eerdmans, 1975.

Lemos, T. M. "Shame and Mutilation of Enemies in the Hebrew Bible." *JBL* 125 (2006): 225–241.

Letellier, Robert Ignatius. *Day in Mamre, Night in Sodom: Abraham and Lot in Genesis 18 and 19.* Biblical Interpretation Series 10. Leiden: E.J. Brill, 1995.

Lewis, Michael. *Shame: The Exposed Self.* New York: The Free Press, 1992.

L'Hour, Jean. "Les Interdits *To'eba* dans le Deutéronome." *RB* 71 (1964): 481–503.

Lipka, Hilary. "Masculinities in Proverbs: An Alternative to the Hegemonic Ideal." In *Biblical Masculinities Foregrounded*, edited by Ovidiu Creangă and Peter-Ben Smit, 86–103. Hebrew Bible Monographs 62. Sheffield: Sheffield Phoenix Press, 2014.

Lipka, Hilary. *Sexual Transgression in the Hebrew Bible*. Hebrew Bible monographs 7. Sheffield: Sheffield Phoenix Press, 2006.

Loader, J. A. *A Tale of Two Cities: Sodom and Gomorrah in the Old Testament, Early Jewish and Early Christian Traditions*. Contributions to Biblical Exegesis and Theology 1. Kampen: J.H. Kok Publishing House, 1990.

Măcelaru, Marcel V. "Saul in the Company of Men: (De)Constructing Masculinity in 1 Samuel 9–31." In *Biblical Masculinities Foregrounded*, edited by Ovidiu Creangă and Peter-Ben Smit, 51–68. Hebrew Bible Monographs 62. Sheffield: Sheffield Phoenix Press, 2014.

Macwilliam, Stuart. "Ideologies of Male Beauty in the Hebrew Bible." *Biblical Interpretation* 17 (2009): 265–287.

Magdalene, F. Rachel. "Ancient Near Eastern Treaty-Curses and the Ultimate Texts of Terror: A Study of the Language of Divine Sexual Abuse in the Prophetic Corpus." In *A Feminist Companion to the Latter Prophets*, edited by Athalya Brenner, 326–352. The Feminist Companion to the Bible 8. Sheffield, UK: Sheffield Academic Press, 1995.

Marböck, J. "נָבָל." In *Theological Dictionary of the Old Testament*, edited by G. Johannes Botterweck, Helmer Ringgren, and Heinz-Josef Fabry, translated by John T. David E. Green and Douglas W. Stott, vol. 9:167–170. Grand Rapids: Eerdmans, 1998.

Matthews, Victor H. "Honor and Shame in Gender-Related Legal Situations in the Hebrew Bible." In *Gender and Law in the Hebrew Bible and the Ancient Near East*, edited by Victor H. Matthews, Bernard M. Levinson and Tikva Frymer-Kensky, 97–112. JSOTSup 262. Sheffield, UK: Sheffield Academic Press, 1998.

Mayes, Andrew D. H. *Deuteronomy*. NCB. Grand Rapids, MI: William B. Eerdmans, 1979.

McCarter Jr., P. Kyle. *II Samuel*. AB 9. Garden City: Doubleday and Company, 1984.

Milgrom, Jacob. *Leviticus 17–22: A New Translation with Introduction and Commentary*. AB3a. New York: Doubleday, 2000.

Miller, Susan. *The Shame Experience*. Hillsdale, NJ: The Analytic Press, 1985.

Morschauser, Scott. "'Hospitality', Hostiles and Hostages: On the Legal Background to Genesis 19.1–19." *JSOT* 27 (2003): 461–485.

Nissinen, Martti. *Homoeroticism in the Biblical World, a Historical Perspective*. Minneapolis: Fortress, 1998.

Novick, Tzvi. "'She Binds Her Arms': Rereading Proverbs 31:17." *JBL* 128 (2009): 107–113.

Olyan, Saul M. "'And with a Male You Shall Not Lie the Lying Down of a Woman': On the Meaning and Significance of Leviticus 18:22 and 20:13." *Journal of the History of Sexuality* 5 (1994): 179–206.

Olyan, Saul M. "Honor, Shame and Covenant Relations in Ancient Israel and Its Environment." *JBL* 115 (1996): 201–218.

Paschen, Wilfried. *Rein und Unrein: Untersuchung zur biblischen Wortgeschichte: Studium zum Alten und Neuen Testament* 24. München: Kösel-Verlag, 1970.

Phillips, Anthony. *Deuteronomy*. Cambridge: Cambridge University Press, 1973.

Phillips, Anthony. "NEBALAH – A Term for Serious Disorderly and Unruly Conduct." *VT* 25 (1975): 237–242.

Pressler, Carolyn. *The View of Women Found in the Deuteronomic Family Laws*. BZAW 216. Berlin: Walter de Gruyter, 1993.

Preuss, H. D. "תועבה." In *Theologisches Wörterbuch zum Alten Testament*, edited by G. Johannes Botterweck, Heinz-Josef Fabry, and Helmer Ringgren, vol. 8: 580–591. Stuttgart: W. Kohlhammer, 1995.

Rofé, Alexander. "Family and Sex Laws in Deuteronomy and the Book of the Covenant." *Henoch* 9 (1987): 131–159.

Roth, Wolfgang M. W. "NBL." *VT* 10 (1960): 401–409.

Stansell, Gary. "Honor and Shame in the David Narratives." *Semeia* 68 (1996): 55–79.

Stiebert, Johanna. *The Construction of Shame in the Hebrew Bible, the Prophetic Contribution*. JSOTSup 346. Sheffield: Sheffield Academic Press, 2002.

Stone, Ken. *Sex, Honor, and Power in the Deuteronomistic History*. JSOTSup 234. Sheffield: Sheffield Academic Press, 1996.

Synnott, Anthony. *Re-Thinking Men: Heroes, Villains and Victims*. London: Ashgate, 2009.

Tigay, Jeffrey H., *Deuteronomy*. JPS Torah Commentary. Philadelphia, PA: JPS, 1996.

Toorn, Karel van der. *Sin and Sanction in Israel and Mesopotamia: A Comparative Study*. Studia Semitica Neerlandica 22. Assen, Netherlands: Van Gorcum, 1985.

Vedeler, Harold Torger. "Reconstructing Meaning in Deuteronomy 22:5: Gender, Society, and Transvestitism in Israel and the Ancient Near East." *JBL* 127 (2008): 461–475.

Washington, Harold C. "Violence and the Construction of Gender in the Hebrew Bible: A New Historicist Approach," *Biblical Interpretation* 5 (1997): 324–363.

Weinfeld, Moshe. *Deuteronomy and the Deuteronomic School*. Oxford: Clarendon, 1972.

Weinfeld, Tsvi. "תועבה." *Beth Mikra* 22 (1977): 230–237.

West, Candace and Don H. Zimmerman. "Doing Gender." In *The Social Construction of Gender*, edited by Judith Lorber and Susan A. Farrell, 13–37. Newbury Park: Sage, 1991.

Wold, Donald J. *Out of Order: Homosexuality in the Bible and the Ancient Near East*. Grand Rapids: Baker Books, 1998.

Yoder, Christine Roy. "The Woman of Substance (אשת חיל): A Socioeconomic Reading of Proverbs 31:10–31." *JBL* 122 (2003): 427–447.

8 Happy is the man who fills his quiver with them (Ps. 127:5)

Constructions of masculinities in the Psalms*

Marc Brettler

Gender, sex, and the Hebrew Bible

The previous paper offers an excellent framework for examining gender in relation to ancient Israel, a multifaceted society that flourished from the late second millennium BCE to the late first millennium CE, and in the (Hebrew) Bible, a complex collection reflecting the beliefs and desires of various subsets of that society.[1] I would like to supplement it in two ways: by offering some discussion of terms concerning gender and sex in the Bible, and by looking at gender, specifically constructions of masculinity, in the Book of Psalms. The initial exploration of sex and gender is important in its own right, and will also serve as background for approaching Psalms. I have chosen Psalms because it is long and well known, and thus complements the previous chapter's focus on a lesser-known, single biblical episode. In addition, several previous scholars have looked at gender and Psalms, so it is possible to enter into a dialogue.

In this study, I will use the standard distinction between "sex" and "gender," where sex is biological and gender is socially constructed.[2] Although only recently have scholars carefully described the distinction between these two, it is certainly possible that premodern societies recognized this distinction in their lexicon. The information about sex, gender, and their intersection is based on the interpretation of a wide variety of biblical texts, since in contrast to, for example, Greek literature, the Bible contains no theoretical discussions of these matters.[3] The Bible recognizes only two sexes: male and female. This is surprising because intersexed babies now comprise between 0.1 percent and 0.05 percent of live births,[4] and there is no reason to believe that antiquity was any different. Before the advent of "corrective surgery," different societies treated intersexed babies in a variety of manners. Rabbinic literature recognizes the sex categories *tumtum* and *androgynous*; the *tumtum* has no observable genitalia; the *androgynous* is a hermaphrodite.[5] (Rabbinic *androgynous* should not be confused with the contemporary use of the word, where it is typically a gender, not a sex term.) The *tumtum* is from a post-biblical Hebrew root "to be covered," while the latter is a Greek word borrowed into Hebrew. The post-biblical origin of these words, especially the Greek origin of androgynous, buttresses the notion that although such people existed, they were ignored by the biblical authors. Intersexed individuals are referred to in Mesopotamian texts contemporary with the Bible.[6] We do not know how different groups in ancient Israel may have treated and categorized intersexed people; we only know that their existence is not recognized in the male-female absolute dichotomy of the Bible.[7]

The two main *sex* terms in the Bible are *zakar* for male, and *neqebah* for female.[8] They are used for both humans and domesticated animals (and nothing else). In rabbinic literature, *zakar* and *neqebah* may refer to grammatical gender, but we do not know how far back this usage extends. Almost all uses of *neqebah* are alongside *zakar*,[9] and thus the two words form a clear polar contrast, as in Genesis 1:27, when people are created *zakar* and *neqebah*, in Genesis 6:19, where the animals *zakar* and *neqebah* are brought into Noah's ark, in Leviticus 3:1 where animal offerings, *zakar* or *neqebah*, are prescribed, or Deuteronomy 4:16, where the making of images, *zakar* and *neqebah*, is prohibited. These cases highlight the fact that *zakar* and *neqebah* cover all sexual categories that the authors wish to recognize, namely that they function as a minimal pair.

As the late James Barr and others have noted, etymology is connected to a word's original meaning, but is usually not very important for understanding how a word continues to function, which may become independent of its etymology.[10] In most cases, he is correct. Yet, the word *neqebah* is unusually transparent etymologically, deriving from the root *nqb*, "to pierce"[11] – it is a biological term similar to the cuneiform munus sign of the female pubic triangle.[12] (When a word's etymology is so transparent, it often continues to influence the word's meaning and use, unlike the cases that Barr focuses on.)

Zakar's etymology is debated, depending on whether or not the root *zkr* is understood as homonymic. Some claim that *zakar* is related to the common word "to remember," though why males should be specifically connected to memory is unclear; others connect it to a different Semitic *zkr* root meaning "phallus,"[13] even though there is no text in the Bible where *zakar* must be translated as penis.[14] The existence of a separate root *zkr* in Hebrew is supported by the many cases where *zakar* (and not a gender "man" word) is used specifically in relation to (male) circumcision (see esp. Genesis 17 and 34). It is almost as if expressions such as *himmol lo kol zakar* (Exodus 12:48, in reference to eating the paschal offering), literally "may every male of his household be circumcised" may be understood as "everyone belonging to him (i.e., the non-Israelite resident) who has a penis must be circumcised." An overliteral, etymological translation might render every *zakar* as "one who possesses a penis" and every *neqebah* as "a pierced one," but I doubt that in ancient Israel, when the average person used *zakar* and *neqebah*, they thought of the words' etymological meaning – instead, they meant "a biological male" or "a biological female." There is no case I can see in the Bible where either term is used in reference to gender rather than sex. This point is easiest to appreciate by comparison to English: someone might tell a "wimp" to "be a man" (in the sense of the hegemonic man discussed by Lipka), since "man" is a gender term, but would not tell a person to "be a male," since "male" is a sex term, and a person either does or does not have the proper genes and/or external sexual physiological characteristics to be male or female. In the Bible, no one is ever told "be a *zakar/neqebah*" for similar reasons – these are dichotomous biological states that in biblical times were unchangeable. Thus, the usages of the words *zakar* and *neqebah*, are more determinative than their etymology, and confirm that these are sex terms.

'Ish and *'ishshah*, both very common biblical words (2198×; 781×), are the typical Hebrew words for "man" and "woman."[15] Although *'ishshah*, with its terminal *-ah*, a common sign of feminine nouns in Hebrew, looks like the feminine form of *'ish*, historically this is not the case. The etymologies of the words are disputed,[16] and neither is transparent (in contrast, e.g., to *neqebah*). It is likely that most ancient Israelites, who were not aware of scientific Hebrew grammar, thought that *ishshah* was merely the feminine form of male *'ish*, much like *par*, "bull" and *parah*, "(female) cow." The frequent use of the word-pair *'ish we'ishshah* "a man and a woman" in a wide variety of contexts and genres (see e.g. Leviticus 13:29; 1 Samuel 27:11; Jeremiah 44:7) supports the idea that together they were all-inclusive, and formed a minimal pair. In English, man and woman are understood as polar binaries of gender, but among some English speakers, there are other, in between categories (e.g. an androgynous person, a butch woman, an effeminate man, etc.).

'ish and *'ishshah* are complicated words. To begin with, *'ish* often has nothing to do with sex or gender, but is a term of affiliation, indicating that a person belongs to a particular group.[17] *'ish*, like pre-1970s English "man" (but not "male"!), and in some cases even now, may be used in a gender-neutral sense. For example, Exodus 35:21 speaks of every *'ish* coming, and in the next verse further divides them into *'anashim* (the plural of *'ish*) and *nashim* (the plural of *'ishshah*). Contextually, in the first case,*'ish* must mean "people, men and women," while in the following verse it refers to men only. Here, context determines the referent *'ish*, and this is frequently the case, especially when it is paired with *'ishshah*, or is used in certain legal contexts where it is certain that women are included.[18] (The masculine *'ish* is suitable for "people" since masculine in Hebrew is prior gender, namely a group of men and women is grammatically masculine, even if women are the majority.)[19] There are, however, many texts where context is ambiguous, and the interpreter must make a careful interpretive choice between "man" and "person."

The preceding remarks have treated *'ish* and *'ishshah* as gender terms. Based on my earlier example of "be a man" as an expression that uses "man" as a gender term, it is clear that *'ish* is, in certain cases, a gender term, as in 1 Kings 2:2, where the dying David tells his son, the crown prince Solomon "you must be strong (*wechazaqta*) and be (*wehayita le*) a man (*'ish*)." The Hebrew idiom is *hayah le'ish* – literally "become/turn into[20] a man," indicating that this is not a biological, but a social category. Using Lipka's term, David is telling Solomon to become a, or even the, hegemonic man, to enact or perform a particular type of masculinity. (Stated differently, it is possible to become a man, but not to become a male in a world that did not know of gender reassignment surgery.) "Be[ing] strong" is a main component of such a man,[21] and the expression of the verse may even be understood as: "Perform your proper role as a hegemonic man (and not a woman or child) by being strong, and eliminating the various enemies of the royal house" (as reflected in verses 5–9). This is one of several cases where *'ish* is best understood as "manly one," a designation for one type of man – the hegemonic man.[22] The expression in Judges 8:21 "strength comes with manhood (*'ish*)"[23] also reflects the use of *'ish* as "(gendered) hegemonic man."

There can, however, be some overlap between gender and sex terms in a language.[24] For example, although in English "male" is usually a sex term, and "man" is a gender term, in the sentence "All men should go to the right, all women to the left" these typical gender terms would most likely be understood as sex terms. The same is true in labeling certain public bathrooms as "men's" or "women's" – this involves "the conflation of gender, sex and sexuality."[25] Given this overlap, it should not be surprising, therefore, that Hebrew *'ish* and *'ishshah* are also used as sex terms. This is very clear in Genesis 2:24, where an *'ish* leaves his parental home to cleave to his *'ishshah*, becoming one flesh. *'Ish* (rather than *zakar*) is used once in reference to circumcision (Genesis 34:14). A eunuch in Jeremiah 38:7 is an *'ish saris*, a castrated male,[26] and the *'ishshah niddah* of Ezekiel 18:6 is a menstruous female – these refer to sex, not gender roles. When various texts suggest that in wars *'ish* and *'ishshah* are or should be killed, the sense is those who are biologically male and female (a definition connected to sex), not those who act like typical men or women (a definition connected to gender). Finally, the frequent use of *'ish* and *'ishshah* to refer to "husband" and "wife" also partakes in a biological, sexual sense of those terms, as does the biblical idiom "an *'ish* did not 'know' her [a woman]."[27] The same is true for Exodus 19:15, which at Mount Sinai prohibits anyone (= any male) from approaching an *'ishshah*.[28] It is therefore not surprising that the post-biblical word for sexual relations is *'ishut*,[29] a noun derived from *'ish* with the suffix *-ut* (often used for abstract entities).

'Ish is thus a very polysemic word. It may be a gender term, a sex term, or neither; in other words, it may be translated in different contexts as "male," "man" or "person." Stated differently, in some cases it would make semantic sense to replace it with *zakar*, while in other cases (e.g. when referring to people) it would not. It seems a bit surprising that sometimes *'ish* is strongly marked for sex ("male") and sometimes totally unmarked for either sex or gender ("person"). Given the composite nature of the Bible, it is possible that different subgroups represented in the text used the term differently,[30] though this is not an obvious or necessary conclusion.

Before approaching Psalms, it is important to look at one final sex and gender term: *geber*. It appears in the masculine (unmarked) form only, and has no grammatically feminine equivalent. The Song of Deborah, considered by many (one of the Bible's) oldest passages,[31] refers to each *geber* capturing a female slave or two – the word used for these women is *racham rachamatayim*, literally "a uterus or two."[32] This strongly suggests that *geber* may be a sex term (and the words *lero'sh geber*, literally "to the head of a *geber*," may include a euphemism for the penis).[33] The use of *geber* in Jeremiah 31:22 with *neqebah* also suggests that it can be used as a sex term, although the text is somewhat obscure.[34] It is set in the eschatological period, suggesting that the sex differences are so established, they will continue in the eschaton as well. Jeremiah 30:6 uses *geber* in parallelism with *zakar*, and as the opposite of a female giving birth. Proverbs 30:19, though part of a somewhat cryptic unit, speaks of "the way of a *geber* with a young woman," another clearly sexual use of the term.

Yet in Job 38:3 (repeated in 40:7), YHWH asks Job to "gird himself like a *geber*." Girding is an activity that hegemonic males partook in before going out to battle,[35] and here and in some other cases *geber* is likely a gender term, referring to a person who acts as a hegemonic male, as determined by particular Israelite cultural norms. This culturally dependent gendered use is not surprising since the noun *geber* is transparently related to the root *gbr*, "to be strong, prevail, be violent" and the noun *gibbor*, "a military hero, champion." I suspect that the term *geber* was originally a gender term referring to the hegemonic man. As we have seen, there can be significant permeability between gender and sex designations – and this would especially be so in societies, like ancient Israel, where there were clear overlapping gender roles and attributes for each sex. Thus, the transfer of *geber* from "man" to "male" would be natural. However, unlike *'ish*, there is no case where *geber* is used in a gender-neutral sense.[36] Context, if it can, determines if it is being used in a gendered or sex sense.

This examination of terminology in the Bible suggests that the biblical Israel reflected in these texts had a clear distinction between sex and gender, as would be expected. Sex was depicted using the terms *zakar* and *neqebah* for male and female, and has no connotations beyond the biological. Other terms were more complicated, and were used for both sex and gender, and even in a non-sex, non-gender sense. The study of the pairs *zakar* and *neqebah* and *'ish* and *'ishshah* also suggests that each of these pairs is dichotomous: a person is either a *zakar* or *neqebah* and a person is seen by culture as either a *'ish* and *'ishshah*. This contrasts with modern gender theory, which sees male and female as poles with many options in between, rather than an absolute dichotomy.[37]

Given the close connection between sex and gender, it is possible that biblical Israel's insistence on two polar genders is based on its perception that there were only two sexes, male and female. Intersexed people, who could provide an easy to follow example for indeterminate genders, were invisible to them. The importance of the binary, dichotomous sex and gender distinctions found in various biblical texts is seen especially in Deuteronomy 22:5, where it is a *to'ebah*, an "extreme taboo," for "a woman (*'ishshah*) to use a man(*'ish*)'s implement, and a man (*'ish)* may not wear a woman (*'ishshah*)'s garment," as discussed in the previous essay.[38] Sexual indeterminacy and the legitimacy of gender bending were simply not recognized in the ancient Israelite texts that have been preserved in the Bible. This does not mean, however, that we must expect each male to always perform a standard set of male roles, and each female to perform a standard set of female roles – in other words, we need not expect the hegemonic male and the subordinate female to be the only types of males and females recognized in and supported by biblical texts.

David Clines's manly psalmists

The most comprehensive previous study of gender in Psalms is by David Clines, "The Book of Psalms, Where Men are Men. . . . On the Gender of Hebrew Piety."[39] He begins by noting:

> all the textbooks represent the Book of Psalms in general as an expression of an ungendered Hebrew piety. No one ever says, This is a male text, this Book of Psalms, and men and women alike should be on their guard in case they learn from it and internalize attitudes and prejudices that are specifically male – and therefore partial and discriminatory. That is what I am saying, though.

His evidence comes from "the rhetoric of war, the ideology of honour and shame, the construction of 'enemies,' the role of women, the concept of solitariness, the importance of strength and height in its metaphorical system, and the practice of binary thinking," which he adduces at length. There is much that I admire in Clines's article and thesis, and I believe that many of his conclusions are correct, but I do not believe that much of the evidence he adduces supports his conclusions.

As far as we know, war was fought almost exclusively by men against men in the ancient world. This may explain why being killed by a woman was considered shameful by men: woman were not considered suitable for war, so being defeated by a woman in war is like an adult being beaten by a child in chess.[40] Cross-culturally, war is almost always associated with males, and there is nothing in the Bible, or in the basic structure of ancient Israel, that would suggest that this was exceptional.[41] Yet Clines ignores the fact that women were deeply affected by war – their husbands and children were maimed and killed, and they had to fill male roles while the men were out at war. They worried that if their husbands and sons were defeated, they might be carried off as spoils of war.[42] This explains why in several places the Bible narrates female victory songs upon the men's return. This is seen, for example, in the Song of Miriam at the end of Exodus 15,[43] Deborah's Song in Judges 5, the account of Jephthah's daughter welcoming her father when he returned from battle, and the song of the women in 1 Samuel 18:7: "The women sang as they danced, and they chanted: Saul has slain his thousands; David, his tens of thousands!" These all indicate a role of women in religious war poetry – namely psalms with a lowercase "p" relating to women and battle – and this role includes lauding and perpetuating this male gender role. Already several decades ago Carol Meyers studied these texts, highlighting women's roles.[44] It matters little if any of these songs or events is historical. What does matter is that the institution they reflect is likely true; otherwise these songs would not have been integrated into texts. Thus, we must consider the possibility that some of these psalms that discuss war, especially psalms of thanksgiving concerning war,[45] are connected to the women's world – recited by, or perhaps in some cases composed by women. The same may be true of communal songs of thanksgiving (but not, e.g., of laments or petitions where the individual asks for personal success in battle). I can even imagine (contra Clines) women understanding and depicting YHWH as a male warrior, hoping that the male divine warrior will participate with the male human warriors of their family, and deliver them home alive.[46]

Clines finds no place in Psalms where women are connected to honor, and asks in general: "Have women, in fact, any honour at all in the Hebrew Bible?" – a question that he answers negatively. Since he notes correctly that Psalms is very interested in honor, he suggests: "What we can be rather sure of is that anyone who makes a fuss about honour is a man, and that the Psalms, so full of anxiety about honour, represent male interests." Lipka's previous essay buttresses his conclusions about the importance of certain types of honor to men, and how men perceived themselves as harmed by certain types of shame. Both Clines and Lipka are likely correct that concerns for honor are especially prevalent among biblical men, but it is not true that this concern is an *exclusively* male concern, as Clines suggests.

Nor is shaming an exclusively male anxiety. The first use of the root *bwsh*, the typical root associated with shame, is in the Eden story, where (Genesis 2:25): "The two of them were naked, the man and his wife, yet they felt no shame," and the root is used at least twice, in Hosea and Jeremiah, with mothers as its subject (Jeremiah 50:12; Hosea 2:7). In over ten places cities or countries, which are gendered grammatically as feminine and depicted as feminine, are shamed – it is certainly not only something that males fear.[47] The situation is similar with *klm*, another "shame" root – it is used in reference to Moses' sister, Miriam (Numbers 12:14) and Ruth (2:15), and is found several times concerning the whore Israel in Ezekiel 16. Clines, in discussing masculinity in Psalms, has not considered sufficiently that this notion is socially and historically conditioned, and has incorrectly assumed that his idea of biblical masculinity, largely derived from his idea of hegemonic masculinity in contemporary society, may serve as a model for biblical masculinity. This is especially frustrating because he notes these theoretical problems in his introduction to an earlier 1994 piece on the masculinity of David – but there too he sometimes uses modern Western norms for constructing David's masculinity.[48]

I do not find many of the other proposals of Clines convincing. For example, "The psalmists need their God to be strong, for that is the quality they most desire for themselves" – and thus the psalms reflect a masculine perspective. Women in antiquity had a vested interest in strong husbands – so they would be protected, and a strong God, so their family and nation would be protected. Similarly, his claim that "binary is a straitjacket of maleness" cross-culturally, and that the psalms are masculine since they think in a binary fashion, is problematic. Although women have been at the vanguard of critiquing binary thinking,[49] I do not know of cross-cultural evidence that supports the idea that binary thinking is exclusively masculine.

In sum, Clines's conclusions that "This is a male text, this book of Psalms" and "the Psalms are male, indefeasibly and unmistakably male" are not proven by the evidence that he adduces. Furthermore, any careful look at Psalms should distinguish sex and gender, and in terms of gender, must distinguish more carefully between such issues as gendered authorship, gendered audience, and gendered recitation of psalms. It is no longer the case that each psalm must be viewed as a cultic composition by men for men.[50]

Furthermore, any study of gender and psalms must consider the possibility, indeed the likelihood, that several, if not many, different conceptions of gender existed in ancient Israel at different times and places. In *In the Wake of the Goddesses*, Tikva Frymer-Kensky "follow[s] the ideology of gender as it changed drastically in biblical thinking" and observes that "Cultural thinking about gender is never static."[51] As many theorists of gender have noted, masculinity and femininity are socially constructed, and change over time, and even at the same time, differ among different classes or groups. The book of Psalms is an anthology – a collection of collections of collections,[52] and it would be wrong to start looking at it with an expectation that it has a single notion of masculinity, that the *geber*, the man I mention in my title, taken from Psalm 127, is, for example, constructed similarly to the *geber* mentioned in v. 4 of the following psalm.

A new look at gender in psalms

Given that Psalms in not a book in the modern sense,[53] it is best to explore the gender issues of each psalm so that a broader picture of various matters concerning gender and psalms may be begin to emerge one psalm at a time. Some studies have done this in reference to particular psalms. For example, Knowles investigates the textually difficult Psalm 131:2b, which is translated in NJPS as "like a weaned child with its mother; like a weaned child am I in my mind."[54] She concentrates on this psalm only, and remarks, very astutely:

> Yet does this female voice, incorporating within it the metaphor of a weaned child with his or her mother, necessarily indicate that this text was written by a woman? Is there enough information in Psalm 131 to distinguish between actual female authorship and the attribution of a quotation to a female? The specific details linked with the speaker's experience (the avoidance of "high matters," the affirmation of humility, and sitting with a weaned child) could be considered stereotypical and public enough to be written about by either a male or a female author. One might also argue that, in its valorization of humility, docility, and childlikeness, the text could have been written by someone (either a man or a woman) intent on teaching women such behavior. No evidence rules out such a possibility. Thus, the portrayal of a woman's prayer in Psalm 131 is not necessarily, though it could be, a record of such a prayer.[55]

This approach is better than the observation that a woman likely prayed this psalm, noting such generalities as "The possible connections between psalm texts and women's lives in ancient Israel are countless" in part, because "The emotions, joys, and concerns found throughout the Psalter are those shared by both men and women."[56] Nor is it correct to assume, as Coetzee does in reference to Psalm 139:13 (NRSV: "For it was you who formed my inward parts; you knit me together in my mother's womb"), that the deity of Psalms must be masculine, therefore any possibly feminine reference reflects the usurping of the female by the male.[57] The opposite is possible, and we may have here, as several times in Isaiah 40–66, YHWH depicted as a woman,[58] or at the very least, depicted very differently from the hegemonic male ideal that Lipka discusses. The psalm does mention enemies (vv. 19–22), which according to Clines makes it male – but as I have argued, this evidence is far from definitive since masculine and feminine images of YHWH may intersect in a single psalm[59] so a masculine God in one section of a psalm does not imply that the entire psalm shares that image. Weaving generally, and in ancient Israel more specifically, was a woman's job,[60] and to use Clines's logic, this image is more likely to originate with a woman. But certainly men know of weaving and could have originated this image as well, just as, based on cultural and familial familiarity, they may have referred to a "weaned child" in Psalm 131. Finally, the verb used for "weave" in Psalms 139:13 is homonymic, and does not necessarily mean "weave."[61] Thus this image proves neither that a male author has appropriated a female image for his male deity, nor that a female-authored psalm has snuck into the psalter.

Rather than trying to generalize from modern attributes to the Psalter (as Clines sometimes does), or by treating the Psalter as a whole (Clines as well), or by looking at images that may reflect a female sphere such as weaning or weaving (even though certain aspects of these spheres were visible to, and of interest to men), I believe it is best to look at psalms that either explicitly contain a clearly gendered term such as *geber* and how he performs or enacts his malehood, or texts that explicitly contrast male and female. As noted earlier, we must use caution with texts that use the word *'ish*, which like the English word "man" in 1960, could be used in a gender-neutral or a gender-specific way depending on the speaker or the context. Only where the biblical context clearly indicates in some other way that the *'ish* under question is a male, may we use that psalm as evidence for masculinity. Similarly, various terms such as "those who fear God (*yir'ei YHWH*)" or "the house of Israel (*beit yisra'el*)" or evildoers (*po'alei awen*) are grammatically male, but may include women within them, and cannot be used in discussions concerning sex and gender in Psalms.

Furthermore, we must be careful in not using secondary material in the psalm as evidence of male authorship and a masculine perspective. Thus, I am assuming with most scholars that the Psalm titles or superscriptions are secondary,[62] and thus the ones attributed to David or to other males such as Korach or Asaph should not automatically be seen as composed by a (particular) male. Furthermore, if a psalm is composite, there is no reason to believe that its authors all had the same notion of gender, so its parts should be looked at separately. These strictures are both good and bad news – bad news since they mean that there are relatively few psalms that can be discussed – but in a sense this is good news, since the long book of Psalms suddenly becomes more manageable.

The term *neqebah*, the sex term for female, is absent in Psalms. This is not especially surprising – the word is only found 22 times in the entire Hebrew Bible, all but one of them in the Pentateuch, mostly in late P literature there, which hardly influences Psalms. The noun *zakar*, more common in the Bible, and a bit more evenly distributed, is also lacking in Psalms. The combined absence of *zakar* and *neqebah* in Psalms probably reflects the book's lack of interest in sexual identity as a category.

Ten of the 66 biblical occurrences of *geber* are in Psalms – this is disproportionate and noteworthy (Psalms 18:26; 34:9; 37:23; 40:5; 52:9; 88:5; 89:49; 94:12; 127:5: 128:4). Five of these texts (34:9; 37:23; 40:5; 89:49; 94:12) use *geber* but do not contain descriptions or prescriptions for what the psalmist's ideal of masculinity was. This is so, for example, for Psalm 34:9, "happy is the *geber* who takes refuge in Him!," and Psalm 94:12, "Happy is the *geber* whom You discipline, O LORD." These psalms, not surprisingly, were written with men (*gebers*) only in their purview. To the extent that the Bible is considered to reflect, by and large, male elites,[63] and to the extent that the Temple service was conducted by and large by male elites,[64] this focus on the *geber*, even though the sentiment expressed is appropriate to women as well, is not at all surprising.

Some of these *geber* psalms do describe and prescribe gender issues. Psalm 18 concerns war,[65] and the psalmist requests from YHWH various means for military victory (see esp. vv. 33–43), so the use of *geber* there is not surprising. Psalm 52:9 reads: "Here was a fellow who did not make God his refuge, but trusted in his great wealth, relied upon his mischief." Given that under normal circumstances women do not inherit property in ancient Israel, and we are not even sure if a married woman retained her dowry in case of divorce,[66] it is logical that wealth should be associated with masculinity, and *geber* was used. In the second part of Psalm 88:5, the petitioning psalmist, who feels almost dead, says "I am a helpless *geber*." Unfortunately, the last word (rendered here "help"), *'eyal*, is hapax in the Hebrew Bible – namely it occurs only here – and the less frequent the word, the more difficult it is to define its meaning. The ancient versions understand it as related to "help," as do most of the modern lexica, though Clines's new lexicon adds "perhaps strength, arbitration."[67] It is therefore difficult to know how the *geber* of this psalm relates to manhood. Thus these ten *geber* verses in Psalms are not very helpful in terms of deciding how each psalmist's (note where ' is) idea of human masculinity, how they believed masculinity should be performed – we may only observe that this may include strength and wealth.

It is very difficult to know whether *'ish* should be translated as "man" or "person" in most of the psalm verses that use this term. For example, Psalm 62:13b reads "[for/when you] reward each *'ish* according to his deeds," and Psalm 34:13–14 reads: "Who is the *'ish* who is eager for life, who desires years of good fortune? Guard your tongue from evil, your lips from deceitful speech." Certainly, it is well within the theology of ancient Israelites to believe that YHWH offers proper recompense for both men and women, and to believe that it is good for women as well as men to avoid deceitful speech. In other words, it is possible either that these verses understand *'ish* in the sense of man and woman, or that the author's focus was on men only. Many newer translations render *'ish* in such contexts as "person," in part because these translations are intended for liturgical use, and attempt to be as gender neutral or gender friendly as possible. (For example, for 63:12, NRSV translates "For you repay to all" and NIV reads "You reward everyone," and the Catholic NJB renders it "You repay everyone." In contrast, NJPS has "man.") A historical-critical translation of these psalms, however, may prefer to translate *'ish* as "man" – though this is not always certain, and depends on the extent that we should believe that all Psalms are by men for men. This issue of translating as "man" or "person" exists in other Semitic languages as well, for example, in some contexts with the Akkadian word *awīlu/amēlu*.[68]

The best way of understanding gender in various psalms is by looking at psalms that contrast men and women, or those that clearly single out one gender, but there are relatively few of these. Significantly, most of these are found in Psalms in the last two books of the Psalter, in Psalms 90–150, which are considered by many scholars to have been written later, that is in the post-exilic time period, after 538.[69] This in itself is an important and previously unnoted fact – gender is more explicit in late psalms. Scholars should explore if this is connected to other changes in gender perception or focus in this period, especially the tirades against intermarriage with foreign women in Ezra-Nehemiah[70] and the warnings against the strange or foreign woman in Proverbs 1–9[71] and perhaps the counterview concerning gender found in Ruth, if the latter is indeed a late book.[72] At various times, due to various socio-historical issues, gender becomes highlighted in society or in groups within society. The post-exilic period is one of these times, and various reasons for this, none certain, have been hypothesized.[73] It is thus not surprising that the psalms in which specifically gendered terms appear are disproportionately late.

Some of these late psalms use gendered terms, but do not elaborate upon them. For example, Psalm 148:12 mentions, uniquely in Psalms, "male youths and maidens alike" praising YHWH – this is rare, important evidence for women's participation in a Psalmist's cult. Psalm 131:2, one of the Songs of Ascent, mentions the highly gendered image, "like a weaned child with its mother," discussed above. 123:2, also from that collection, notes: "As the eyes of slaves follow their master's hand, as the eyes of a slave-girl follow the hand of her mistress, so our eyes are toward the LORD our God, awaiting His favor." When combined with the longer gender references in Psalms 127–128 that I will discuss later, the 15 Psalms of ascent (120–134) have a disproportionate interest in gender. The recent studies of these psalms have not noted this fact, which should be taken into consideration when understanding the origin, reworking, and nature of this collection, and the meaning of its enigmatic titles, "The Song of Ascents" and its variants.[74]

I wrote on Psalm 128 a decade and a half ago, in *Gender and Law in the Hebrew Bible and the Ancient Near East*,[75] where I noted:

1 This psalm warns us that many psalms that seem gender neutral are not, and do have a male audience. Although this psalm opens by noting "Happy are all (*kol*) who fear the LORD," suggesting that all genders are included, its continuation in v. 3, *'eshtecha*, "your wife," and v. 4, "the man (*geber*) who fears the LORD," suggests otherwise. I do not wish to overgeneralize that all psalms that may initially seem gender-inclusive reflect the masculine, as Clines does, but want to use this psalm as a warning that Psalms that initially seem gender neutral are not necessarily so.
2 No psalm specifically deals with women's life-cycle issues. In other words, in contrast to ancient Near Eastern and later Jewish prayers, there is no psalm of thanksgiving for successful childbirth, or petition for the birth of a (male) child. I will modify this point a bit in my discussion of Psalm 113, below.
3 It is clear from 1 Samuel 1–2 and other contexts that women prayed. Hannah's prayer in 1 Samuel 2 is a psalm (lower case p), whose subject is the (male) king's military victory. The fact that an editor could put it in a woman's mouth indicates that in some situations, women may have

recited psalms that were written by males for males, and when women wanted to pray, they did the best they could with prayers that were written by men for men.

4 The psalm offers clear gender roles. Men do the hard work in the field – as v. 2 notes, "You shall enjoy the fruit of your labors"; this may be a paraphrase of the curse in Eden in Genesis (3:19), "By the sweat of your brow shall you get bread to eat." The Psalm offers and perpetuates these gender roles. Liturgical texts may have been widely recited, and the perpetuation of this division of labor through this text may have been widely felt – in other words, such texts (continue to) prescribe these roles as they describe them. These gender roles are not, however, identical to the role of the hegemonic male described by Lipka.

5 The assignment and perpetuation of gender roles continues in the next verse that I translate as: "your wife is like a fruitful vine in the corner of your house," where *yarketei*, "corner," (NJPS "within,") refers to where the wife weaves and cooks inside the typical four room house. This contrasts spatially sharply with the continuation of the verse, where the children surround the table. The man is the focus of the psalm, the woman is peripheralized, while the children are central.

6 This God-fearing man gets a reward at the end of the psalm – grandchildren or grandsons (the Hebrew is ambiguous). His wife is the fruitful vine, but *he* gets the grandchildren. Various biblical texts and contemporary realia suggest that vines themselves are useless – they are weak, and don't burn efficiently – they cannot even be used for kindling. Thus the image of the wife as a vine coalesces with the image of her as within the house. Little work, however, has been done by biblical scholars on the well-known dichotomy of men in public vs. women in private spaces in the Bible, and the frequent stereotype of women inside private spaces may not automatically be assumed for ancient Israel.[76]

In sum, Psalm 128 is a man's psalm for men. Women are mentioned only to bolster the men's place. Men produce agriculture, with the result (v. 2), "you shall be happy and you shall prosper." Nothing is good for the vine-woman in the corner, who does not even get to eat the food she likely prepared. This psalm reinforces one well-known set of gender roles in some patriarchal societies. In this psalm, and in the one that precedes, "gendered language serves as an ideological tool expressing, justifying, and maintaining asymmetrical relationships of power."[77]

Psalm 127,[78] from which the title of this talk is taken, is similar. Its last three verses[79] read in the NJPS translation:

(3) Sons are the provision of the LORD; the fruit of the womb, His reward.
(4) Like arrows in the hand of a warrior are sons born to a man in his youth.
(5) Happy is the man who fills his quiver with them; they shall not be put to shame when they contend with the enemy in the gate.

This psalm, that focuses on the *geber*, the male (v. 5),[80] is more ambiguous than the translation suggestions. "Sons" of v. 3 could also be gender-neutral children. (The word is the same as used in 128:3.) It is unclear why children of the youth are so important, though these may offer help in the field or may reflect on the virility of the *geber*. JPS translates the fourth from last Hebrew word in v. 5 as "contend" – the root *dbr* is homonymic, and can mean "to speak" (verbally contend) or, as NJPS rendered it, "to put down using physical force" (physically contend).[81] I believe that the latter is most likely, and the image is of useful boys, who in the man's old age, when he is barely a *geber*, can be good *geber*s by defending him physically. Such is the reward given by YHWH. Women are needed to produce these children, but are never mentioned – this psalm is like many biblical genealogies where men beget men. In fact, the word for "provisions" in v. 3 is the feminine *nachalah* – males fulfill the function of this feminine entity here.

The beginning of v. 5 presents a case of what Gloria Steinem, Phyllis Chessler, and others call "uterus or womb envy," based on the earlier work of the psychologist Karen Horney who critiqued Freud's understanding of women.[82] She notes that men's womb envy is stronger than women's penis envy, leading to the fact that "men are evidently under a greater necessity to depreciate women than conversely."[83] V. 5, which sees the quiver, which is grammatically female, holding the grammatically male arrows, is a case of uterus envy. It gets rid of females (I am intentionally using the sex term) by giving the warrior man both arrow and quiver = penis and vagina. Men function, and even reproduce sexually, in an all-male warrior society.

If uterus or womb envy is present in Psalm 127, it is even more radical than Psalm 128. In Psalm 128, women are peripheralized; in 127, they are made to disappear. To the extent that the men get the quiver, however, there is nothing in the psalm that suggests that they lose their hegemonic masculinity. They become masculine, male hermaphrodites. Both psalms together suggest that bearing children with a weak or absent wife is one role of some masculinities in Psalms.

A final male-female contrast in the Psalter is found in Psalm 144:12, which contains a clear *ben-bat*, son-daughter contrast (NJPS renders the verse, which has some textual problems, as "For our sons are like saplings, well-tended in their youth; our daughters are like cornerstones trimmed to give shape to a palace.") This verse, with its contrasting similes is especially helpful, although it is uncertain how, and how extensively, its open-ended similes should be interpreted.[84] The dynamic nature of the sons is especially striking – they are living saplings that grow, while the daughters are a rock that is carved by others. Males have agency, females lack it – a well-known "cross-cultural idea."[85] This was likely part of many constructions of masculinity in ancient Israel. In addition, males are well-tended over time,[86] and this helps them prosper, while the girls are only tended to once, when they are shaped by the rock-cutter. Saplings are out in the sun; the women may be inside, as part of the house. (See the discussion about men/women outside/inside above.) It is hard to know how to understand "cornerstone" – a hapax word, perhaps borrowed from Akkadian via Aramaic.[87] Does it emphasize the "cornerness," the "insideness" of the female, as in Psalm 128? Was it part of the foundation that was covered up? Or is it a description of centrality and importance, as recently suggested by Schroer, and is this further highlighted by it being part of a temple or *heikal* – a well-known loanword from Sumerian via Akkadian, which may refer to either a palace or a temple?[88]

Women appear in one additional late psalm – at the end of Psalm 113, which I discuss in detail in the Adele Berlin festschrift.[89] It has long been recognized that this psalm overlaps with a section of Hannah's prayer from 1 Samuel 2, which I noted was originally a royal war psalm. Various pieces of evidence suggest that Psalm 113 knows 1 Samuel 2, and is later than it, and recontextualizes it. In its recontextualization, its climactic, concluding verse says (v. 9 – my translation): "He sets the childless woman in the household as a happy mother of children. Hallelujah." Yet, the psalm is not primarily a song of thanksgiving for giving birth to a child. Although it still may have been used for that purpose, this has been downplayed when it was given a new introduction that reframed how it should be understood. Thus, the themes reflected in Psalm 113 have quite a prehistory: they belong originally to a royal war psalm, and were secondarily turned into a psalm of thanksgiving upon giving birth to a child, but then were given new meaning when they were turned into Psalm 113, a general song of thanksgiving by *'avdei YHWH*, "YHWH's servants," whoever these may be.[90] The changing fate of the woman in the psalm underscores some of the complexities that should be noted in understanding gender and Psalms. Psalms may be composed by one gender and used by another, and gendered language may have been accentuated or deemphasized as individual psalms were reworked.

Concluding observations

I have said much less than Clines, but I believe that my more restrictive method has allowed a more correct sense of sex and gender in Psalms to emerge. Psalms is a masculine book in the sense that it never deals with rituals that were specific for females. Clines may be correct that most of the psalms were composed by men for men and reflect masculine notions – but this cannot be shown by Clines's methods, or any method that I can see. Although these are very difficult to tease out, it is likely that Psalms reflects several of the different conceptions of masculinity that existed in ancient Israel. We know from the example of Hannah's Song in 1 Samuel 2 that women recited psalms written by men for men by recontextualizing them – even if they we not originally intended for women – so we must be extra careful in completely removing women from Psalms. The Psalter shows little interest in women, except for within the Song of Ascent collection and some other late psalms. This absence in earlier psalms needs to be discussed and explained more extensively, as does the change seen in later psalms. Finally, although some late psalms do discuss both men and women, they do so, as far as I can see without exception, to maintain and reinforce the patriarchal role of men, who are central and active and seem to produce children without the aid of women.

I have little to say concerning the gender of God in the Psalter. I remain uncertain how to tell if each psalmist viewed God as male. All psalmists used male grammatical gender for God, but was this a mere convention, or did it suggest that God was envisioned as male?[91] Some psalms explicitly view YHWH as king, and thus these images in these verses are of God as male, but as I have shown elsewhere, biblical authors mix their metaphors in a single context, so I cannot be sure that the entirety of these psalms views YHWH as a male king.

The idea that YHWH is not typically or always male or masculine in the Psalter may be supported by the paucity of references where YHWH is called *'ab*, "father." Significantly, Psalm 27:10, via figurative image, imagines YHWH as both mother and father: "Though my father and mother abandon me, the LORD will take me in" – YHWH takes up the slack of the abandoning father *and* mother. Psalm 103:13, in a simile, is one of the very few psalms that explicitly calls YHWH a father: "As a father has compassion (*kerachem*) for his children, so the LORD has compassion for those who fear Him." It is very striking that here the father is the compassionate one, even though many scholars identify the root *rchm* with *rechem*, womb, as uterine or motherly compassion. This identification may be incorrect in terms of proper, scientific etymology, but may have functioned as a popular etymology.[92] Might this be another case of uterus envy, and the subsequent uterus stealing? And might Psalm 2:7, which notes concerning the Davidic king and YHWH "You are My son, I have begotten you this day" be similar? Or does the compassionate father of Psalm 103:13 reflect a notion of masculinity that differs from the hegemonic male? Such multiplicities should not be surprising, and it is even possible that if the *'ish* of Psalm 1 refers to men rather than people more generally,[93] it offers a very different model of the Israelite man: he spends his time not at war, and not peripheralizing women or making them disappear, but in an all-male environment, studying Torah day and night.[94]

In the last few decades Psalms scholars have become interested, in addition to individual psalms and their prehistory and function, in how clusters of psalms function, how the Psalter was edited, and thematic movement within the Psalter, for example, the movement from psalms of lament, which predominate at the beginning, to hymns, concentrated at the end.[95] Much of this study has been influenced by the canonical methods of the late Brevard Childs. In this context, I would note that the Psalter (1) is more concerned with gender at its end than at its beginning, and (2) may at its very end reflect some loss of total focus on men. We earlier saw Psalm 148:12, the third from last psalm, which mentions male youths and maidens. Perhaps it is significant that Psalm 1 opens with a description of *ha'ish*, who given the context of Torah study is likely "the male" or "the man,"[96] while the Psalter closes (150:6) with the much more gender-inclusive "Let all that breathes praise the LORD. Hallelujah,"[97] and two verses earlier mentions "timbrel and dance," which elsewhere are associated with women.[98] Thus, a birds-eye view of the Psalter suggests that its first part cares little about women, while toward the end it focuses on men, peripheralizing women, though at the very end, in contrast to the beginning, it recognizes both male and female. This fact should be incorporated into the vexed questions concerning the composition and organization of the Psalter, and offers an important counterview to Clines, especially for those (male and female) who wish to incorporate the Psalter into their contemporary religious life.

Notes

* This chapter has gone through many revisions, though it has been impossible to keep it fully updated. In addition to the useful comments from the various participants in the conference, I would like to thank the Hebrew Bible faculty and students at the University of Göttingen, who heard a later version of this chapter, Mr. Lenny Prado and Dr. Max Strassfeld. Of the extensive new literature that I wish I had a chance to fully incorporate, I would like to highlight the forthcoming work by Erica L. Martin, *Lovely Tents of Jacob: The Vagina in Scripture*.

1 One of the most significant contributions of feminist studies of biblical texts is the appreciation that the Bible is not an accurate mirror of ancient Israelite beliefs and practices; see e.g. the studies of the last two decades by William Dever (e.g. *Did God Have a Wife? Archaeology and Folk Religion in Ancient Israel* [Grand Rapids: Eerdmans, 2008]; *The Lives of Ordinary People in Ancient Israel: When Archaeology and the Bible Intersect* [Grand Rapids: Eerdmans, 2012]), and concerning women, Jennie R. Ebeling, *Women's Lives in Biblical Times* (London: T & T Clark, 2010).

2 See e.g. Amy Blackstone, "Sex Versus Gender Categorization" in *Encyclopedia of Gender and Society*, ed. Jodi A. O'Brien (Thousand Oaks, CA: SAGE, 2008), 786–788. Finer distinctions, such as between gender, gender identity, and gender role (e.g. Patricia Wheelan, "Cross-Cultural Sexual Practices" in *Encyclopedia of Women and Gender*, ed. Judith Worell [San Diego, CA: Academic Press, 2001], 291–302), will be noted as necessary.

3 See e.g. Sabina Lovibond, "An Ancient Theory of Gender: Plato and the Pythagorean Table" in *Women in Ancient Societies*, ed. Léonie J. Archer, Susan Fischler, and Maria Wyke (Houndmills: Macmillan, 1994), 88–101.

4 Ami Lynch, "Intersexual, Intersexuality" in *Encyclopedia of Gender and Society*, ed. Jodi A. O'Brien (Thousand Oaks, CA: SAGE, 2008), 470–472.

5 See Charlotte E. Fonrobert, "Gender Identity in Halakhic Discourse," http://jwa.org/encyclopedia/article/gender-identity-in-halakhic-discourse; "Androgyne, Androgynous Beings: IV Judaism," *EBR* 1.1144–1146; "Regulating the Human Body: Rabbinic Legal Discourse and the Making of Human Gender" in *The Cambridge Companion to the Talmud and Rabbinic Literature*, ed. Charlotte Elisheva Fonrobert and Martin S. Jaffee (Cambridge: Cambridge University Press, 2007), 270–294. For more details, see now Max Strassfeld, "Classically Queer: Eunuchs and Androgynes in Rabbinic Literature," PhD diss., Stanford University, 2013.

6 Pirjo Lapinkivi, "Androgen, Androgynous Beings: I Ancient Near East," *EBR* 1.1137–1140.
7 On the problems created by such dichotomies, see e.g. Lorraine Code, "Dichotomies" in *Encyclopedia of Feminist Theories*, ed. Lorraine Code (London: Routledge, 2000), 135.
8 A more complete version of this chapter may also include discussion of the term *'adam*, which according to some is also a male sex term; see J. Barr, "One Man, or All Humanity?" in *Recycling Biblical Figures: Papers Read at a NOSTER Colloquium in Amsterdam, 12–13 May 1997*, ed. Athalya Brenner and Jan Willem van Henten (Leiden: Deo, 1999), 3–21 and the contrary view, which I find more satisfactory, by Johannes C. de Moor, "The First Human Being a Male? A Response to Professor Barr," ibid., 22–27. Part of the problem by deciding if *'adam* is a sex term is that, unlike *zakar* (and *neqebah*), it is not part of a dichotomous pair.
9 This is noted in J. Scharbert, "*nqb*," *TDOT* 9.552.
10 James Barr, *The Semantics of Biblical Language* (London: Oxford University Press, 1961), esp. 107–160.
11 Contrast Scharbert, ibid., who associates its meaning with "deflower."
12 René Labat and Florence Malbran-Labat, *Manuel D'épigraphie Akkadienne: Signes, Syllabaire, Idéogrammes* (6 ed.; Paris: Geuthner, 1995), 228–229, sign number 554.
13 BDB does not see the root as homonymic; HALOT does. See also the discussion in R. Clements, "*zkr*," *TDOT* 4.83.
14 See the discussion of biblical terms for penis in Lipka, above, and Athalya Brenner, *The Intercourse of Knowledge: On Gendering Desire and 'Sexuality' in the Hebrew Bible* (Leiden: Brill, 1997), 36–39.
15 This study is looking at Hebrew words only and is not exploring the situation in biblical Aramaic texts.
16 See *HALOT*, 43, 93.
17 David E. S. Stein, "The Noun איש ('ÎŠ) in Biblical Hebrew: A Noun of Affiliation," *JHS* 8.1, http://www.jhsonline.org/cocoon/JHS/a078.html/, accessed 13 April 2016
18 Mayer I. Gruber, "Women in the Cult According to the Priestly Code" in his *Motherhood of God and Other Studies* (Atlanta: Scholars, 1992), 49–68.
19 On masculine as prior gender, see Gesenius §122g, and esp. WOC p. 108 (6.5.3a). This grammatical principle, and thus the usage of *'ish* for both "man" and "person," continues in post-biblical Hebrew as well. Better terminology, used in David E. S. Stein, "The Grammar of Social Gender in Biblical Hebrew," *Hebrew Studies* 49 (2008), 16, is "*gender-inclusive by default.*"
20 The Hebrew idiom *hayah le* (instead of plain *hayah*) typically means "to become"; see BDB *hyh* 2d,e,f.
21 See Lipka's article, above, and Ami Lynch, "Hegemonic Masculinity" in *Encyclopedia of Gender and Society*, ed. Jodi A. O'Brien (Thousand Oaks, CA: SAGE, 2008), 412–414.
22 See *HALOT* 43. Other cases cited there are 1 Samuel 4:9 and 26:15.
23 Here and elsewhere, the translations typically follow NJPS, or are a modification of that translation.
24 Ruth Hubbard, "Gender and Genitals: Constructs of Sex and Gender," *Social Text* 46/47 (1996), 157–165.
25 http://thesocietypages.org/socimages/2010/09/02/guest-post-go-where-sex-gender-and-toilets/, accessed 16 May 2012.
26 On biblical eunuchs, see most recently Jacob L. Wright and Michael J. Chan, "King and Eunuch: Isaiah 56:1–8 in Light of Honorific Royal Burial Titles," *JBL* 131 (2012), 99–119.

27 See e.g. Genesis 19:8.
28 For the significance of this verse, see Judith Plaskow, *Standing Again at Sinai: Judaism from a Feminist Perspective* (San Francisco: Harper & Row, 1990).
29 Elieser Ben Iehuda, *Thesaurus Totius Hebraitatis* (Tel-Aviv: La'am, nd; Hebrew), 201.
30 See the discussions of the nature of biblical Hebrew surveyed in Ian Young and Robert Rezetko, *Linguistic Dating of Biblical Hebrew* (2 vols.; London: Equinox, 2008).
31 On its date, see the discussion in Marc Zvi Brettler, *The Book of Judges* (London: Routledge, 2002), 64–65.
32 See esp. Charles L. Echols, *Tell Me O Muse: On the Song of Deborah (Judges 5) in the Light of Heroic Poetry* (New York: T & T Clark, 2008), 43.
33 See the likely sexual use of "head" in Song of Songs 5:2. Other parts of the body that stick out, such as legs and hands, are used euphemistically that way in the Bible, and it would not be surprising if "head" were used similarly.
34 See William W. Holladay, *Jeremiah 2* (Hermeneia; Minneapolis: Fortress, 1989), 193, 195; and Jack R. Lundbom, *Jeremiah 21–36* (AB: New York: Doubleday, 2004), 451–452.
35 See David J. A. Clines, *Job 38–42* (Word; Nashville: Nelson, 2012), 1096: "Loin girding is a gendered activity."
36 Some scholars, e.g. HALOT, 176 and Clines *CDH* 313, find such uses in wisdom literature, but this is extremely unlikely, since the main addressee in this literature is the male student; this explains, in part, the xenophobia of these books.
37 *Aleksandra Djajic Horvath*, "Gender Transgression" in *Encyclopedia of Gender and Society*, ed. Jodi A. O'Brien (Thousand Oaks, CA: SAGE, 2008), 383–386.
38 See p. 178.
39 This essay, presented at SBL, was formerly on David Clines's website, and is forthcoming in his *Play the Man! Biblical Imperatives to Masculinity.*
40 See Judges 9:53 and 2 Samuel 11:21.
41 *Encyclopedia of Sex and Gender: Men and Women in the World's Cultures*, s.v. "War and Gender", accessed 13 May 2012, http://resources.library.brandeis.edu/login?qurl=http%3A%2F%2Fwww.credoreference.com/entry/sprsg/war_and_gender
42 Susan Niditch, *War in the Hebrew Bible: A Study in the Ethics of Violence* (New York: Oxford University Press, 1993), 84–86.
43 For this song as Miriam's rather than Moses's, see Phyllis Trible, "Bringing Miriam out of the Shadows," *Bible Review* 5/1 (Feb. 1989): 14–25, 34.
44 "Of Drums and Damsels: Women's Performance in Ancient Israel," *BA* 54 (1991), 16–27, and more recently "Mother to Muse: An Archaeomusicological Study of Women's Performance in Ancient Israel," in *Recycling Biblical Figures*, ed. Brenner and van Henten (Leiden: Deo, 1999), 50–77.
45 The number of relevant psalms would increase considerably if the sensible thesis of Williamson, that many psalms labeled as "laments of the individual" are really psalms of thanksgiving, is accepted; see H. G. M. Williamson, "Reading the Lament Psalms Backwards" in *A God So Near: Essays on Old Testament Theology in Honor of Patrick D. Miller*, ed. Brent A. Strawn and Nancy R. Bowen (Winona Lake, IN: Eisenbrans, 2003), 3–15.
46 On the male warrior ideal, see e.g. Jacob L. Wright, "Making a Name for Oneself: Martial Valor, Heroic Death, and Procreation in the Hebrew Bible," *JSOT* 36 (2011), 131–162.
47 On cities as female, see Christl M. Maeier, *Daughter Zion, Mother Zion: Gender, Space, and the Sacred in Ancient Israel* (Minneapolis: Fortress, 2008).
48 David J. A. Clines, "David the Man: The Construction of Masculinity in the Hebrew Bible," in *Interested Parties: The Ideology of Writers and Readers of*

the Hebrew Bible (JSOTSup205; Sheffield: Sheffield Academic Press, 1995), 212–243.

49 See e.g. Maggie Humm, *The Dictionary of Feminist Theory* (second edition; Columbus: Ohio State University Press, 1995), 22–23 ("binary thinking").

50 For different understandings of the origin of specific psalms, see S. E. Gillingham, *The Poems and Psalms of the Hebrew Bible* (Oxford: Oxford University Press, 1994), 173–189. Pp. 177–184, "The Psalmists as Liturgical Poets Serving the Cultic Community," discuss only one possible view concerning the Psalter's origin. On Psalm 113, see now Marc Z. Brettler, "A Woman's Voice in the Psalter: A New Understanding of Psalm 113" in *Built by Wisdom, Established by Understanding: Essays on Biblical and Near Eastern Literature in Honor of Adele Berlin*, ed. Maxine L. Grossman (Bethesda, MD: University Press of Maryland, 2013), 131–146.

51 Tikva Frymer-Kensky, *In the Wake of the Goddesses: Women, Culture, and the Biblical Transformation of Pagan Myth* (New York: Free Press, 1992), 31.

52 Marc Zvi Brettler, *How to Read the Jewish Bible* (New York: Oxford University Press, 2007), 219–220.

53 John Barton, "What Is a Book? Modern Exegesis and the Literary Conventions of Ancient Israel" in *Intertextuality in Ugarit and Israel: Papers Read at the Tenth Joint Meeting of the Society for Old Testament Study and Het Oudtestamentische Werkgezelschap in Nederland en België, held at Oxford, 1997*, ed. J. C. de Moor, Oudtestamentische Studiën 40 (Leiden: Brill 1998), 1–14.

54 Melody D. Knowles, "A Woman at Prayer: A Critical Note on Psalm 131:2b" *JBL* 125 (2006), 385–391.

55 Ibid., 388.

56 Lisa W. Davison, " 'My Soul Is Like the Weaned Child That Is with Me': The Psalms and the Feminine Voice," *HBT* 23 (2001), 166, 158. Yet, as Athalya Brenner and Fokkelien Van Dijk-Hemmes, *On Gendering Texts: Female and Male Voices in the Hebrew Bible* (Leiden: Brill, 1993) have shown, it is important to distinguish between a women's voice and female authorship. For other discussions about women's voices entering into the Psalter, see the following studies, some of which are more compelling than others: Klara Butting, " 'Die Töchter Judas frohlocken' (Ps 48,12): Frauen beten die Psalmen," *Bibel Und Kirche* 56 (2001), 35–39; Ulrike Bail, "Die Klage einer Frau. Zu sprechen gegen das Schweigen: Eine feministisch-sozialgeschichtliche Auslegung von Psalm 55," *Bibel Und Kirche* 51 (1991), 116–118 (this article is esp. problematic in its lack of citation of terms that must refer to rape); Erhard S. Gerstenberger, "Weibliche Spiritualität in Psalmen und Hauskult" in *Ein Gott Allein?*, ed. Walter Dietrich and Martin A. Klopfenstein (Freibourg: Universitätsverlag, 1994), 349–363 (a good, careful survey by a major Psalms scholar).

57 Johan Coetzee, " 'Silence, Ye Women! God at Work in the Womb: Psalm 139 as Illustration of Israel's Embodied Patriarchal Theology of Containment," *OTE* 18 (2005), 521–530.

58 Gruber, "The Motherhood of God in Second Isaiah" in *The Motherhood of God*, 3–15; Hanne Løland, *Silent of Salient Gender? The Interpretation of Gendered God-Language in the Hebrew Bible Exemplified in Isaiah 42, 46 and 49* (FAT 32; Tübingen: Mohr Siebeck, 2008).

59 Marc Zvi Brettler, "Incompatible Metaphors for YHWH in Isaiah 40–66," *JSOT* 78 (1998), 97–120, and more extensively, Sarah J. Dille, *Mixing Metaphors: God as Mother and Father in Deutero-Isaiah* (*JSOT*Sup 398; London: T & T Clark, 2004).

60 See e.g. Prov. 31.19 and Philip J. King and Lawrence E. Stager, *Life in Biblical Israel* (Louisville: Westminster John Know, 2001), 152: "They [spinning and weaving] were typically women's work performed at home while tending the

children." For a later period, see Miriam B. Peskowitz, *Spinning Fantasies: Rabbis, Gender, and History* (Berkeley: University of California Press, 1997).

61 See *HALOT* 754 and Clines, *DCH*, 6.153–154.

62 Note Stephen A. Geller's term "Pseudepigraphical Headings" in his "Psalms" in *The Oxford Encyclopedia of the Books of the Bible*, ed. Michael D. Coogan (New York: Oxford University Press, 2012), 2.196.

63 Though never stated explicitly, this is certainly the view that emerges from various studies of writing and scribal practices in ancient Israel, such as Karel van der Toorn, *Scribal Culture and the Making of the Hebrew Bible* (Cambridge, MA: Harvard University Press, 2007).

64 I am assuming that guilds were responsible for composing most psalms (see Nahum M. Sarna, "The Psalm superscriptions and the Guilds" in his *Studies in Biblical Interpretation* [Philadelphia: Jewish Publication Society, 2000], 335–356), and all the recorded names of guild members are male. The main functionaries were male as well (see e.g. Menahem Haran, *Temples and Temple-Service in Ancient Israel* [Oxford: Clarendon, 1978], 58–111), though two texts (Exodus 38:8; 1 Samuel 2:22) mention minor female functionaries whose roles are unknown.

65 See for example Erhard G. Gerstenberger, *Psalms Part 1 with an Introduction to Cultic Poetry* (FOTL; Gand Rapids: Eerdmans, 1988), 96, who characterizes the psalm as "Messianic Thanksgiving Song; Royal Victory Hymn."

66 On property, see Zafrira Ben-Barak, *Inheritance by Daughters in Israel and the Ancient Near East* (Jaffa: Archaeological Center, nd) and Raymond Westbrook and Bruce Wells, *Everyday Law in Biblical Israel* (Louisville: Westminster John Knox, 2009), 54 (though I am doubtful concerning their generalization from Proverbs 31); and on the dowry, see ibid., 99–100 and Raymond Westbrook, *Property and the Family in Biblical Law* (JSOTSup 113; Sheffield: JSOT Press, 1991), 142–164 ("The Dowry").

67 Clines, *DCH* 1.212; *HALOT* 1.40 renders it "strength."

68 *CAD* A/2 48.

69 I will discuss this issue in my forthcoming commentary on Psalms 91–119.

70 For a new interpretation of the rituals in Ezra and Nehemiah, see Yonina Dor, *Have the "Foreign Women" Really been Expelled: Separation and Exclusion in the Restoration Period* (Jerusalem: Magnes, 2006; Hebrew).

71 See most recently Nili Shupak, "Female Imagery in Proverbs 1–9 in the Light of Egyptian Sources," *VT* 61 (2011), 310–323.

72 See the discussion in Mary Joan Winn Leith, "Ruth" in *The Oxford Encyclopedia of the Books of the Bible*, 280–281.

73 See e.g. Joseph Blenkinsopp, "The Social Context of the 'Outsider Woman' in Proverbs 1–9," *Biblica* 72 (1991), 457–473.

74 See e.g. Loren D. Crow, *The Song of Ascents (Psalms 120–134): Their Place in Israelite History and Religion* (SBLDS 148; Atlanta: Scholars, 1996); and Michael D. Goulder, *The Psalms of the Return (Book V, Psalms 107–150)*, JSOTSup 258 (Sheffield: Sheffield Academic Press, 1998).

75 "Women and Psalms: Toward an Understanding of the Role of Women's Prayer in the Israelite Cult," *Gender and Law*, JSOTSup 262, ed. Victor Matthews and Bernard Levinson (Sheffield: Sheffield Academic Press, 1998), 25–56; for documentation, see the notes there.

76 See the many questions raised by Karla G. Bohmbach, "Conventions/Contraventions: The Meaning of Public and Private for the Judges 19 Concubine," *JSOT* 83 (1999), 83–98, and especially Carol Meyers, "'Women of the Neighborhood' Ruth 4:17: Informal Female Networks in Ancient Israel," in *Ruth and Esther: A Feminist Companion to the Bible*, ed. Athalya Brenner (Sheffield: Sheffield Academic Press, 1999), 110–127, who questions the viability of the public-private dichotomy in the Bible.

77 Cynthia R. Chapman, *The Gendered Language of Warfare in the Israelite-Assyrian Encounter* (HSM 62; Winona Lake: Eisenbrauns, 2004), 3.

78 For a recent treatment and discussion on history of interpretation of Psalm 127 see Elie Assis, "Psalm 127 and the Polemic of the Rebuilding of the Temple in the Post Exilic Period" *ZAW* 121 (2009), 256–272. Quite usefully, on pp. 269–272, he notes certain similarities between Pss. 127 and 128, but does not deal at all with issues of gender, and how they bridge these two compositions.

79 Scholars debate whether or not vv. 1–2 and 3–5 are separate psalms, or separate sections of a single psalm; see Daniel J. Estes, "Like Arrows in the Hand of a Warrior (Psalm CXXVII)," *VT* 41 (1991), 304–311, and more recently, Frank-Lothar Hossfeld and Erich Zenger, *Psalms 3* (Hermeneia; Minneapolis: Fortress, 2011), 383. This issue has no bearing on my analysis of v. 3–5.

80 Though missing in some LXX manuscripts, *geber* is retained by most commentators.

81 See e.g. *HALOT* 209–210; see Hossfeld and Zenger, *Psalms 3*, 381, n. h.

82 Karen Horney, *Feminine Psychology* (New York: Norton, 1967); Gloria Steinem, "Womb Envy, Testyria, and Breast Castration Anxiety: What if Freud were Female?" Ms. 4/5 (March/April 1994), 48–56; Phyllis Chessler, *About Men* (New York: Simon and Schuster, 1978).

83 Ibid., 62.

84 To use the language of George Lakoff, how many of the entailments of the metaphor are being called up in this context? Chapman, *The Gendered Language* offers helpful illustrations of the intersection of gender and the study of metaphors and similes.

85 Mary E. Kite, "Gender Stereotypes" in *Encyclopedia of Women and Gender*, ed. J. Worrell (San Diego: Academic Press, 2001), 562.

86 This is especially true if the readings or interpretations preserved in the Targum and Peshitta are preferred to the MT.

87 Hayim ben Yosef Tawil, *An Akkadian Lexical Companion of Biblical Hebrew: Etymological-Semantic and Idiomatic Equivalents with Supplement on Biblical Aramaic* (Jersey City, NJ: Ktav, 2009), 90.

88 Concerning *heikal*, see ibid., 83. See also the lengthy exploration of this image in Silvia Schroer, "Frauenkörper als architektonische Element. Zum Hintergrun on Ps 144,12" in *Bilder als Quellen/Images as Sources: Studies on Ancient Near Eastern Artefacts and the Bible Inspired by the Work of Othmar Keel*, ed. Susanne Bickel, Silvia Schroer, René Schurte, and Christoph Uehlinger (Fribourg: Academic Press, 2007), 425–450.

89 Marc Zvi Brettler, "A Women's Voice in the Psalter: A New Understanding of Psalm 113." That article offers the documentation for the arguments adduced here concerning Ps 113.

90 See the broader discussion in Edward J. Bridge, "Loyalty, Dependency and Status with YHWH: The Use of 'bd in the Psalms," *Vetus Testamentum* 59 (2009), 360–378. It is unclear if this is a specific group in the Israelite cult, and if so, who comprised them, or if it may refer to many different groups, depending on context, as suggested by Hossfeld and Zenger, *Psalms 3*, 182.

91 I find myself totally unconvinced by scholars who claim that YHWH was genderless or above/beyond gender, such as Brevard S. Childs, *Old Testament Theology in a Canonical Context* (Philadelphia: Fortress, 1986), 39–40. I also believe that most scholars discussing this issue have not taken into account more recent psycholinguistic studies of the Whorf-Sapir hypothesis; see e.g. http://www.edge.org/3rd_culture/boroditsky09/boroditsky09_index.html accessed on 12 ay 2012, with further references there.

92 Gruber, "The Motherhood," 6.

93 The same ideal may be expressed in Psalm 111; see Marc Zvi Brettler, "The Riddle of Psalm Ps 111" in *Scriptural Exegesis: The Shapes of Culture and the Religious Imagination: Essays in Honour of Michael Fishbane*, ed. Deborah A. Green and Laura S. Lieber (Oxford: Oxford University Press, 2009), 62–73.

94 I am completing this article in May 2012, in Israel, as the Tal Law concerning exemption of Yeshivah students from army service is being debated. I am thus very conscious of two very different, competing ideas of masculinity within contemporary Israeli society: the hegemonic man who serves in the army, and the more elite and combat-oriented the unit the better, and the male Yeshivah student, who studies (inside) day and night, is exempt from the army, and often has a wife who is the primary breadwinner.

95 Much of this was stimulated by Gerald Henry Wilson, *The Editing of the Hebrew Psalter* (SBLDS 76; Chico, CA: Scholars, 1985). See also J. Clinton McCann, ed., *The Shape and Shaping of the Psalter* (JSOTSup 159; Sheffield: JSOT Press, 1993) and the judicious survey in S. E. Gillingham, *The Poems and Psalms of the Hebrew Bible*, 232–255 and Erich Zenger, ed., *The Composition of the Book of Psalms* (BETL 238; Leuven: Peeters, 2010).

96 Given the focus on Torah study and the possible connections of this psalm to wisdom literature, the translation "the man" is more likely here.

97 This includes animals (male and female) as well; see Brent A. Strawn and Joel M. LeMon, "'Everything That Has Breath': Animal Praise in Psalm 150:6 in the Light of Ancient Near Eastern Iconography" in Susanne Bickel et al. eds., *Bilder als Quellen* (Fribourg: Academic Press, 2007), 451–485.

98 See Exodus 15:20; Judges 11:34 and 1 Samuel 18:6, and n. 44, above.

9 Relative masculinities in the Hebrew Bible/Old Testament

Martti Nissinen

Relative masculinities

> *"[G]ender in antiquity was mapped not as a binary of two fixed and 'opposite' sexes – but rather as a dynamic spectrum or gradient of relative masculinities."*[1]

If we were to compile a "Historical Atlas of Masculinity," we would soon realize that, while there is a good selection of literature negotiating masculinity in modern times, the mapping of masculinities in the ancient world is still in the making. The ancient Near Eastern texts in particular appear as a still largely unexplored terrain. The interrogation of ancient Near Eastern masculinities does not need to begin *ex nihilo*, however. A fair number of studies has been written to examine many white spots in the maps of Classical Antiquity and the New Testament,[2] and even the exploration of the Hebrew Bible/Old Testament has recently begun.[3] Thanks to the existing studies of men and masculinity in modern and premodern times, we can – to use a "masculine" expression – start penetrating the unexplored terrain with the help of the theoretical and methodological tools developed in previous scholarship.

The first "map" I used in my own expedition to the texts of the Hebrew Bible/Old Testament was the introductory article to the volume *Mapping Gender in Ancient Discourses* (2007) written by Virginia Burrus.[4] It is from her article that I adopted the idea of "relative masculinities" and the titles of the subheadings of this chapter: masculinity, sexuality, body, empire, and religion.

The second map I used was R. W. Connell's book, *Masculinities*,[5] which informs the concept of "relative masculinities" with important theoretical viewpoints concerning the social practice of gender featuring hegemonic, subordinate, and marginalized masculinities. Hegemonic masculinity corresponds to the cultural ideal of male performance in a male-dominated society, defined and legitimated by those in privileged positions of power. Subordinate masculinity appears always in relation to hegemonic masculinity. It refers to male performance that lacks or differs in some crucial characteristics of hegemonic masculinity and signifies a lower status in male hierarchy, often implying repulsion, violence, and social exclusion. Marginalized masculinity is the type of subordinate masculinity that "is always relative to the *authorization* of the hegemonic masculinity of the dominant group,"[6] representing a "wrong" and illegitimate type of male performance.

Finally, I have adopted the idea of physical, social, and cosmic bodies from Dale Launderville's book, *Celibacy in the Ancient World*.[7] Physical body refers to the human body's individual characteristics, while social body is the body as interpreted, legitimized, and positioned by the community. Cosmic body means "the man before God," that is, the body as interpreted in relation to the cosmic order, deities, religious doctrines and institutions. The cosmic body, therefore, does not need to conform to the ideals of hegemonic masculinity, and non-hegemonic masculinities may be idealized if they are serving even higher ideals.[8]

Defining masculinity is a hazardous exercise, of course, since masculinity is not a coherent object but, rather, a configuration of gender practices.[9] The basic distinction of masculinity and femininity is shared by humanity at large;[10] however, perceptions of masculinity are culture-specific, and setting criteria for masculinity in any given text or society different from one's own is prone to anachronisms and questionable transfers of meanings. Ancient cultures cannot be experienced by a modern scholar, the only thing we can do is to read texts and other artifacts produced by ancient cultures and to try to understand them.

In ancient texts which, as a rule, are products of a patriarchal world, socially defined constructs of masculinity – what it means to be male and how to perform ideal manhood – set an important, sometimes marked but often unmarked standard for human life and institutions. It is rather the deviations from this standard that were pointed out as exceptions to the rule. The problem, of course, is how to typify the ideal construct of masculinity without falling to an essentialist trap. Masculinities are always performed within a setting, social as well as literary, hence what we can do is to compare different masculinities and attitudes towards them in different literary contexts of the Hebrew Bible/Old Testament, describing patterns of male performances and their interpretation. This, I believe, can be done without presupposing normative ideas about what men in general ought to be.

Using the concept of relative masculinities, I attempt to explore the ground between differing constructs of masculinity, contending that in the Hebrew Bible/Old Testament, there are different kinds of masculinities which are not appreciated equally in the texts. Studies in masculinity in the ancient world have shown that gender in antiquity "was mapped not as a binary of two fixed and 'opposite' sexes – but rather as a dynamic spectrum or gradient of relative masculinities."[11] In spite of (or perhaps *because* of) the absence of the absolute binary of male and female, there was a permanent and significant concern for *ideal* masculinity. Where the "ethos of penetration and

Figure 9.1 In public domain. http://www.loc.gov/pictures/item/2002712088/ (accessed 26 Oct 2015).

domination"[12] pervaded, being a man was not an inborn quality. There were ideals of male performance as well as variations and divergences from these ideals; men were both made and unmade, not all men met the ideal standards: "Normative definitions of masculinity . . . face the problem that not many men actually meet the normative standards."[13] It is precisely the *spectrum* of masculinities that made it important to signify and identify acceptable ways of masculine performance. In fact, manhood was a vulnerable quality that was constantly endangered and had, therefore, always to be demonstrated, done, and accomplished by means of a proper male performance: "Be a man and do it!"[14]

At the first sight, the idea of relative masculinities seems to be difficult to reconcile with the declaration "male and female (*zākār û-nĕqēbâ*) he created them" (Gen 1:27), which seems to leave little room for anything but a strict dichotomy between the sexes.[15] By introducing the concept of relative masculinity I do not wish to erode the male/female dichotomy and the notion of ideal masculinity, which were and still are actively upheld by patriarchal (and even postpatriarchal) cultures everywhere. What I want to say is that masculinity is not essential but relational. Relative masculinities exist even in cultures where the social and ideological dichotomy between sexes prevails, but constructs of ideal masculinity need to be constantly negotiated with different kinds of male performances.

The absolute binary, hence, turns into a spectrum of masculinities that can be monitored from the perspectives of body, social hierarchy, and performance. Male bodies are not all the same. Some men are strong, others are physically weak, some are married while others live outside the conventional family structure, some are physically disabled, others appear to be castrated, and yet others are born as hermaphrodites. Social hierarchy is not all about dominating men and subordinated women, because some men are clearly overpowered and marginalized. Men can be found as passive partners in sexual encounters, which typically indicates a subordinate position. Men living outside the conventional family structures have a special status and varying degree of appreciation in the reproductive society. Finally, male performance is not all about aggression and domination; men can behave in a way that does not meet the expectations of hegemonic masculinity but is still considered legitimate. All of this happens even in the Hebrew Bible/Old Testament.

Masculinity and sexuality

> *"Sexuality may often best be understood as a site for the inscription of gender in antiquity."*[16]

"Sexuality" is a word with many meanings, and it is often unclear which parts of the broad semantic field of this rather slippery word are covered by each discourse.[17] In this chapter, I use it to refer to physical sexual activity, or the lack thereof, and its significance in constructing masculinities: who is allowed and/or supposed to interact sexually with whom and how, and how the sexual activity determines a man's masculinity relative to the hegemonic ideal. The standard ideal in a patriarchal society is that of the procreating male who performs an active, dominant, and penetrative role in the sexual relationship – preferably, but not exclusively, with legal partners.[18] However, there are many exceptions to this "inscription of gender" in the Hebrew Bible/Old Testament, some of them less tolerated than others. The following three cases – *a.* male-to-male intercourse, *b.* love between two men, and *c.* prophetic celibacy – serve as examples of masculine (non)sexual performances beyond the conventional family structures.

a. The "ethos of penetration and domination" implies the question "who's on top?,"[19] which, again parallels the structures of social practice. In the Hebrew Bible, legal relations of penetration are clearly defined in Leviticus 18 and 20:10–26, mirroring the patriarchal family structure.[20] The implied addressee of the Levitical proscriptions is the procreating *paterfamilias* who is supposed to perform an active sexual role, but whose sexual practice is strictly restricted within the bounds of the patriarchal family. The potential but forbidden sexual partners include even another male person: "You shall not lie with a male as with a woman; it is an abomination" (Lev 18:22); "If a man lies with a male as with a woman, both of them have committed an abomination; they shall be put to death; their blood is upon them" (Lev 20:13). These prohibitions of male-to-male sexual intercourse include two important expressions:

1 To "lie with a male as with a woman," literally "to lie the lyings of a woman" (*šākab miškěbê 'iššâ*), mirrors the expression "lying of a man" (*miškab zākār*) which implies the loss of virginity (cf. Num 31:17–18; Judg 21:11–12),[21] hence the expressions indicate the act of penetration seen from the active and the passive partner's perspective, respectively. In male-to-male intercourse, this causes a change in the passive partner's status from the active (male) to the passive (non-male) role – in other words, from hegemonic to subordinate masculinity. The same change is presupposed also by the Middle Assyrian laws which impose on the active partner the punishment of not only to be penetrated himself, but also turned into a eunuch, that is, to suffer a permanent change in his masculine performance.[22]

2 Male-to-male penetration is defined as "abomination" (*tô'ēbâ*),[23] that is, the severest possible transgression of sacred borders, from which there is no purification – hence the death penalty for both partners in Lev 20:13, unlike the Middle Assyrian laws lacking a similar religious ideology. This transgression is forbidden, because "the inhabitants of the land, who were before you, committed all of these abominations, and the land became defiled" (Lev 18:27). Committing them threatens

the purity of the "Land" irrespective of the social or sexual status of the transgressors; therefore, in this setting, even the hegemonic masculine performance of the penetrating party is condemned.

The Levitical proscriptions imagine a male-to-male penetration that constitutes an illegal performance of hegemonic and subordinate masculinities. The subordination of a man's masculinity is criminalized also by the Middle Assyrian laws, which imply that the penetrated partner's physical body is violated and his social body degraded because of the change of sexual status caused by the penetration. The penetrated partner as the victim of such an action is not punished in the Middle Assyrian laws, but Lev 20:13 – probably interpreting and expanding Lev 18:22 – goes further in punishing both parties. Defining the act of penetration as a *tôʿēbâ* condemns *both* partners' *cosmic* body, which leads to the ultimate marginalization of their masculinities by means of capital punishment.

b. An entirely different case of male-to-male intimacy is provided by the narrative of David and Jonathan in the books of Samuel (1 Samuel 18–20; 2 Samuel 1). The unmistakably homoerotic traits of this story have been acknowledged long ago[24] – indeed, the story of David and Jonathan has played a significant role in the genealogy of the very notion of homosexuality.[25] To be sure, David and Jonathan have usually not been interpreted as violating the Levitical proscriptions – not only because they may be of later date and represent different societal ideals[26] but also because the expressions of intimacy between these two men have been interpreted as telling a story totally different from Leviticus.[27] Many interpreters have considered the relationship of David and Jonathan as another example of male bonding comparable to Gilgameš and Enkidu in the *Epic of Gilgameš* or to Achilles and Patroclus in Homer's *Iliad*.[28] These are tales of "real men" who perform hegemonic masculinity in every respect, without confining themselves to conventional family structures. Their male bonding is characterized by mutual love and affection constructed differently from the standard patriarchal pattern of male-female relationships: there is no differentiation between active and passive sexual roles, and the partners are described as equals without, however, sharing a similar social background.

Even David, by any criteria, serves as a model of hegemonic masculinity: "From the start to the finish of the biblical narrative, the success of David is dependent upon his conformity to heteronormative masculine ideas,"[29] such as military prowess and marriage. Jonathan, however, is a more nuanced figure with regard to his masculinity. He is depicted as performing the ideals of hegemonic masculinity as a warrior (1 Samuel 13–14); however, in relation to David his "daring commitment to intimacy and connectedness with a friend over family ties smacks of the 'gay way of relating.' Which is counternormative to all things traditionally masculine."[30] Even in this relationship, Jonathan is not stripped of his masculinity and placed in the feminized position; however, it is the narrative strategy of the text to legitimize David's kingship by making Jonathan to relinquish the status superiority that would belong to him on account of his birth.[31] In terms of masculinity, David and, most of the time, Jonathan, represent hegemonic masculinity; nevertheless, "the idea that there is a status relationship to be negotiated between David and Jonathan is never abandoned."[32] This does not cause Jonathan's masculinity to become subordinate, the issue is more about the relative status of the social bodies of the two males. Seen against the background of Near Eastern royal ideology, the king was considered the embodiment of hegemonic masculinity,[33] and there was only room for one such royal body. In relation to this quintessential social body, every other body was subordinate. It is not sexuality that makes David's masculinity distinct from Jonathan's, or their relationship different from other male bondings, but David's narrative role as the one destined for kingship.

c. One variation of masculinity in relation to the physical, social, and cosmic body still needs to mentioned: the unmarried man. While not a constituent of the ideal of hegemonic masculinity, the unmarried status does not immediately deprive a man of his masculinity but, depending on his socioreligious position, makes it nevertheless distinctive within what R. W. Connell calls the "reproductive arena."[34] The non-married status is often associated with the lack of legitimate offspring which was considered a social and personal failure all over the Near East.[35] In the Hebrew Bible, there is only one person who is not allowed to marry: Jeremiah the prophet.[36] God forbids him to marry and procreate in order to make him a living symbol of the fate of the unfaithful people of Judah and their morbid life in the foreign land (Jer 16:1–21). Within the literary context of the Hebrew Bible that does not endorse celibacy and asceticism as virtues of (masculine) self-control, Jeremiah's unmarried status can be regarded as a subversion of conventional gender structures,[37] queering his social body[38] and raising the question of his masculinity.

Jeremiah cannot be called a prime example of hegemonic masculinity; in fact, he is often presented as everything else but a self-determined and goal-oriented man in fulfilling his prophetic role.[39] Jeremiah is reluctant to assume the role of a prophet, becomes the victim of maltreatment by his community, and complains about his fate in his numerous laments. In one of the laments, he says to God: "O Lord, you have enticed me, and I was enticed; you have overpowered me, and you have prevailed" (Jer 20:7). The verbs *pth* and *ḥzq* are suggestive of a sexual connotation (cf. Exod 22:15; Hos 2:16; Job 31:9 [*pth*]; Deut 22:25–27; 2 Sam 13:11 [*ḥzq*]), thus Jeremiah has become seduced and subdued, becoming a passive partner.

In the case of Jer 20:7, the hegemonic male is God, while the prophet plays the role of the sexually passive partner. This pattern is reminiscent of the divine-human gender matrix, in which the humans, whether as a community or as individuals, assume a subordinate role in relation to the hegemonic divine party.[40] Jeremiah's celibacy is "a discipline that forces him to depend more fully on Yhwh,"[41] hence his masculinity is presented primarily in relation to God.[42] He might be made a fortified city, an iron pillar, and a bronze wall (Jer 1:18; 15:20), but all this epitomizes God's strength, not Jeremiah's. Jeremiah, like any prophet, appears as the vehicle of the divine agency, but in his case this happens not only verbally but also by way of bodily performance. While Jeremiah's social body is marginalized and his masculinity queered, his cosmic body is justified as a sign from God, embodying the people of Judah and thus having a subordinate position in the divine-human gender matrix.

Masculinity and body

> *"The body encountered as a site of human fragility leads to particularly complex articulations of gender. . ."*[43]

Body is the site of the practice and performance of gender, and at the same time, it is the site of human fragility and vulnerability. "Gender is social practice that constantly refers to bodies and what bodies do, it is not social practice reduced to the body,"[44] hence the male body is not simply biologically determined. The physical appearance of a man can place him differently within the network of relative masculinities depending on how he fulfills the expectations of whatever is considered to signify ideal masculinity. Bodily defects and disabilities, as well as impotence, illness and old age, would generally count as physical markers of subordinate or marginalized masculinity.[45] The physical body becomes a social body in which the marks of various constructs of masculinity are inscribed.

As a case study, I have chosen the eunuchs, whether "eunuchs who have been so from birth," or "eunuchs who have been made eunuchs by others," to use the classification put in the mouth of Jesus of Nazareth in Matt 19:12. The eunuchs (Heb. *sārîs*) constitute a group of non-female people who are not just an imaginary category but who demonstrably existed in the texts' social world, and whose social body is characterized by their lack of a procreative power, a key component to the performance of hegemonic masculinity. We do not know what exactly turned a male person into a eunuch in the early times; according to the common imagination based on later evidence[46] and some biblical verses (Lev 21:20; Deut 23:2), it had to do with mutilation or manipulation of male genitalia, probably castration by crushing or removing the testicles. However, not every castrate was called a eunuch, and perhaps not everyone called eunuch was castrated. Whatever the technical operation was, it was a symbolic act that permanently changed the status of the physical, social, and cosmic body of the persons in question.

Even without an act of castration, eunuchship appears as a status that, as I would argue, still *was* considered a kind of masculinity. However, eunuchs appear as queering figures who challenge stable gender identities and transgress fixed gender categories.[47]

A eunuch can be called a "dry tree" (Isa 56:3; see below) because of his incapability of procreating which easily places him in marginal positions within the network of relative masculinities. In Wisdom of Solomon a eunuch who has been faithful to God's law is juxtaposed with an infertile but faithful woman (Wis 3:14).[48] This text does not say eunuchs are otherwise equal to women; rather, it identifies the defective and marginalized social bodies of the barren woman and the eunuch as cosmic bodies acceptable to God, to whom faithfulness matters more than the social status of the body: "Better than this is childlessness with virtue" (Wis 4:1).

The eunuchs were seen as unable to emulate the active and penetrative sexual role of a fully masculine man, and this gave reason to statements like the following in the book of Ben Sira: "Like a eunuch lusting for intimacy with a maiden is he who does right under compulsion" (Sir 20:4). A similar point is made elsewhere in Ben Sira (Sir 30:20): "So is one punished by the Lord; he sees with his eyes and groans as a eunuch groans when embracing a girl." Interestingly, both texts take it for granted that even a eunuch has physical desires and emotions attached to a female object: a eunuch can be sexually attracted by a girl but, despite his male desire, is not able to perform the deeds of a man. Ben Sira, hence, regards the eunuchs as males and not as women; however, they represent a kind of masculinity that he considers non-functional.[49]

In some legal texts, men with mutilated genitalia appear in a different light; technically, they are not called eunuchs, but they do appear as a stigmatized and marginalized group.[50] According to Deut 23:2, "No one whose testicles are crushed or whose member is cut off shall be admitted into the congregation of the Lord." No reasons are given for this ban. It may simply grow out of repulsion for such defects projected to God himself;[51] ideologically, it seems to represent the priestly ideal of bodily integrity which, more than anything, aims at reducing the influence of impurity, both of the temple and of the "Land." The priests had to be physically intact: "For no one who has a blemish shall draw near, one who is blind or lame, or one who has a mutilated face or a limb too long, or one who has a broken foot or a broken hand, or a hunchback, or a dwarf, or a man with a blemish in his eyes or an itching disease or scabs or crushed testicles" (Lev 21:18–20). All this, needless to say, concerns men, not women, and the priests had to fulfill the strictest criteria. In the case of the priests, the social body becomes a cosmic body, symbolizing the purity of the Land as a guarantee of its intact and undisturbed relationship with its God.

A totally divergent discourse concerning eunuchs is to be found in Isa 56:3–4:

> Do not let the foreigner joined to the Lord say, 'The Lord will surely separate me from his people'; and do not let the eunuch (*sārîs*) say, 'I am just a dry tree.' For thus says the Lord: To the eunuchs who keep my sabbaths, who choose the things that please me and hold fast my

> covenant, I will give, in my house and within my walls, a monument and a name (*yad wā-šēm*) better than sons and daughters; I will give them an everlasting name that shall not be cut off.

From the point of view of masculinity, this passage is noteworthy for several reasons: (1) It presumes that the community to whom the prophetic speech is addressed includes eunuchs. (2) It compares the status of a eunuch to that of a foreigner, without implying that eunuchs *had* to be foreigners.[52] (3) It contests directly, if not knowingly, the view of Deut 23:2, according to which eunuchs have no access to Yhwh's congregation;[53] on the contrary, (4) it promises the eunuch who observes the Sabbath and keeps the covenant a full membership and good standing in Yhwh's congregation. (5) The eunuchs' inability to procreate keeps affecting their relative status of masculinity, but the lack of sons and daughters does not impede them from receiving divine favors; rather, (6) the lack of progeny is compensated for by the *yad wā-šēm*, "a monument and a name." The marginal socio-religious status of the eunuch is removed and his body, both cosmic and social, is rehabilitated: he will be given "an everlasting name that shall not be cut off," an obvious pun referring to the manipulation of their physical bodies.[54] As Jacob Wright and Michael Chan have shown, this passage, interpreted against the background of the evidence of eunuchs in Near Eastern imperial courts, "turns a major symbol of royal power on its head by transferring absolute devotion to the empire, which eunuchs both symbolize and physically embody, to fidelity to YHWH."[55] As the eunuchs' masculinity in the Near Eastern courts was seen primarily in relation to the king instead of the average male citizen, so is the eunuch's masculinity in Isa 56:3–4 related first and foremost to God. This reinterpretation of the eunuchs' social and cosmic bodies transforms the symbol of foreign power into an honorific monument in the city and temple of Jerusalem. The eunuch's social body is, hence, programmatically demarginalized, and his cosmic body restored.

Masculinity and empire

> *"Empire sets the stage for the performances of gender. . ."*[56]

In the ancient patriarchal world, the empire was a male-dominated institution. As such, it was the stage for hegemonic and marginalized masculinities, marginalization being "relative to the *authorization* of the hegemonic masculinity in the dominant group."[57] The hierarchy of masculinities emerged as a system of relations of hegemony, authorization, and marginalization both in the ancient Near East and in the Hebrew Bible. This system produced a spectrum of masculinities dependent on the social class, age, and the religious and political status. I use as an example the case of the Assyrian court official called *ša rēši*. Several sources suggest that these men lacked beards and testes, two physical markers of being biological adult male and two social markers of the hegemonic construct of masculinity. At the same time, however, they appear as active, respected, and powerful members of their societies. I will argue that the same can be said of *sārîsîm* in the Hebrew Bible.

There has long been a virtual consensus that Hebrew word *sārîs* is derived from the Akkadian *ša rēši* (LÚ.SAG). The meaning of this Akkadian expression has been disputed, however. While many Assyriologists hold the view that *ša rēši* generally denotes a eunuch,[58] some scholars would rather interpret it as a designation of royal attendants who may or may not have been castrated.[59] The very existence of the eunuchs in the Assyrian court has not been denied even by the representatives of the latter group; the question is rather whether the equation of *ša rēši* with eunuchs is valid even in cases that do not render it immediately evident.

That *ša rēši* generally denotes a eunuch is suggested most persuasively by the Old Babylonian omen which presents the *ša rēši* as infertile men: "May your semen dry up like that of *ša rēši* who cannot beget" (*CT* 23 pl. 10:14: *kīma šūt rēši lā alidi nīlka lībal*). Indirectly, the omen may refer to them as being castrated; the point, however, is the permanent inability to have children. Also in the Middle Assyrian laws, an adulterous man and a man having a sexual intercourse with another man are punished by turning them into *ša rēši* (MAL A §§ 15, 20). This law makes sense if the punishment is balanced with the crime according to the talionic principle, as imposing a permanent change on the perpetrator's social status and body as a retribution for his abuse of hegemonic masculinity.[60]

Furthermore, as Kazuko Watanabe has observed, the usual phrase in the clause of penalties for litigation in Neo-Assyrian sale documents, "his sons or grandsons," is routinely omitted in the case of *ša rēši*[61] who, consequently, seem not normally have had children – something to be expected of the eunuchs. This does not exclude the possibility of adoption, and indeed, there are a few documents that mention sons and grandsons of a *ša rēši*.[62] Finally, the characteristic appearance of the eunuchs is frequently depicted on Assyrian reliefs and seals showing a beardless person worshipping a deity, often the goddesses Ištar or Gula.[63] Almost all Assyrian seals identifying the owner as a *ša rēši* have a depiction of a beardless worshipper.[64] In fact, the Assyrian officials appear as divided into two groups: the *ša rēši* and the *ša ziqni*, the latter designation meaning "bearded courtiers." Since the beard is a significant social marker of masculinity, this is quite revealing: The use of the beard as the distinctive feature between the two groups implies that the *ša rēši* represent a class of masculinity distinct from the bearded men.

All this scattered evidence deriving from different periods strongly suggests that *ša rēši* generally denotes a eunuch. This, of course, cannot be inferred from every reference to the people thus designated, but the cases where this meaning is not immediately visible do not yield any additional information about the sexual status of the *ša rēši*, and, hence, do not prove the contrary.

In the Hebrew Bible it is clear that the word *sārîs* is very often used of royal officials, but there is no unanimity about whether the noun always denotes a eunuch. If, however, the Akkadian term normally means a castrated court official, as I think can be demonstrated, then it would be a strange development to adopt the term in Hebrew denoting something different, especially since *sārîs* in some cases *is* indisputably used of an eunuch (Isa 56:3–4; Sir 30:20).[65] The most probable period of the linguistic borrowing of the Akkadian term is the Neo-Assyrian period when there cannot have been any uncertainty in Judah and Israel what kind of people the *ša rēši* were.[66]

Translations of the Hebrew Bible tend to conceal the fact that eunuchs appear dozens of times in the Hebrew Bible – virtually always translated as *eunoukhos*, "castrated man,"[67] in the Septuagint[68] – plus a few times in the Apocrypha. The reason for this is that when the word *sārîs* is used of a royal official, it is usually not translated as a "eunuch" but as "official," "officer," and the like. The translation "eunuch" is used consistently only in cases where the non-procreative sexual status of the *sārîs* is made apparent (Isa 56:3; Sir 30:20) – sometimes, and quite revealingly, also of royal officials who are clearly of non-Judahite origin, such as the Persian and Babylonian *sārîsîm* in the books of Esther and Daniel, and a few individual cases such as Ebed-Melech the Ethiopian in Jer 38:7. The distinction appears in all major Hebrew dictionaries, where the meanings "official" and "eunuch" are regularly separated from each other, although this translation practice has no linguistic grounds whatsoever. Rather, the translation "eunuch" is used in cases considered queer, pitiful, or foreign, but it is avoided when a non-foreign person occupies a respectable position in the king's service, as if it were the common assumption that there simply cannot have been so many "real" eunuchs in high positions in the Kingdom of Judah, whose laws (to judge from Deut 23:2) did not even admit such persons into Yhwh's congregation. It is true that the texts in which the *sārîsîm* appear as royal officials, their gender performance plays no role and their status as eunuchs is not thematized by any means. This does not imply that they were not eunuchs but rather that there was no need to explain or defend their status.

Whether we go to Assyrian, Persian, or Hittite sources,[69] eunuchs feature as high officials, king's personal attendants, and as functionaries related to the women's quarters. The idea and concept of the "harem" has been rightly questioned with regard to the Assyrian court;[70] nevertheless, an important feature of the role of the eunuchs is their relationship to the kings' wives and other royal women.[71] In Assyrian sources, the eunuchs can be found working under the authority of the palace women or serving the queen's staff, several of them bearing the designation "the queen's eunuch" (*ša rēši ša issi ekalli*).[72] Other than that, eunuchs are to be found in high positions performing administrative and military roles in the service of the ruler all over the ancient Near Eastern world.

As was already mentioned, the Assyrian officials were divided into two groups: eunuchs (*ša rēši*) and the "bearded courtiers" (*ša ziqni*). In contrast to the *ša ziqni*, the *ša rēši* formed a distinctive group within the Assyrian society with a special status (*ša rēšuttu*, "eunuchship") involving an overseer, the chief eunuch (*rab ša rēši*). The Neo-Assyrian eunuchs could be appointed city overseers or provincial governors, and the chief eunuch counted among the king's primary magnates.[73] The chief eunuch was a military officer of the highest rank and, at times, headed the Assyrian army. One of the chief eunuchs, Sin-šumu-lešir, even ruled Assyria for a few months, probably in 627 after the death of Aššur-etel-ilani, son of Assurbanipal.[74]

In the Hebrew Bible, the *sārîsîm* appear in roles similar to the ancient Near Eastern eunuchs. Throughout the biblical evidence, they belong to the entourage of the king, whether Judean, Egyptian (Gen 37:36; 39:1; 40:2, 7), Assyrian, Babylonian, or Persian. The Judean *sārîsîm* seem to form a distinct group among officers (*śārîm* etc.), even though the title "chief eunuch" (*rab-sārîs* 2 Kgs 18:17; Jer 39:3, 13; Dan 1:3, or *śar has-sārîsîm* Dan 1:7) is only used of Assyrian and Babylonian officials, probably translating the Akkadian title *rab ša rēši*. A *sārîs* may, for example, act as the king's messenger (1 Kgs 22:9//1 Chr 18:8; 2 Kgs 8:6; cf. Jdt 12:11). It is not unusual to find the *sārîs* is in one way or another connected with women – the eunuchs in the Persian royal women's quarters (Esther *passim*), the *sārîsîm* in Queen Jezebel's room (2 Kgs 9:32) and those associated with the Judean king's mother and wives in 2 Kgs 24:15 and Jer 29:2. As military leaders, we find not only the Assyrian and Babylonian chief eunuchs (2 Kgs 18:17; Jer 39:3, 13) but also the *sārîs* who was in command of the soldiers and was brought to Babylonia in 2 Kgs 25:19//Jer 52:5. The juxtaposition of the *sārîs* and military officers is also suggested by *has-sārîsîm we-hag-gibbôrîm* in 1 Chr 28:1.

If the Hebrew *sārîs* should consistently be understood as denoting a eunuch,[75] then the masculinity of a eunuch appears in an entirely different light as in the previously discussed texts which focused on the non-reproductive, and in this sense non-masculine, status of the eunuch. It appears that the Judean eunuchs, much in the same way as their Assyrian colleagues, occupied leading positions in the state bureaucracy, including military leadership conventionally thought of as hegemonic masculine performance *per definitionem*. In these functions, in fact, the sexual otherness of the eunuchs is never mentioned as if it constituted no problem whatsoever in seeing the eunuchs as fully functional leaders and members of the royal court.

The only gender-related aspect that deserves attention is some eunuchs' proximity to the royal women – again, a feature that the *sārîsîm* shared with their Near Eastern counterparts. Such a position between the male and female spheres is usually, and probably correctly, explained by the eunuchs' sexual status. Being unable to reproduce, and not expected to have any sexual interest in women (*pace* Ben Sira), they constituted no threat to the king's dominion over his women and could function within the women's quarters of the royal court. One could even imagine that the eunuchs could serve the women's interests by mediating between the royal women and the king and his male courtiers.

The case of the eunuchs is quite revealing in demonstrating how the spectrum of relative masculinities works in the ancient Near Eastern and biblical texts. Being a eunuch meant a divergent masculinity in terms of bodily appearance and sexual performance, but it hardly signified non-masculinity in the realm of power and empire where it fulfilled fully masculine functions. The eunuchs seem to form a category of their own, whether a distinctive gender[76] or, rather, a special position in the network of relative masculinities and within the structures of the masculinized imperial authority. On the stage of the empire, the masculinity of the eunuchs who served the royal court was certainly subordinate to the king's masculinity, but at the same time, it was authorized as a part of the machinery of hegemonic masculinity: the eunuchs, "as bodily extensions of the king, often represent imperial rule."[77] This, however, does not mean a universal acceptance of their masculinity at all levels of the society, as will be demonstrated by the realm of religion.

Masculinity and religion

> "*. . . gender played a strong role in the agonistic articulation of nascent religious identity and difference.*"[78]

Many texts discussed thus far are significantly about religion, whether the issue is the maintenance of the purity of "Israel," that is, the religious community worshipping Yhwh, or that of the sacred boundaries marked by "abominations" (*tôʿēbôt*) ascribed to other people. The contradictory attitudes towards physically manipulated male bodies in Deut 23:2 and Isa 56:3–4 provide contradictory examples of the treatment of relative masculinities in this religious community, possibly going back to the controversies of the Second Temple period.

The religious status of the eunuchs in the monarchical period is unknown even if Deut 23:2 dated back to the late preexilic period – which is to be doubted for the very reason that the existence of the *sārîsîm* does not seem to constitute any problem for the Deuteromistic writers of the Books of Kings, and no word is uttered concerning their relationship to the worship of Yhwh. We do not even know whether they were of foreign origin, except for the case of Ebed-Melech the Kushite/Ethiopian (Jer 38:17). Since, however, the word *sārîs* is derived from Assyrian, and since the Judahites may have known by their own experience that the Assyrian eunuchs had a special devotion to the goddess, it is thinkable that the male performance of a eunuch was seen by some circles as representing foreign socioreligious influence. Furthermore, not every male with "crushed testicles" was necessarily understood as a *sārîs*.[79] Deut 23:2 does not use the word *sārîs*, perhaps to avoid restricting the proscription to a specific construct of masculinity. If this is the case, then the absolute exclusion of all kinds of men with mutilated genitalia from Yhwh's congregation in Deut 23:2 may serve as another example of the "agonistic articulation of nascent religious identity and difference" prohibiting practices that could be interpreted as signifying a devotion to a deity other than Yhwh.[80] If this is the case, the manipulation of the physical bodies of the persons in question is seen as an act of transforming their cosmic bodies in way that Deut 23:2 does not tolerate.

The man whose testicles are crushed is discussed in Deut 23:2 together with a *mamzēr*, whatever it means (the usual translation is "bastard" – whatever that means),[81] and the Ammonites and the Moabites, which places him in the same category with foreigners without necessarily implying that the man in question *is* a foreigner. The same juxtaposition appears in Isa 56:3–4, where proselytized eunuchs and foreigners appear together as being welcomed to the congregation of the worshippers of Yhwh, as if this was not their original status. This, as we have seen, requires an interpretation of the social and cosmic bodies of eunuchs and foreigners different from what Deut 23:2 implies.

The Hebrew Bible does not unequivocally recognize people comparable to the genderwise ambiguous *assinnu*, *kurgarrû* and other devotees of Ištar known from Mesopotamia.[82] Their existence had a mythological explanation, and they had a religious function in the worship of the goddess, hence their kind of masculinity had a place in the divine order. All this serves as an example of a cosmic body very different from that of the Jerusalemite priests of the Hebrew Bible. It is possible, though, that the Deuteronomic prohibition of bending or queering masculinity or femininity in the form of cross-dressing (Deut 22:5) echoes the existence and gender performance of the *assinnu* type of devotees.

Something similar has been detected in the function of the people called *qādēš* (pl. *qĕdēšîm*), "holy, consecrated." These persons were conventionally interpreted as remnants of the so-called Canaanite fertility cult in Judahite worship, a class of male homosexual cult prostitutes who probably functioned in the service of the goddess Asherah rather than Yhwh (*KJV*: 'sodomites'). Phyllis Bird has argued that this class of temple functionaries lacks any historical basis.[83] According to Bird, the *qādēš* was first created as a masculine counterpart to the feminine *qĕdēšâ* in Deut 23:18, and the other occurrences, all but one (Job 36:14) to be found in the Deuteronomistic History, are dependent on Deut 23:18. Bird argues convincingly that there is no historical evidence of male (or even female) cultic prostitution in the temple of Jerusalem.[84]

Even in the absence of any historical proof of the existence of *qĕdēšîm* as a distinct class, the religious and sexual role of the people thus designated is worth investigating as a part of the textual strategy. Precisely as a Deuteronomistic construction, the texts mentioning the *qĕdēšîm* are part of a literary context which, again, can very well be characterized as an "agonistic articulation of nascent religious identity and difference."

The sexual innuendo in the portrait of a *qādēš* comes first and foremost from Deut 23:18–19: "None of the daughters of Israel shall be a *qĕdēšâ*;

none of the sons of Israel shall be a *qādēš*. You shall not bring the fee of a prostitute or the wages of a dog into the house of the Lord your God in payment for any vow, for both of these are abhorrent (*tôʻēbâ*) to the Lord your God." The mention of the male and female *qādēš* is followed by "the fee of a prostitute and the wages of a dog," which is usually understood as characterizing their role in negative sexual terms. It used to be commonplace to interpret the "whoring" in concrete terms as cultic prostitution, but it can also be understood as a metaphor similar to that employed in the prophetic books of the Hebrew Bible, as indicating the worship of deities other than Yhwh. The economic transaction connected to the paying of vows has been understood as the fee of a woman who has prostituted herself in payment of vows;[85] it can be wondered, however, how paying vows and buying sex are imagined to happen in the case of the *qādēš*. What, in my view, matters more is that all this is called *tôʻēbâ*, the term used also in Lev 18 and 20 for transgressions of sacred borders, usually religious and sometimes (as in the case of the male-to-male intercourse discussed above) sexual with a strong religious coloring. Hence, Deut 23:18–19 uses sexual language in the context of worship, but it is not at all evident how the reader is expected to interpret the nature of the sexual activity of the *qĕdēšîm*. It is not even clear if "wages of a dog," in fact, refer to their activity at all; Phyllis Bird has recently argued for a metaphorical understanding of both the "whore" and the "dog."[86]

In other texts mentioning the *qĕdēšîm*, it is clearly the religious aspect that matters, while the sexual aspect goes entirely unmentioned. In the time of Rehoboam, according to 1 Kgs 14:24, "the *qādēš* was in the land," but nothing at all is told about his sexual function. It is important to notice, however, that the *qādēš* is mentioned immediately after the statement that the Judahites had established cult places, *maṣṣēbôt*, and *ʼăšērîm*, "on every high hill and under every green tree." This is the common phrase for the worship condemned by the Deuteronomists, but no reference is made to physical sexual activity here. Whatever is done on these cult places is, again, called *tôʻēbôt* which places the activity of the *qādēš* in the realm of the forbidden and presents his cosmic body as perverted – sexually and otherwise.

Finally, in the account of King Josiah's religious reform (2 Kgs 23:7) we are told that he broke down the houses of the *qĕdēšîm*, where the women were weaving "houses" for the goddess Asherah. This texts suggests more directly a connection with the worship of the goddess, even though the role of the *qĕdēšîm* remains as difficult to fathom as the activity of the female weavers. What is actually abolished here, and how are the women supposed to relate to the group of *qĕdēšîm*? For the purposes of this chapter, it is worth paying attention to the preceding text describing the removing and burning of the symbol of Asherah. What matters again is worship, not sexuality, especially if we abandon the long-cherished idea of the sexual depravity of the "Canaanite religion." As Bird correctly states, "the Deuteronomists, through whom alone we encounter the *qdš(ym)*, permit us no reliable access to any institutionally meaningful phenomenon behind them."[87]

Returning to the issue of masculinity, we have to put forward the question of whether the *qĕdēšîm* are at all relevant in mapping relative masculinities in the Bible. The biblical texts do not provide us with the slightest image of what kind of masculinity the *qĕdēšîm* performed and what kind of sexual activity, if any, belonged to their job description. If we want to reconstruct it anyway, all we can do is try to resort to comparative circumstantial evidence, keeping in mind that it is the religious rather than sexual aspect that characterizes the negative description of the *qādēš*. After all, the designation means "holy, consecrated," which implies a permanent religious function.

In my book *Homoeroticism in the Biblical World*, I cautiously compared the *qĕdēšîm* with the Syrian *galli*, who were called "holy" (*hieroi*), and with the Mesopotamian *assinnu*s whose logographic designation UR.SAL can be read as "dog-woman" (cf. the "wages of a dog" in Deut 23:19). If the Deuteronomists had something like this in their minds (note that the *qĕdēšîm* are presented as something foreign, "*tô'ēbôt* of the nations," 1 Kgs 14:24) – then, to quote myself, "it is possible that the *qĕdēšîm* were thought of as men who had assumed an unusual gender role and thereby expressed their lifelong dedication to a deity."[88]

At any rate, in terms of gender and religion, the texts provide us with an interesting case of unauthorized and marginalized masculinity. Historically, the *qĕdēšîm* are probably an imaginary construction, but they do feature in the Deuteronomistic texts as an example of male practitioners of a *tô'ēbâ* which, from the point of view of the religious identity advocated by the Deuteronomists, placed them into the extreme margin of the society constructed in their cultural memory. If the description of the *qĕdēšîm* really has sexual overtones in Deut 23:18–19, the most important characteristic of their sexual role is that it was wrong. In addition, associating the *qĕdēšîm* with the goddess Asherah implies an idea of the dedication to the goddess, which in sexual terms, at least metaphorically, was interpreted a quasi-sexual relationship with the goddess. This, in the eyes of the Deuteronomists, was perceived as something distinctly queer and made the *qĕdēšîm* representatives of a wrong type of "holiness"[89] and a damned kind of a cosmic body.

Conclusion: masculinities of physical, social, and cosmic bodies

I hope to have demonstrated in this chapter that masculinity in the Hebrew Bible/Old Testament is not just a unidimensional scale of different degrees of masculinity but, rather, a network of relations of physical, social, and cosmic bodies on the one hand, and hegemony, subordination, and marginalization on the other hand. The individual physical body was interpreted within a social context, and this interpretation produced the social body. Physical qualities and sexual behavior were important signifiers of masculinity, but they interacted with the person's status in the social hierarchy. The cosmic body, again, was interpreted in relation to the person's religious status, which defined his masculinity within the belief system and religious order.

When negotiating relative masculinities in the biblical texts, it makes a difference whether the man in question is a king, slave, priest, prophet, or eunuch. David and Jonathan are both given a royal and hegemonic role, Jonathan as the king's son and David as the one for who the kingship was destined. Their camaraderie is that of two equals without a distinction of sexual roles or any contamination of their physical bodies. However, since there can only be one king and the narrative gives this position to David, Jonathan's otherwise hegemonic masculinity becomes subordinate to David.

A prophet like Isaiah could walk naked and barefoot for three years, because God told him to do so (Isa 20), hence, it is his cosmic and not social body that was displayed to the people. His performance was to be interpreted as a sign and a portent in the same vein as the unmarried status of the prophet Jeremiah. Most of the time, Jeremiah's masculinity is distinctly non-hegemonic, and his social body often appears as marginalized, but all this is justified because his cosmic body functions as the vehicle of divine-human communication.

The maintenance of sacred boundaries could also push certain performances to the extreme margins of the network of relative masculinities. This is the case with the (imaginary) *qĕdēšîm*, whose performance in the cultural memory of the Deuteronomistic writers was an illegitimate transgression of sacred boundaries (*tôʿēbâ*) and, therefore, forbidden by Yhwh. Consequently, their masculinity is marginalized to the utmost and their cosmic body condemned. Similarly, the Levitical proscriptions against male-to-male intercourse condemn the cosmic body of the male persons whose physical bodies are contaminated by a forbidden fusion of hegemonic and subordinate masculinities.

Finally, the eunuchs provide an interesting example of the complexity of the network of relative masculinities. The male performance of the eunuchs seem not to have presented a problem in the case of *sārîsîm* who occupied high positions in the royal court, hence their social body was authorized by the social hierarchy in spite of the appearance of their physical body which, from the point of view of the priestly ideology, made their cosmic body intolerable. The image of the eunuchs, therefore, depends on which text we are reading. In some texts the cosmic body of the eunuchs is abhorred, while in others, their cosmic body, together with their marginalized masculinity, is rehabilitated, and in yet another texts, they form an integral part of the male-dominated imperial hegemony.

Notes

1 Burrus (2007, 4).
2 See, e.g., Gleason (1995); Moore and Anderson (ed.) (2003); Rosen and Sluiter (ed.) (2003); Conway (2008); Krondorfer (ed.) (2009); Williams (2010, 130–176).

3 See especially Creangă (ed.) (2010) and Creangă and Smit (ed.) (2014); cf. Clines (1995) and (2002); Washington (1997); Chapman (2004).
4 Burrus (2007).
5 Connell (2005, 67–86).
6 Connell (2005, 80–81); emphasis original.
7 Launderville (2010, 252).
8 See Asikainen (2014, 181–183); Nissinen (2014: 275–276).
9 Connell (2005, 72, 81).
10 For ancient Near Eastern expressions of the masculinity-femininity divide, see the article of Joan Westenholz and Ilona Zsolnay in this volume and cf., e.g., Asher-Greve (1998); Zsolnay (2009).
11 Burrus (2007, 4).
12 Halperin (1990, 35).
13 Connell (2005, 79).
14 United States Navy recruiting poster from 1917 (www.lilesnet.com/ourmilitary/navy/recruiting.htm).
15 For the dichotomy of *zākār* and *nĕqēbâ*, see Mark Brettler in this volume.
16 Burrus (2007, 6).
17 As Michel Foucault has shown, the idea of an individual "sexuality" as a deep-seated domain in human body and mind is essentially the product of the sexological research of the nineteenth century CE; see Foucault (1978).
18 For the significance of procreation, especially of producing a male child, as a means of perpetuating one's name, see Wright (2011).
19 Cf. Halperin (1990, 29–38).
20 For these chapters from the point of view of sexual transgression, see, e.g., Lipka (2006, 49–62).
21 Both texts mention two kinds of women: those who have experienced the *miškab zākār*, and those who have not, i.e., the virgins.
22 MAL A §20: "If a man has sex with his comrade and they prove the charges against him and find him guilty, they shall have sex with him and they shall turn him into a eunuch (*ana ša rēšēn utarrūš*)." The "comrade" (*tappā'u*) means a person of the same social standing. See my analysis in Nissinen (1998, 24–28); cf. Cooper (2002, 82–85).
23 For *tô'ēbâ*, see, e.g., Lipka (2006, 253–254).
24 The last couple of decades have seen a profusion of literature on the homoerotic traits of the relationship of David and Jonathan; see, e.g., Schroer and Staubli (1996); Nissinen (1999); Ackerman (2005, 151–231); Römer and Bonjour (2005, 61–102); Heacock (2010); Harding (2013).
25 See Harding (2013, 274–365).
26 Thus Römer and Bonjour (2005, 79).
27 The question whether or not the relationship of David and Jonathan is to be interpreted as "homosexual" has led to an anachronistic imposition of the concept of homosexuality onto the narrative ignorant of modern categories of human sexuality; however, even when this is acknowledged, it has turned out to be difficult to become altogether free from such transfers of meaning; cf. the criticism of Nissinen and Ackerman by Stone (2001) and Heacock (2007). An alternative focus on the text is provided by queer reading that aims at deconstructing heteronormative presuppositions and challenging the unspoken norm of hegemonic masculinity in the reading of biblical texts.
28 For these interpretations, see Heacock (2010, 49–55).
29 Heacock (2010, 144).
30 Heacock (2010, 144).
31 Ackerman (2005, 222). In Ackerman's reading, the narrative aims at feminizing Jonathan, who assumes a wifelike role, hence making him unworthy of

the kingship which now belongs to David; cf. my review of Ackerman's book (Nissinen 2007) for an argument against Jonathan's feminization.

32 Ackerman (2005, 217).

33 See Chapman (2004, 20–59).

34 See Connell (2005, 71–74).

35 Asher-Greve (1998, 28).

36 See Huffmon (2002); Davis (2010); Launderville (2010, 375–384).

37 Thus Huffmon (2002, 246–250).

38 For queering Jeremiah, see Macwilliam (2002).

39 To be sure, enough aggressive and abusive language has been found in the book of Jeremiah to make the prophet a proponent of male dominance (Davis 2010, 200). However, this language typically belongs to the divine discourse, hence representing God's, rather than Jeremiah's, masculinity.

40 For the divine-human gender matrix, see Carr and Conway (2008). See also Davis (2010, 206): "While the specific roots of Jeremiah's reputation for lament remain obscure and speculative, [. . .] this aspect of the prophet's persona is most plausibly informed by the feminine imagery supplied from the Book of Lamentations, and it is ascribed to Jeremiah through personification of the nation of Judah and its reflection on the destruction of Jerusalem."

41 Launderville (2010, 395).

42 Even the he-man's masculinity is subordinate in relation to God; cf. Haddox (2010, 15): "While the biblical text in many ways reflects and supports the categories of hegemonic masculinity, in the realm of the relation with God, these norms are frequently subverted, because no human can assume the position of ultimate power. That position is left to God."

43 Burrus (2007, 7).

44 Connell (2005, 71).

45 Cf, e.g., the double downgrading of the blind and the lame in 2 Sam 5:6–8. For disability and masculinity, see Hentrich (2007); Strimple and Creangă (2010).

46 See, e.g., Bullough (2002); Lightfoot (2002). It is noteworthy that, as far as I have been able to observe, the act of castration as the method of eunuch-making is not mentioned in the ancient sources before Herodotos 8:105: "Now among the many whom Panionius had castrated (*exetame*) in the way of trade was Hermotimus, who was not in all things unfortunate; for he was brought from Sardis among other gifts to the king, and as time went on he stood higher in Xerxes' favour than any other eunuch." Cf. Herodotos 6:32: ". . . for when they [scil. the Persians] had gained the mastery over the cities, they chose out the comeliest boys and castrated them (*exetamnon*), making them eunuchs instead of men . . ."

47 Burke (2011, 181): "The inability to stabilize the gender of such eunuchs troubled the boundaries between the categories of male and female."

48 Some commentators understand the Greek word *eunoukhos* as a childless man rather than a eunuch (e.g., Hübner 1999, 57), but I see no reason not to read the word in its usual meaning.

49 In fact, castrated men can sometimes achieve a functional erection. Greenstein, Plymate, and Katz (1995) demonstrated that, while castration is generally associated with marked decrease in libido and erectile function, 25 percent of their patients who were castrated surgically for prostatic cancer responded to visual erotic stimulation with functional erection.

50 Cf. Olyan (2008, 33).

51 Olyan (2008, 35): "Restrictive cultic texts such as Lev 21:17–23, Deut 23:2 (Eng. 1), and 2 Sam 5:8b, texts that seek to separate persons with "defects" from the deity's presence to a greater or lesser degree, may well assume the idea that Yhwh despises such persons, even though it is not stated explicitly."

52 To be sure, eunuchs seem often (but not exclusively) to have been recruited from among foreigners, possibly in Assyria (cf. Grayson [1995, 95]; Julia Assante in this volume), and probably in Persia (cf. Llewellyn-Jones 2002, 33). Herodotos (3.92) says the Persians imported five hundred boy-eunuchs from Babylonia and Assyria in the reign of Darius I.

53 Isa 56:3–5 is often read as directly challenging Deut 23:2 (thus, e.g., Olyan 2008, 28; Launderville 2010, 322); however, Wright and Chan (2012, 100–102) demonstrate the different scope of the two texts, arguing that the authors of Isa 56:3–5 did not have Deut 23:2 in view. Nevertheless, "[t]his combination of the issues of ethnicity and physical integrity makes Deut. 23.2–9 and Isa. 56.3–8 close parallels" (Schramm 1995, 124).

54 Cf. Schramm (1995, 124–125 n. 6). A part of the pun is that *yad* can also mean a standing stone, a 'memorial'; see the archaeological and iconographic analysis of de Hulster (2009, 144–168).

55 Wright and Chan (2012, 119).

56 Burrus (2007, 8).

57 Connell (2005, 80–81) (emphasis original).

58 See, e.g., Grayson (1995); Radner (1997, 155–157); Tadmor (1998, 2002); Deller (1999); Mattila (2000); Bonatz (2008); Wright and Chan (2012); Julia Assante in this volume.

59 E.g., Dalley (2001), according to whom *ša rēši* refers to eunuch only in the late phase of the Assyrian empire; and Siddall (2007), according to whom "the firm connection between the title *ša rēši* and court eunuchs is not as concrete as often indicated" (p. 225); similarly Pirngruber (2011), who argues against the routine equation of *ša rēši* with a "eunuch." Cf. also *AHw* 974 ("keine Eunuchen!") and *CAD* R 296.

60 Cf. Pirngruber (2011, 292). Given the context, I remain unconvinced that this would mean turning the person over to the *ša rēši* officials, as suggested by Dalley (2001, 200–201); cf. Siddall (2007, 228).

61 Watanabe (1999, 317–319).

62 Postgate (1976) nr. 9:14 (= ND 3426:14) mentions the sons and grandsons of Šamaš-šarru-uṣur identified as a *ša rēši* on line 6; see also Pirngruber (2011, 305).

63 See the inventory in Watanabe (1999, 324–331). For more depictions of beardless men in Assyrian art, see Bonatz (2008).

64 Of the eighty-eight seals discussed by Watanabe, eighteen are bearing a readable inscription. One seal shows a bearded worshipper together with a beardless one. "So far, however, there are no seals of *ša rēši* which have depictions of only bearded worshippers without any beardless ones" (Watanabe 1999, 319).

65 Cf. *rab-sārîs* as an equivalent of the Akkadian *rab ša-rēši* in 2 Kgs 18:17; Jer 39:3, 13. Even in postbiblical texts, both Hebrew and Aramaic use a verb *srs* (derived from the noun *sārîs*) to denote castration or causing impotence. See Jastrow (1926, 1028–1029).

66 Tadmor (1998, 324).

67 See *LSJ* ad loc. It has been argued that the word *eunoukhos* does not always refer to a castrated male but can be used as a professional title of a high official (see, e.g., Pirngruber 2011, 279, 309); however, as in the case of the *ša rēši*, whenever the use of the word reveals anything about its bearers' sexuality, it evokes a castrated male. See Burke (2011, 178), who has not found "one example in Greek texts from the fifth century BCE to the second century CE or in Greek-Jewish texts from the second century BCE to the first century CE in which *eunoukhos* was used to refer to a person who was *clearly not* castrated" (emphasis original).

68 Only in Jer 34:19 (LXX 41:19) and in 1 Chr 28:1, *sārîsîm* seem to be rendered with *dynastas*, but in both cases the translation is so far from the MT that it

cannot be taken for certain which word actually stood in the Hebrew *Vorlage* of the LXX.

69 Assyrian: Grayson (1995); Deller (1999); Mattila (2000); Tadmor (2002); Bonatz (2008, 133–138); Launderville (2010, 339–345). – Persian: Briant (2002, 268–277); Llewellyn-Jones (2002); Launderville (2010, 339–345); Pirngruber (2011, 280–284). – Hittite: Hawkins (2002).

70 On the women's quarters, see Svärd (2015, 109–120).

71 Cf. Llewellyn-Jones (2002); Launderville (2010, 343–345).

72 See Svärd (2015, 72–73).

73 See Mattila (2000, 61–76, 131, 153–154).

74 For Sin-šumu-lešir, see Mattila (2000, 64; 2002, 1148).

75 I agree with Everhart (2002, 143): "Translating all instances of biblical *sārîs* with the English term 'eunuch' is faithful to the historical evidence and allows the eunuch's unique status to emerge."

76 Thus Everhart (2002).

77 Wright and Chan (2012, 118).

78 Burrus (2007, 9–10).

79 Wright and Chan (2012, 101).

80 For the devotion of Assyrian eunuchs to Ištar and other goddesses, see Watanabe (1999, 322–323).

81 In the Hebrew Bible, the word may be a "quasi-gentilic for a non-Judean" (*DCH* 5: 330). The Septuagint translates it as *allogenēs* in Zech 9:6, and as *ek pornēs* in Deut 23:3 (cf. Vulgate: *mamzer hoc est de scorto natus*). The latter translation seems to designate a person born as a result of illicit sexual act or, perhaps, a mixed marriage.

82 For the *assinnu*, *kurgarrû*, and other similar devotees of the Goddess, see, e.g., Nissinen (1998, 28–33); Gabbay (2008); Teppo (2008); Assante (2009, 34–49).

83 Bird (1997).

84 For recent criticism of the idea of "cult/temple prostitution" as belonging to an oriental or Canaanite "fertility cult," and its alleged traces in the Hebrew Bible, see also Stark (2006); Assante (2009); Wacker (2009).

85 Cf. van der Toorn (1989).

86 Bird (2015: 362): " 'Harlot's wage' and 'price of a dog' do not tell us in any specific terms what the prohibited sources of income are, but brand a class of revenue as unacceptable by identification with common symbols of dishonor and disgust." See also Stark (2006, 156–160); cf. Wacker (2009, 72).

87 Bird (1997, 74); cf. Stark (2006, 147).

88 Nissinen (1998, 41).

89 I agree with Brodsky (2006, 96), according to whom "we are not dealing with a dichotomy between the realms of the sacred and the profane, (. . .) so much as we are dealing with a dichotomy within the sacred itself. Within the aspect of the sacred lies the possibility for its equally potent opposite. The opposite of the holy is not the unholy but the 'anti-holy.' "

Bibliography

Ackerman, Susan. 2005. *When Heroes Love: The Ambiguity of Eros in the Stories of Gilgamesh and David*. New York: Columbia University Press.

Asher-Greve, Julia M. 1998. The Essential Body: Mesopotamian Concepts of the Gendered Body. Pages 8–37 in *Gender and the Body in the Ancient Mediterranean*. Edited by Maria Wyke. Oxford: Blackwell.

Asikainen, Susanna. 2014. "Eunuchs for the Kingdom of Heaven": Matthew and Subordinated Masculinities. Pages 156–188 in *Biblical Masculinities Foregrounded*.

Edited by Ovidiu Creangă and Peter-Ben Smit. Hebrew Bible Monographs 62. Sheffield: Sheffield Phoenix Press.

Assante, Julia. 2009. Bad Girls and Kinky Boys? The Modern Prostituting of Ishtar, Her Clergy and Her Cults. Pages 23–54 in *Tempelprostitution im Altertum: Fakten und Fiktionen*. Edited by Tanja S. Scheer. Oikumene: Studien zur antiken Weltgeschichte 6. Oldenburg: Verlag Antike.

Bird, Phyllis. 1997. The End of the Male Cult Prostitute: A Literary-Historical and Sociological Analysis of Hebrew *qādēš-qĕdēšîm*. Pages 37–80 in *Congress Volume Cambridge 1995*. Edited by J. A. Emerton. Supplements to Vetus Testamentum 66. Leiden: Brill.

———. 2015. Of Whores and Hounds: A New Interpretation of the Subject of Deuteronomy 23:19. *Vetus Testamentum* 65: 352–364.

Bonatz, Dominik. 2008. Bartlos in Assyrien: Ein kulturanthropologisches Phänomen aus Sicht der Bilder. Pages 131–153 in *Fundstellen: Gesammelte Schriften zur Archäologie und Geschichte Altvorderasiens ad honorem Hartmut Kühne*. Edited by Dominik Bonatz, Rainer M. Czichon, and F. Janoscha Kreppner. Wiesbaden: Harrassowitz Verlag.

Briant, Pierre. 2002. *From Cyrus to Alexander: A History of the Persian Empire*. Translated by Peter T. Daniels. Winona Lake, IN: Eisenbrauns.

Brodsky, David. 2006. *A Bride without a Blessing: A Study in the Redaction and Content of Massekhet Kallah and Its Gemara*. Texts and Studies in Ancient Judaism 118. Tübingen: Mohr Siebeck.

Bullough, Vern L. 2002. Eunuchs in History and Society. Pages 1–17 in *Eunuchs in Antiquity and Beyond*. Edited by Shaun Tougher. London: Classical Press of Wales and Duckworth.

Burke, Sean D. 2011. Queering Early Christian Discourse: The Ethiopian Eunuch. Pages 175–189 in *Bible Trouble: Queer Reading at the Boundaries of Biblical Scholarship*. Edited by Teresa J. Hornsby and Ken Stone. Society of Biblical Literature Semeia Studies 67. Atlanta: Society of Biblical Literature.

Burrus, Victoria. 2007. Mapping as Metamorphosis: Initial Reflections on Gender and Ancient Religious Discourses. Pages 1–10 in *Mapping Gender in Ancient Religious Discourses*. Edited by Todd Penner and Carolne Vander Stichele. Biblical Interpretation Series 84. Atlanta: Society of Biblical Literature.

Carr, David M., and Colleen M. Conway. 2008. The Divine-Human Marriage Matrix and Constructions of Gender and "Bodies" in the Christian Bible. Pages 275–303 in *Sacred Marriages: The Divine-Human Sexual Metaphor from Sumer to Early Christianity*. Edited by Martti Nissinen and Risto Uro. Winona Lake, IN: Eisenbrauns.

Chapman, Cynthia R. 2004. *The Gendered Language of Warfare in the Israelite-Assyrian Encounter*. Harvard Semitic Monographs 62. Winona Lake, IN: Eisenbrauns.

Clines, David J. A. 1995. David the Man: The Construction of Masculinity in the Hebrew Bible. Pages 212–243 in *Interested Parties: The Ideology of Writers and Readers of the Hebrew Bible*. Edited by David J. A. Clines. Journal for the Study of the Old Testament Supplement Series 205. Sheffield: Sheffield Academic Press.

———. 2002. He-Prophets: Masculinity as a Problem for the Hebrew Prophets and their Interpreters. Pages 311–328 in *Sense and Sensitivity: Essays on Reading the Bible in Memory of Robert Carroll*. Edited by Alastair G. Hunter and Philip R. Davies. Journal for the Study of the Old Testament Supplement Series 348; Sheffield: Sheffield Academic Press.

Connell R. W. 2005. *Masculinities*. Second edition. Berkeley: University of California Press.

Conway, Colleen M. 2008. *Behold the Man: Jesus and Greco-Roman Masculinity*. Oxford: Oxford University Press.

Cooper, Jerrold S. 2002. Buddies in Babylonia: Gilgamesh, Enkidu, and Mesopotamian Homosexuality. Pages 73–85 in *Riches Hidden in Secret Places: Ancient Near Eastern Studies in Memory of Thorkild Jacobsen*. Edited by Tzvi Abusch. Winona Lake, IN: Eisenbrauns.

Creangă, Ovidiu, ed., 2010. *Men and Masculinity in the Hebrew Bible and Beyond*. The Bible in the Modern World 33. Sheffield: Sheffield Phoenix Press.

Creangă, Ovidiu, and Peter-Ben Smit, ed. 2014 *Biblical Masculinities Foregrounded*. Hebrew Bible Monographs 62. Sheffield: Sheffield Phoenix Press.

Dalley, Stephanie. 2001. Review of Raija Mattila, *The King's Magnates: A Study of the Highest Officials of the Neo-Assyrian Empire*. *Bibliotheca Orientalis* 58:197–206.

Davis, Patrick C. J. 2010. Jeremiah, Masculinity and His Portrayal as the "Lamenting Prophet." Pages 189–210 in *Men and Masculinity in the Hebrew Bible and Beyond*. Edited by Ovidiu Creangă. The Bible in the Modern World 33. Sheffield: Sheffield Phoenix Press.

de Hulster, Izaak J. 2009. *Iconographic Exegesis and Third Isaiah*. Forschungen zum Alten Testament II/36. Tübingen: Mohr Siebeck.

Deller, Karlheinz. 1999. The Assyrian Eunuchs and Their Predecessors. Pages 303–311 in *Priests and Officials in the Ancient Near East: Papers of the Second Colloquium on the Ancient Near East – The City and Its Life Held at the Middle Eastern Culture Center in Japan (Mitaka, Tokyo) March 22–24, 1996*. Edited by Kazuko Watanabe. Heidelberg: Universitätsverlag C. Winter.

Everhart, Janet. 2002. Hidden Eunuchs of the Hebrew Bible. *Society of Biblical Literature 2002 Seminar Papers*. Society of Biblical Literature Seminar Papers Series 41. Atlanta: Society of Biblical Literature.

Foucault, Michel. 1978. *The History of Sexuality*, Vol. 1: *An Introduction*. Translated by Robert Hurley. New York: Vintage Books.

Gabbay, Uri. 2008. The Akkadian Word for 'Third Gender': The *kalû* (gala) Once Again. Pages 49–56 in *Proceedings of the 51st Rencontre Assyriologique Internationale Held at the Oriental Institute of Chicago, July 18–22, 2005*. Edited by Robert D. Biggs, Jennie Myers, and Martha T. Roth. The Oriental Institute of the University of Chicago Studies in Ancient Oriental Civilizations 62. Chicago: The Oriental Institute.

Gleason, Maud W. 1995. *Making Men: Sophists and Self-Presentation in Ancient Rome*. Princeton: Princeton University Press.

Grayson, A. Kirk. 1995. Eunuchs in Power: Their Role in Assyrian Bureaucracy. Pages 85–98 in *Vom Alten Orient zum Alten Testament: Festschrift für Wolfram Freiherr von Soden zum 85. Geburtstag am 19. Juni 1993*. Edited by Manfried Dietrich and Oswald Loretz. Alter Orient und Altes Testament 240. Kevelaer: Butzon and Bercker and Neukirchen-Vluyn: Neukirchener Verlag.

Greenstein, Alexander, Stephen R. Plymate, and P. Gary Katz. 1995. Visually Stimulated Erection in Castrated Men. *Journal of Urology* 153: 650–652.

Haddox, Susan E. 2010. Favoured Sons and Subordinate Masculinities. Pages 2–19 in *Men and Masculinity in the Hebrew Bible and Beyond*. Edited by Ovidiu Creangă. The Bible in the Modern World 33. Sheffield: Sheffield Phoenix Press.

Halperin, David M. 1990. *One Hundred Years of Homosexuality and Other Essays on Greek Love*. New York: Routledge.

Harding, James E. 2013. *The Love of David and Jonathan: Ideology, Text, Reception*. BibleWorld. Sheffield: Equinox.

Hawkins, J. D. 2002. Eunuchs among Hittites. Pages 217–233 in *Sex and Gender in the Ancient Near East: Proceedings of the 47th Rencontre Assyriologique Internationale, Helsinki, July 2–6, 2001*. Edited by Simo Parpola and Robert M. Whiting. Helsinki: The Neo-Assyrian Text Corpus Project.

Heacock, Anthony. 2007. Wrongly Framed? The "David and Jonathan Narrative" and the Writing of Biblical Homosexuality (sic), *The Bible and Critical Theory* (www.epress.monash.edu/bc).

———. 2010. *Jonathan Loved David: Manly Love in the Bible and the Hermeneutics of Sex*. The Bible in the Modern World 22. Sheffield: Sheffield Phoenix Press

Hentrich, Thomas. 2007. Masculinity and Disability in the Hebrew Bible. Pages 73–87 in *This Abled Body: Rethinking Disabilities in Biblical Studies*. Edited by Hector Avalos, Sarah J. Melcher, and Jeremy Schipper. Semeia Studies 55. Atlanta: Society of Biblical Literature.

Hübner, Hans. 1999. *Die Weisheit Salomos*. Das Alte Testament Deutsch, Apokryphen 4. Göttingen: Vandenhoeck & Ruprecht.

Huffmon, Herbert B. 2002. Gender Subversion in the Book of Jeremiah. Pages 245–253 in *Sex and Gender in the Ancient Near East: Proceedings of the 47th Rencontre Assyriologique Internationale, Helsinki, July 2–6, 2001*. Edited by Simo Parpola and Robert M. Whiting. Helsinki: The Neo-Assyrian Text Corpus Project.

Jastrow, Marcus. 1926. *A Dictionary of the Targumim, the Talmud Babli and Yerushalmi, and the Midrashic Literature*. New York: Traditional Press.

Krondorfer, Björn, ed. 2009. *Men and Masculinities in Christianity and Judaism: A Critical Reader*. London: SCM Press.

Launderville, Dale. 2010. *Celibacy in the Ancient World: Its Ideal and Practice in Pre-Hellenistic Israel, Mesopotamia, and Greece*. Collegeville: MN: Liturgical Press.

Lightfoot, J. L. 2002. Sacred Eunuchism in the Cult of the Syrian Goddess. Pages 71–86 in *Eunuchs in Antiquity and Beyond*. Edited by Shaun Tougher. London: Classical Press of Wales and Duckworth.

Lipka, Hilary. 2006. *Sexual Transgression in the Hebrew Bible*. Hebrew Bible Monographs 7. Sheffield: Sheffield Phoenix Press.

Llewellyn-Jones, Lloyd. 2002. Eunuchs and the Royal Harem in Achaemenid Persia (559–331 BC). Pages 19–49 in *Eunuchs in Antiquity and Beyond*. Edited by Shaun Tougher. London: Classical Press of Wales and Duckworth.

Macwilliam, Stuart. 2002. Queering Jeremiah. *Biblical Interpretation* 10: 384–404.

Mattila, Raija. 2000. *The King's Magnates: A Study of the Highest Officials of the Neo-Assyrian Empire*. State Archives of Assyria Studies 11. Helsinki: The Neo-Assyrian Text Corpus Project.

———. 2002. Sīn-šumu-lēšir. Page 1148 in *The Prosopography of the Neo-Assyrian Empire*, Volume 3, Part I. Edited by Heather D. Baker. Helsinki: The Neo-Assyrian Text Corpus Project.

Moore, Stephen D., and Janice Capel Anderson, ed. 2003. *New Testament Masculinities*. Semeia Studies 45. Atlanta: Society of Biblical Literature.

Nissinen, Martti. 1998. *Homoeroticism in the Biblical World: A Historical Perspective*. Translated by Kirsi Stjerna. Minneapolis: Fortress Press.

———. 1999. Die Liebe von David und Jonathan als Frage der modernen Exegese. *Biblica* 80: 250–263.
———. 2007. Review of Susan Ackerman, *When Heroes Love. Journal of the History of Sexuality* 16: 307–312.
———. 2014. Biblical Masculinities: Musings on Theory and Agenda. Pages 271–285 in *Biblical Masculinities Foregrounded*. Edited by Ovidiu Creangă and Peter-Ben Smit. Hebrew Bible Monographs 62. Sheffield: Sheffield Phoenix Press.
Olyan, Saul M. 2008. *Disability in the Hebrew Bible: Interpreting Mental and Physical Differences*. Cambridge, UK: Cambridge University Press.
Pirngruber, Reinhard. 2011. Eunuchen am Königshof: Ktesias und die altorientalische Evidenz. Pages 279–312 in *Ktesias' Welt/Ctesias' World*. Edited by Josef Wiesehöfer, Robert Rollinger, and Giovanni B. Lanfranchi. Wiesbaden: Harrassowitz.
Postgate, J. N. 1976. *Fifty Neo-Assyrian Legal Documents*. Warminster: Aris & Phillips.
Radner, Karen. 1997. *Die neuassyrischen Privatrechtsurkunden als Quelle für Mensch und Umwelt*. State Archives of Assyria Studies 6. Helsinki: The Neo-Assyrian Text Corpus Project.
Römer, Thomas, and Loyse Bonjour. 2005. *L'homosexualité dans le Proche-Orient ancien et la Bible*. Essais bibliques 37. Geneva: Labor et fides.
Rosen, Ralph M., and Ineke Sluiter, ed. 2003. *Andreia: Studies in Manliness and Courage in Classical Antiquity*. Mnemosyne Supplement Series 238. Leiden: Brill.
Schramm, Brooks. 1995. *The Opponents of Third Isaiah: Reconstructing the Cultic History of the Restoration*. Journal for the Study of the Old Testament Supplement Series 193. Sheffield: Sheffield Academic Press.
Schroer, Silvia, and Thomas Staubli. 1996. Saul, David und Jonathan – eine Dreiecksgeschichte? Ein Beitrag zum Thema "Homosexualität im Ersten Testament. *Bibel und Kirche* 51: 15–22.
Siddall, Luis R. 2007. A Re-examination of the Title *ša rēši* in the Neo-Assyrian Period. Pages 225–240 in *Gilgameš and the World of Assyria: Proceedings of the Conference Held at Mandelbaum House, the University of Sydney, July 21–23, 2004*. Edited by Joseph Azize and Noel Weeks. Ancient Near Eastern Studies Supplement 21. Leuven: Peeters.
Stark Christine. 2006. *"Kultprostitution" im Alten Testament? Die* Qedeschen *der Hebräischen Bibel und das Motiv der Hurerei*. Orbis Biblicus et Orientalis 221. Fribourg: Academic Press and Göttingen: Vandenhoeck & Ruprecht.
Stone, Ken. 2001. Homosexuality and Bible or Queer Reading: A Response to Martti Nissinen. *Theology and Sexuality* 14:107–118.
Strimple, Cheryl, and Ovidiu Creangă. 2010. "And His Skin Returned Like a Skin of a Little Boy": Masculinity, Disability and the Healing of Naaman. Pages 110–126 in *Men and Masculinity in the Hebrew Bible and Beyond*. Edited by Ovidiu Creangă. The Bible in the Modern World 33. Sheffield: Sheffield Phoenix Press.
Svärd (Teppo), Saana. 2008. Sacred Marriage and the Devotees of Ištar. Pages 75–92 in *Sacred Marriages: The Divine-Human Sexual Metaphor from Sumer to Early Christianity*. Edited by Martti Nissinen and Risto Uro. Winona Lake, IN: Eisenbrauns.
———. 2015. *Women and Power in Neo-Assyrian Palaces*. State Archives of Assyria Studies 23. Helsinki: The Neo-Assyrian Text Corpus Project.
Tadmor, Hayim. 1998. Was the Biblical *sārîs* a Eunuch? Pages 317–325 in *Solving Riddles and Untying Knots: Biblical, Epigraphic, and Semitic Studies in Honor of*

Jonas C. Greenfield. Edited by Ziony Zevit, Seymour Gitin, and Michael Sokoloff. Winona Lake, IN: Eisenbrauns.

———. 2002. The Role of the Chief Eunuch and the Place of Eunuchs in the Assyrian Empire. Pages 603–611 in *Sex and Gender in the Ancient Near East: Proceedings of the 47th Rencontre Assyriologique Internationale, Helsinki, July 2–6, 2001*. Edited by Simo Parpola and Robert M. Whiting. Helsinki: The Neo-Assyrian Text Corpus Project.

Tougher, Shaun, ed. 2002. *Eunuchs in Antiquity and Beyond*. London: Classical Press of Wales and Duckworth.

van der Toorn, Karel. 1989. Female Prostitution in Payment of Vows in Ancient Israel. *Journal of Biblical Literature* 108: 193–205.

Wacker, Marie-Theres. 2009. "Kultprostitution" im Alten Israel?: Forschungsmythen, Spuren, Thesen. Pages 55–84 in *Tempelprostitution im Altertum: Fakten und Fiktionen*. Edited by Tanja S. Scheer. Oikumene: Studien zur antiken Weltgeschichte 6. Oldenburg: Verlag Antike.

Washington, Harold C. 1997. Violence and the Construction of Gender in the Hebrew Bible: A New Historicist Approach. *Biblical Interpretation* 5: 324–363.

Watanabe, Kazuko. 1999. Seals of Neo-Assyrian Officials. Pages 313–366 in *Priests and Officials in the Ancient Near East: Papers of the Second Colloquium on the Ancient Near East – The City and Its Life Held at the Middle Eastern Culture Center in Japan (Mitaka, Tokyo) March 22–24, 1996*. Edited by Kazuko Watanabe. Heidelberg: Universitätsverlag C. Winter.

Williams, Craig A. 2010. *Roman Homosexuality*. Second edition. Oxford: Oxford University Press.

Wright, Jacob L. 2011. Making a Name for Oneself: Martial Valor, Heroic Death, and Procreation in the Hebrew Bible. *Journal for the Study of the Old Testament* 36: 131–162.

Wright, Jacob L., and Michael J. Chan. 2012. King and Eunuch: Isaiah 56:1–8 in Light of Honorific Royal Burial Practices. *Journal of Biblical Literature* 131: 99–119.

Zsolnay, Ilona. 2009. Do Divine Structures of Gender Mirror Mortal Structures of Gender? Pages 85–120 in *In the Wake of Tikva Frymer-Kensky*. Edited by Steven Holloway, JoAnn Scurlock, and Richard Beal. Gorgias Précis Portfolios 4. Piscataway, NJ: Gorgias Press.

10 The masculinity of male angels on the make

Genesis 6:1–4 in early nineteenth-century Gothic imagination[1]

Steven W. Holloway

This chapter is an exercise in the reception history of the English Bible that treats four poetic compositions penned between 1813 and 1823, and six illustrations created between the 1790s and 1860. Our beacon is the notorious Genesis 6:1–4. Despite the fact that the first full translation of *First Enoch* into a modern European language was published in 1821, and a tangible fascination with those parts of the work already available had gripped the British imagination years earlier, all of the many literary and visual incarnations of Enoch focused on the aforementioned male-angel female-human "gallantries," so I feel justified in treating the Enochian artistic renditions as at base a concern with, and exposition of, the biblical text.

The gendered assimilation of Judeo-Christian "angels" in Victorian-era art to the subordinationist ideal of the wife as "the angel in the house" (Coventry Patmore ballad, 1854) pushed popular iconography toward the familiar prepubescent and epicene entities mass marketed as hand-tinted lithographs by the Currier & Ives New York City studio (1834–1907). During the years between 1813 and 1823 in Hanoverian England, however, angels as literary and visual presences regularly assimilated masculine and even hypermasculine characteristics. As a conceptual grid upon which our angelic masculinities can be analyzed, we will map them against the categories of the classical hero, the chivalrous knight, the *paterfamilias*, and the warrior.[2]

Genesis 6:1–4 and the Romantic poets

Genesis 6:1–4 in its doctrinal 19th-century context: the contemporary exegetical imagination was as parched as the Sahara desert. In scouring various commentaries, universal histories, and preaching helps, I encountered a total of four shopworn options for the passage:

1 the enigmatic *bĕnê hā-'ĕlōhîm* are the god-fearing descendants of Seth, whereas the *bĕnôt hā-'ādām* stem from the wicked Cain (Pseudo-Clementine *Recognitiones*, Chrysostom, Cyril of Alexandria, Theodoret);[3]
2 the sons of God are angels (Book of Enoch, LXX, Palestinian Targums, Philo, Josephus, the earliest Church Fathers);[4]

3 the sons of God are members of the nobility, the daughters of men are "the people of the land" (Targum Onkelos, Greek Symmachus, Samaritan Bible, fairly consistent rabbinic interpretation);[5]
4 the expressions "sons of God" and "daughters of men" are figures of speech meaning nothing more than "human beings" (an early Christian denationalization of the rabbinic reading of "sons of God" as shorthand for "Israel").[6]

Barring odd flights of fancy, like Henry Rawlinson's imagined parallel between the biblical passage and a cuneiform text "demonstrating" that the fall of man was due to negritude, that's it in a nutshell;[7] it is pointless to rehash the circular arguments undergirding these ancient exegetical positions.[8] Whereas the British exegetical imagination went catatonic over Genesis 6:1–4, poetic fancy took dizzying flight. From 1813 to 1823, no fewer than five major poems concerning the antediluvian misadventures of Genesis 6 appeared, uncorking a veritable deluge of review articles, satires, sermons, a renewed theological interest in angelology, and literary imitations on the Continent.

In 1813 the Scottish poet and hymn-writer James Montgomery (1771–1854) published *The World before the Flood, a Poem, in Ten Cantos*. A child of Moravian missionaries, Montgomery, with an extensive collection of poetry written by his 15th birthday, chafed under parochial education and ran away, ultimately securing the editorship of the *Sheffield Iris*, a newspaper whose sometimes radical views twice landed Montgomery in jail for sedition. A tireless sponsor of social justice issues in Sheffield, he moved freely between the Baptist, Methodist, and Anglican churches of the city, and was readmitted to Moravian fellowship in 1814. The publication of *The Wanderer of Switzerland and other Poems* in 1806 gained Montgomery fulsome praise from Robert Southey and young Lord Byron, and succeeded in bringing Montgomery to public attention. His poetry is rarely anthologized today, and few outside of English literature researchers care to plow through the 200 pages of *The World before the Flood*, but he was a poet rockstar in his age, constantly sought-after on the lecture circuit and as a periodical reviewer.[9]

The World before the Flood, at 200 pages of heroic couplets, whisks the reader into a sphere of lush bowers, antediluvian biography, savage giants, and Christological prophetic narrative only tenuously related to Genesis 6:1–4. The poem begins *in medias res* with the tale of Javan, the master bard of the Cainites, adopted by holy Enoch and raised in the blessed land surrounding the approaches to the forbidden Garden of Eden. The warlike Cainites, having subdued the entire world save for the defenseless pocket of Patriarchs who dwell near the tomb of Adam and Eve, prepare their anti-conquest of Ur-Canaan even as Javan, who had earlier won fame among the giants, returns to the fount of his spiritual nativity. "What the world needs now, is love, sweet love" crooned the Burt Bacharach melody from the 1960s, and indeed *The World before the Flood* turns upon the spiritual ascent of Javan, from his carnal (and unconsummated) love for Zillah, to his allegiance to the Patriarchal clan through corporate love, to the vision of divine love that bloodlessly liberates the Patriarchs even as it compels the thwarted race of giants into a suicidal assault on the angelically fortified Garden of Eden.

> Early and joyful, o'er the dewy grass,
> Straight to their glen the ransom'd Patriarchs pass;
> As doves released their parent-dwelling find,
> They fly for life, not cast a look behind;
> And when they reach'd the dear sequester'd spot,
> Enoch alone of all their train "*was not*."[10]

A sustained effort to revive the Miltonian Restoration biblical epic, Montgomery's theologically innocuous poem eschewed concupiscent angels or any overtly titillating allusion to sensual love. Montgomery's Moravian heritage is probably responsible for his keeping the manly weapons of war out of the hands of Enoch & Company, whereas "good" angels, like their counterparts in the Book of Revelation, wage ruthless battle for the sake of preserving the purity of Eden's real estate. The *World Before the Flood* is dominated by the patriarchy of the Patriarchs, a world in which sexually chaste men sing songs of valor while women tend the sheep and, if need be, expire on cue, even as Eve gives up the ghost within seconds of Adam's.[11]

The biography of the evil Giant-King (Canto VII) casts him and his Cainite followers in the role of Milton's Satan in *Paradise Lost*, who vows

> To range the universe from pole to pole,
> Rule the remotest nations with his nod,
> to live a hero, and to die a god.
> (Canto VII p. 99)

In contrast the Patriarchal clan, a righteous nation that knew not Cain, in

> manly vigor till'd the unfailing soil;
> Green sprang the turf, by holy footsteps trod,
> Round the pure altars of the living God
> (Canto I p. 18)

The manly heroism that Montgomery believed available to biological men living evangelical lives has naught to do with martial pursuits. As for women, in perfect Miltonian gender ordering, "He for God only, she for God in him" (*Paradise Lost* IV 297). Genesis 4:19–22, describing the genealogy of Lamech, is referenced only by the "genealogy" of Jubal's gift of the harp to Javan, whose music evokes tranquility: it is the giants and Cainites who wield metallic instruments of death, broadly reinforcing Montgomery's division between "advanced" social and technocratic organization (evil, or at least morally suspect) and "traditional" subsistence farming, with a nod to poetry and spiritually uplifting instrumental music.

In 1822 the Irish poet Thomas Moore (1779–1852) published *The Loves of the Angels, a Poem*. One of the first Catholics to be admitted to Trinity College in Dublin, Moore successfully prosecuted classical studies there while he clandestinely participated in Irish nationalist affairs, having befriended Robert Emmet who was later executed for treason. Moore enjoyed a brilliant career as a public intellectual and salon personality, scoring triumphs as a playwright, actor, lyricist, satirist, biographer, but above all as a poet who used Romantic Orientalism as a vehicle to explore Irish nationalist politics. Among his many poems, *Lalla Rookh*, published by Longmans in 1814 for the colossal sum of 3000 guineas, went through innumerable editions and remains his most widely anthologized work. Today he is chiefly remembered for his indispensable biography of Lord Byron. His taste for eroticism, mild to the point of blandness by 21st-century standards, and his biting anti-British satires brought him both celebrity and obloquy. An erudite man of letters, he read the Greco-Roman classics in their originals, the Church Fathers, and the Septuagint, and quoted extensively from the translations of the Qur'ān, the *Avestas*, rabbinic literature, and the *Zohar*.[12]

The *Loves of the Angels* consists of tales of three different male angels, the first two narrated in the first person, confessional style.[13] Written in imitation of the Ovidian erotic *epyllion*, the poem was supplied by Moore with a studiously ponderous introduction and critical notes detailing his sources, whose primary purpose, one suspects, was defensive – they mostly deal with non-Christian authors and legends, thereby shielding Moore from lawsuits for blasphemous libel by the likes of the conservative Constitutional Association, a fate that shadowed John Murray for publishing Byron's controversial biblical drama *Cain*.[14] The first angel's story reworks the Islamic legend of *Hārūt and Mārūt*, wherein two angels accept a challenge from the Almighty that immortal beings could walk the earth and resist the weaknesses of the flesh. Once there, Hārūt and Mārūt speedily succumb to wine, women, and homicide, and spend eternity hung up by their heels in a well in Babylon.[15] Moore's first angel, smitten by the beauty of a bathing woman, moons over her in a platonic friendship strictly enforced by her frosty chastity. Imprudently joining her in a banquet, the amorous angel tastes forbidden wine, and all is lost. The woman easily extracts from him the magical password known only to angels, and immediately levitates to the star formerly inhabited by the angel, grounded eternally thereafter for his indiscretion. "Why, why have hapless Angels eyes? | Or why are there not flowers to cull, | As fair as Woman, in yon skies?" laments the abandoned angel.[16]

The second angel's story is a patent retelling of the classical myth of Zeus and Semele. His narrative dwells on the differences between human males and females, which are fundamentally intellectual and motivational.

Women, more weakly endowed with reason, are the more easily gulled by an honest demeanor, hence the biblical Fall:

> I had seen this; had seen Man – arm'd
> As his soul is with strength and sense –
> By her first words to ruin charm'd;
> His vaunted reason's cold defence,
> Like an ice-barrier in the ray
> Of melting summer, smil'd away![17]

Adding gilded physical beauty to nature, the power of womankind is to "bewitch," and that power is what the second angel sought to explore through his congress with a daughter of Eve. In Moore's hands a literary exploration of the angelic psychology of an Enochian Watcher, the second angel instructs the woman in knowledge forbidden to humankind, fatally stoking her curiosity.

> There's nothing bright above, below,
> In sky – earth – ocean, that this breast
> Doth not intensely burn to know,
> And thee, thee, thee, o'er all the rest!
> Then come, oh Spirit, from behind
> The curtains of thy radiant home,
> Whether thou would'st as God be shrin'd
> Or lov'd and clasp'd as mortal, come![18]

Nothing loath to thwart such an offer, the yielding angel is compelled to reveal himself in his full heavenly splendor. As he embraces her, the angel watches in horrified fascination as his human lover is reduced to fly-ash. Worse still, as she succumbs, the angel glimpses the hellish sin of pride, and is permanently branded by her dying kiss.

The final tale recounts the rather more innocent love of a seraph for a woman, and their subsequent doom, rendered by a God who "never did . . . look down | On error with a brow so mild"[19] – to roam the earth together like the Wandering Jew in stereo, suffering every human vicissitude, until doomsday when they will be brought to heaven with, presumably, their transgressions forgiven. Whereas the first two angels are seduced by ocular visions of women, the seraph falls prey to the dulcet song of his human beloved:

> Oh Love, Religion, Music – all
> That's left of Eden upon earth –
> The only blessings, since the fall
> Of our weak souls, that still recall
> a trace of their high, glorious birth[20]

Moore goes out of his way to level the differences between seraph and female in this light-hearted vignette.

Despite the elevated diction and supernatural protagonists, Moore's *Loves of the Angels* reads more like a drawing-room comedy of manners, with the subverted Hollywood formula Angel Chases Girl, Angel Loses Girl, Angel Loses Wings. To be fatally human, from an angelic standpoint, is to engage in fatally masculine behavior by craving the company of womankind, and Moore exercises devastating wit in toying with the impossibility of his angels performing the role of *paterfamilias* or adopting the code of chivalry, whereas he eschews warriorhood and heroism altogether for his angelic narrative.

In 1822 a 25-year-old Church of England clergyman and educator by the name of Thomas Dale (1797–1870) published *Irad and Adah, A Tale of the Flood*. Publication of a well-received collection of poetry before he entered Corpus Christi College, Cambridge, helped finance his academic career and secured him employment as a tutor. In 1828 he was appointed professor of English language and literature at University College, London, the first such position in England. A stalwart evangelical, he abandoned the job in 1830 on account of the "godless" nature of the institution, and concentrated his talents on various parochial educational ventures and preaching. Although described by a contemporary as a "a queer-looking man, who bent low over his manuscript, and read rapidly for more than an hour without once looking up," his preaching garnered large audiences and appointments to prestigious London positions, including St. Pancras.[21]

Irad and Adah, A Tale of the Flood, originally published with specimens of his translations of the Psalms, relates the forbidden love of the humans Irad and Adah, with the unusual twist of making the woman, Adah, a Sethite and the man, Irad, a Cainite. The frame narrative, quoted on the title page, is not Genesis 6 but the words of Jesus in Matthew 24:38–39: "In the days that were before the flood they were eating and drinking, marrying and giving in marriage, until the day that Noë entered into the ark, and knew not until the flood came, and took them all away." In one hundred and ten pages of Spenserian couplets divided into three uneven parts: "Guilt," "Prophecy," and "Judgment," Dale recounts the fatal error of this antediluvian pair, the sonorous, didactic preaching of Noah, and the consequences of sin, a retelling of the biblical flood story with a heavy-handed overlay of Christian eschatology. Lest there be the slightest doubt concerning the source of evil, our author drums repeatedly the deadly, two-syllable word: WOMAN:

> But know'st thou not, rash youth! that Falsehood's lure
> Is ever framed the stamp of Truth to bear,
> That Man is weakest still, when more secure,
> And Beauty's smile oft falsest, when most fair?
> A woman tempts thee, but a Fiend is there![22]

A single line alludes to angelic misconduct with the fairer sex: this is a tale of forbidden human love and its punishment, including vignettes about the idolatrous, doomed giants thrown in as moralizing foils, with precious little of the Orientalizing vamp of Moore's *Loves of the Angels*.

To be a manly man in the world that Dale begot is to manage power: power to prophesize doom (Noah), power to handle weapons even in a bad cause (the doomed giants), power to seduce a weak but superior woman (the Cainite Irah). The ultimate loss of power is to listen to the dulcet voice of – you guessed it – a woman, basically any woman will do. Who needs concupiscent male angels to wreak moral havoc when even the daughters of pious Seth can't keep their hands off the handsome sons of Cain?

Irah, an exiled murderer like his grandsire Cain, with rugged good looks and an eye for the ladies, exhibits masculine temperament by his capacity to brave climactic extremes and the ostracizing frowns of heaven itself. With superhuman strength, he carries his weakening lover to the last mountain peak left standing above the crescendo seas – "his manly might Endured through all" (Part 3 stanza 50), where she dies of exposure. Fending off the carrion birds, the waters overwhelm man and corpse, whose troubles have only begun, given the blazing hell fires of Christian eschatology set to consume them both.

Our last poem, *Heaven and Earth, A Mystery*, was published in 1823 by the one poet whose name remains a household word, Lord Byron (1788–1824). Byron, iconic Romantic author, skeptic, and rake, altered the course of English letters through lyrical dramas like *Sardanapalus*, book-length poems like *Childe Harold* and *Don Juan*, brief works like *The Destruction of Sennacherib*, and merciless, trenchant satire ladled out with respect for neither person nor office. Despite his religious skepticism, his extraordinary familiarity with the Bible impelled him to keep abreast of scientific controversies that impinged on biblical authority, and, in the case of *Cain* and *Heaven and Earth*, prompted him to rework the Bible itself with bold, deft strokes. A philohellenist and political idealist, he invested his person and property in the Greco-Turkish conflict, dying in Missolonghi in 1824 at the age of 36.[23]

Heaven and Earth, an unfinished lyrical drama, that is to say, a drama never meant for stage performance, consists of some 1200 lines in three unequal acts. The *dramatis personae* consists of Noah and his sons Japhet and Shem, two women of the line of Cain, Anah, and Aholibamah, the angels Samiasa, Azaziel, and Raphael, and choruses of spirits and mortals. The time is the eve before the Deluge; the action takes place in the vicinity of Mount Ararat. Anah and Aholibamah summon their respective angelic lovers through solemn invocations aimed at their heavenly abode.

Descend and share my lot!
Though I be formed of clay,
And thou of beams

More bright than those of day
On Eden's streams,
Thine immortality can not repay
With love more warm than mine. . . .[24]

The angelic lovers are only too happy to oblige. The denouement occurs in a gloomy cavern, where the jilted Japhet confronts the human women together with their angelic paramours, the flood waters gurgling ominously just beyond the cave's mouth. The scandalized archangel Raphael gives Samiasa and Azaziel the equivalent of five minutes to report back for duty before the heavenly throne, and a bad-tempered Noah apostrophizes the epic housekeeping to be accomplished by the flood and threatens Japhet with drowning for his effeminate sympathy for the doomed Cainites.

Wouldst thou have God commit a sin for thee?
Such would it be
To alter his intent
For a mere mortal sorrow. Be a man!
And bear what Adam's race must bear, and can.
(III ll.690–695)

The two human women, maintaining the moral innocence of their interspeciation with angels, are flown off bodily by their respective lovers, presumably to safety, happiness, and the joys of requited love.[25] The anonymous chorus of spirits are simply champing at the bit to witness the miserable race of mortals snuffed out.[26] Like Montgomery's *World Before the Flood*, Byron's *Heaven and Earth* celebrates love, sweet love; unlike Montgomery, it is carnal love between species that walks away with the laurels. Byron sets up an epistemological showdown between the morose Noah, the embodiment of blind faith in revealed religion, and the human women and their angelic lovers, who in good Romantic fashion trust their senses and impulses as empirically responsible as they jointly venture into uncharted waters of consuming, forbidden love.

Although these four poems addressed a host of contemporary issues, I believe the fundamental reason that Genesis 6:1–4 became such sizzling real estate was its ready applicability to the Gothic imagination. Gothic literature, retrospectively kicked off by Horace Walpole's *Castle of Otranto* in 1764, gained incredible momentum from the excesses of the French Revolution and the Napoleonic wars, spawning iconic texts like Mary Shelley's *Frankenstein*, Edgar Allen Poe's macabre poetry and fiction, Bram Stoker's *Dracula*, and continues to thrive to this day in the genres of, among others, horror fiction, splatter films, acid-rock iconography, and zombie apocalypse.

Formal English literature parlance restricts "Gothic" to a set of novels written between the 1760s and the 1820s, with an emphasis on psychological and physical terror, archaic settings, exploitation of the supernatural, and prominent use of suspense as a plot motif.[27] Omnipresent features in this fiction additionally include secrecy, hereditary family curses usually evinced by the sins of the fathers visited on the children, moral and physical decay of the aristocracy, lurid depictions of church and clergy, tortured maidens or femmes fatale, occult technicians, demonic beings, Byronic heroes, darkness, death, melodrama, and madness. Explanations for the extraordinary popularity of the Gothic novel range from crude pandering to a taste for sex and sensationalism, to the triumph of narrative unreality in a prosaic age, to a mechanism through which subversion of authority could be imaginatively explored.[28] Of particular note here was the capacity of the early Gothic imagination to explore gender-constructed realities through the deliberate destabilization of tradition. In the world of letters, men and women alike could claim masculinities by courting Gothic anxieties that would have baffled the culture-bearers of Georgian England, or contrariwise they could opt to reaffirm the traditional verities of hearth, church, and plow.

Between the writing of Milton's *Paradise Lost* and Montgomery's *World Before the Flood*, "[male] angels had come to be the dinosaurs of Christian legacy – useless, cumbersome, embarrassing, extinct."[29] The Gothic imagination changed all that. Genesis 6:1–4, courtesy of 2,000 years of exegetical history, dished up secret, forbidden sex, hereditary evil, sinister angels, wicked giants, femmes fatale (or persecuted maidens), the in-breaking of the supernatural, and infinite melodramatic possibility in the guise of the universal destruction of the Deluge. For example: Montgomery's *World Before the Flood* augments the wickedness of the Cainite giant-king by making him a protégé of a demonic sorcerer, and invents an Orphic hero, Javan, who mediates between the semi-divine Enoch and the pacifist Sethites. While giving and taking in marriage is tolerated among the Patriarchal clan, chaste masculine love (unlike the lusts of the Cainites) garners better press. Soldiering is the proper affair of archangels and God.

Moore's *Loves of the Angels* exults in the Romantic possibilities of interspeciation or, if you prefer, cosmic miscegenation, tabooed sex being a Gothic staple. We are made privy to details of the angelic realm, witness the ontological transformation of a mortal woman into an angel (and the corresponding ontological degradation of a male angel), voyeuristically thrill to the disintegration of another woman by unshielded angelic radiation, and vicariously participate in angelic fall induced by wine, women, and song – but mostly women. All of Moore's women are femmes fatale, and any angelic attempt to "save" them results in loss of masculine angelic abilities – wings that no longer achieve flight, a transparent castration symbol. All of the first-person narratives in *Loves of the Angels* make much of the artifice of secrecy that the angels engage in to preserve their liminal gendering caused by the creation of Woman. Brinks believes that "the gothic secret stands as a communal emblem for the hero's psyche, an emblem that necessarily reflects back on the communal psyche as well."[30] Given the extent that Byron and other Gothic writers made use of secrecy to explore gender-crossing and same-sex desire, Moore's angels are deeply problematized as masculine constructs, failing nearly all the later Victorian "tests" of chaste heroism, chivalry, *paterfamilias*, and soldier. In keeping with certain Gothic sensibilities, *Loves of the Angels* is darkly satirical, making fun of angelic accessories, magic words, nuptial vows, and the entire notion that angels are pure intelligences *à la* Aquinas. Moore's lush verbal canvass seethes with exoticist flourishes culled from Islamic, Jewish, and Zoroastrian legend, a literary mirror of the Orientalist paintings just then coming into vogue.[31] The third angel's narrative ventures closest among these four compositions to exploring the role of fallen but constant angel as potential *paterfamilias*.

Whereas Thomas Dale's *Irad and Adah* chastely eschews titillating his readers with lustful angels, the details of the horrific extinction wrought by the Deluge are sketched with unabashed pornographic relish. Evangelical fervor for the biblical Last Judgment was explored by various artists, Dale included, through apocalyptic visions of the fall of western civilization or global disasters like the Noahide flood.[32] Seemingly irresistible changes in society and nation brought on by the tidal waves of the Napoleonic wars and the industrial revolution surfaced in Gothic fiction in tales of irreversible decay, calamitous disaster, and the creation of monstrous beings, and Dale's reworking of antediluvian sin and its nemesis should be classified accordingly. And let's not forget his didactic use of terror – what would a Gothic yarn be without a spine-tingling dose of terror, and who better to deliver the goods than a hellfire evangelical preacher?

Despite the "manly might" of the Cainite Irad, he is ultimately feminized by his inability to save his lady-love any more that the desperate mothers, clinging to the same rocky eminence, could preserve their infants from drowning. Dale foreshadows the Victorian encoding of masculinity as the power of the family patriarch to weather the economic cancer of spreading industrial and social chaos, destitution and the workhouse signaling the eclipse of manhood[33] even as Irad expired beneath the waves, helpless to save Adah from the Deluge. Similarly, though Irad sought to "slay" the chaos waters and save his woman as Perseus speared the dragon and freed Andromeda in countless late Victorian artworks,[34] the Cainite's physical heroism failed the test, as did his lack of scruples where chastity was concerned. Dale certainly made no bones about painting womankind in *Irad and Adah* as *succubi* at least as fatal to the naïve man as John Keats's *La Belle Dame sans Merci* (1819), linking biblical idolatry with romantic love.

Byron's *Heaven and Earth* sports a veritable Gothic fiction checklist, groaning under the weight of concupiscent angels, alluring, strong-willed women who will not take no for an answer, a Byronic hero in the guise of the morally conflicted Japhet, and the sinister, clock-watching martinets Raphael and Noah. The work as a whole flouts conventional piety every step of the way by its challenge to divine compassion. If, as modern theorists maintain, Gothic literature is defined by transgressive discourse, then *Heaven and Earth* takes the prize among these four poems by stunningly subverting the Genesis narrative.[35] Byron, quintessential Romantic who engaged in radical social critique, comes closest in our poets' lineup to re-visioning the heroic masculine role as one capable of acknowledging female libido without condemnation, a stance at loggerheads with the high Victorian image of the Greco-Roman mythological and medieval chivalric hero as chaste.[36] "Manliness" plays out as stolid endurance against feelings of pity and fear of death, and certainly the possession of power to choose one's destiny, even (or especially even) in the face of divine displeasure. Unlike many of his other compositions, Byron fails to exploit the possibility of gothic secrecy in the unraveling of Anah and Aholibamah's yearning for angelic congress, though it is evident that the Cainite women, and not Japhet, wear the pants in the story. It is Japhet who is dispossessed of masculine identity by the angelic lovers, the latter openly reveal their interspecies liaison to Raphael and the enraged Patriarch Noah, and act decisively on their erotic passions. Unhappily, the final half of *Heaven and Earth* was never penned, and we are left with guesses as to the postdiluvian fates of Anah, Aholibamah, and their angelic swains.

A lesser but salient explanation for the waxing topicality of Genesis 6:1–4 was excitement building due to the recovery of the full text of the apocryphal *Book of Enoch*. The intrepid Scottish explorer James Bruce obtained three Ethiopic copies of the (*First*) *Book of Enoch* in 1773, confirming centuries' old rumors that copies of the lost revelations by the antediluvian hero who cheated death resided in Abyssinia/Ethiopia.[37] Bruce published his travelogue in five sumptuous volumes in 1790, a text that inspired much Romantic interest in Africa.[38] In 1800 the Orientalist Silvestre de Sacy described the Ethiopic copy Bruce gave to Louis XV and published a Latin translation of chapters 1–3, 6–16, 22–23 (an English retelling of de Sacy's translations appeared the following year),[39] but the first translation of the entire Ethiopian *Enoch* into a modern European language, English, was published by the former Oxford Regius Professor of Hebrew Richard Laurence in 1821,[40] just in the nick of time to be seized upon by Thomas Moore for his *Loves of the Angels*. Centuries earlier, parts of the *Book of the Watchers* (chapters 7–10:15), preserved in Georgius Syncellus' *Chronographia*, had been transmitted to Europe in Latin and Greek by J. J. Scaliger in 1606, scornful of the state of the text and the perceived vulgarities it described. An English synopsis of Scaliger's translation was published by Samuel Purchas as part of his ecclesiastical geography in 1614,[41] while a full English translation of Scaliger's Enoch materials appeared in 1715 under the picturesque title *The History of the Angels and their Gallantry with the Daughters of Men, Written by Enoch the Patriarch*.[42] The mathematician William Whiston assiduously collected all of the apocryphal Enoch texts in Greek or Latin and translated them (or borrowed translations) together with the massive corpus of Jewish and Christian traditions beginning with Genesis in his widely circulated volumes on the Old and New Testaments (1727–28).[43] In terms of exact knowledge of *First Enoch*, the poetical works of Montgomery, Dale, and Byron,[44] with the possible exception of Moore, give evidence of nothing that any attentive reader of Whiston could not have trotted out by 1727 at the latest. Laurence's translation in 1821 made no critical contribution to any of these, and as we shall see with our visual artists, fallen angels and the Book of Enoch were all the rage in the 1790s. What with the translation of the dualistic Zoroastrian *Avesta*s by Anquetil-Duperron and the circulation in Europe of Islamic angelic legends like *Hārūt and Mārūt*, the cryptic verses in Genesis 6, nourished by the Gothic imagination, could blossom into darkly fecund tales of libidinous angels, hot women, superheated heroics, and cataclysm as gratifyingly destructive and inescapable as the hydrogen bomb.

Genesis 6:1–4 and its visual scribes

The passage was eschewed by every woodcutter or metal engraver of 19th-century illustrated Bibles, save one, whose works I could lay hands on. The usual sequence of illustrations was to skip from the *Murder of Abel by Cain* to the crowd-pleasing *Noah's Ark*, with the occasional artistic license of a tear-jerking *Eve Finds the Body of Abel*; no giants, no Nephilim, certainly no sex, at least where this passage was concerned, figured in your Moroccan leather-bound parlor Bible. One must turn to other sources for visual examples.[45]

Little commented on is the fact that three well-known British artists illustrated this passage (or its equivalents in Enoch) by 1827 at the latest. The second edition of Moore's *Loves of the Angels* (1823) included four octavo-size illustrations by the prolific Royal Academician Richard Westall (1765–1836), one for each of the three stories plus a fourth for the title page.[46] Westall specialized in portraits and historical tableaux, illustrating editions of Shakespeare, Milton, and Walter Scott; in his last years he served as drawing master to the young Queen Victoria.[47]

In this engraving of Moore's first tale, an angel pleads his troth with one of the daughters of men, both assuming hackneyed theatrical poses. Lop off the wings and doff the classicizing garb, and the illustration could easily pass for "an elegant pastoral shepherd and his coy mistress."[48] It is the sentimental style in the mode of Francis Wheatley's pastorals that gives Westall's actors an androgynous cast, a trait amplified by the handiwork of the popular engraver Charles Heath.[49]

The second story, a reworking of the Zeus and Semele myth, depicts the cherub Rubi, literally standing on a pedestal/altar, acceding to the fatal prayer of the mortal Lilis, begging the "idol of my dreams"

> Let me this once but feel the flame
> Of those spread wings, the very pride
> Will change my nature, and this frame
> By the mere touch be deified![50]

Figure 10.1 First angel pleading with one of the daughters of men. Drawn by Richard Westall, engraved by Charles Heath. From Thomas Moore, *Loves of the Angels* (4th edition, 1823), page 23. In the public domain.[51]

No monstrous Watchers or wicked daughters of Cain here, only very human love-torn souls comfortably reinforcing visual gender stereotypes.

Another Royal Academician, John Flaxman (1755–1826), was a sculptor and draughtsman best known for his exquisite line drawings published in

Figure 10.2 Cherub Rubi appearing to Lilis. Drawn by Richard Westall, engraved by E. Portbury. From Thomas Moore, *Loves of the Angels* (4th edition, 1823), page 61. In the public domain.

translations of Homer, Hesiod, Aeschylus, and Dante.[52] His iconic style so defined the genius of neoclassicism that it was imitated throughout Europe, yet his Romantic art played a pivotal role in England's Gothic Revival. Flaxman and his wife befriended fellow artist William Blake, moving in a congruent orbit of intellectual coteries and theosophical experimentations.

Flaxman prepared rough sketches for the *Book of Enoch*, unpublished in his lifetime. Most art historians date the drawings between 1821 and his death in 1826 under the assumption that Flaxman was unfamiliar with the text prior to Laurence's translation in 1821, despite the well-publicized fact that Flaxman signed and dated a drawing "And Enoch Walked with God and he was not for God took him" in May 1792![53]

Irresistible muscular Watchers swoop out of the sky to seize the recumbent daughters of men in a composition that could be titled "Rape of the Sabines," though "Enoch" appears in Flaxman's hand at lower right (Huntington Library copy).[54] Another sketch of the same scene is inscribed "Angels descending to the daughters of Men" (Fitzwilliam Museum copy); a more finished detail figures in a manuscript with the legend "Angels descending to the daughters of men / Enoch" (University College, London). Other sketches with "Enoch" labels depict wingless muscular male figures in downward flight. The Renaissance masterpieces that Flaxman studied during his seven-year sojourn in Rome (1787–94) notably Michelangelo's Sistine Chapel, might have inspired his treatment, though it is worth noting that William Young Ottley (1771–1836), a lifelong friend of Flaxman's, sketched numerous midair angelic battles after Cimabue, Signorelli, and Michelangelo around the time that they were together in Italy,[55] suggesting that the apocalyptic tales of fallen angels exercised particular attraction for many in the politically turbulent years of the 1790s.

Flaxman prepared a number of illustrations for Emanuel Swedenborg's *Arcana Coelestia*, at least two of which dealt with the mystic's exegesis of the Enoch passages in Genesis.[56] Flaxman and his wife were active in the

Figure 10.3 John Flaxman, Angels descending to the daughters of men. 4.5 × 9 inches, pen and brown wash over pencil. Inscribed "Enoch" lower right. Huntington Library Collection, San Marino, California (66.51). © Courtesy of the Huntington Art Collections, San Marino, California.

Swedenborg-friendly theosophical societies that ultimately led to the organization of the London New Jerusalem Church in January 1788. Although Flaxman did not join the New Jerusalem Church until 1797, his lifelong engagement in Swedenborgian thought manifested itself in visual and textual expressions that include sepulcher reliefs[57] and a 26-page manuscript, "The Knight of the Blazing Cross" (1796).[58] In 1810 Flaxman together with his friend Charles Augustus Tulk became founding members of *The Society for Printing and Publishing the Writings of the Hon. Emmanuel Swedenborg*.[59] Like Blake, Flaxman was exposed to synopses of the *Book of the Watchers* and esoteric speculations on the figure of Enoch decades before the publication of Laurence's translation in 1821, hence some or all of Flaxman's Enoch sketches could have been created in the mid-1790s.

Flaxman's angels claim the later Victorian masculinity of the soldier, albeit using Renaissance modeling and composition. They are muscular though beardless (the latter the fashion in Regency England), warlike without weapons, active in the face of passive earthbound women, though assuredly not chaste as the Victorian reworking of Arthurian legend would have it be.

The eccentric mythographer, engraver, and Bible-intoxicated mystic William Blake (1757–1827)[60] left a series of six unfinished pencil sketches of the *Book of Enoch*, with no hint of an accompanying poem.[61] The figure of Enoch had preoccupied him for years.[62] The subject matter of *First Enoch* – forbidden sexual congress between angelic beings and human women, apocalypticism, and secret lore from before the Flood – appears repeatedly in Blake's oeuvre, so it is unsurprising that he would try his hand at it. Yet in order to grasp something of the complexity and intent of these works, however, the milieu in which the Enoch sketches were created must be sought. The ongoing scholarly effort to contextualize Blake within contemporary society is situating him in a culture of radical Christianity and revolutionary politics. His mother belonged to the Moravian Fetter Lane congregation in London at the height of Count Zinzendorf's avant-garde experimentations combining mystical-body piety, liberal education for both sexes, and openness to the sacramental possibilities of martial sex. The artistic society that Blake frequented, Royal Academicians like John Flaxman and Richard Cosway, playwrights and literati like William Hayley and George Cumberland, and patrons of the arts like Charles Augustus Tulk and Thomas Butts, swam through the turbulent seas of speculative Christian thought and theosophical esotericism in the guise of Free Masonry, Rosicrucianism, Swedenborgianism, Christian Kabbalah, animal magnetism, and seditious critiques of European monarchy and colonial adventures abroad.[63]

Blake's lifelong love/hate relationship with the thought of Emanuel Swedenborg is undoubtedly ingredient in the artist's engagement with *First Enoch*. Swedenborg was positive that the manuscripts of lost biblical books, including *Enoch*, were to be discovered in Africa, and that innocent and godly races dwelled on the Dark Continent that it behooved fallen Europe to contact, a variant of the medieval Prester John myth. Bruce's announcement in 1773 of the recovery of *Enoch* MSS in Ethiopia signaled to the Swedenborgian faithful that the rest of his African predictions could come true, an assumption that lead to African exploration and an effort to establish a utopian colony in Sierra Leone under a constitution espousing Swedenborgian ideals, with conjugal (patriarchal) bliss as its fulcrum. William and Catherine Blake attended the four-day Great East Cheap Swedenborg conference April 13–17, 1789, as subscribers to but not members of the New Jerusalem Church in London. The full list of participants was recently published. In the words of David Worrall, "the common thread to these 1789 East Cheap connections are their intricate links to abolition, Africa, colonization projects and the presence of black people."[64] Carl Bernhard Wadström, one of the chief architects of the conference, published that same year *A Plan for a Free Community Upon the Coast of Africa*, and had given eye-witness evidence of the inhuman slave conditions in Guinea 1787–88. Another attendee, Augustus Nordenskjöld, would perish in Sierra Leone in 1792 after an abortive expedition to discover Swedenborg's blessed races in central Africa. Another attendee, William Spence, a Swedenborg apologist, wrote that "Mr. Bruce has been the means, under God, of bringing to Europe . . . the long lost book of Enoch or Chanoch according to the Hebrew. According to all the quotations I have seen of it, it truly answers Mr. Swedenborg's description," and advocated further African searches for other obscure texts hinted at in the Bible.[65] Blake's subsequent engagement in making anti-slavery illustrations for John Gabriel Stedman (1792), the abolitionist themes in his own compositions, and the role of the divinity in Africa in his illuminated works of the 1790s, especially the *Song of Los* (1795), has been much studied.[66] That Blake was specifically influenced by Swedenborg's writings regarding the figure of Enoch is proven by the poems *Milton* and *Jerusalem*, where the patriarch Enoch is identified as the seventh "church," a concept pivotal to Swedenborg's exegesis of the Enochian passages in the *Arcana Coelestia*, the same texts that Blake's friend, patron, and working colleague John Flaxman illustrated in 1792.[67]

Interpreting the *Book of Enoch* sketches of Blake,[68] had they been finished works within an illustrated poem, would have been taxing enough, given the artist's penchant for staging dialogue with polarizing conversation partners through single, overdetermined symbols. Given the rough state of the drawings, their uncertain order and the intended composition, if any, the following remarks are provisional at best.

Figure 10.4: A nude Watcher (sans halo?) descends from the sky with his left hand reaching for a woman's pubis, who is evidently pleased by the attentions, judging by the placement of one hand on his probing arm and other on her thigh below the genital region, taken together with her untroubled facial expression. The right hand of the Watcher at his side could be holding something; his face is next to her left ear, which, with the inclination of the head, suggests that he is whispering to her and she is attentive, perhaps the "eternal secrets" (*First Enoch* 9:6) that, practiced on earth, led to

Figure 10.4 William Blake, A Watcher seducing a daughter of men. 20.75 × 14.57 inches, pencil on paper watermarked "W ELGAR / 1796." Inscribed "from the Book of Enoch" and "2. Enoch." Lessing J. Rosenwald Collection, National Gallery of Art, Washington, DC (1944.14.6). Courtesy National Gallery of Art, Washington.

oppression and bloodshed (*First Enoch* 7:1b, 8:1–3). Flanking either side of the woman are two grotesque humanoid figures sketched with faces that are inclined toward hers. Flames may be emanating from them. They are outsized in relation to the women and the Watcher, a fact that most commentators suggest is taken to indicate that they are the gigantic offspring of the sexual congress between divinities and humans (*First Enoch* 7:2–5, 9:9) – they could be allegories, they could be something altogether unconnected with *First Enoch*. Tendrils of vines with leaves reach from the ground to her buttocks and around her back, spilling down the other side, whereas a long tendril of vine with a different leaf structure reaches *down* from the Watcher to the ground. Is this visual evidence of the lessons the Watchers inculcated concerning "the cutting of roots" (*First Enoch* 7:1b, 8:3), or is this simply another mechanism by which Blake associates the actors with "vegetative life," a delusive state in which mind and spirit are reduced to earthly, literal cognition without the vivifying fourfold vision that reveals spiritual truths for what they are? The woman is squarely posed before a steep Gothic spire with a smaller spire on her right and possibly on her left as well; the linear lines of the spires cut through the "flames" of the right-hand grotesque, indicating that they are not part of the same detail, but constitute an independent iconographic symbol.[69] Blake employs vertical Gothic architectural motifs in many of his drawings, including the Enoch lithograph of 1806–7, which functions there as a symbol of the seventh "church" that Enoch represents *à la* Swedenborg. Blake critics are uniform in treating his use of Gothic architecture as a sign of authentic Christianity, versus Greco-Roman designs that depict the evils of the contemporary state church. Is this a symbol of uncorrupted, prelapsarian revealed religion crumbling under the inbreaking of the Watchers? A sign of coming redemption?[70]

Figure 10.5: Two Watchers with halos(?) accost a daughter of man. They flank her menacingly, her head level with their groins, their heads craning down toward her. The gigantic corkscrew appendages on the Watchers' genital regions are thought to be phalluses radiating jagged beams of lust that fill much of the sketch surface. The woman's exposed breasts and vulva are prominent. One of her hands appears to be caressing one phallus while she eyes the other. Her facial expression is one of terror or anguish, the overwhelming emotion echoed by her agitated, Medusa-like hair and writhing body. The downward-pointing fingers of her right hand are elongated like tree roots, as if the arms were transforming into part of a single vegetative organism rooting the phallus she caresses to the earth. Undulating "rivers" flow downward from the Watchers around her feet, overlaying dim outlines of what might be a horizon. The sketch, unfinished as it is, powerfully communicates the savage, predatory experience of rape.

Figure 10.6: Often called "The Daughter of Men Becomes a Siren" with no textual basis in Blake, Syncellus' version of *First Enoch* or Ethiopic *First Enoch* shows three figures in intensely contrastive postures: a recumbent figure, gender uncertain, lies supine before a tree or pillar; a female figure with

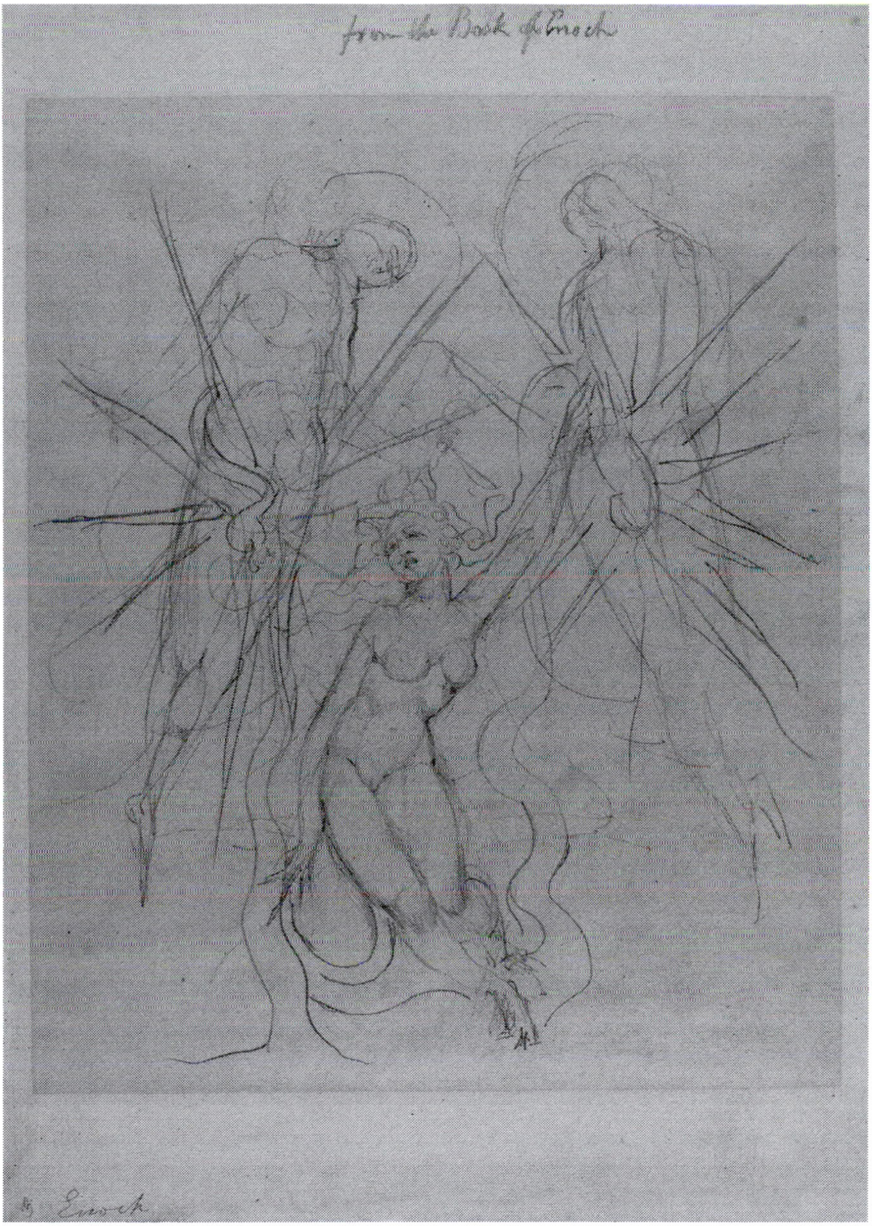

Figure 10.5 William Blake, Two Watchers accosting a daughter of men. 20.75 × 14.57 inches, pencil on paper watermarked "W ELGAR / 1796." Inscribed "from the Book of Enoch" and "3. Enoch." Lessing J. Rosenwald Collection, National Gallery of Art, Washington, DC (1944.14.5). Courtesy National Gallery of Art, Washington.

Figure 10.6 William Blake, Two daughters of men and supine figure. 20.75 × 14.57 inches, pencil on paper watermarked with an elaborate crest. Inscribed "B. of Enoch," "4," "102," and "[No 27 *deleted*] No 26 next [?] at p. 43." Lessing J. Rosenwald Collection, National Gallery of Art, Washington, DC (1944.14.7). Courtesy National Gallery of Art, Washington.

scales levitates above the body with powerful, sinuous grace; another female on the far side of the tree holds up both hands and arms in alarm, shrinking away from the scene. The facial features of the scaly woman communicate self-absorption or triumph, not terror. Scaly women are best avoided in Blake's mythos:

> A Woman Scaly & a man all Hairy
> Is such a Match as he who dares
> Will find the Womans Scales Scrape off the Mans Hairs[71]

The nature-goddess Vala is described by Luvah in the *Four Zoas* as

> She grew
> A scaled serpent, yet I fed her tho' she hated me.[72]

There is nothing in the *Book of the Watchers* or the entire Ethiopic *First Enoch* that matches the dramaturgy of this scene. It is wholly speculative to interpret the scene as a transformation of a daughter of men into a monstrous being following her relations with fallen angels.[73]

Taking the unfinished, contextless sketches as a whole, I will guardedly follow Rowland who builds on the work of Helen P. Bruder in seeing here a tableau of primordial male violence against women and its propagation as a mythologization of the evil fruits of masculine social control.[74] The irresistible violence of the rape in Figure 10.5 becomes internalized (Figure 10.4), with monstrous offspring as a result and women who consequently are transformed into bestial predators in their own right (Figure 10.6). If this interpretation of Blake has any merit, then, we have been given a retelling of the Fall story with male-authored violence at its core, not female wiles or weakness as in canonical Genesis or Swedenborg's *Arcana Coelestia*.[75] Blake spun out several versions of the myth of original violence and the terrifying way that it can impose its value system within the human situation. For instance, in *The Vision of the Daughters of Albion* (1791), Bromion, a type of Reason or Law, rapes and impregnates Oothoon while she is seeking her love Theotormon (Desire), the latter whom binds them back to back in manacles of bitter hatred. Oothoon's experience yields insight into the false consciousness of patriarchy, "the chain of life in weary lust" and pities the wretched offspring of such loveless unions, while Bromion, a slave owner, learns nothing and repents of nothing; Theotormon laments his loss (but never unlocks the manacles). Said to have been inspired by Mary Wollstonecraft's *Vindication of the Rights of Women* (1792),[76] *The Vision of the Daughters of Albion* grants them insight without reprieve from their subjugation. Did the nameless women victimized in Blake's sketches for the *Book of Enoch* even have that much to show for their pain?

The unspeakable Genesis 6:1–4 inspired few 19th-century exegetes but fueled a formidable collection of English poems and illustrations in the early decades of that century. Publication of an English translation of Enoch in 1821 was ingredient to this creative ferment, but I contend that the major stimulus is to be located in the nexus between the traditional exegetical possibilities of the passage, the ascendant Gothic imagination, and the political and social fallout of the Napoleonic wars, Utopian dreams of Africa, the industrial revolution, and Evangelical anxieties concerning liberal thought and shifting social mores.

What does it mean to say that an angel inhabits masculine space? The exegetical options for Genesis 6:1–4 dictated, for the most part, the masculinities constructed by three of our four poets. Montgomery's *World Before the Flood* piously re-enforces the Patriarchal order, even as the evangelical Dale manages male anxieties by tallying up conclusive evidence for the incorrigible depravity of womankind. Moore's baroque tales of angelic peccadillo tease the gender fault-lines, but in the end reinforce the platitude that Father God knows best and his boy angels must play the chaste man or suffer the consequences. Byron characteristically subverts the exegetical dead hand of the past, and seems to enjoy watching his watcher-angels engage in topping-and-bottoming power-exchanges with the virile daughters of Cain. On the visual score, Westall and Flaxman serve up hackneyed tableaux of male dominance, with allowances for stylistic canons. William Blake's unfinished *Enoch* sketches, painfully enigmatic, may encode another statement of his critique of patriarchal social control, subverting the received Protestant reading of the Genesis Fall story as well as exposing the shortcomings of Swedenborg's theosophy surrounding conjugal love and divine theodicy.

Like the endlessly recursive expressions of a mathematical fractal, the artistic and literary reception of Genesis 6:1–4 in pre-Victorian England constitutes an extraordinarily rich window into the ongoing power of the Bible to extrude architectonic forms that mirror the regnant masculine constructs of the day, gripped by the Gothic imaginary.

Notes

1 I wish to thank Ilona Zsolnay for massaging this workshop into existence, and for graciously inviting me to take a place at the table, and for the sundry funding agencies that made this show happen. The portion of this chapter dealing with four British Romantic poets is a heavily reworked version of a Midwest SBL regional paper published in *Proceedings, Eastern Great Lakes Midwest Region of the Society of Biblical Literature* 28 (2008): 25–40; I gratefully acknowledge permission for republication. The latter portion of this chapter that deals with three illustrators is almost entirely new research. I would like to thank Jennifer Jesse for her luminous and unstinting help with John Flaxman and William Blake.

2 In this I am dependent on the study by Joseph A. Kestner, *Masculinities in Victorian Painting* (Brookfield VT: Scolar Press and Aldershot: Ashgate Publishing Company, 1995), making due allowances for the fact that all of our poems and most of the illustrations were created prior to the accession of Queen Victoria.

3 George Bush, *Notes, Critical and Practical, on the Book of Genesis: Designed as a General Help to Biblical Reading and Instruction* (6th edn; 2 vols.; New York: Dayton & Newman, 1842) 1:115–116; Philip Smith, *An Ancient History from the Earliest Records to the Fall of the Western Empire, Vol. 1: From the Creation of the World to the Accession of Philip of Macedon* (London: James Walton, 1868) 22–23; Henry Charles Groves, *Commentary on the Book of Genesis for the Use of Readers of the English Version of the Bible* (Cambridge and London: Macmillan and Co., 1861) 86–88.

4 Johann Heinrich Kurtz, *History of the Old Covenant* (trans. Alfred Edersheim; Philadelphia: Lindsay and Blakiston, 1859) 95–101.

5 George Smith, *Patriarchal Age: Or, the History and Religion of Mankind, from the Creation to the Death of Isaac: Deduced from the Writings of Moses, and Other Inspired Authors* (New York: Carlton & Lanahan, 1847) 164–167; François Lenormant, *The Beginnings of History According to the Bible and the Traditions of Oriental Peoples: From the Creation of Man to the Deluge* (trans. from the 2nd French edn by Mary Lockwood; New York: Charles Scribner's Sons, 1882) 295–381.

6 William Henry Green, *The Unity of the Book of Genesis* (New York: Charles Scribner's Sons, 1895) 51–56. Reginald Stuart Poole and Edward William Lane, *The Genesis of the Earth and of Man or, the History of Creation, and the Antiquity and Races of Mankind Considered on Biblical and Other Grounds* (2nd revised & enlarged edn; London: Williams and Norgate, 1860) 75–84, consider the daughters of men to be Adamite humanity, and the sons of God a veiled reference to pre-Adamite humanity.

7 Henry Creswicke Rawlinson, pioneer Assyriologist, East India Company bureaucrat and diplomat, argued prior to 1869 that cuneiform parallels to the Genesis passage reveal that the ancient Babylonians divided the antediluvian world into two races, black (sons of Adam, thus imputing original sin to negritude) and white, a position naively adopted by George Smith but soundly debunked and buried by Friedrich Delitzsch and François Lenormant; Lenormant, *Beginnings of History*, 310–316.

8 For contemporary surveys of the exegetical possibilities, see Johann Heinrich Kurtz, *Die Ehen der Söhne Gottes mit den Töchtern der Menschen: Eine theologische Untersuchung zur exegetischen historischen, dogmatischen und praktischen Würdigung des biblischen Berichtes Gen. 6, 1–4* (Berlin and New York: J.A. Wohlgemuth, 1857); William Rainey Harper, "The Sons of God and the Daughters of Men: Genesis VI," *Biblical World* 3 (1894): 440–448.

9 "James Montgomery," in Robert Chambers (ed.), *Cyclopædia of English Literature; a History, Critical and Biographical, of British Authors, from the Earliest to the Present Times* (2 vols.; Edinburgh: William and Robert Chambers, 1844) 2:363–366; G. Tolley, "Montgomery, James (1771–1854)," in *Oxford Dictionary of National Biography* (2004–14), http://www.oxforddnb.com/view/article/19070 (accessed 1 January 2015).

10 James Montgomery, *Verses to the Memory of the Late Richard Reynolds; The World Before the Flood* (Romantic Context: Poetry; New York and London: Garland Pub., 1978), canto 10 p. 197; see the analysis in Gayle Shadduck, *England's Amorous Angels, 1813–1823* (Lanham MD: University Press of America, 1990) 187–212.

11 Montgomery, *World Before the Flood*, 76–78.

12 "Thomas Moore," in Chambers (ed.), *Cyclopædia*, 2:363–366; Geoffrey Carnall, "Moore, Thomas (1779–1852)," in *Oxford Dictionary of National Biography* (2004–14), http://www.oxforddnb.com/view/article/19150 (accessed 1 January 2015).

13 English editions of *Loves of the Angels* appeared in 1823 (including a pirated one in Philadelphia), 1824, 1826, 1844, 1873, two French versions in 1824, Dutch in 1835, Spanish in 1843, and Italian in 1873; G. E. Bentley, Jr., "A Jewel in an Ethiop's Ear," in *Blake in his Time*, edited by Robert N. Essick and Donald Pearce (Bloomington, IL: Indiana University Press, 1978) 221. It was also arranged for choral music within the first years of its publication.

14 After listing his formidable canon of sources, Moore sniffs that, in these texts, "the reader will find all that has ever been fancied or reasoned, upon a subject which only such writers could have contrived to render so dull." Thomas Moore, *The Loves of the Angels, a Poem* (London: Longman, Hurst, Rees, Orme, and Brown, 1823) 130.

15 G. Vajda, "Hārūt wa-Mārūt," in *Encyclopedia of Islam* (2nd edn.; Leiden: Brill, 2004) (CD-ROM version).

16 Moore, *Loves of the Angels*, 19.

17 Moore, *Loves of the Angels*, 44.

18 Moore, *Loves of the Angels*, 58–59, and see Shadduck, *England's Amorous Angels*, 242–293. Elia [pseudonym], "The Child Angel: A Dream," *The London Magazine* (June 1823): 677–678, is a contemporary satire that directly alludes to Moore's poem.

19 Moore, *Loves of the Angels*, 114.

20 Moore, *Loves of the Angels*, 111.

21 Arthur Burns, "Dale, Thomas (1797–1870)," in *Oxford Dictionary of National Biography* (2004–14), http://www.oxforddnb.com/view/article/7019 (accessed 1 January 2015).

22 Thomas Dale, *Irad and Adah, A Tale of the Flood. Poems. Specimens of a New Translation of the Psalms* (2d edn.; London: J. M. Richardson, 1822), 12 (part I, stanza 23); Shadduck, *England's Amorous Angels*, 309–330.

23 "Lord Byron," in Chambers (ed.), *Cyclopædia*, 2:386–395; Jerome McGann, "Byron, George Gordon Noel, sixth Baron Byron (1788–1824)," in *Oxford Dictionary of National Biography* (2004–14), http://www.oxforddnb.com/view/article/4279 (accessed 1 January 2015).

24 George Gordon Byron, in Jerome J. McGann, and Barry Weller (eds.), *Lord Byron: The Poetical Works* (Oxford English Texts 6; Oxford and New York: Clarendon Press, 1991) 6:349 (scene I ll.96–102); Shadduck, *England's Amorous Angels*, 109–113, 213–241.

25 Byron at one point contemplated resettling the two women and their angelic lovers on the moon, but later planned to kill them off in melodramatic fashion by the Flood, judging from the text of a conversation published by Thomas Medwin in 1824; McGann and Weller (eds.), *Lord Byron: Poetical Works*, 6:688–689.

26 The spirit chorus express contempt for Japhet and his relations who crave life, knowing that the bulk of the human race will expire – the spirit chorus claims superiority to humanity on the basis of their solidarity, a nod toward a masculine ideal of comradeship in adversity (III 135–159).

27 The prehistory of the classic Gothic novel in the so-called graveyard poetry of the 18th century and the cult of sentimentality, does not concern us. Similarly, the term "Gothic" as a genre category, expanded to cover American fiction by, among others, Joyce Carol Oates and Flannery O'Connor, modern horror fiction and film of any sort, and of course the "Goth" phenomenon in contemporary youth culture, mercilessly commodified, will also be ignored.

28 Works consulted include David G. Punter, *The Literature of Terror: A History of Gothic Fictions from 1765 to the Present Day, Vol. 1: The Gothic Tradition* (New York: Longman, 1996); David G. Punter and Glennis Byron (eds.), *The Gothic* (Blackwell Guides to Literature; Malden, MA: Blackwell Publishing, 2004) 3–75; George E. Haggerty, *Gothic Fiction/Gothic Form* (University Park:

Pennsylvania State University Press, 1989); Benjamin Eric Daffron, *Romantic Doubles: Sex and Sympathy in British Gothic Literature, 1790–1830* (New York: AMS Press, 2002); Dani Cavallaro, *The Gothic Vision: Three Centuries of Horror, Terror and Fear* (London and New York: Continuum, 2002).

29 Shadduck, *Amorous Angels*, 11.

30 Ellen Brinks, *Gothic Masculinity: Effeminacy and the Supernatural in English and German Romanticism* (Blackwell Studies in Eighteenth-Century Literature and Culture; Lewisburg and London: Bucknell University Press/Associated University Press, 2003), 69.

31 The quintessential Orientalist painting, Eugène Delacroix's *The Death of Sardanapalus* (*La Mort de Sardanapale*), would be exhibited in 1827.

32 For visual analogues, see the provocative work Morton D. Paley, *The Apocalyptic Sublime* (New Haven: Yale University Press, 1986).

33 Kestner, *Masculinities in Victorian Painting*, 149–157.

34 Kestner, *Masculinities in Victorian Painting*, 65–75.

35 Among its mind-teasing gems, the chorus of spirits draws Japhet's and the readers' attention to the contemporary geological debates raging over the chronology and universality of the Noahide Flood:

Howl! howl! oh Earth!
Thy death is nearer than thy recent birth:
Tremble, ye mountains, soon to shrink below
The ocean's overflow!
The wave shall break upon your cliffs; and shells,
The little shells, of ocean's least things be
Deposed where now the eagle's offspring dwells.

McGann and Weller (eds.), *Lord Byron: Poetical Works*, 6:362 (scene III ll. 234–240).

36 Kestner, *Masculinities in Victorian Painting*, 48–140.

37 The Orientalist Guillaume Postel (1510–1581), a French member of a monastic community of expatriate Ethiopians living in Rome, declared that Enoch's antediluvian prophecies were part of the canonical scriptures of the Ethiopian church. Postel also translated portions of the *Zohar* into Latin, a text whose mystical exegesis of Genesis expands on the character of Enoch as privy to primordial secrets; Ariel Hessayon, "Og, King of Bashan, Enoch and the Books of Enoch: Extra-Canonical Texts and Interpretations of Genesis 6:1–4," in *Scripture and Scholarship in Early Modern England*, edited by Ariel Hessayon and Nicholas Keene (Aldershot: Ashgate, 2006) 23–24.

38 James Bruce, *Travels to Discover the Source of the Nile, in the Years 1768, 1769, 1770, 1771, 1772, and 1773* (5 vols.; London: Printed by J. Ruthven, for G. G. J. and J. Robinson, 1790).

39 John Beer, "Blake's Changing View of History: The Impact of the Book of Enoch," in *Historicizing Blake*, edited by Steve Clark and David Worrall (New York: St. Martin's Press, 1994) 167–168.

40 Richard Laurence, *The Book of Enoch the Prophet: An Apocryphal Production, Supposed to Have Been Lost for Ages, but Discovered at the Close of the Last Century in Abyssinia: Now First Translated from an Ethiopic Ms. In the Bodleian Library* (Oxford: At the University Press for the Author, 1821).

41 Samuel Purchas, *Pvrchas His Pilgrimage. Or Relations of the Vvorld and the Religions Observed in All Ages and Places Discouered, from the Creation Vnto This Present. In Fovre Parts. This First Containeth a Theological and Geographical Historie of Asia, Africa, and America, with the Islands Adiacent. Declaring the Ancient Religions before the Flovd, the Heathnish, Jewish, and Saracenicall in All Ages since, in Those Parts Professed, Vvith Their Seueral Opinions, Idols,*

Oracles, Temples, Priests, Fasts, Feasts, Sacrifices, and Rites Religious: Their Beginnings, Proceedings, Alterations, Sectes, Orders and Successions (2nd edn. London: Printed by William Stansby for Henrie Featherstone, 1614) 36–37.

42 Johann Ernest Grabe, *The History of the Seventy-Two Interpreters: Of Their Journey from Jerusalem to Alexandria, Their Entertainment at the Egyptian Court, Their Version on the Septuagint: With All the Circumstances of That Illustrious Transaction* (Trans. into English by Thomas Lewis; London: Printed for J. Hooke, and T. Caldecott, 1715) 177–196.

43 William Whiston, *A Collection of Authentick Records Belonging to the Old and New Testament. Translated into English. By William Whiston, M. A. Sometime Professor of the Mathematicks in the University of Cambridge* (London: Printed for the author: and are to be sold by the booksellers of London and Westminster, 1727): "EXTRACTS OUT OF THE First Book of Enoch, CONCERNING The Egregori: [or fallen Angels.]," 1:262–269; "A DISSERTATION, TO PROVE, That this Book of Enoch, whose Fragments we have here produc'd, was really genuine, and was one of the Sacred Apocryphal or Concealed Books of the Old Testament," 1:270–293. E. Isaac, "1 (Ethiopic Apocalypse of) Enoch (Second Century B.C. – First Century A.D.): A New Translation and Introduction," in *The Old Testament Pseudepigrapha, Vol. 1: Apocalyptic Literature and Testaments*, edited by James E. Charlesworth (New York: Doubleday, 1983) 8, knows little of the history of the textual transmission apart from the Dead Sea scrolls fragments.

44 Indeed, Byron in the poem *Manfred* (1816–17) gives a synopsis of the *Book of the Watchers* in a single stanza; *Manfred* 3:II:4–9.

45 Treatments of William Etty's *The World Before the Flood* or *A Bevy of Fair Women* (1828) and Schnorr von Carlosfeld's *Die Kinder Gottes vermischen sich mit den Kindern der Welt*, in *Das Buch der Bücher in Bildern* (1851–60) were cut due to manuscript limitations; the preprint version posted in the James Madison University institutional repository retains the text.

46 Reproduced in Bentley, "A Jewel in an Ethiop's Ear," 222–226, pls. 122–225.

47 Richard J. Westall, 'Westall, Richard (1765–1836)', *Oxford Dictionary of National Biography*, (2004–14) http://www.oxforddnb.com/view/article/29106 (accessed 1 January 2015).

48 Bentley, "A Jewel in an Ethiop's Ear," 223.

49 Charles Heath, working from Richard Westall's designs, produced engravings for an edition of the KJV that are indistinguishable in style from those that adorn Moore's *Loves of the Angels*; *The Holy Bible, Containing the Old and New Testaments, and the Apocrypha* (London: White, Cochrane & Co., 1815).

50 Moore, *Loves of the Angels*, 83.

51 http://www.archive.org/details/lovesofangelspoe00mooriala (accessed 1 January 2015).

52 Sarah Symmons, "Flaxman, John (1755–1826)," *Oxford Dictionary of National Biography*, (2004–14) http://www.oxforddnb.com/view/article/9679 (accessed 1 January 2015).

53 Bentley, "A Jewel in an Ethiop's Ear," 239 n. 35.

54 John Flaxman, "Enoch," 4.5 x 9 inches, pen and brown wash over pencil, Huntington Collection 66.51, http://emuseum.huntington.org/media/view/Objects/3035/547?t:state:flow=d13a3194-56f4-4008-bc57-31fa8e30b531 (accessed 1 January 2015); Robert R. Wark, *Drawings by John Flaxman in the Huntington Collection* (San Marino: Henry E. Huntington Library and Art Gallery, 1970) no. 25. Bentley, "A Jewel in an Ethiop's Ear," 226–229, pls. 126–138.

55 Hugh Brigstocke, "William Young Ottley in Italy," in *John Flaxman and William Young Ottley in Italy*, edited by Hugh Brigstocke, Eckart Marchand and A. E. Wright (The Walpole Society 72; Wakefield: Walpole Society, 2010) 347–349,

363–365 nos. 12–19, most dated 1796 or 1798. "[The *Battle of the Angels*], neo-mannerist in their distortions and exaggerated forms, seem to take us rapidly away from the aesthetic values Ottley hitherto had shared with Flaxman into a visionary extravagant world. Beyond the *terribilità* of Signorelli and Michelangelo . . . we are involved in a romantic experience matched only by Fuseli, who was also obsessed with Milton, and by Blake" (351).

56 For all of the illustrations and their link to the *Arcana Coelestia*, see Martha Gyllenhaal, "John Flaxman's Illustrations to Emanuel Swedenborg's *Arcana Coelestia*," *Studia Swedenborgiana* 9 no. 4 (1996): 1–71; the two Enoch illustrations for *Arcana Coelestia* §464 appear as plates 1–2. Flaxman owned a copy of the 1749 Latin first edition, volume one (he of course as a classicist artist read Latin). Gyllenhaal's plate 1 is the aforementioned Gen. 5:24 drawing with the May 1792 date, executed while Flaxman was in Rome. A drawing of a different subject bears the inscription "J. Flaxman from memory of three drawings of Blake, June 1792." Evidently, Blake was on Flaxman's mind at the time; whether there was any direct connection between Flaxman's treatment of the ascension of Enoch in *AC* §464 and Blake's interest in the apocryphal story must remain conjectural. Several of the Flaxman's *AC* illustrations deal with evil spirits and spirits held captive.

The drawings and, exceptionally, one watercolor, are located in the British Museum and formerly in the private collection of Christopher Powney; in addition to Gyllenhaal, see David Bindman, "Drawings Not Connected with Sculpture," in *John Flaxman, R.A.*, edited by David Bindman (London: Royal Academy of Arts, 1979) 126 no. 152 (*Arcana Coelestia* §1272), 127 no. 153 (bearing legend "AC" but paragraph number is cut off).

57 Mary Webster, "Flaxman as Sculptor," in *John Flaxman, R.A.*, edited by David Bindman (London: Royal Academy of Arts, 1979) 100–111.

58 Bindman, "Drawings Not Connected with Sculpture," 120 no. 140.

59 See Raymond H. Deck, Jr., "New Light on C. A. Tulk, Blake's Nineteenth-Century Patron," *Studies in Romanticism* 16 no. 2 (1977): 217–236.

60 Of the making of Blake biographies there is no end. See, for starters, the masterful G. E. Bentley, Jr., *The Stranger from Paradise: A Biography of William Blake* (New Haven: Yale University Press, 2001), and Robert N. Essick, "Blake, William (1757–1827)," *Oxford Dictionary of National Biography*, (2004–14) http://www.oxforddnb.com/view/article/2585 (accessed 1 January 2015).

61 Five of the sketches were sold from the John Linnell collection in 1918 and are currently located in the US National Gallery of Art, part of the Lessing J. Rosenwald collection (Butlin 827.1–5). William Michael Rossetti identified them in 1880 as "five designs to the Book of Enoch." Two of the folio sheets bear the legend *from the Book of Enoch*, two have *Book of Enoch*, and one, *B. of Enoch* (the handwriting is not Blake's); Allan R. Brown, "Blake's Drawings for the Book of Enoch," *Burlington Magazine for Connoisseurs* 77 no. 450 (1940): 80. A sixth sketch bearing the legend "Enoch" was drawn on the verso(?) of the Dante series piece, *The Circle of the Gluttons, with Cerberus* (Butlin 812.11, located in the Fogg Art Museum of Harvard University).

62 Blake made a watercolor of Enoch in his youth (1780–85) and illustrated the figure of Enoch holding a scroll with Cain and Abel behind in the epitome of James Hervey's *Meditations Among the Tombs* (1820). Blake's only stab at lithography is a tableau with "Enoch" written in Hebrew characters on a book held by the central figure, dated 1806–7, though Enoch is mentioned in the genealogies of *Milton* 37:36 and *Jerusalem* 7:25, 75:11; Morton D. Paley, *The Traveller in the Evening: The Last Works of William Blake* (Oxford and New York: Oxford University Press, 2003) 269–270.

Two of the *Book of Enoch* sketches bear a watermark dated 1796. One of these was sketched on the back of a Dante drawing, a series Blake made for

John Linnell between 1824 and 1827. Dating the creation of the *Book of Enoch* sketches at the end of Blake's life, the path most Blake commentators follow, is a matter of triangulating between 1821, the year the first full English translation of the Ethiopian *First Enoch* manuscripts was published, Blake's unfinished poem *Genesis*, with some leaves watermarked 1826, and his death in 1827. All that the "watermark argument" can establish is the *terminus post quem*, 1796. The impoverished artist blazed off his preliminary studies on whatever scraps of paper stock were at hand – the Dante/Enoch piece could just as well attest to an Enoch drawing made in the 1790s with a Dante study added on the recto thirty years later. Arguing a late date for the *Enoch* drawings from access to Ethiopic *First Enoch* via Laurence's translation is a broken reed that ignores the febrile intellectual diet that Blake consumed throughout his career. Rowland adds to the Laurence translation argument his impression that the art of the Enoch sketches is "late" and then goes on to adduce importance thematic parallels with *The Visions of the Daughters of Albion* (1793); Christopher Rowland, *Blake and the Bible* (New Haven: Yale University Press, 2010) 116–119. Other Blake specialists draw attention to visual and thematic parallels with *Vala/The Four Zoas* (1796–1807?); Brown, "Blake's Drawings for the Book of Enoch," 80–81, 83–85; Bentley, "A Jewel in an Ethiop's Ear," 234; Paley, *Traveller in the Evening*, 274–275. To my knowledge, Schuchard is the only scholar to openly defend a dating of the *Book of Enoch* sketches in the 1790s, based on access to translations of the Syncellus versions and heavy Swedenborgian interest in Africa, Kabbalistic Enoch, and the recovery of the lost text; Marsha Keith Schuchard, *William Blake's Sexual Path to Spiritual Vision* (Rochester VT: Inner Traditions, 2008) 250–258. Schuchard's interpretations of Blake's poetry and marital life must be used with caution. The strength of the book, as noted by various reviewers, lies in the archival research she has conducted on the Moravian, Swedenborgian, and theosophical backgrounds of Blake's London, and her work on Enoch is no exception. It does not pay to be dogmatic about the dates of the *Book of Enoch* drawings, in my opinion – 1796 to 1827 are all possible dates of composition – but effectively limiting the sphere of inquiry to the last six years of Blake's life poses a serious methodological shortcoming to the interpretation of these arresting pieces. Beer, "Blake's Changing View of History," 159–178, an unusually sensitive reading of the sketches, tends to date them to the first decade of the 19th century.

63 Robert Rix, *William Blake and the Cultures of Radical Christianity* (Aldershot: Ashgate, 2007) is weak on British Moravianism but strong on the other movements mentioned above. Schuchard, *William Blake's Sexual Path*, 12–53 has done substantial archival research on the history of the Fetter Lane Moravian congregation. On the political background of the times, see Saree Makdisi, *William Blake and the Impossible History of the 1790s* (Chicago and London: University of Chicago Press, 2003). Magnus Ankarsjö, *William Blake and Religion: A New Critical View* (Jefferson NC: McFarland & Co., 2009) attempts to navigate between the latest findings on Blake's relationships to Unitarianism, Swedenborgianism and Moravianism. Jennifer G. Jesse, *William Blake's Religious Vision: There's a Methodism in His Madness* (Lanham MD and Plymouth UK: Lexington Books, 2013) identifies Blake as a theological moderate, working broadly within the Wesleyan tradition, who was in polemical dialogue with both radical and rationalistic exponents of British Christianity.

64 David Worrall, "Blake, the Female Prophet and the American Agent: The Evidence of the 1789 Swedenborg Conference Attendance List," in *Blake and Conflict*, edited by Sarah Haggarty and Jon Mee (Hampshire and New York: Palgrave Macmillan, 2009) 58.

65 Quoted in Worrall, "Evidence of the 1789 Swedenborg Conference," 54.

66 Rix, *William Blake*, 94–98; Ankarsjö, *William Blake and Religion*, 26–31; David Worrell, "Thel in Africa: William Blake and the Post-Colonial, Post-Swedenborgians Female Subject," in *Blake, Nation and Empire*, edited by Steve Clark and David Worrall (Hampshire and New York: Palgrave Macmillan, 2006) 40–62. Africa, for Swedenborg, was a place of lost wisdom and innocence that Europeans desperately needed to access. In his 1798 novel *Captive of the Castle of Senaar*, George Cumberland, Blake's confrère, makes a similar point. Both Bruce and Cumberland cautiously extol the virtues of polygamy; Swedenborg is dead-set against it. Susan Matthews, "Africa and Utopia: Refusing a 'Local Habitation'," in *Reception of Blake in the Orient*, edited by Steve Clark and Masashi Suzuki (London: Continuum, 2006) 109–111.

67 *Arcana Coelestia* §§463–64 (Gen 5:21–24). *Arcana Coelestia* §§554–98 (Gen 6:1–9) "Sons of God are the doctrinals of faith . . . lusts are called the daughters of man" (§570). Swedenborg conceives of the biblical patriarchs and primeval history as a record of the perversions of original revealed religion, with the chief protagonists representing religious sects ("heresies and doctrines") as it were. Lust for the daughters of men causes the watcher/doctrines to go astray into destructive heterodoxy, that is to say, the mischief in Gen 6:1–4 is the fault of womankind.

Other early drivers behind Blake's engagement with *First Enoch* could have included contact with Benjamin Henry La Trobe, who was hired to edit James Bruce's African travelogue, and a Kabbalistic disquisition by General Rainsford on Enoch based in part on a translation by Charles Woide of the Ethiopic *Enoch* manuscript given to Louis XV by Bruce, both of whom moved in the artistic circles frequented by Blake; Schuchard, *William Blake's Sexual Path*, 251–252. William Hayley, whose patronage of Blake went badly sour in the first years of the nineteenth century, wrote an erotic satire based on an English version of Syncellus' account of the *Book of the Watchers* and the quintessential 18th-century novel *Clarissa*, positing an antediluvian virgin capable of resisting the seductive blandishments of a most persistent Watcher; William Hayley, *A Philosophical, Historical, and Moral Essay on Old Maids* (London: Printed for T. Cadell, 1785) 2:6–37; Susan Matthews, "Blake, Hayley and the History of Sexuality," in *Blake, Nation and Empire*, edited by Steve Clark and David Worrall (Hampshire and New York: Palgrave Macmillan, 2006) 92–94 (the form of the Watcher's names in Hayley's satire is proof positive that he used one of the extant English or French translations of Syncellus/Scaliger and did not gain an early preview of the Ethiopic text in translation, *pace* Matthews); idem, *Blake, Sexuality and Bourgeois Politeness* (Cambridge Studies in Romanticism; Cambridge: Cambridge University Press, 2011) 95–97.

68 The three sketches not shown or described here, omitted in consideration of (my) time and (this volume's) space, may be found in Bentley, "Jewel in an Ethiop's Ear," pls. 139, 143–144. The open-access images posted by the National Gallery of Art are can be zoomed for detailed examination (http://www.nga.gov/fcgi-bin/tinfo_f?object=30673, http://www.nga.gov/fcgi-bin/tinfo_f?object=30674, http://www.nga.gov/fcgi-bin/tinfo_f?object=30672) (accessed 14 August 2015); as of 15 Aug 2015, the online William Blake Archive has yet to mount them (http://www.blakearchive.org/blake/).

69 I am greatly indebted to Professor Jennifer Jesse for bringing this feature to my attention. To my knowledge, she is the first Blake specialist to have noted it. Once it is recognized in the sketch, it is impossible to view the tableau without "seeing" the linear Gothic design as a major structuring element.

70 Note that the "cathedron" is the body of woman, particularly the womb, where the golden looms of Los weave mortal bodies doomed to die; S. Foster Damon, *A Blake Dictionary: The Ideas and Symbols of William Blake* (Revised edn;

Hanover and London: University Press of New England, 1988) 74. In one of Blake's most obscure works, a female figure with a seven-pointed crown identified by some as the Whore of Babylon/Rahab bears a Gothic facade superimposed over her genitals (*Four Zoas*, Night III, MS p. 44 E323).

71 From the *Notebook* poems, cited in Paley, *Traveller in the Evening*, 274.

72 Brown, "Blake's Drawings for the Book of Enoch," 114, and Paley, *Traveller in the Evening*, 275. Rowland, *Blake and the Bible*, 114 calls attention to an illustration of a bescaled woman caressing a dragon head, probably to be identified with Rahab, "reveald Mystery Babylon the Great: the Abomination of Desolation Religion hid in War: a Dragon red, & hidden Harlot" (*Jerusalem* 75:18–20).

73 I note in passing that Blake required nothing for these sketches from *First Enoch* beyond the contents of *First Enoch* 6–9, freely available since 1727 in English translation based on Syncellus' *Chronographia*.

74 Helen P. Bruder, *William Blake and the Daughters of Albion* (New York: St. Martin's Press, 1997) 73–89 (the book as a whole contextualizes contemporary European sexual mores and politics with compelling examples); Rowland, *Blake and the Bible*, 116–119. See also Matthews, "Blake, Hayley and the History of Sexuality," 83–101, that deals substantively with rape in Blake. Bruder's work is ground-zero for Blake gender studies, and I can recommend her essays and edited volumes: Helen P. Bruder, "Blake and Gender Studies," in *Palgrave Advances in William Blake Studies*, edited by Nicholas M. Williams (Houndmills, Basingstoke, Hampshire and New York: Palgrave Macmillan, 2006) 132–165; Helen P. Bruder (ed.), *Women Reading William Blake* (Basingstoke England and New York: Palgrave Macmillan, 2007); idem and Tristanne J. Connolly (eds.), *Queer Blake* (Basingstoke and New York: Palgrave Macmillan, 2010).

75 In fact, an earlier dating of the sketches opens one avenue of interpretation as combining a polemic against Swedenborg's sexual esotericism and his uniformly positive assessment of angels as helpful spiritual mediators. *The Marriage of Heaven and Hell* (1793) openly satirizes Swedenborg's doctrine of angels and inspiration in general, but the animus of Blake's critique seems to turn on Swedenborg's fundamental misconstrual of the nature of evil.

76 Damon, *Blake Dictionary*, 438.

Bibliography

Ankarsjö, Magnus. *William Blake and Religion: A New Critical View*. Jefferson NC: McFarland & Co., 2009.

Beer, John. "Blake's Changing View of History: The Impact of the Book of Enoch." In *Historicizing Blake*, edited by Steve Clark and David Worrall. New York: St. Martin's Press, 1994, 159–178.

Bindman, David. "Drawings Not Connected with Sculpture." In *John Flaxman, R.A.*, edited by David Bindman. London: Royal Academy of Arts, 1979, 120–130.

Brigstocke, Hugh. "William Young Ottley in Italy." In *John Flaxman and William Young Ottley in Italy*, edited by Hugh Brigstocke, Eckart Marchand and A. E. Wright. The Walpole Society 72. Wakefield: Walpole Society, 2010, 341–370.

Brinks, Ellen. *Gothic Masculinity: Effeminacy and the Supernatural in English and German Romanticism*. Blackwell Studies in Eighteenth-Century Literature and Culture. Lewisburg and London: Bucknell University Press/Associated University Presses, 2003.

Brown, Allan R. "Blake's Drawings for the Book of Enoch," *Burlington Magazine for Connoisseurs* 77 no. 450 (1940): 80–81, 83–85.

Bruce, James. *Travels to Discover the Source of the Nile, in the Years 1768, 1769, 1770, 1771, 1772, and 1773*. 5 vols. London: Printed by J. Ruthven, for G. G. J. and J. Robinson, 1790.

Bruder, Helen P. "Blake and Gender Studies." In *Palgrave Advances in William Blake Studies*, edited by Nicholas M. Williams. Houndmills, Basingstoke, Hampshire and New York: Palgrave Macmillan, 2006, 132–165.

Bruder, Helen P. *William Blake and the Daughters of Albion*. New York: St. Martin's Press, 1997.

Bruder, Helen P. (ed.), *Women Reading William Blake*. Basingstoke England and New York: Palgrave Macmillan, 2007.

Bruder, Helen P. and Tristanne J. Connolly (eds.). *Queer Blake*. Basingstoke and New York: Palgrave Macmillan, 2010.

Burns, Arthur. "Dale, Thomas (1797–1870)." In *Oxford Dictionary of National Biography*, Oxford University Press, 2014.

Bush, George. *Notes, Critical and Practical, on the Book of Genesis: Designed as a General Help to Biblical Reading and Instruction*. 6th edn. 2 vols. New York: Published by Dayton & Newman, 1842.

Byron, George, Gordon Byron, Jerome J. McGann, and Barry Weller, eds. *Lord Byron: The Poetical Works*. Oxford English Texts 6. Oxford: Oxford University Press; New York: Clarendon Press, 1991.

Carnall, Geoffrey. "Moore, Thomas (1779–1852)." In *Oxford Dictionary of National Biography*, Oxford University Press, 2014.

Cavallaro, Dani. *The Gothic Vision: Three Centuries of Horror, Terror and Fear*. London and New York: Continuum, 2002.

Chambers, Robert, ed. *Cyclopædia of English Literature; a History, Critical and Biographical, of British Authors, from the Earliest to the Present Times*. 2 vols. Edinburgh: William and Robert Chambers, 1844.

Daffron, Benjamin Eric. *Romantic Doubles: Sex and Sympathy in British Gothic Literature, 1790–1830*. New York: AMS Press, 2002.

Dale, Thomas. *Irad and Ahah, a Tale of the Flood. Poems. Specimens of a New Translation of the Psalms*. 2d edn. London: J. M. Richardson, 1822.

Damon, S. Foster. *A Blake Dictionary: The Ideas and Symbols of William Blake*. Revised edn. Hanover and London: University Press of New England, 1988.

Deck, Raymond H., Jr. "New Light on C. A. Tulk, Blake's Nineteenth-Century Patron," *Studies in Romanticism* 16 no. 2 (1977): 217–236.

Elia [pseudonym]. "The Child Angel: A Dream," *The London Magazine* (June 1823): 677–678.

Essick, Robert N. "Blake, William (1757–1827)," In *Oxford Dictionary of National Biography*, Oxford University Press, 2014.

Grabe, Johann Ernest. *The History of the Seventy-Two Interpreters: Of Their Journey from Jerusalem to Alexandria, Their Entertainment at the Egyptian Court, Their Version on the Septuagint: With All the Circumstances of That Illustrious Transaction*. Translated by Thomas Lewis. London: Printed for J. Hooke, and T. Caldecott, 1715.

Green, William Henry. *The Unity of the Book of Genesis*. New York: Charles Scribner's Sons, 1895.

Groves, Henry Charles. *Commentary on the Book of Genesis for the Use of Readers of the English Version of the Bible*. Cambridge and London: Macmillan and Co., 1861.

Gyllenhaal, Martha. "John Flaxman's Illustrations to Emanuel Swedenborg's *Arcana Coelestia*," *Studia Swedenborgiana* 9 no. 4 (1996): 1–71.

Haggerty, George E., *Gothic Fiction/Gothic Form*. University Park: Pennsylvania State University Press, 1989.

Hayley, William. *A Philosophical, Historical, and Moral Essay on Old Maids*. Vol. 2. London: Printed for T. Cadell, 1785.

Hessayon, Ariel. "Og, King of Bashan, Enoch and the Books of Enoch: Extra-Canonical Texts and Interpretations of Genesis 6:1–4." In *Scripture and Scholarship in Early Modern England*, edited by Ariel Hessayon and Nicholas Keene. Aldershot: Ashgate, 2006, 5–40.

Isaac, E. "1 (Ethiopic Apocalypse of) Enoch (Second Century B.C. – First Century A.D.): A New Translation and Introduction." In *The Old Testament Pseudepigrapha, Vol. 1: Apocalyptic Literature and Testaments*, edited by James E. Charlesworth. New York: Doubleday, 1983, 5–89.

Jesse, Jennifer G. *William Blake's Religious Vision: There's a Methodism in His Madness*. Lanham MD and Plymouth UK: Lexington Books, 2013.

Kestner, Joseph A. *Masculinities in Victorian Painting*. Brookfield VT: Scolar Press; Aldershot: Ashgate, 1995.

Kurtz, J. H. *History of the Old Covenant*. Translated by Alfred Edersheim. Philadelphia: Lindsay and Blakiston, 1859.

Laurence, Richard. *The Book of Enoch the Prophet: An Apocryphal Production, Supposed to Have Been Lost for Ages, but Discovered at the Close of the Last Century in Abyssinia: Now First Translated from an Ethiopic Ms. In the Bodleian Library*. Oxford: At the University Press for the Author, 1821.

Makdisi, Saree. *William Blake and the Impossible History of the 1790s*. Chicago and London: University of Chicago Press, 2003.

Matthews, Susan. "Africa and Utopia: Refusing a 'Local Habitation'." In *Reception of Blake in the Orient*, edited by Steve Clark and Masashi Suzuki. London: Continuum, 2006, 109–111.

Matthews, Susan. "Blake, Hayley and the History of Sexuality." In *Blake, Nation and Empire*, edited by Steve Clark and David Worrall. Hampshire and New York: Palgrave Macmillan, 2006, 83–101.

Matthews, Susan. *Blake, Sexuality and Bourgeois Politeness*. Cambridge Studies in Romanticism. Cambridge: Cambridge University Press, 2011.

McGann, Jerome. "Byron, George Gordon Noel, Sixth Baron Byron (1788–1824)." In *Oxford Dictionary of National Biography*, Oxford University Press, 2014.

Montgomery, James. *Verses to the Memory of the Late Richard Reynolds; the World before the Flood*. Romantic Context. Poetry; New York and London: Garland Pub., 1978.

Moore, Thomas. *The Loves of the Angels, a Poem*. London: Longman, Hurst, Rees, Orme, and Brown, 1823.

Paley, Morton D. *The Apocalyptic Sublime*. New Haven: Yale University Press, 1986.

Paley, Morton D. *The Traveller in the Evening: The Last Works of William Blake*. Oxford and New York: Oxford University Press, 2003.

Punter, David G. *The Literature of Terror: A History of Gothic Fictions from 1765 to the Present Day, Vol. 1: The Gothic Tradition*. New York: Longman, 1996.

Punter, David G. and Glennis Byron (eds.), *The Gothic*. Blackwell Guides to Literature. Malden MA: Blackwell Publishing, 2014.

Purchas, Samuel. *Pvrchas His Pilgrimage. Or Relations of the Vvorld and the Religions Observed in Alsl Ages and Places Discouered, from the Creation Vnto This Present. In Fovre Parts. This First Containeth a Theological and Geographical Historie of Asia, Africa, and America, with the Islands Adiacent. Declaring the Ancient Religions before the Flovd, the Heathnish, Jewish, and Saracenicall in All Ages since, in Those Parts Professed, Vvith Their Seueral Opinions, Idols, Oracles, Temples, Priests, Fasts, Feasts, Sacrifices, and Rites Religious: Their Beginnings, Proceedings, Alterations, Sectes, Orders and Successions.* 2nd edn; London: Printed by William Stansby for Henrie Featherstone, 1614.

Rix, Robert. *William Blake and the Cultures of Radical Christianity.* Aldershot: Ashgate, 2007.

Rowland, Christopher. *Blake and the Bible.* New Haven: Yale University Press, 2010.

Schuchard, Marsha Keith. *William Blake's Sexual Path to Spiritual Vision.* Rochester VT: Inner Traditions, 2008.

Shadduck, Gayle. *England's Amorous Angels, 1813–1823.* Lanham MD: University Press of America, 1990.

Smith, George. *Patriarchal Age: Or, the History and Religion of Mankind, from the Creation to the Death of Isaac: Deduced from the Writings of Moses, and Other Inspired Authors.* New York: Carlton & Lanahan, 1847.

Smith, Philip. *An Ancient History from the Earliest Records to the Fall of the Western Empire, Vol. 1: From the Creation of the World to the Accession of Philip of Macedon.* London: James Walton, 1868.

Symmons, Sarah. "Flaxman, John (1755–1826)." In *Oxford Dictionary of National Biography*, Oxford University Press, 2014.

Tolley, G. "Montgomery, James (1771–1854)." In *Oxford Dictionary of National Biography*, Oxford University Press, 2014.

Vajda, G. "Hārūt Wa-Mārūt." In *Encyclopedia of Islam.* Leiden: Brill, 2004.

Wark, Robert R. *Drawings by John Flaxman in the Huntington Collection.* San Marino: Henry E. Huntington Library and Art Gallery, 1970.

Webster, Mary. "Flaxman as Sculptor." In *John Flaxman, R.A.*, edited by David Bindman. London: Royal Academy of Arts, 1979, 100–111.

Whiston, William. *A Collection of Authentick Records Belonging to the Old and New Testament. Translated into English. By William Whiston, M. A. Sometime Professor of the Mathematicks in the University of Cambridge.* London: Printed for the author: and are to be sold by the booksellers of London and Westminster, 1727.

Worrall, David. "Blake, the Female Prophet and the American Agent: The Evidence of the 1789 Swedenborg Conference Attendance List." In *Blake and Conflict*, edited by Sarah Haggarty and Jon Mee. Hampshire and New York: Palgrave Macmillan, 2009, 48–64.

Worrell, David. "Thel in Africa: William Blake and the Post-Colonial, Post-Swedenborgians Female Subject." In *Blake, Nation and Empire*, edited by Steve Clark and David Worrall. Hampshire and New York: Palgrave Macmillan, 2006, 40–62.

General index

Terms index

Texts index